Contents

Sophia Wilhelmina Williams

Casanova's daughter; Princess Augusta's
Private Almoner

Chapter One

1820–1831

Wherever we attach it, the word "orphan" has a melancholy ring and a name less welcoming for any seat of learning than "The Adult Orphan Institution" would be difficult to find, compete though it would with "The Protestant Dissenters' Grammar"[1] and "The Royal Naval Female School".[2]

An Institution so described once stood in Regent's Park. A trust governed it, comprising two Committees: one of Ladies; the other, of Gentlemen, called the Managing; and it depended for support on about 1,200 patrons, donors and subscribers. The Gentlemen included the Rev. Dr Edward Burrow of Magdalene College, Cambridge, and of Trinity College, Oxford, with books to his name on conchology—seashells and shellfish—the Elgin Marbles, with forty plates drawn and etched by himself, some hefty tomes on Christian faith and practice and translations from the German of Zschokke;[3] it was he who wrote the preface to their Annual Report, recording the origin and purpose of the school: having first published it in 1823, he revised it in 1831 and from then until at least 1880 it read little changed.

The Adult Orphan Institution derives its origin from the benevolent endeavours of a private individual to rescue, from a situation of much difficulty and danger, some few among the many young persons who have, by birth, great claims upon society; and who, unfortunately, have but too often the greatest need that these claims should be strongly urged on their behalf. Mrs Sophia Williams, who was already advantageously known to the public as the active promoter of more than one charitable work, especially as the foundress of an excellent establishment at Cheltenham, the Old School of Industry, was led, some years ago, by accidental circumstances which powerfully called forth her feelings of sympathy and commiseration, to entertain the hope that she might be enabled, by the bounty of the public, to prevent in some cases, and to alleviate in others, such sufferings as she had then been obliged to witness. She formed the design of establishing an Asylum for those Orphan Daughters of the Clergy, and of Military and Naval Officers, who should be left friendless or

[1] 1808–1868; since then Mill Hill.

[2] Founded in Richmond in 1840 "for the Daughters of Naval and Marine Officers", it kept its title till in the 1890s "Female" was omitted. In 1942 it moved to Haslemere.

[3] Johann Zschokke, 1771–1848, German turned Swiss, best known for his morally instructive plays and stories.

unprovided to contend with the hardships and temptations to which they might be exposed. The plan was honoured with the approbation of Her Majesty Queen Charlotte; and this high distinction, together with the intrinsic merit of the design and Mrs Williams's unremitting exertions, gradually obtained, in favour of the projected establishment, a considerable list of royal and noble names.

On the 24th of June 1820, with HRH Princess Augusta[4] as its sole Patron, the Institution newly formed found a temporary home at 32 and 33 Mornington Place,[5] off the Crescent adjoining the Hampstead Road, and there, Dr Burrow continues and concludes:

Sixteen wards, who had been strongly recommended, and were deemed worthy of election, were admitted without delay; and the ladies by whose agency the establishment was to be conducted, under the direction of Mrs Williams, entered upon the discharge of their respective functions.

From this period, until the time of her death, which took place just three years afterwards,[6] the Institution was chiefly indebted to the judicious management of Mrs Williams, who was appointed Honorary Secretary and Sub-Treasurer, for all the gratifying proofs, which were from time to time exhibited, of the improvement which took place in the young persons committed to her care; and not less was it indebted to her unwearied zeal and benevolent exertions for a regular and very considerable increase in the numbers of the friends and contributors to the establishment.

*Owing to the favourable opinion entertained of the Institution by his late Majesty, who had become an Annual Subscriber of One Hundred Pounds towards its support, and conferred on it the additional honour of consenting to be its Patron, a grant was made, in the year 1823, of a piece of ground in the Regent's Park, of sufficient extent to answer all the purposes of the Institution, in a most desirable situation, and on the most reasonable terms. On this a house having been built according to a plan gratuitously furnished by Mr Nash,[7] the Committee were enabled to remove the Institution into a permanent residence, every way suited to and becoming its character, at Michaelmas in the year 1824. The cost of this building, together with that of a subsequent enlargement in the year 1829, and of the necessary furniture, has been entirely defrayed to the amount of between £6000 and £7000; and, notwithstanding some temporary inconvenience has been occasioned by this outlay, the advantages expected to result from it have been fully realized. There has been a diminution of annual expence [*sic*] by the saving of rent; and a degree of publicity and*

[4] Sixth of the fifteen children and second of the six daughters of King George III and Queen Charlotte.

[5] Vestiges of a street once elegant remain. The area is derelict.

[6] 25.6.1823.

[7] John Nash, 1752–1835, the King's architect.

respectability has also been obtained for the Institution, which has occasioned a gradual increase of the number of its patrons, and a considerable extension of the sphere of its utility.

It should be observed, that a peculiar feature in the plan of this Institution is the Adult *age which the Wards must have attained before they can be admitted. A proportionate proficiency in the rudiments of knowledge is therefore to be expected in all Candidates. "It is to be remembered", to use the words of Mrs Williams, in her last Report, just before her death, "that the Institution was formed, not to educate Children but to finish the education of Young Women and to forward them in their way through life." To train them, therefore, for a most respectable occupation in life, to become Governesses in private families, or Assistants in schools, was the object at which Mrs Williams chiefly aimed and which is now exclusively pursued; their attention being confined to those branches of education in which all governesses of children, in respectable families, are expected to be well versed. Among these, a superior course of religious instruction is provided, under clerical superintendence, and in strict accordance with the principles of the Established Church.*

Thus this Institution not only affords an Asylum to the Orphan Daughters of Clergymen, and Military and Naval Officers, at the period of their lives when they most stand in need of counsel and protection, during the five or six years previous to their arrival at confirmed womanhood, and enables them to procure for themselves a sufficient maintenance, without descending from the rank in life in which they have been born, but it repays, with large interest, whatever it derives from the bounty of the public, by making a secure and effectual provision for the education of the children of those who have most influence on the habits of society. In other words it is not only the fatherless daughter who reaps an immediate advantage, but through her the best interests of many families are in the end more certainly promoted than they could be by any other means; and this must be acknowledged as giving the Institution the strongest title to benevolent and charitable consideration.

For a century and a half little more was known or told about Sophia Wilhelmina Williams than Dr Burrow here relates. Her address in April 1821 was that of the Dowager Viscountess Sydney:[8] 2 Chapel Apartments, Grosvenor Square, where the Ladies' Committee sometimes met: *The Gentleman's Magazine* gave her place of death as the house of the same Viscountess Dowager in Chapel Street, off South Audley Street;[9] and Lord Sydney[10] referred to her as one of his forebears when he spoke at a fund-raising dinner for the school in 1880. Information at some time appeared, and was handed down, that she was small, mild and submissive; played the

[8] Elizabeth, widow of the first Viscount, Thomas, the statesman after whom Sydney, Australia, was named. She died in 1826.

[9] Obituary, 25.6.1823.

[10] John, third Viscount; the first and the last Earl.

harp and sang; that her mother was a rich and famous lady of fashion, who fell on evil days and had to leave her children to learn as best they could how to earn themselves a living; and that the young Sophia was appointed governess in various noble families till at last she served as Private Almoner to Princess Augusta. The account, though meagre, was mostly or all correct; and a tendency to refer to Mrs Williams as "Mistress" or more usually "Miss",[11] when in 1920 the school celebrated its hundredth birthday, makes it likely that someone, at least, knew rather more than he was willing to divulge.

The truth about the mother did not lie buried deep. An "Obituary of remarkable Persons", published in *The Gentleman's Magazine* of 1797, tells how the lady of fashion rose and fell; the memoirs of Casanova[12] provide almost all that we can find about her early and middle years; to which Horace Walpole's letters add (1732–97); Dr E. F. Rimbault's *Soho and its Associations* (edited and published in 1895) reflects the lustre of her fame; and John Taylor, in his *Records of my Life* (1832), scornfully exposes and perhaps distorts her character and folly.

Though born in Venice in 1723 and reared there, the daughter of an actor, Giuseppe Imer, himself a Genoese, it is said that she was German, fair-haired, and called Teresa. An ageing senator, Malipiero, took her as his *protégée*. She was then 17. Thirteen years later, having married a dancer, Angelo Pompeati, and borne him a son, she had become the mistress of the Margrave of Bayreuth. Karl Alexander, Prince of Lorraine, Governor of the Austrian Netherlands (now Belgium) engaged her for a time to control its theatres. In Amsterdam, singing in opera or concerts, she appeared as Madame Trenti, till she borrowed the name of her next lover (Casanova says that she ruined him): Cornelis (de Rigerboos). Yet in London in 1746, performing at the Haymarket in Gluck's *La Caduta de' Giganti*,[13] she was again known as Madame Pompeati. In 1753, the year in which Angelo, her husband, took his life (disembowelling himself with a razor), she lived in Venice but with Casanova's help (100 ducats) had returned to London by 1759, where she acquired the palatial Carlisle House in Soho Square[14] and there began providing the most lavish imaginable balls and masquerades: twelve a year, Casanova says, for nobility and gentry, and another

[11] Elderly spinsters were often still called "Mrs" in the early 1820s.

[12] The Chevalier de Seingalt, born in Venice, novitiate (expelled), diplomatist, soldier, adventurer, spy. His complete and revised memoirs, *Histoire de ma vie*, 12 vols, were published in France in 1962.

[13] Dr Charles Burney, Fanny Burney's father, in Vol. IV of his *General History of Music*, 1776–89, recalls that in that production she had "such a masculine and violent manner of singing that few female symptoms were perceptible".

[14] Dr Rimbault thinks it likely that Mrs Cornelys bought it from the Howards. It had belonged to General Charles Howard, third Earl of Carlisle, under whose colonelcy the Yorkshire Regiment, the 19th Foot, had acquired the grass-green facings to its uniform and the name, Green Howards. The house was taken down in 1788 and the site has since been occupied by St Patrick's Roman Catholic Church.

twelve for commoners, up to six hundred guests all together in one big room, paying two guineas a head. "A singular dame", writes Horace Walpole, in a letter to Sir Horace Mann:[15]

in her fairy palace . . . she pretended to take no money, and had the assurance to advertise that the subscription was to provide coals for the poor, for she had vehemently courted the mob and succeeded in gaining their princely favour. She then declared that her masquerades were for the benefit of commerce—I concluded that she would open a bawdy house next for the interests of the Foundling Hospital, and I was not quite mistaken, for they say, one of her maids . . . affirms that she could not undergo the fatigue of making the beds so often.

Karl Abel[16] and Johann Christian Bach,[17] housemates, conducted her concerts after 1765. The Prince of Monaco, the King of Denmark, the Duke of Gloucester and other members of the royal family honoured her with visits. Her future looked better than secure. But the cost of repeated alterations to the house, its comfort and embellishment (including almost 4,000 wax lights), wages (about 100 musicians at a time were employed) and ton upon ton of food and drink, ran her into debt—she had landed there before: in 1763 or 64, when she sat awaiting trial, Casanova had paid for the bailiff to release her, trusting £50 in bank-notes to her daughter, Sophie, then aged 10. In 1771 the Bow Street magistrate's court fined her for keeping "a common disorderly house". Bankruptcy followed and the contents of the house were auctioned. In 1776, having meanwhile kept a hotel in Southampton and catered for a grand regatta on the Thames, she returned for a while to Soho Square and may still have occupied the abode in rural Hammersmith where, in her heyday, she had employed at least thirty-two servants and two or three secretaries and kept six horses and a pack of hounds. But again her fortune must have waned. She withdrew from the public eye, assuming the name of Mrs Smith, as she was called in it seems about 1790, when John Taylor, with his friend, Edward Jerningham, the poet,[18] discovered her again, selling ass's milk in Knightsbridge:

She had a large brood of the long-eared sisterhood in her service, and despatched them daily to several parts of the town. She was not, however, though far advanced in years, and as might be supposed, subdued by adversity, without a hope that she should possibly regain her influence in

[15] 27.2.1771.

[16] The famous player of the viola da gamba. Born in 1725, he died of drink in 1787.

[17] The "Milanese" or "English" or "London" Bach, 1735–82, the youngest surviving son of Johann Sebastian.

[18] Fanny Burney, letter of May 1780: "a mighty delicate gentleman: looks to be painted, and in all daintification in manner, speech and dress". He charmed Horace Walpole. But his verse did not find favour: William Gifford, in his satirical poem, *The Baviad*, derides "snivelling Jerningham", who weeps "o'er love-lorn oxen and deserted sheep"; and his publisher, heir to all his manuscripts, printed none.

the fashionable world; for she aspired to the honour of having a public breakfast, under the patronage of his late Majesty, then Prince of Wales, at her humble dwelling, which might be aptly styled Assinine Hall. She seemed delighted at the idea of being reintroduced to any part of a family who had known her in better times. She then took us into the room intended for the morning fête that was to take place under royal patronage. It exhibited a melancholy proof of the total loss of that taste, which had produced such a variety of elegant arrangements at Carlisle House; and consisted of a small room ornamented on all sides, as well as on the ceiling, with bits of variously coloured looking-glass.[19]

The venture had to fail and, being pressed by her creditors, she found herself a refuge in the Fleet Prison, then reserved for debtors only, where more comfortable rooms could be rented for those who could afford to pay—their debts notwithstanding—and died there in 1797, aged 74. An obituary reads:

*Such was the fate of the once-celebrated Mrs Cornelly [*sic*], whose melancholy end holds forth a warning to the imprudent; for, with common discretion, she might have closed her life in affluence. It is not as has been said, that Mrs C. [*sic*] subsisted upon the bounty of her fellow-prisoners in the Fleet. She had a liberal allowance from a lady related to the family of Lord Cowper, who would have increased that allowance, and have settled it on her for life, if she would have renounced her* projecting turn, *which flattered her with the hope of reviving all her influence in the fashionable world. These visionary prospects, however, she would not resign, and, while she was dreaming of a palace, she died in a gaol!*[20]

Casanova had put her son, Giuseppe, to a Monsieur Viar's boarding-school in Paris. A "false, secretive", ungrateful "little rascal" he found him, so deceitful as to be "incapable of friendship"; "to inspire respect" he had successfully posed there as le Comte d'Aranda (and had had his way with the headmaster's daughter). Returned by Casanova to his mother, and now called Joseph—to which one day he added "Sir"—he would change his name to Altorf[21] after her disgrace; but she still enjoyed his support. For a few years he tutored George Fermor, the future third Earl of Pomfret,[22] who "held him in esteem", John Taylor says, "for his talents, attainments and moral character". After that he went abroad, where—or so it was reported—he died, still young.

[19] John Taylor, *Records of my Life*, 1832.

[20] *The Gentleman's Magazine*, 1797.

[21] Mr Joseph Cornelys being greatly admired not only as a scholar but also as a flautist, it is interesting to find that his adopted name—not at all as German as it sounds—anagrammatises the Latin *flator*, a player of woodwind.

[22] His father, also George, second Earl, reputedly one of Mrs Cornelys's lovers, is said to have bought Carlisle House for her, then tried and failed to recover either it or the money in court.

Wilhelmine Friederike, his first sister, he had lost when she was only a few years old. Sophie, his second, Sophia Wilhelmina, Mrs Williams or Miss, still lived.[23]

Casanova, who had pleaded but in vain to be allowed to bring Sophie up, always believed that she was born his child. Her mother had told him so and although, later, she would claim that the girl's real father was the Marquis of Montperny, major-domo to the Margravine of Bayreuth, he could only see in her a likeness to himself, as did many others, if we take his word.[24] It was he who paid for her education—in Harwich, he writes, but Hammersmith is meant ("we went there"—from London—"after dinner")—at a boarding-school which a Catholic noblewoman[25] ran for fifteen or sixteen girls, where she stayed till, aged 15, she returned to her mother, in Hammersmith perhaps or in Soho Square.

Teresa Cornelys

Printed "from a caricature of the period" in E.F. Rimbault's *Soho and its Associations*, 1895.

Casanova

Memoirs not always accurate, but truthful. Almost certainly father of Teresa's daughter, Sophie.

[23] *The Gentleman's Magazine*, obituary, 25.6.1823: "The daughter is still alive, and, under another name, has long been patronised by some noble families, who knew her in better days . . . her musical talents procure her an easy introduction in polite circles."

[24] Teresa and he were old friends, his father and her mother had been lovers, and Sophie was conceived at about the time when she met him in Venice in May 1753.

[25] John Taylor, ibid.: "The daughter was placed in a Roman Catholic seminary at Hammersmith, generally known by the name of 'The Nunnery' . . ." Horace Bleackley, *Casanova in England*, 1923, identifies its Lady Superior as Frances Gentil, of the Sisters of the Institute of Mary, in the Broadway. The school was founded in 1669. In

Mr Taylor knew both daughter and son. The son he admired, "a very amiable and accomplished young man". His sister was "of a different description":

She had cultivated her musical talents with success, and performed very well upon the piano-forte, the harp, and the common guitar. She had a fine voice, and sang with great taste and expression. After her mother's fall, she began to think the connexion not very creditable to her; and when she once visited her mother in the Fleet, told her that she was sure she was not her daughter, but of noble origin in Germany, and desired to know who really were her parents. It was in vain that the mother, depressed with misfortune, and shocked at such an unnatural application, with tears in her eyes assured her that her suspicion was wholly unfounded. Sophy resolved to believe the contrary, and, I fear, deserted her unhappy parent. Finding it expedient to give herself a noble extraction, she reported that she was a natural daughter of Prince Charles of Lorraine by a lady of quality, and was base enough to insinuate that Mrs Cornelys wanted to sacrifice her to Lord Pigot,[26] who lived in Soho Square, and was a patron of her mother; though the mother, knowing that Lord Pigot was a man of gallantry, actually sent her daughter to a convent abroad, that she might be out of the way of temptation. It is proper to add, that I have no reason to believe she ever, to use the words of Pope, "broke Diana's law".

For some time the present Mr Charles Butler,[27] well known for his legal knowledge, his attachment to the Roman Catholic religion, his literary talents, and the benevolence of his disposition, allowed her a provision, which enabled her to take apartments near Bedford Row, Bloomsbury. He had known her in her prosperity, was fond of music, and admired her talents. I remember to have heard her sing an air, the words and music of which were composed by that gentleman, of which I reminded him many years afterwards, when I had the pleasure of meeting him at the late Dr Kitchener's.[28]

1780, when it closed, the pupils were dispersed. The Bar Convent (St Mary's) in York, which the same order had founded, may well have taken some. In 1975 its school was absorbed by All Saints, a Roman Catholic maintained comprehensive. The convent stands where it has always stood since 1677.

[26] Pigot, George, unmarried father of at least six children, became an Irish peer in 1766, having twice served as Governor of Madras. His famous diamond, the Pigot, was sold in 1818 for £30,000 to Ali Pasha, the Albanian despot, who dying of wounds in 1822 had it brought before him and crushed into a powder.

[27] Scholar and biographer, 1750–1832; disqualified from a career at the bar by his faith, he chose conveyancing instead and campaigned eloquently for Catholic emancipation.

[28] Kitchiner (not Kitchener), William, seems meant. Although English (and an Etonian) he could not with a Glasgow degree practise medicine in London, where he lived, so switched to optics, writing many books. Also known and admired for the music which he played, sang and collected and for the lunches which he cooked for his special friends, with an eye as much to their health as to their pleasure.

During many months, while Sophy Cornelys was endeavouring to procure a situation as teacher to young ladies in a private family, for which she was well qualified by her musical talents, and her knowledge of the French and Italian languages, it was her custom to come after breakfast to our house in Hatton Garden, where she continued the remainder of the day, and I always escorted her home at night. She was a very agreeable companion, and by her talents well rewarded my parents and the family for the humble protection which she received.

Lady Caroline Harrington, wife of the second Earl, took her under her wing "at the Stable Yard, St James's—she had recommended the boarding-school in Hammersmith and would recall the beauty of Sophy's "moonlight voice"[29]—followed first by her daughter, Anna Maria, the future Duchess of Newcastle, then by Margaret, widow of the first Earl Spencer, who bequeathed her £100 a year.[30]

On the death of the latter, she returned to town, and renewed her acquaintance with some of her earlier friends, but being introduced to the present Princess Augusta, she gradually dropped all intercourse with her old connexions, and even denied that she ever knew them. I forgot to mention in the proper place, that on the fall of her mother, she was anxious not to be known as Miss Cornelys; and one night when a knock was heard at our street-door, to quiet her fears lest a stranger should hear her name, she begged that I would go to the door myself and prevent intrusion. The person who knocked, happened to be an inquisitive little friend, who was too intimate with the family to be excluded; and asking who was in the parlour, a common name occurred to me, and I told him a Miss Williams. From that time she adopted this name, and retained it amidst all her vicissitudes till her death.

She was totally void of sensibility, but affected great feeling. She was

[29] John Taylor, ibid.: "it had a soft, calm, plaintive sound, which, like the 'sweet echo' of the lady in Comus, was more suited to the stillness of night than 'to the garish eye of day'."

[30] Mr Taylor's chronology is doubtful and incomplete. Lady Cowper too had provided Miss Williams with a home (and would leave her an annuity), as had the Marchioness of Tweeddale and the Duchess of Beaufort.

Horace Walpole refers to a Miss Williams in a letter, 4.11.1789, to his friend, Hannah More, asking whether she is with the Duchess of Beaufort at Stoke. And so does Fanny Burney in her journal, 12.1791: "I was pleased in seeing Miss Fanny Williams, as she is called; the young person who was left an Infant at the door of Lady Amherst, and who is reported to be Daughter of every woman of Rank whose character, at that date, was susceptible of suspicion. She looks a modest and pretty young Creature, and Lady Amherst brings her up with great kindness and propriety."

Mr Walpole's Miss Williams and Miss Burney's Fanny may well have been the same. But Miss Burney's "young Creature" cannot have been Williams, Sophia Wilhelmina, who was born between 12.1753 and 1.3.1754, and so, like Miss Burney herself, in her late thirties. Mrs Williams's daughter would be less unlikely, if any evidence that she had one could be found.

kindly harboured some time by Mrs Mayor, the wife of Mr Mayor, formerly Member of Parliament for Abingdon, who was an accomplished lady, and at whose house[31] *I was a frequent visitor. One evening when Miss Williams was present, a story of a recent domestic calamity was related, which drew tears from all the company, while Miss Williams forgot herself so much, as to continue her needle-work with apparent indifference. Mrs Mayor, observing her so unmoved, could not help expressing her surprise that she should hear so lamentable a story, which had so deeply affected all the company, without emotion. Miss Williams, who then thought it time to "assume a virtue, if she had it not", twisted the hair upon her forehead, looked wildly, exclaimed, "Oh! it is too much," and rushed hastily out of the room, to give vent to the violence of her sympathy.*

At length she withdrew from all intercourse with those who were likely to have known her in early days, and, obtaining the patronage of the present Princess Augusta, was employed by that amiable branch of the royal family in the distribution of her charities, to whom, no doubt, she submitted cases of calamity that never existed, and allotted the bounties to herself. She was so artful, so suspicious, and so unforgiving, that a lady who was also patronised by the same Princess for her talents as an artist, and who had painted a portrait of her Royal Highness, assured me she was obliged to pay the most cautious homage to Miss Williams, lest she should deprive her of the royal patronage.

It may be thought that I am too harsh in describing one of my early connexions; but I feel it to be a moral duty not to suffer artifice, hypocrisy, and ingratitude, to put themselves forward as virtuous qualities. Besides, Miss Williams was many years older than I was at the time, and I knew too little of the world to be able to pierce through the veil of practised subtlety and dissimulation which she assumed. Far from regretting that I have thus unmasked an artful hypocrite, who has not left any relations to lament her death, I conceive it but just that I should undeceive those whom her cunning might have ensnared into friendship, and hold out a warning to amiable credulity.

So Williams was not Mrs Williams's real name and we may wonder how Lord Sydney had been led to understand that someone whose mother was a German lady born in Venice and whose father was most likely Casanova could be numbered with his forebears. But did Mrs Williams dissemble and embezzle? We cannot be sure, for all we have is the word of Mr Taylor, who scoffs, filling his book with highly entertaining, discreditable gossip. Dr Burrow could be right, who has nothing to say of Mrs Williams but good; we can hardly doubt that she it was who founded "the old School of Industry in Cheltenham", or at least one or two of the

[31] John Mayor, a London brewer, MP 1774–82, and his wife lived at Lacy Court, near Abingdon.

hundreds of subscribers would have challenged the claim, who for almost sixty years were supplied with Dr Burrow's account; or that the bright idea was hers, of a school where girls might learn how to teach, and earn their living, too many of whom would have otherwise been destitute; and that "Sophia Wilhelmina Williams" stood a better chance than "Sophie Cornelys" of success. "By their fruits ye shall know them," Dr Burrow might have said, "St Matthew, chapter vii, verse 15."

A volume of the Managing Committee's Annual Reports, 1823, 1826 and 1827,[32] includes her silhouette, its distinctive features a big poke bonnet and a stick of a nose; and in her portrait in oils, which Princess Augusta presented to the school in 1826, we see a young woman, dressed in white, altogether more appealing, with sandalled feet and peeping toes, fingering a harp, and seated on a red-upholstered bench or stool, with a pillar to her right, under dark storm-clouds, where the sun breaks through, a symbol. The portrait hangs where the school came to stand, at Temple Dinsley in Hertfordshire. Mrs Williams's employer, the Princess, also in oils, but gilt-framed, looks down towards her from half way up the stairs.

Silhouette of Mrs Williams added to a presentation copy of the first Annual Reports.

[32] A Mr Daniel Hipwell, of 65 St John's Wood Terrace, had sold it to the school in 1894, restored and embellished. It was presented, he said, by Mrs Williams—after her death?—to the Rev. Mr John Joseph Ellis, Rector, 1821–55, of St Martin's Outwich, in the City, and a founding member of the Gentlemen's Committee. A "brief printed biography of Mrs Williams" and "three autograph letters in her hand", addressed to Mr Ellis and accompanying the book, have long since disappeared.

Ellis, John Joseph . . . Joseph Cornelys . . . Were the two connected? It can as yet no more be proved that Cornelys, *alias* Altorf, died young and abroad, as we are told, and did not return, *alias* Ellis and relieved of the stigma of his mother's shame, to beget a son and heir, than that Sophie Cornelys, *alias* Williams, bore no one a daughter.

Mrs Williams's school was and would remain in one respect unique. A Clergy Orphan Girls' School had stood at St John's Wood, just the other side of the Park,[33] since 1812; in 1824 the Clergy Daughters' School[34] began at Cowan Bridge in Lancashire; its Naval equivalent had followed and its Military[35] much later; but the Adult Orphan Institution was the first and last of its kind housing daughters of the Clergy and of Officers Army, Naval and Marine under one roof. Almost all its pupils had to be elected, as was common practice among such schools. The Secretary drew up a list of candidates, which the Committee of Ladies pruned, each girl being vouched for, "if of the Church, by the Corporation of the Sons of the Clergy, the Clergy Orphan Society or two beneficed Clergymen; if of the Army, by two General Officers of His Majesty's regular service; if of the Navy or Marines, by two Flag Officers"; and donors, subscribers and other benefactors to the school were given postal votes, proportional to their bounty—in 1831 Messrs Broadwood got eight, in return for their "two excellent horizontal grand pianofortes"—to be cast in favour of the candidates who and whose families they thought were most deserving, every six or seven months.

"Daughter of an Officer" was narrowly defined. Cordelia Rishton had to be disqualified, whose father was no longer in the Army when he died; and so did Anna Conquer, the daughter of an assistant master attendant at Plymouth Dockyard and former master RN, and Miss Cupples and Miss Illingsworth, who had each had a surgeon RN father, the surgeons RN remaining non-commissioned till 1837; a Dr Quarrie wrote objecting to the rule but in vain. By 1828 the daughters of officers holding His Majesty's Commission in the East India Company were accepted, so long as they were "born of European parents", a change the Committee seemed later to forget: though still enshrined in a footnote to their Laws, in 1858 it was announced as if new policy.

It had always been understood that the only eligible candidates for election were those who intended to be governesses and that wards would be returned to their mothers or their friends if they decided not to teach, or if they suffered from some disability that would jeopardise their prospect of being appointed to a post, or if they misbehaved; but some who found the work rather too difficult remained, if they were diligent and virtuous.

The first fifteen of the elected wards admitted, on the 11th of May 1820, were of the Church five: Octavia Langhorne, Clara Bingham, Mary and Frances Bussell and Harriet Williams; of the Navy two: Eleanor

[33] Lord's cricket-field now occupies the site. A ward went and taught there in 1826. In 1897 the school became St Margaret's, Bushey.

[34] Now Casterton. Its first year's pupils included four of the five Brontë sisters. Elizabeth Gaskell's account of its harsh régime in her *Life of Charlotte Brontë*, 1857, may be too severe.

[35] The School for Daughters of the Army, at Bath, in 1865, when it narrowly missed being called "the Military Female School". It continued to accept only Protestants till as late as 1920.

Campbell and Amelia Kendall; of the Royal Marines one: Emma Middleton; and of the Army seven: Amelia Bennet, three sisters Ross—Margaret, Mary Anne and Jane—Eliza Elliott, Arabella Battley and Alicia Sills. In July four of the nineteen listed were aged 14, two 15, four 16, three 17, two 18, one 19, one 20 and one 21. Seven of these had also lost their mothers and had guardians, called "friends". Four were "pennyless", having no other means of support but the Institution. The mothers or friends of the rest paid fees of £12 a year, called a "stipend", and sixpence a week for their laundry, in quarterly instalments. They arrived wearing long dresses and a poke bonnet, of their own choice, and were then each issued with a dessert-spoon, a tea-spoon, a pair of sheets and six towels. There was no uniform, but "the greatest neatness and simplicity" was required, "at all times".

Mrs Williams was impressed by all her pupils, their obedience, gratitude, morale and their eagerness to help and to progress:

*The Wards admitted have all come into the Institution at their own requests and have implicitly followed the regulations laid down for them with the greatest Cheerfulness. They behave with infinite cordiality and affection to each other and appear fully convinced that, being equally the children of misfortune, it is an indispensable Duty to assist and feel for each other. They draw Lots every week for their places at Church, Dinner, Tea and every six weeks for their Domestic employment . . . and the thorough knowledge they are enabled and seem desirous to obtain of their Religious and Moral Duties insures [*sic*] the continuance of that Opinion.*

The certainty that if the Institution succeeds, and they are deserving of its Protection, they will at all times find an asylum in it endears it to them and makes them delighted in lending their assistance in every way that can promote its prosperity.

A more demanding course of education was proposed than the accomplishments of music, dancing, needlecraft and painting; these remained, but as much was introduced as would enable the wards to earn themselves a living independently; as Mrs Williams put it: "as Teachers of different Branches of Education or Artists, or as useful Members of Society in domestic Concerns", they having all learnt how to manufacture and spin lace thread—"two certain and productive ways of securing constant employment"—"to be made perfect Mistress", as far as in them lay, "of the English Language and Arithmetic, to write and read French grammatically, to be well grounded in sacred and profane History, Chronology, Ancient and Modern Geography and the use of the Globes, perfect in the rudiments of Drawing and Theory of Music, so as to be capable of teaching others", as well as for their own satisfaction, and to be "neat plain workers and well instructed in the minutest parts of family Economy".

The earlier staff often taught free of charge and the wards themselves could help to support the Institution, giving private lessons. Amelia Kendall (18), the daughter of a captain RN, had two pupils for music ("on

Mr Logier's[36] system"); her sister, Mary (19), gave lessons too; Mary Ann Ross (17), whom Mr Jenkins taught dancing, had by 1822 acquired five "scholars", had "already divided with the Institution £3-10s.-od., the first fruits of her exertions", and would soon offer French, at a Miss Darby's school in Argyll Place; Eliza Elliott (19)—"designed for an English teacher"—taught *locum tenens* in Bromley, Kent, where she was paid "remuneration for her trouble"; Caroline Ginn (22), "having a taste for landscape" and "received as a *gratis* pupil by Mr Papendick",[37] would teach "in his style of Drawing"; and Charlotte Roby (15), another daughter of a naval captain, painted miniatures for sale.

The spinning of cambric and thread "as samples", Mrs Williams explained, was "too recently brought to perfection for the proper market or to afford great hopes of an early profit"; but had yielded £50. And a pair of ruffles which the wards had made, from lace manufactured by the inmates of the Princess Elizabeth Cottage, Clay Farm, Windsor, from flax grown at Winkfield nearby, and which they now presented to His Majesty, King George IV, brought a handsome promise of support from the King which he eventually honoured.

"The Wards all work", Mrs Williams reported, "with assiduity, in order to proeme[38] to themselves some independence and to the Institution some little profit . . ." Not one of them displayed false pride: "they one and all appear convinced that nothing is below the Dignity of a Gentlewoman but doing wrong."

Their earnings helped to keep the school afloat and it was partly to benefit more from the employment of the wards that Mrs Williams recommended that the age of admission be raised from 14 to 16. But the scheme fell through—Mornington Place did not then lie within the best of catchment areas for private pupils, though it seems that it was only for a year or two that wards were employed to help finance their own education.

Princess Augusta pinned her hopes on the ruffles and the King. She had been much encouraged by his undertaking to espouse the orphan cause, and was quick to write Mrs Williams a letter, announcing what appeared to be splendid news.

Buckingham House
May 24. 1822

My dear Mrs Williams,

I have the pleasure to inform you that I was with the king this morning who expressed himself in the most gracious and the kindest manner

[36] Johann Bernard Logier, 1777–1846, a Palatine German of French descent, inventor of the chiroplast, a hand-rest correctly positioning the hand to the piano, and whose method was to teach up to twelve or more pupils at as many pianos, playing all together, which financially at least was a huge success.

[37] George Ernesti Papendiek [*sic*]; born in Windsor in 1788; painter and diplomat; and appointed British Consul in Bremen in the year of his death, 1835.

[38] To preface or introduce (OED). Obsolete, rare, and here, it seems, misused.

respecting the Adult Orphan Institution. He has commanded me to assure you, my dear Mrs Williams, how truly interested he is in its welfare and that he shall subscribe annually one hundred pounds towards its support. My Brother added how much he admired the Lace Ruffles which were presented to him by the whole Institution.

Be assured I feel myself particularly happy in thus communicating the King's gracious intention and that he dwelt much upon his support and interest, proceeding greatly from his respect and veneration to the memory of our excellent Mother, who had so benevolently entered into and approved of the Plan.

Believe me my dear Mrs Williams
Your very sincere friend
Augusta

Princess Augusta did much to support Mrs Williams. The Committee of Ladies continually looked to her for guidance and approval, especially when they appointed staff. She did much to secure the patronage and bounty of the royal and famous, to her own contribution of £150 being added: from her mother, the late Queen Charlotte, and Prince Leopold of Saxe-Coburg[39] £200 each; £50 each from her brother, the Duke of Cambridge, and the Archbishop of Canterbury;[40] and from the young Lord Palmerston[41] £20. An example was set to the charitable public and, although King George IV's intention had not yet become hard cash, it too might give a lead.

The books have disappeared which she presented to the school, Alison's *Modern Europe*, and other works, "peculiarly well adapted for the reading and instruction of the wards", and her only monuments now visibly remaining are her gilt-framed portrait, perhaps by the artist Mr Taylor refers to, and a disfigured lithograph by R. J. Lane,[42] taken from a miniature by W. C. Ross,[43] a copy of which she gave to each of her staff, shortly before she died in 1840. The portrait tells little, but the lithograph says more, and no one is deceived who thinks that it reflects a kind and honest soul. She was prodigally generous. "Her benevolence has been extended to all around her," an obituary reads, "her left hand knew not what her right gave away; and never was her charity marred by ostentation on the part of the giver."[44] Having nothing to bequeath, she left no will.

[39] Widower of Princess Charlotte, only daughter of George IV and Caroline of Brunswick.

[40] Dr William Howley, 1828–48.

[41] Then Secretary-at-War under Liverpool.

[42] Grand-nephew of Gainsborough, the painter, well known for his chalk and pencil sketch of the young Princess Victoria and for his prints after Winterhalter and Chalon.

[43] Till 1857, when he was paralysed, the most sought-after of miniaturists, producing well over 2,000 pieces, his patrons including Queen Victoria, Prince Albert and Prince Louis Napoleon Bonaparte, afterwards Emperor.

[44] *The Gentleman's Magazine*, 11.1840.

At the same time, telling right from wrong, she could be firm, not only gentle, as her brother found when late in his reign he pressed her to dine with him in the company of a lady of whom she disapproved. "If you command my attendance as *King*, I will obey you; but, if you ask me as a *brother* to come, nothing will induce me."[45]

In 1821, when the school was a year old, the Princess had foreseen that it would take Mrs Williams two years more to set it on its feet. Her two years passed and in June 1823, at the house of the Dowager Countess of Harcourt[46] in Portman Square, Mrs Williams reported to the donors and subscribers. The progress of the school had been "most favourable" and, although she bore in mind "the possibility" of her death before she had "matured" her plans in detail, she would "exclusively" guide the school and manage it, if invited so to do, assisted by the two Committees, and "with undiminished zeal" she would "obey their Mandate".

Princess Augusta

Sixth of George III and Queen Charlotte's fifteen children.

It was then proposed and agreed without dissent that Mrs Williams be thanked "for her indefatigable exertions" and that her "Powers of Management" be continued "for the space of one year".

But five days later, on the 25th of June, the doubts that Mrs Williams appears to have alluded to were confirmed, for she was dead.

A meeting of the Gentlemen had already been arranged. Six of them

[45] Ibid.

[46] Elizabeth, widow of the second Earl, George Simon, and first President of the Ladies' Committee.

attended it: Mr Rowley Lascelles, lawyer, antiquary and zealous Anglican, the Rev. Dr T. T. Walmesley,[47] Dr Burrow, Mr Samuel Bosanquet and his brother, Charles,[48] of the Huguenot family of London merchants,[49] and Mr James Mure, they one and all resolving:

that this Committee, impressed with a painful sense of the loss the Adult Orphan Institution has sustained . . . cannot proceed to the performance of the duties assigned them without first expressing their cordial Esteem and Veneration for the Character of the Individual to whom the Institution owes its existence, as well as their unfeigned regret for the melancholy event which has deprived it of her inestimable services.

In bearing testimony to the extraordinary zeal, ability and benevolence with which the Establishment was originally formed, and to the persevering efforts and assiduous care with which, amidst many difficulties, it has been, for three years, directed and sustained, the Committee do but bare justice to that excellent person whose name the Orphan and the Friendless will long have ample cause to bless.

They are however most anxious to pay the best tributes to the Memory of her who laid the foundation of so great a benefit to Society, by confirming, as far as their delegated powers extend, the superstructure to her plans and wishes. They are desirous that nothing should be altered, which can properly, under the present unfortunate change of circumstances, remain the same. That the same objects should be still pursued and similar measures be now adopted in the conduct of the Institution as have hitherto been followed under the successful guidance of Mrs Williams, is their primary design in any provisions they may be called upon to make for the stability and welfare of the Institution, and for the due appropriation of the Funds.

Princess Augusta reiterated and amplified their tributes and proposals. A letter that she wrote to the Dowager Countess of Harcourt was read to the Gentlemen, then entered in the minutes:

July 8th 1823

My dearest Lady Harcourt,

Most sincerely do I lament the loss of that excellent good Mrs Williams. Her worth was great. She was humble and yet persevering in doing good. I am all anxiety about the Adult Orphan Institution, and I must entreat you to call a Committee of the Gentlemen together, or if you

[47] Walmesley, Tindal Thompson, Rector of Hanwell, Middlesex, and St Vedast, a Wren church in Foster Lane in Cheapside, bombed and wrecked in World War II but fully restored by 1962.

[48] Chairman of the Exchequer Bill Office and Sub-Governor, later Governor, of the South Sea Company.

[49] Casanova found and admired a kind and helpful Bosanquet when he visited Mrs Cornelys in London. Horace Bleackley, ibid., identifies him as Jacob, son of David, and a great-uncle of Samuel and Charles.

cannot, to see any one or two of the members, and to beg them in my name to do what they think the best for the advantage of the Institution which they have so kindly undertaken to assist. That I must beg that all Mrs Williams's Plans and Directions may be kept to most implicitly, and that no Person may be placed about the young Ladies, or any Girl admitted amongst them whose principles have not been well sounded; and also that no religious books may be put into their hands which deviate in the minutest point from the Church of England. Besides the interest which I naturally must take from duty as well as inclination for an Institution which was approved of and sanctioned by my Mother I also owe it to the attention and zeal of the Gentlemen of the Committee to place my entire confidence in them for the support of the Institution at this particular period when they have lost that good and excellent Mrs Williams to whom the Members of it must, with all those concerned in its welfare, feel such gratitude for her exertions, and such regret for her loss.

I shall also be much obliged to the Gentlemen of the Committee if they would acquaint Mrs Oliver[50] *that I am much pleased to desire them to tell her, that dear Mrs Williams mentioned her in her last Letter to me, as acting in a most satisfactory manner; and that as I know she was placed there at the recommendation of Mrs Williams, she is only called upon to go on as she has done, and on no account whatever to alter anything however trifling it may be, or seem to be, without the full approbation of the Committee and the Subscribers, who are all informed of the excellent rules laid down for the good of the Institution.*

Adieu my dear Lady Harcourt.
Ever your most truly affectionate friend,
Augusta

The Gentlemen responded, assuring the subscribers, in their Annual Report, that "the cultivation of the fine arts and sciences as professional occupations" was "never permitted to interfere with daily religious exercises, with general education, or with regular attention to work and the family avocations of the Institution", and laid it down, in the "Regulations for the Internal Management":

That all the Wards . . . be diligently and carefully instructed in the principles and duties of the Christian Religion, according to the Church of England as by law established; and do all constantly attend Divine Service on Sundays, either at the Parish Church or an Episcopal Chapel, unless prevented by illness or other sufficient reason . . . that the business of each day begin and end with prayers; and that no Religious Books or Tracts be admitted . . . but such as are contained in the catalogue of the Society for

[50] Mrs Oliver, Matron, died in office only two and a half years later, after sick-leave in Leamington Spa, "using the Bath" and for "continuance to bathe . . . maybe of essential service to her".

Promoting Christian Knowledge, or have the written sanction of both the Ladies' and Gentlemen's Committees.

The wards first worshipped at St James's Chapel[51] in the Hampstead Road, in the parish of St Pancras, where they were allowed to occupy two pews, *gratis*, till in 1825 Charles, third Lord Southampton came of age. It was more than enough time, for in 1824 the Institution moved from its rates-free, but confined and inconvenient, temporary premises to the new building which the King's architect, John Nash, had designed, it occupying land on the west side of Regent's Park, thereafter to be known as 11 St Andrew's Place, costing £3,950 and subject to ground rent of £100 a year, payable to His Majesty's Commissioners of Woods and Forests.[52]

Mrs Williams had set the Institution on its feet, its Honorary Secretary, Sub-Treasurer and factotum remarkable. Its early meetings took place at the rooms of the Hon. Mrs Ariana Egerton,[53] in St James's Palace, when Ladies outnumbered Gentlemen, and at the Dowager Countess's home in Portman Square, where and near where so many of them lived. Princess Augusta watched over it. She visited the school in 1825 and was pleased to express Her approbation of the progress made by the Wards, in the different branches of education and accomplishments, as well as of the management of the whole", in touch with her friend, among other titled ladies, the Marchioness Cornwallis,[54] a member of the Ladies' Committee by 1828 and its President from 1831 till 1850.

It was Gentlemen, however, who mainly now took charge. The Ladies vetted candidates for election; sat and listened to the wards read English and French, converse with Mademoiselle and play their music, looked at their drawings, handwriting, watched them dance, were satisfied to learn of their progress in arithmetic ("as far as the ladies can judge from the accounts they have received"); recommended them for posts (recalling that Mrs Williams had not intended that they should all teach—almost all, however, did); admonished the ill-behaved; visited the sick; inspected pianos; and hired domestic staff. The Gentlemen decided what seemed to them important. They called for the estimates, reviewed expenditure, signed drafts for the payment of the quarterly bills, negotiating and remonstrating through their Clerk, Mr Jesse, with baker, butterman, cheesemonger, greengrocer, tea-dealer, brewer—or cooper and malt-and-hopster,

51 1791 (Sir Thomas Hardwick)–1956, opposite the end of Robert Street.

52 The Commissioners of Woods, Forests and Land Revenues, which in 1923 became the Commissioners of Crown Lands and in 1956 the Crown Estate Commissioners.

53 Lady of the Bedchamber to the late Queen Charlotte; unmarried daughter of William, Lt.-Col.; niece of John, Bishop of Durham; and cousin to the Henry, eighth Earl of Bridgwater, scholar and crank, who filled his Paris house with dogs and cats, dressing some as folk, and its garden with small game to be shot and potted.

54 Louisa, daughter of the fourth Duke of Gordon; a tireless friend of the needy and of the village school, which she governed and supported, at Culford, where she lived, near Bury St Edmunds.

when the beer was brewed at the school—poulterer, butcher, hatter, undertaker—when a ward or servant had died—chinaman, looking-glass maker, silversmith, colourman, tallow-chandler, coal-merchant, laundry, bookseller, music shop . . . and who dealt with the neighbours who complained about the smoke from the wash-house and their view of the privy and with the nuisance to the wards of the stench rising from the cesspool. The Ladies put the Gentlemen right when they decided to have the privy converted into a tool-shed for the gardener—the privy could not be done without, so a covered way was built to it instead—but it was clearly understood that, whatever the Ladies might propose, the Gentlemen disposed, whose word almost always prevailed.

Expenditure had to be contained, income pleaded for and the £100 a year extracted which His Majesty had promised in May 1822. No £100 forthcame. In April 1824 the Committee wrote to the King's Private Secretary, Sir William Knighton,[55] and asked him "to ascertain the proper course to be pursued for the receipt of the same". No luck. Another month passed by and, having still not heard from Sir William, they decided to address to the King himself this obsequious memorial:

May it please your Majesty

Your Majesty's most humble and dutiful servants the Managing Committee for the Adult Orphan Institution presume to lay at your Majesty's feet their respectful thanks for the high honour conferred on the Adult Orphan Institution by your Majesty's distinguished Patronage and to entreat a continuation of your Majesty's most gracious Benevolence by a command that the Annual Munificent Donation may be transmitted to the Funds of the Institution.

Your Majesty's
most humble and dutiful subjects

The approach appeared to work. On the 30th of June 1825 Chairman Earl Manvers[56] could report that the King's £100 had been received, indeed 100 guineas, "with a gracious message that a Report of the Charity might be sent in annually to his Majesty's Privy Purse".

A fund-raising concert was arranged next year. Princess Augusta, the Duchess of Kent[57] and Prince Leopold patronised it, which ensured success, and themselves undertook each to sell ten tickets of the hundred issued, the Ladies and the Gentlemen dealing with the rest. Recitals were

[55] Physician to the Prince of Wales till the Prince became King, then his Private Secretary and Keeper of his Privy Purse.

[56] Charles, the second Earl, MP for Nottinghamshire, 1801–16, and founder in 1851 of St Mary's Hospital, Paddington.

[57] Victoria, youngest daughter of the Duke of Saxe-Coburg, widow of Prince Emich Charles of Leiningen, wife of Edward Augustus, George III's fourth son, and mother of his only child, Victoria, Princess and future Queen.

given, for no fee, by fifteen musicians of repute and even fame, including Madame Pasta, soprano,[58] but not a Madame Laborde Bussoni, whose offer to appear was "respectfully declined"; Ignaz Moscheles, the Czech pianist and composer;[59] Mr Franz Cramer[60] and Charles de Bériot,[61] violinists; and His Majesty's Band, which Mr Thomas Greatorex conducted, Organist at Westminster Abbey. The receipts totalled £750 (£629–8s.–6d. net) and in the words of the next Report "the pecuniary means of the Institution" were "materially promoted and its interests essentially advanced by the public being more extensively made acquainted with its claims for their support".

Legacies helped: £1,000 from a late Mrs Vernon financed an extension housing twelve more wards; and a collection made in India by the Marquess of Hastings[62] was felt to be a godsend. But, as fast as capital accumulated, expenditure depleted it. More regular income was needed than donations and legacies could provide and the Managing Committee had continually to appeal to the subscribers themselves to solicit more subscriptions.

The Gentlemen's Reports were dated June or July. A thousand copies were printed and distributed in 1834, including one each for the United Services Club, the Naval and the Oxford and Cambridge. Luke and James Hansard[63] asked for three, and for other information, in 1847. By 1871, 1,500 were required. They tell us much about the school in Regent's Park. And more has survived in the minutes, just legible, of the separate meetings of the Gentlemen's and Ladies' Committees.

The earlier Reports read like Dr Burrow's. As Honorary Secretary, and link between the two Committees, taking endless pains over the appointment of the wards to their teaching posts, he was highly esteemed, and the Gentlemen, at least, seemed almost inconsolable when in 1827 a school in Exeter appointed him its head and he had to withdraw his services: "Dr Burrow's resignation is dictated by imperious motives which cannot be controuled [*sic*] by remonstrance or entreaty . . . The evil must be met, for it

[58] Pasta, Giuditta, the young Jewish-Italian soprano, a regal figure, on stage, and as mistress, years later, of her villa near Lake Como, entertaining. Her uneven but impassioned voice ran from low A to top D.

[59] His name subordinately minuted by the Gentlemen: he had only just reached London, there to stay till in 1841 Mendelssohn invited him to head the piano division at the Paris Conservatory.

[60] From a musically gifted Mannheim family; like his father, Wilhelm, he would direct King George IV's own band.

[61] A Belgian, aged 24, who made as well as played the violin; composer, craftsman, landscape painter, poet and sculptor; second husband of Maria Malibran, he would design her tomb, casting her on it as St Cecilia.

[62] Francis, first Marquess of Hastings and second Earl of Moira; Governor of Bengal, 1813–22.

[63] Two younger sons of Luke, who in 1828 succeeded him as printers to the House of Commons.

cannot be palliated . . ." They gave him an ink-stand, bearing his and the school's names and the names of all the Ladies and their own.

Events overtook the sorrow, gift and tributes. Dr Burrow resigned from his new post or was dismissed, after only a term, falling out with his employers; and in 1830 he returned to the school in Regent's Park, no longer however as its Honorary Secretary, but as Clerical Superintendent, empowered to organise, control, and if possible improve, its methods of instruction.

But joy at the news of his return was as premature as dismay had been at the news of his departure. For although, as Clerical Superintendent, he was allowed to communicate directly with the wards ("free admission"), under Regulation XI it had been laid down that he might only do so when "one of the Ladies of the Establishment was present".

Dr Burrow may not have thought the rule important, having long ago allowed Mr Papendiek to teach Miss Ginn perspective and landscape, all alone, when none of the Gentlemen, whom he had taken the precaution of informing, appear to have demurred; but the Ladies were displeased and, once it was reported that he had spoken to the wards unchaperoned, he felt himself honour-bound to resign his office.

The Gentlemen stood by him, but failed to change his mind, and the Ladies agreed that the Dowager Duchess of Newcastle[64] should be asked to invite Princess Augusta to review the regulations, if necessary consulting the Archbishop of Canterbury,[65] and so perhaps to construe it as to relieve Dr Burrow's conscience and persuade him to continue. But all in vain: Archbishop and Princess conferred and agreed that the rule should be adhered to; Dr Burrow resigned, followed by Mr Ellis, now Secretary, Dr Walmesley and five of the Ladies; then escaped notice until, after five years, he was posted to Gibraltar as a civil chaplain, finding time perhaps to collect more shells, and was appointed Archdeacon there in 1842.

We can be sure that he was missed. Control of the school was already discontinuous, with no one on the premises for long who from day to day took charge. The first Lady Governess was Mrs Mackenzie, widow of Thomas, the Admiral,[66] who answered all enquiries. A Lady Manager was also appointed, Mrs Gascoigne, who might have been described as housekeeper, were it not that she also organised the teaching. Their functions overlapped.

In 1823, Mrs Williams having died, the Gentlemen asked the King's Private Secretary, Sir William Knighton, to obtain "His Majesty's commands for the future conduct of the Institution by the Managing

[64] Anna Maria, daughter of the second Earl of Harrington and widow of Thomas, third Duke.

[65] Still Dr Howley, the second Earl Grey's "poor miserable creature", opposed to bills for the emancipation of Catholics and Jews and the reform of Parliament.

[66] His rather piratical career was only half complete when in 1793 something undisclosed went wrong and he began to feel unwanted. He died aged 60 in 1813—Norie's *Naval Gazetteer* (1842): "secluded from the world . . . of a broken heart".

Committee". Sir William enquired; then replied that the King had heard "a very favourable report of Mrs Mackenzie", whom he therefore recommended as worthy to succeed the late Mrs Williams. But Mrs Williams, the Gentlemen explained, had held no office (they were wrong: she had been Honorary Secretary and Sub-Treasurer), so had left no vacancy; Mrs Mackenzie had resigned anyway; and a lady of whom Mrs Williams had approved, a Mrs Wickes, had been appointed in her stead.

Mrs Wickes, however, was no longer in her prime and only half a year later was "elected to Bromley College", a home for clergymen's widows.[67] A *locum* followed her, Miss Goodspeed—"Lady Resident"—who stayed four or five months while the school still occupied its temporary quarters. Miss Larkin was appointed next, nominee of Lady Harcourt, her duties being to supervise "the education, conduct and manners of the wards", but she too only stayed five months. Miss Watson took Miss Larkin's place in 1825, who had soon to be dismissed—somehow ineffective—a Miss Douglas was found—another *locum*—then Miss Mary Charlton, returning from Paris, whose sister, Elizabeth, became the Lady Manager—she had once taught the wards to paint on velvet, and had charged no fee. After three years the Charltons were dismissed by the Ladies, whereupon they both resigned, writing grateful letters, but only to the Gentlemen. Miss Daniel replaced Mary, the Ladies "highly approving of her manner and appearance", and remained till 1830, when her health failed; and Miss Richards replaced Elizabeth, the Lady Manager to be now called Matron.

Miss Richards believed that she as Matron would outrank the Lady Governess and, although she was mistaken, her mistake was not ill-founded, for the Regulations, 1823, had made it clear that the Lady Manager had had as much to do with education as with keys, bed-linen and cod-liver oil, and it was matrons, her successors, who inspected the letters and parcels the wards received and sent, and who reported on their conduct to the Ladies' Committee, as well as on their health and on the tradesmen.

By 1828 either all or almost all the staff were paid. There was no fixed scale. The Italian Master, Mr Ziliani, got more than the French. Monsieur Grégoire found out that this was so and felt upset, he "being of opinion that a perfect acquirement of the French language" was "an object of primary importance"; but the Managing Committee accepted his complaint, for he was "very indefatigable in his attention to the wards", and raised his yearly salary to forty guineas. When Gentlemen taught, Matron had to sit through all their lessons, especially no doubt now that Regulation XI had been invoked and upheld.

The day's routine began at 8.0 a.m., with Prayers, followed by Breakfast at 8.30, Work (Needlework or Lace) from 9.30 to 11.0, Religious Instruction from 11.0 to 11.30, Lunch at 1.0 p.m., "Masters or Exercises

[67] Founded by Dr John Warner, Bishop of Rochester, in 1666, and as his will reads: "for twenty poore widowes (of orthodoxe and loyall clergymen)".

and Translations" (Italian and French), or Religion again, from 2.30 to 4.0, Tea at 5.0, most of the academic subjects from 6.0 to 8.0, Dancing from 8.0 to 9.0, then renewed Prayers. For their evening lessons the girls were divided into Classes I and II (we are not told how) and by 1829 this was their time-table:

Class I

	Monday	Tuesday	Wednesday	Thursday	Friday
6–7 p.m.	Geography and Globes	Arithmetic	Geography and Globes	French Dictation	Arithmetic
7–8 p.m.	History and Chronology	Bible and Chronology	History	Bible	History

Class II

	Monday	Tuesday	Wednesday	Thursday	Friday
6–7 p.m.	Bible and Chronology	Arithmetic	History	Bible and Chronology	Arithmetic
7–8 p.m.	Geography and Globes	Writing and Composition	Dictation	Geography	Dictation

What else we learn of what was taught, and how, is fragments. The Ladies agreed that "it would be advantageous to the Wards if they were permitted to read Poetry occasionally" and "the Works of Milton were named" by the Gentleman "as being unexceptionable". No more was heard of poetry, however, till Cowper was announced in 1857. A Mme Mongredin had early taught French ("a person of great respectability"), giving two days a week, on the one two hours of written, on the next two hours of speech. Corneille was read, who offered heroes to admire, and Molière, light relief. Miss Daniel asked that the wards be allowed to read the History of France from *The London Encyclopaedia*. The Gentlemen decided on a separate text. Yearly examinations began in 1828 or earlier and in 1829 were presided over by Mr Charles Blomfield, Lord Bishop of London, a formidable scholar, in the presence of HRH Princess Augusta. Dr Burrow proposed £5 worth of books, which may have been awarded, for diligence and good conduct. Monsieur Grégoire awarded his own, who could now perhaps afford to—"tokens of merit" for his best pupils—a *fait*

accompli which Miss Daniel reported to the Managing Committee, who then blessed it.

In her last report, presented at a General Meeting of Donors and Subscribers, Mrs Williams had insisted that a high standard prevail both of work and behaviour, and emphasised how much that standard would depend on quality of intake; for the object of the school was "not to give talents, but to cultivate them; not to combat bad habits, but to encourage and confirm good ones; not to correct erroneous ideas but to instil just ones". And thus designed the Institution would reserve to itself the right of returning to their friends any wards who were not "fit objects; that is, as not being qualified either in point of character or ability to profit by the advantages offered them".

The Institution's Laws, about aims, finance, votes, officers and meetings, were amplified in its Bye-Laws, one of which laid down that the elected ward's first year was probationary and that no one might continue as a pupil who could not or would not learn. It was first applied in 1824. Miss Emily Dade, though impeccably behaved, had fallen far behind in class. The Gentlemen had reprieved her "for reasons of humanity". But now they decided to remove her after all, Dr Burrow being called upon "to take such means of informing her Mother of the determination of the Committee as may be least unpleasant to her feelings". Another ward, Ann Foley, the daughter of a lieutenant in the 58th Regiment of Foot, who in 1807 had been lost aboard a mail-boat, the *Prince of Wales*, found the work too difficult. She asked to be allowed to be apprenticed to a mantua-maker, but stayed at school till her friends could no longer pay towards her keep, when she remained free of charge till a post for her was found as governess with the family of Mr Frederick Coventry, of Killy Lodge, Great Glen, in Leicestershire.

A new Bye-Law was approved in 1828 after two mothers, acting "out of selfish considerations", had reclaimed their daughters, whereby the too indulgent mother, or sometimes friend, had to undertake to repay to the school a sum of £20 for each year of tuition and board which the pupil had received. For if a girl was to justify a training which her family could not otherwise have found or afforded, and return to society the benefits which she had enjoyed, her mother's wish "to have for her own comfort the Society of her Child" should be resisted.

After Laws and Bye-Laws, Regulations followed, for the Internal Management of the Institution, about religion, worship, the curriculum, visitors, gratuities and mail. They allowed family visitors in the presence of the Governess or Matron, including uncles and brothers, if they came between the hours of two and five o'clock and on Saturdays only, "so as not to interfere with the avocations of the wards", but other kinsmen, and women friends, had first to apply for "an order" from a member of one of the Committees; a ward was not allowed to leave the premises "on any pretence whatever", unless accompanied by staff or by someone approved of by any one member of the Managing Committee or of the

Sub-Committee of the more important Ladies; gratuities, "on what pretext soever, to any servants or officer of the Institution", were "expressly forbidden"; and letters and parcels to and from the wards had first to be received by Matron, inspected by Matron and the Governess, then delivered or posted or withheld as the two saw fit.

Authority and the rules were circumvented and defied. Miss Richards found the wards too independent. And so did the Gentlemen, who disapproved of the "great and improper expence [*sic*]" which the wards and servants had incurred over the year "in the celebration of several Festivities"—"the most rigid economy would have to be observed". Misses Elliott, France, Grisdale—the Rev. Mr Solomon Grisdale's Anne—Mackay, Mascall, Morgan, Roberts, Pratt and Vallance—almost one in four of the junior (resident) wards in 1830 and four of the nine of them daughters of the cloth—were insubordinate and, being summoned to appear, were reproved—Mrs Pratt then took away her unhappy Elizabeth—and as many others misbehaved and were removed as were withdrawn by their family or friends. Jane Kirk, "repeatedly admonished without any good effect", was returned to her mother, Princess Augusta approving, as was Jane Chamberlayne, the daughter of the Rector of Charlton in Kent, who had twice written to her sister on the sly, and was sent home, "guilty of prevarication and falsehood by denying the fact". The cook and the upper housemaid, who had aided and abetted Miss Chamberlayne, were also dismissed. The Rev. Mr George Cambridge,[68] Archdeacon of Middlesex, and Mr Joshua Watson,[69] his friend, protested that the Committee had acted too severely[70] but the Ladies and the Gentlemen saw it as their duty "to hold out as an example to the Establishment the consequences of such insubordination" and would not relent.

The rules were strict and they were rigorously enforced. Applications for leave, however, were considered more indulgently. Alicia Sills and Emma Middleton could each have a month at home with their mothers—Mrs Middleton was dying; Amelia France, a visit to hers, now "supposed to be very near her dissolution"; Laura Elliott, a day or two with a brother about to leave for India, for a continuous period of seventeen years; and Georgina Roberts, three days with a sister she might never see again. But

[68] Son of the poet, Richard (1717–1802).

[69] A rich wine-merchant, a leader of the high church party, a founder of the National Society for the Education of the Poor, the Church Building Society and King's College, London, Secretary of a fund for the relief of German victims of the Napoleonic Wars and Treasurer of the Society for the Promotion of Christian Knowledge—with Mr Cambridge—and of the Clergy Orphan School.

[70] It may have seemed to Mr Cambridge that the Committee's decision to remove Miss Chamberlayne had failed the test which his father implies—

What is the worth of anything,
But for the happiness t'will bring?

—in his poem, *Learning*, which till 1979 *The Oxford Dictionary of Quotations* continued to enshrine.

Mary Ann Ross, who wished to go and visit her sister, Jane, employed by the Wagners of Herstmonceux, had to stay at school; Mr Benjamin Gibbon[71] was not allowed to come and see his sister, Martha,[72] outside the hours prescribed—Martha was thought to be "brainsick"; or Mrs Donne, widow of the Rev. Mr Theophilus Donne, "late of the Island of Jamaica", to have her Mary with her for Christmas ("contrary to the rules"). Holidays had yet to be declared but in June 1829, when the house needed to be painted, the wards went home, all but five who had nowhere to go—Miss Richards took them to Hastings, given £30 to cover all her outlay. Mary Donne went home next August "to spend a few days in the Country with her Mother", to be nursed. No more of her was heard until the few days had become ten months, when the Ladies refused to allow her to return. The Gentlemen resolved to approve and confirm what the Ladies had already decided, "on account of her protracted absence . . . without leave, her advanced age also rendering it improbable that she would become qualified in due time"—she was 20 or 21—"to undertake a situation as Governess".

The school took pains to ensure that candidates for election were morally and physically dependable, so that no opportunity to learn, then teach, would be wasted on a ne'er-do-well or invalid, the mother or a friend of any applicant for a wardship having first to produce a certificate, which the minister and churchwardens of her parish had signed, stating her age and whether she had had whooping-cough, cow-pox or measles; that she had had small-pox or been vaccinated against it; that she was not subject to scrofula[73] or any other constitutional disease; and had no defect of intellect, impediment of speech or immoral habit; but enjoyed good health, was of sound character and "in every respect . . . a proper object to be elected into the Adult Orphan Institution".

Physicians and surgeons gave their services free, among them Mr William Wadd, Surgeon Extraordinary to King George IV—known also for his etchings—till in 1829, on holiday in Ireland, he was killed jumping from a runaway vehicle; Dr James Johnson, Physician Extraordinary to King William IV; Mr Robert Keate—from 1823 to 1858—brother of the ferocious John, Headmaster of Eton, President of the College of Surgeons, the King's Serjeant-Surgeon Extraordinary, then Serjeant-Surgeon to Queen Victoria—in later life he is said to have said: "I have attended four sovereigns, and have been badly paid for my services. One of them, now deceased, owed me nine thousand guineas"; Dr William Chambers, Physician in Ordinary to Queens Adelaide and Victoria, in his time London's leading physician, earning over £10,000 a year, whose death occurred in 1855,

[71] A renowned line-engraver, once a pupil at the Clergy Orphan School, he lived round the corner in Albany Street, where in 1851, aged 49, he died of cholera.

[72] A Mrs Heathcote employed her, at her home in the New Forest, but "serious misconduct" led to her dismissal, when the Gentlemen disowned her and returned her to the care of the Clergy Orphan Corporation.

[73] A disease thought to have been tubercular, known also as the king's evil; it typically affected the lymphatic glands.

some six or seven years after a medical journal had already reported it; and Mr Samuel Cartwright, ivory turner become a dental surgeon, dispatching up to fifty patients in a regular twelve-hour day, thus earning even more than Dr Chambers.

In 1827 Mr Rumball, an apothecary, analysed the bread and found it to contain "a very considerable quantity of alum . . . very injurious to the health of the wards". Custom was transferred from Rogers to Glendinning. The diet improved: "Cook makes very good bread", Mrs Richards reported, "when she has good flour." The beer was brewed in the house and fresh vegetables were grown in the school's own garden, where the gardener supplied his own manure, gravel and tools in return for a wage of £70 a year.

Sanitation from time to time offended, especially the garden privy and the sewers. Hygiene was otherwise as good as could be hoped for in the 1820s. The wards took a bath every night. Dr Keate recommended high-back chairs, which, the Ladies agreed, were "highly necessary". "A uniform temperature of sixty degrees" was prescribed for Clara Bingham's room. Sickness was mostly treated on the premises. The seriously ill were taken home, if they could travel, and if those who survived had friends wealthier than their widowed mothers they might go and convalesce in the country or at the seaside. Martha Gibbon, however, who had lost both parents in her first two years of life, and was "destitute of friends", all but her brother, he unable to accept her, was allowed to stay at school. There she recovered. The Rev. Mr Richard Frizell's Eliza, from Ilfracombe in Devon, who had topped the poll with 805 votes in the election to her wardship, was found to be "decidedly consumptive"; RM Capt. William Steele's Victoria had "pulmonary disease" and lateral curvature of the spine; Victoria and Eliza were removed; and Mary Bone, daughter of Capt. William Bone of the Royal York Rangers—killed in Tobago in 1814—had to leave her post, with failing eyesight.

The Managing Committee had by now decided that all candidates should be "presented to the Gentlemen"—no doubt the physicians—a month before the votes were cast, but preliminary screening did little to restrict the number of girls admitted who would later be returned, hopelessly ill, to their mothers or their friends. Miss Sarah Hildyard, one of the eleven children of the Rev. Mr John Hildyard, of Bonby in Lincolnshire, was "in delicate health" but "free from disease" in 1829, fell seriously ill next year and was allowed to go and stay with her mother (she survived and would teach Queen Victoria's children). The condition of nine other wards was reported "unobjectionable". But three died: RM Lt.-Col. Middleton's Emma (21), having just lost her mother, RN Lt. Talbot's Catherine (20), who like Emma was consumptive, and Army Lt. Elliott's Eliza (25),[74] at Mrs Hodgett's seminary, Bath.

[74] Of the Elliott four, Eliza, Jane, Laura and Matilda, only Eliza and Matilda were sisters.

Wards aged 21, called seniors, took posts, if their health, character and work were satisfactory. Alicia Sills, daughter of a captain in the Prince of Wales's Leicester Fencibles, crossed the Park and became an assistant governess at the Clergy Orphan School. Another Army captain's daughter, Eloisa Drury, was offered to Lady Willoughby d'Eresby[75] but refused to go; she accepted instead a Mrs Henry, who valued her services; returned exhausted, after three years, to 11 St Andrew's Place; recovered; and was then transferred. Octavia Langhorne, whose father had been Vicar of Little Grimsby, near Louth, travelled all the way to the home of the Rev. Mr Charles Leicester, of Westbury in Shropshire, but could not stay, for she had no Latin. General the Hon. John Brodrick[76] and his wife, Anne, took Eliza, daughter of Army Captain Walsh—later she accepted posts without permission; her name was twice deleted from the senior list; but she disarmingly repented and her name was twice restored.

Dr Burrow having left, it was the Ladies who now placed wards with employers; they considered "highly blamable" anyone who transferred herself to another family of her own free will; and when Caroline Ginn left the Rev. Mr Norton's children in Southwold, and Georgina Roberts went to Dr James Monk, Bishop of Gloucester,[77] their names were removed. Miss Roberts herself though had already been withdrawn by her guardian, Dr Scratchley, and Miss Ginn, who only a few months later returned uninvited to her old school and was there severely chidden, remained unabashed.

In 1827 the Gentlemen's Report betrayed anxieties. Did the high standard Mrs Williams had set, it was asked, still prevail?

*Education, whether literary or scientific, is not all that is requisite for a Ward to acquire in order to do justice to her employers, the Institution, or herself. A young person may be capable of teaching the early branches of Education, may therefore be useful in a family, and capable of assisting herself, and of relieving the Institution of the expence [*sic*] of her maintenance, who may not yet have acquired sufficient command of her own temper, be sufficiently schooled in moral and religious duties, to bear with patience the mortifications to which her situation as a Governess will probably expose her; and unless the Wards from the Institution continue to support the character which has already been acquired for them by their predecessors, they will lose that pre-eminent estimation in which they are now held; and it will cease to be considered a privilege to obtain a Governess from this Establishment.*

[75] Priscilla, Lady Willoughby, was then aged 66 and would die within a year. Eloisa may have taught her grandchildren, at Gwydir in Caernarvonshire or at Grimthorpe Castle in Lincolnshire.

[76] Fourth son of George, third Viscount Midleton, and Albinia, sister of the first Viscount Sydney. John, their eldest child, was now 15. It is more likely that Eliza taught Anne, Mary and Maria.

[77] A brilliant scholar and a friend of Mr Blomfield. He had three daughters and a son called Charles. It is not known how long he kept Georgina. The little boy did well: a future MP for Gloucester and Chancellor of Bristol University.

So far, however, as their progress was concerned, "in the several branches of Education and accomplishment, in religious instruction, Arithmetic, Geography, and the use of the Globes, French and Italian, History, Music and Drawing", results in the May examinations had been "most satisfactory" and were "not less creditable to the diligence and good will of the scholars, than to the zeal and ability of the Instructors".

Demand for the services of the wards was more than the school could satisfy, as the Lindsays of Haigh Hall, Wigan, the Allgoods of Tynemouth, South Shields, and the Carrutherses of Mitchells, Tunbridge Wells, each found. It all reflected Mrs Williams's success. After ten years 1,106 benefactors had accumulated 1,970 votes and 82 or so wards now received, or had completed, a course of education which boys had long either suffered or enjoyed, while their sisters were denied it; and although the school in Regent's Park would struggle, and almost perish, in the end it would endure.

Chapter Two

1831–1842

Miss Hervey, "a lady highly recommended and eminently qualified", was appointed Lady Governess in 1831. She had taught in the family of the Rev. Mr Vere John Alston, Rector of Odell, in Bedfordshire, and would remain in office for eleven years.

The Committees knew that her inheritance was difficult. In the words of the Gentlemen's Report:

from the period of Mrs Williams's death until the year 1829 the offices of Governess and Matron had been filled by persons who proved very unequal to the proper discharge of their duties, and a gradual relaxation had in consequence taken place in the observance of many of the original rules.

The rules were now to be enforced and tightened. Only two visitors at a time would be allowed each ward and, "to avoid much inconvenience", uncles and brothers were limited to only one hour every three months. But one relaxation was confirmed, which the Ladies had appeared to overlook, whereby after four years a ward might spend a month at home with her mother or with friends, the practice to continue "should her general conduct merit that indulgence".

A problem arose. Too many of the wards employed as governesses were dissatisfied with their pay and returned to the school expecting to be accommodated free of charge, as its bye-laws promised. Not all could be received. An improved minimum salary was therefore prescribed: £50 a year, rising by £10 steps to £80,[1] intended to keep them happier at work, and off the premises, till they were thirty years old and mature enough to bargain independently. But rumour having spread, and got the better of denial, that board and lodging were about to be withheld, fifteen seniors decided to resign.

Their departure may have helped, but not their protest, which did nothing to provide more space and beds, and five years later the Committee had to rule that only two seniors at a time could be accepted and that all who had reached the age of 25 would have to turn instead to their families or friends.

Another change was proposed and agreed, which, it was hoped, might improve the wards' behaviour. A decision taken only two days before the death of Mrs Williams, to raise the age of entry from between 14 and 17 to

[1] This was £20 more than the most that Miss Hervey would earn as Lady Governess.

between 16 and 20, was reversed; there would be "more docility, more willing submission to the rules . . . and fewer confirmed habits to correct", if the elected wards were admitted two or three years younger. But the change, if it worked, could not work fast; and as the years went by it appeared to make no difference. Lt.-Col. Skinner's Marianne, who had topped the poll in 1830 (1,023 votes), attended church without permission, it seems to meet her brother, who wrote her a letter which Miss Hervey and the Ladies thought unfit for her to read. The Gentlemen decided to exclude her brother from the premises, but Marianne was allowed to complete the course and, after taking posts at Cowesby in remote North Yorkshire and near Swansea, she settled in Australia. Jane McInnes, however, the daughter of a lieutenant in the 8th Veteran Battalion, was removed, exposed by her aunt, who had written to say that she was still corresponding with a young man whom she had known before she had been enrolled. The Ladies then discovered that her sister, a Mrs Hanson, had aided and abetted her, and so "highly reprehensible" did they find her conduct, she having "for a considerable period denied the facts notwithstanding the existence of the most satisfactory evidence", that the Gentlemen agreed—Earl Manvers, Mr James Mure, now Treasurer, and the Very Rev. Dr James Webber, Dean of Ripon,[2] Clerical Superintendent—that it was "absolutely necessary that she should be removed from the Institution as early as possible". Subscribers protested; Messrs Chippendale and Hoghton withdrew their support, Mr Hoghton explaining that, although he disapproved of Miss McInnes's behaviour, the Committee could have taken other steps—"coercive measures"—designed to mend her ways.

Behaviour as a whole seemed good to the Committee in 1834, the subscribers were informed:

From the Governess, Miss Hervey . . . they learn that the deportment of her pupils has . . . been most regular and attentive; and that by their cheerful compliance with her wishes and steady application to their studies they have uniformly evinced a due sense of the advantages offered by the Institution and an earnest desire to profit by them to the best of their power. In fact, not a single instance of misconduct has occurred to require the least interference or animadversion of the Managing Committee.

Assistant Commissary General (West Indies) Harold France's Louisa, however, was removed at about the time that their Report was being printed, whose complaint by way of her sister, Amelia, that Miss Hervey had ill-treated her, was investigated and dismissed; then Sophia Rule,

[2] Also Vicar of Kirkham in Lancashire, one of twelve Prebendaries of Westminster Abbey, thus Curate of St Margaret's, Westminster—a wealthy pluralist. His memorial in Ripon Cathedral records in Latin how five of his children died: one drowning in the Thames, one suddenly collapsing, one accidentally shot, one in her cot and another (but he at least was 65 years old) mountaineering in Switzerland.

daughter of a surgeon in the Glengary Fencibles, who did not appear to have the makings of a governess and who pertly declared that her friends were free to withdraw her when they chose; and RN Lt. Cyrus Elliott's Jane, whose "spirit of obstinate resistance" to Miss Hervey's authority disturbed the otherwise prevailing atmosphere of "harmony, order and regularity".

It may have been true, as the Ladies believed, that the wards were almost all happy and grateful. Mr John Turner, however, a Managing Gentleman, appeared not to think so, giving notice of a motion he proposed to introduce "as to the propriety of enlarging the means of communication of the Wards with Society", thus perhaps implying that they lived too confined, had exhausted their repertoire of talk and fun and yearned to escape and enjoy a change of scene. But the Ladies disagreed, who had heard about the impending motion from Mr Jesse, the Clerk; the Marchioness Cornwallis, the Hon. Mrs Bowles,[3] Miss Hall and Mrs Lonsdale[4] begged to state, as "their unqualified opinion", that any alteration to the rules affecting discipline "would be prejudicial to the Wards": the wards were now "perfectly satisfied", enjoying as they did "the liberty of visiting the several Ladies of the Committee"; furthermore: "the Situations in which the Wards are for the most part placed do not render necessary any more extensive acquaintance with Society".

It does not seem that the Ladies understood, or many of the Gentlemen, how cloistering 11 St Andrew's Place might feel, to a young woman 18 years old to 21, or how provocatively difficult. The need to repair or decorate the house continued to provide a summer break, but only once a year, Christmas and Easter being spent at school, and even that had still to be deserved, as Army Capt. Parker's Eleanor discovered, and the Rev. Mr Charles Woodd's Anne, when in 1841 they had to stay behind when the other girls departed.

At the time of the Ladies' satisfaction with morale the Gentlemen could report to the subscribers that the wards had eased Miss Hervey's task with conduct almost saintly:

the general behaviour . . . has been such as to render her labours light in comparison . . . they evince towards her that deference and respect, grateful attention and affectionate attachment, which must be acknowledged as her due, and which re-act upon the Wards themselves by giving increased facility to their reception of her instruction . . . and . . . towards each other they exhibit a kindness and tenderness of feeling proper to their sex, and such a readiness to assist each other as the sameness of misfortune which has qualified them for admission might be expected to excite, and the nature of the religious instruction they receive to foster and promote.

[3] Frances, born Temple, sister of Lord Palmerston, the statesman; and wife, till her early death in 1838, of Admiral William Bowles of the Managing Committee, its future Chairman.

[4] Sophia, wife of John, Bishop of Lichfield.

It was rather too good to be entirely true. Eight of the wards were removed in Miss Hervey's last six years, including Mary Ellison, who had been guilty of "numerous acts of the most serious insubordination", in particular a secret correspondence with a male cousin, and who "in the presence of the Wards had declared her decided intention not to use any attempts to learn, and also her determination not to remain in the house". A meeting was therefore held of both Committees, they one and all resolving that Miss Ellison be instantly dismissed and her mother summoned to collect her—she too appeared to incur displeasure, being privy to the secret correspondence and aware of her daughter's general misconduct.

The Gentlemen reported Mary's fate to the subscribers in a favourable light, calculated, perhaps, to assuage disappointment, uphold confidence, consolidate support and turn what seemed like failure into triumph:

It affords the Committee much satisfaction to have learned, that the conduct of this Ward was strongly reprobated by all the others who were of an age to understand the folly it betokened in herself, and the injury it might have occasioned to the Institution; and that her short association with them, instead of having been attended with any evil result, has only been the means of trying and proving the solidity and correctness of their principles. They indulge the hope also, from the sense of her fault which she manifested upon her removal, that this mark of censure, which could not consistently with the nature and regulations of the Society be less severe, will, by the Divine blessing, prove useful to her for the future; that it will show her the necessity of observing, though in a different situation from what she might have here attained, candour, circumspectness, and self-control; and that hereafter she will acknowledge it as a happy circumstance that she was received, though but for a short time, into this Institution, where, owing to the vigilance and discipline exercised, a timely check was given to her in a course of folly and indiscretion, from which, if persisted in, the worst consequences might be apprehended.

Illicit correspondence alarmed the Ladies most, as a source or proof of mischief, even more than did uncles and brothers on the premises. But a new rule, minuted in 1840 and forbidding visitors to read or hand a letter to a ward, seems to have gone unprinted.

Lucy Bartlett, daughter of the Vicar of Newark on Trent and of Stoke, father of nine, and RN Lt. Hambly's Elizabeth, were charged with "a continuance of very obstinate conduct". Removal threatened them; their mothers were informed. Lucy had to leave within ten months. Elizabeth improved ("a very satisfactory alteration") but returned home ill in 1839. A year later she had died, aged 17, when her mother wrote to the Gentlemen's Committee and blamed Miss Hervey and the Ladies for her loss, alleging harsh treatment. The Ladies investigated; they satisfied themselves that Miss Hervey enjoyed the support of wards and staff; the charges against her were dismissed as "cruel and calumnious"; and the two

Committees commiserated with her and commended her effort to be firm as well as fair.

Miss Hervey may have felt consoled. But she was ill-prepared to withstand a further blow. The Rev. Mr James Endell Tyler,[5] now Clerical Superintendent, and the Rev. Mr R. S. B. Sandilands, Honorary Secretary, dealt it. A complaint from a ward must have reached them, into which they decided to enquire, disregarding, however, Regulation IX, which had toppled Dr Burrow. Miss Hervey protested and an unpleasant altercation appears to have ensued. The clergy were determined to speak to the ward privately; but in vain did they insist: Miss Hervey stood her ground and the two Reverend Gentlemen withdrew, she refusing to apologise.

Another two wards were removed or withdrawn from Miss Hervey's care: Georgiana Skinner, a sister of Marianne, and Annabel Appleton, the "obstinate and impertinent" daughter of a captain in the Royal Marines. Mrs Skinner wrote a letter to the Marchioness Cornwallis, requesting permission to withdraw her Georgiana. The Ladies refused: Miss Skinner had been most disobedient, "in fraction of the rules respecting visitors", barred from having any visitors at all till her behaviour had improved, and "impertinent and insubordinate . . . for a considerable period". It was imperative that Miss Skinner be removed, and not that her mother be allowed to withdraw her. But the Gentlemen demurred. They alone were empowered to authorise what measures the Ladies might propose, and they did not see how they could now remove a ward who, it appeared, had already been taken home.

Miss Hervey resigned in 1839, "in consequence of the great fatigue and anxiety being more than her health" was "equal to"; then changed her mind; the Hambly ordeal followed, then the Sandilands-and-Tyler; but she stayed in office till in February 1842 she at last retired, no doubt exhausted.

The two clergymen had continued to censure Miss Hervey in committee: if she had not behaved "improperly" she would not have since decided to resign. Other Gentlemen supported them. But the Ladies recognised Miss Hervey's worth, "tendering . . . their unanimous thanks for the very excellent manner in which she discharged . . . the arduous and important duties of Governess of the Institution, and for the anxiety evinced by her for the welfare and happiness of the Wards". And the writer of the Gentlemen's Report to the Subscribers, Mr Sandilands most likely, who now himself resigned, seemed to mumble in what might have been his beard that the Governess had done her well-intentioned best ("zeal"); order and regularity had been restored; she had done her masters' bidding; was at least sound on doctrine ("efficient furtherance of the directions of the Clerical Superintendents for the *religious instruction*"—his italics); and

[5] Tutor and Fellow of Oriel College, Oxford, Vicar of St Giles in the Fields and a Canon of St Paul's. Endell Street, Long Acre, was named after him by his admiring parishioners.

would leave assured of "the respect and esteem of the two Committees, and of their earnest wishes for her welfare and happiness".

Miss Hervey's task had been to supervise the wards, patiently and firmly, and to report to the Ladies on their health, behaviour and progress or lack of it. The Ladies, as before, inspected, discussed, requested and advised. Earl Manvers and the rest of the Gentlemen still dealt with finance, they appointed all but the lowliest of staff, decided their terms of employment, surveyed the fabric of the house, consulting Mr Nash, attended to "the evil . . . respecting the pipes from the water-closets"—the indoor privy was put outside—and had the carpenter drill holes in the bedroom doors to improve ventilation.

The neighbours in Albany Street complained to them about the poplars, which rose above the eastern wall and spoilt their outlook over Regent's Park: Mr Stephens first, and Mr Wyatt next, from 1833 till 1839, who pruned the trees himself, unasked, but wrote and apologised, and paid to have the wall trellissed, then continued remonstrating, with occasional success, followed and supported by Mr Menteath, Mr Combes and Mr Ritterbandt. The trees kept growing.

Some five years later the owners and occupiers of houses in Albany Street and St Andrew's Place made common cause, complaining of "the serious nuisance occasioned by the Pupils of the Rev. Mr Hutton's School"[6] nearby, and requested "the concurrence of the Committee in their endeavours to obtain a removal of the evil". The Committee agreed and a memorial was presented to the Royal Commissioners of Woods and Forests. But nothing worked, whether majesty of crown agents, or broken glass on top of wall, or wood or iron fence, or hurdles or hedge all round. Boys would be boys, especially those let loose by Mr Hutton. And neighbours would continue to plead for a better view—the Rev. Mr William Upton Richards, Perpetual Curate[7] of All Saints, Margaret Street, a Mr Hodson and a Lady Bell—into the fifties and the sixties.

A more serious threat to privacy—"so indispensably necessary"—than boys climbing over wall or gentleman with pruning-hook arose when in 1835 alterations were proposed to the Colosseum: a vast, circular exhibition hall, with glazed cupola and a massive portico, which then stood in the south-east corner of the Park. Entertainments were there to be arranged "of a superior quality", the Committees understood, and a stage or bridge erected which would overlook the school. But the Gentlemen protested; the architect agreed to raise his wall, separating the public and its noise from the pupils and their studies; and anyway: the hall was ill-conceived, it would fall into disuse, a plan to convert it into an opera-house miscarrying, and forty years later it would have to be demolished.

In 1836 burglars made off with a cash-box, containing £27–15s.,

[6] Hutton, Francis, lived somewhere in the Place, who by 1849 was Vicar of Leckford, Stockbridge, in Hampshire.

[7] Appointed by a Patron and licensed by the Bishop; today called Vicar.

which Matron had left in the sitting-room downstairs, with £22–10s. of her own, stolen with it. A man stood trial, who had pawnbroker's tickets for two articles, a watch and a silk handkerchief belonging to the cook. He was acquitted, however, the pawnbroker feeling less sure than he had been of the man's identity. A further £10–16s. slipped away, the prosecution's costs. And a few years later, when another thief took silver and linen, enquiry again came to worse than nothing: the police inspector interrogated and upset all seven of the domestic staff, six of whom walked out, none returning.

A gardener was dismissed. He had failed to deliver a good supply of greens and his conduct, "conversing with persons over the garden wall", had been "very improper". Mr Fendale, the butcher, replaced Mr Baker. Mr Allen replaced Mr Fendale. Mr Allen thought himself "a considerable loser" by his contract but Matron reported that his meat was "not as good as it might be" and the Committee resolved that Mr Jesse "do see Mr Allen and remonstrate with him on the subject" and that if need arose "a special Meeting be summoned to consider the same". The grocer too was haggled with, poor man, which saved half a penny on a pound of butter. The brewer had been told how much beer (18 gallons) he should make from a given quantity of malt (8 bushels), for which he would be paid 10s., but the Committee now decided that the school should brew its own and a malt-mill was acquired, a 75-gallon copper, coolers and 10-gallon casks. Mr Jones delivered coal; his was cheaper than Dalgleish's, Stephens's and Horne's; but after four years it was declared to have been "for some time past very objectionable"; Mr Pope's best Wall's End was bought instead, until it too was found unsatisfactory; then the Gentlemen decided to go back to Mr Jones.

Each item of expenditure was checked: firewood, tin cans for taking hot water upstairs, brown footbaths, a clothes-horse, renovation of beds containing "bad feathers", horse-hair mattresses, ticks, baskets from the school for the blind, window-blinds—roller and brown Holland—bladders of lard—9d. a bladderful in 1839—sherry and port—medicinal—malt, hops, flower-seed, dripping-pan, iron spoons, coffin, for ward or staff, hassocks and bench, where the servants could kneel and pray at bedtime and again when day began, and a French prayer-book for Mlle Muller—the assistant governess was always French and "great advantage derived to the Wards from their constant and familiar intercourse with her as an inmate of the Institution".

Resources were strained when the house needed to be painted or rooms furnished or furniture repaired. But the school seemed secure, cushioned by its holdings of shares in the Regent's Canal and a good £1,000 of Mr Bosanquet's Exchequer bills, and in their 1836 Report the Committee could rejoice that "an institution calculated to produce so much benefit to society, as well as comfort and proper independence to the distressed female orphan of gentle birth", would not "be permitted to droop for want of support from a generous and Christian Public".

The wards now all had mothers or friends who paid towards the cost of their board and tuition—all were "contributory", none was "gratuitous"—and Miss Mary Heath not only had a mother, she owned a horse and, when she fell from the horse and hurt herself, she could also afford to take a holiday at the seaside.

The Royal Family continued its support: King William IV[8] became the school's Patron in 1832, giving £50 a year from the Privy Purse; and the Managing Committee responded to the news with deference most prostrate, almost anguished:

To the King's Most Excellent Majesty

May it please your Majesty

Your Majesty's most humble and dutiful Servants the Members of the Managing Committee for the Adult Orphan Institution presume to lay at Your Majesty's feet their respectful thanks for the high honour conferred on the Adult Orphan Institution by your Majesty's distinguished Patronage and to express their most grateful sense of your Majesty's most gracious benevolence in having commanded that the Munificent Donation of £50 be annually transmitted to the funds of the Institution.

King William died in 1837. Governess, matron and wards were given black to wear as mourning and the Annual Report was printed on mauve. In 1841, his wife, Adelaide,[9] who as queen had asked for a copy to be sent her of the Rules and Regulations of the school, offered to involve herself more closely in its affairs ("a more immediate patronage").

The Committee hoped that her successor, Queen Victoria, would shed upon the school the lustre of her name (who had known what it meant for a child to grow up without a father, having lost her own when only eight months old); and they were not disappointed: in 1838 she became its Patron and the same, £50-a-year "munificent donation" continued till her death in 1901.

The two Archbishops and the Bishop of London helped, as trustees of the Cholmondeley charities. An orphan unnamed sent in £100. Mr Joseph Neeld, Conservative MP for Chippenham, was continually generous, who by 1841 had given £341, thus amassing thirty-seven votes. Another concert, at the Hanover Square (King's Concert) Rooms,[10] Franz Cramer again and Niccolo Paganini both contributing,[11] and three fancy-dress

[8] George III's third child and son; as Duke of Clarence he was crowned in 1830.

[9] Princess of Saxe-Meiningen, 1792–1849.

[10] Built by Vanbrugh and called the Queen's when it was opened in the Haymarket in 1705, the King's 1714–1837, then Her Majesty's. Almost all Handel's operas and oratorios were first played there. Twice destroyed by fire: in 1789, when a bigger hall replaced it, with concert-room adjoining, and in 1867. The original façade remained till 1895, when the building was taken down and the present Her Majesty's Theatre built in Charles II Street.

[11] A breakfast arranged for the same day, 27.6.1831, in Wimbledon, by Edward, eleventh Duke of Somerset, having threatened its success, the Gentlemen, supported

balls, together yielded nearly £2,000; but they were not to be repeated, the Committee having felt or been persuaded that fund-raising could be too much enjoyed to be genuinely charitable, as their Report to the subscribers explained in 1840:

No extraordinary mode of recommending this Institution to public notice has been adopted for the last three seasons. No ball; no concert given in aid of its funds. No such attempt made to excite charity, as, after all, produces perhaps but little charity *towards any Institution, whatever addition it may make to its means of existence.*

Instead they would appeal to the enlightened self-interest of "that better class of society" whose bounty would ensure them a continuing supply of "well-principled Governesses", trained to impart "solid and valuable instruction".

But judgement was required of "that better class" when it cast its votes in the election of the wards, if a good supply of the right calibre of governess was to be guaranteed and it was not to waste its bounty on sow's ears that would never make silk purses. The subscribers having asked what it was that made a candidate deserve their support, the Committee replied:

as this is an Institution for the reception of adults, *whose education is to be* completed *and not* commenced, *those deserve the best support who . . . have been previously well instructed in proportion to their age and who cannot have contracted habits at variance with those of the class of society to which, from their father's station, they are supposed to belong and in which this Institution is to enable them to maintain themselves. Where the father has been long dead, and the orphan left in extreme poverty and indigence, there her education will have been much, if not entirely, neglected; there, inured to privation from her infancy, she will have grown up insensible of her loss, and have become so accustomed to very inferior society as to render it far from probable that she can ever be imbued with those feelings, or acquire that gentlewomanly carriage, which are especially requisite in respectable families. Where, on the other hand, the death of the father is but recent, or the orphan has been left under good guardianship, though with circumscribed means, there . . . her mind will in all probability have been duly cultivated, and she will have become best qualified for appreciating and availing herself of the advantages of this Institution . . . and there the protection of this charitable asylum will be extended with the best prospect of producing benefit to the orphan admitted and of deriving it, through her, to society at large.*

by Princess Augusta, asked the Duke to postpone it. It is unlikely that he agreed, given at the most only nine days' notice. His breakfast, however, may have suffered more from the concert than the concert did from the breakfast, so much did Paganini enrapture his London public. In a letter of the 12th of August next, where he complains of "excessive and noisy admiration", Paganini writes: "I can never leave my home without being mobbed by people who . . . even feel me, as if to find out if I am flesh and blood. And this not only the common people but even the upper classes."

Mistakes, however, continued to be made and, the better to avoid the pain which removal entailed, not only for the wards but also for their families and friends, it was decided that applicants for admission would now be interviewed in London before they were allowed to stand as candidates, when half the cost of their journey would be paid, and the whole sum if the Committee offered them a place and they accepted it.

A ward who had failed to be elected could often try again. Louisa France polled bottom vote but one at her first attempt in 1832 and succeeded next year—although she was then too old to be an eligible candidate, the Gentlemen had made her an exception to the rule, having heard that she had now lost both parents. But Eliza Primrose, who in 1833 polled a record low vote of only 2, remained unlucky, polling 21 at her second attempt and 420 at her third, which was still too few.

Some more bye-laws had now been enacted, the purpose of which was to exclude girls who, elected out of kindness, could not or would not learn. A Sub-Committee was appointed, three Ladies and three Gentlemen, to examine the wards each quarter of a year and assess their proficiency "in the rudiments of Education, more especially English Grammar, Reading, Writing, Arithmetic and the principles of the Christian Religion"; they had power to declare an election null and void and admit instead the unsuccessful candidate with the next highest vote; and further to improve the quality of intake the certificate of fitness, which the Minister and Wardens of her parish church had had to sign on the candidate's behalf, would now declare that, to their best knowledge and belief, neither of her parents had suffered from insanity.

A demanding course of study was prescribed: Holy Scriptures, the Evidences and Peculiar Doctrines of Christianity, Ecclesiastical History—text after chillingly entitled text: *Catechetical Exercises* "by a Country Clergyman", *Geographical Exercises on the New Testament, A Translation of Josephus in Holy Numbers, A History of the Colonial Church*—other History and other Geography, the works of Racine, Corneille and Millot in the French and of Dante, Tasso, Alfieri and Metastasio in the Italian.

Not all the wards could bear the strain. Dr Webber found four unsatisfactory: Henrietta Grant, Ann Knight, Caroline Reid and Sarah Tucker,[12] whom the Gentlemen instructed Miss Hervey to admonish and threaten with removal. Sarah remained and was allowed to go to Paris to improve her French, with her sister, and so did Henrietta, though only to become a "preparatory governess" ("a very inferior description of charge"). Ann and Caroline did not outlast their probationary year and some fifteen other of Miss Hervey's pupils were defeated by the course, who had then to be returned to their friends or mothers. But calibre and standard on the whole stood high and in the summer of 1834, conducting their yearly

[12] Her father, Richard, Captain RN, had been killed by smugglers at Lulworth, Dorset, in 1832.

examination of the top class, the Committees liked what they heard and saw:

The readiness and precision with which these Wards answered almost every question proposed them, and more particularly in Religious Knowledge, History, and Geography, joined with a diffidence of manner peculiarly befitting their sex, obtained from the Lord Bishop of London, who kindly undertook the examination, and from all present, expressions of the warmest approbation.

Queen Adelaide had intended to honour the occasion with her presence, with Princess Augusta, who appeared regularly. The visit was postponed—two of the wards having only just recovered from the measles, it was feared that the young Prince Ernest Leiningen[13] might be infected, "the object of Her Majesty's immediate care"—but in May of the following year she kept her promise, when disappointed juniors turned senior were allowed to come back and witness the proceedings.

Her Majesty was met, on this occasion, by Her Royal Highness the Princess Augusta (Co-Patroness with Her Majesty of the Institution), and her Royal Highness the Landgravine of Hesse Homburg;[14] *and was received by the Marchioness Cornwallis, the Earl Manvers and the other members of the two Committees, together with His Grace the Archbishop of Canterbury*[15] *and the Lord Bishop of London; the latter of whom, with his usual kindness, undertook the examination.*

At the conclusion Her Majesty was pleased to notice, in most flattering terms, the Wards who had been examined, and after presenting the prize-books, which are annually given by the Institution to the most deserving, to select from their drawings, which lay on the table, several which Her Majesty graciously condescended to accept as specimens of their proficiency in that department of their education. At the same time the Archbishop of Canterbury, in a short and most kind address to the Wards, assured them of the very great satisfaction His Grace, no less than Her Majesty, their Royal Highnesses, and the other visitors, had derived from observing their perfect and critical acquaintance with the different subjects to which the examination extended, as proved by the correctness of their replies to the questions proposed; some of which questions, students of a much longer period and of much more mature age might hardly have been expected to answer. His Grace added, that the modesty and diffidence of

[13] Son of Charles, Prince of Leiningen, he was then aged 4. Grandson of Victoria, Duchess of Kent, Queen Victoria's mother, by her first marriage, to Prince Emich Charles Leiningen, therefore Queen Victoria's step-nephew.

[14] Princess Elizabeth, seventh child, third daughter, of George III. Like her sister, Augusta, a true philanthropist, who in 1808 had founded at Windsor a society awarding marriage portions to virtuous girls; and a gifted artist. The Landgrave having died in 1829, she had left Hesse-Homburg and now lived in Hanover.

[15] Dr Howley.

their manner, and the timidity under which they evidently laboured, threw a peculiar charm, in his opinion, over the whole scene, and greatly enhanced his pleasure in witnessing it; and he forcibly impressed upon their attention, that these were ornaments of the female character, for the loss of which, no accomplishments nor attainments in knowledge, however great and desirable in themselves, could sufficiently compensate.

In that same year the Bishop of London, Mr Blomfield, either asked or agreed to be designated Visitor[16] and, the honour conferred, he was "empowered to visit the Wards' department and examine them whenever it" might "suit his convenience to do so". He did not, in the event, conduct spot checks, but he continued to examine the wards each summer term, Princess Augusta being usually present, together in Miss Hervey's later years with her sister, Mary, Duchess of Gloucester.

Dr Charles Longley, a former Headmaster of Harrow,[17] now Bishop of Ripon[18] and a future Archbishop of Canterbury,[19] took the Visitor's place in 1840 but he arrived late, detained by the Address of the House of Lords to the Queen, so that Holy Scripture was all that time allowed. Next year Bishop Blomfield returned. He, and the Duchess, the two Committees, "and a few of their friends", were impressed:

the manner in which the first class acquitted themselves . . . proved their perfect acquaintance with the subjects of examination . . . the Bishop of London expressed his perfect satisfaction; and he was understood to remark, that the amount of religious knowledge and general information which he perceived them to possess, was not only such as would render their services very valuable in that occupation in life for which they had been trained, but such as fully qualified them, as far as mental acquirements could do so, to maintain their place in society as Christian gentlewomen.

Employers' needs determined the curriculum, albeit slowly. A start was made on Latin in 1835, seven years after lack of it had lost Octavia Langhorne a post, some grammars being purchased "for the use of those Wards who, in the opinion of the Governess, may be enabled to pursue the study of that Language without interference with their other occupations", and it was well established by 1842, when Mr Tyler took it over, "to enable them . . . to take the charge of little boys". The Ladies' Committee asked for singing to be taught—"now so generally pursued"—but no class-singing book was introduced till 1844. A Mrs Wilson was employed "to provide for the constant, instead of, as heretofore, the occasional instruction of the Wards in Dancing", which the Ladies had felt to be

16 Dorothy, his second wife, who bore him eleven children, was now a member of the Ladies' Committee.

17 1829–36, when numbers rose from 115 to 165 but discipline grew lax.

18 1836–56, then of Durham till 1860 and of York till 1862.

19 1862–68.

"absolutely necessary for the Wards' advantage", "considering its tendency to give them a lady-like carriage . . . in their situation as Governesses". There was little call for the harp, despite Mrs Williams's example, and Miss Jessie Campbell was refused lessons, even though her mother and friends would have met the extra cost, the Ladies advising the Gentlemen not to introduce any new course, or any new masters to the staff. But Science glimmered: Mr D. F. Walker, "the celebrated lecturer on Experimental Philosophy",[20] introduced it free of charge and in return was declared to be an honorary subscriber, with the privilege of casting one vote in the elections, and in 1835 he invited the wards to attend his lecture on astronomy at the Strand Theatre,[21] "every proper arrangement" being made "for their accommodation".

The wards, whom their Visitor, the Bishop, examined, had been selected as candidates by the Ladies, the Subscribers had elected them, they were or appeared to be mostly well-behaved—blessed were the meek—and were not to be defeated by arithmetic or Latin. But one great obstacle had still to be avoided or survived: disease and disability; and a surprisingly high proportion of the admitted pupils were returned unfit, often dying, to their mothers or their friends, despite "the usual certificates of good health" which they had all had to produce. Miss Clara Parker, the daughter of the Rev. Mr Marcus Parker, Curate of Wanborough in Wiltshire, was the first of many, in Miss Hervey's years, whose hopes were thus disappointed. The Ladies had accepted her as a candidate, one of ten applicants, in April 1831; then three months later her guardian, Miss Seymour, of Speen Hill, Berkshire, informed them that Miss Parker's eyes had a slight and perhaps disqualifying cast. It was now too late to annul her candidature; arrangements for the ballot had been put in hand; Miss Parker stood and was elected, coming fourth in the poll with 437 votes, and was provisionally admitted, the Ladies tending to think or hope that her impaired eyesight was "not at present very objectionable". But the Marchioness Cornwallis must have wanted to be sure, for she took her to be seen by Mr Henry Alexander,[22] who tested her eyes and reported that their weakness arose from "a Scrofulous habit of body", for which no cure was known, and that in his view the duties of a governess were such as could only make her difficulties worse. The Gentlemen agreed. Miss Parker's election was declared invalid; her brother protested in vain; and Mr Sandilands arranged her return to Miss Seymour.

Charlotte Crawford filled Clara's place, the candidate who had polled the next highest vote in the election. Her need was great: RN Lt. Moses

[20] Walker, Deane Franklin, who lectured on his subject at Eton, Harrow and Rugby, like his father before him.

[21] Not today's, at the corner of Catherine Street, built in 1905 and first called the Waldorf, but one put up in 1826 by a Mr Rayner, in the Strand itself, on a site now occupied by the underground railway-station.

[22] A surgeon gentleman: for thirty-seven years he charged no fee.

Crawford had died in 1828 and his widow, who had seven children to support on only £70 a year from the Compassionate Fund,[23] supplementing "the usual pension", had now suffered a paralytic stroke, losing speech and mobility.

But a year later Miss Crawford too had fallen ill, "of a very serious and increasing affection of the spine"; "an invisible back" had been recommended for her, to cost about four guineas; but she could not be cured, so her friends were asked to remove her straight away.

Another nineteen, making roughly one in six of Miss Hervey's juniors, were invalided out: Elizabeth Mackay, sent back to her guardian, the Rev. Mr George Cambridge; Eleanor Tetley, transferred to the care of her mother, a Matron at Greenwich Hospital; Indiana Gray; Caroline Williams; Amelia Hopwood, who then died—"the Ladies . . . took it upon them to give directions for the funeral upon an economical scale", her mother being "wholly incapable of incurring any expense"; Eleanor Hamilton; Charity Ross—but her name was restored, "the young Lady being perfectly convalescent"; Harriet Radford; Mary Savory; Betsy Dowell, Dr Gregory[24] advising that confinement in the Adult Orphan Institution would not help the scrofulous disorder in her system but rather was "too well calculated to renew it", and the Gentlemen agreeing with the Ladies that her admission was "originally disqualified" and "therefore that her Election be declared void and her Friends be requested to remove her . . . forthwith"; Harriet Keily; Mary Roberts, daughter of Capt. William Roberts RN, formerly Governor of the Island of Ascension, and of another Matron at Greenwich Hospital; Emma Farrant ("hopeless state . . . of health"); Emily Street, who died aged 15; Lydia Helpman ("very delicate health"); Mary Prattent ("very subject to fits"), whose father had lost his life when his ship, the *Chameleon*, was rammed by the *Castor* and sank, off Deal; Elizabeth Morris ("decidedly scrofulous"); Anne Little, dead at 16; Jane Mould; Frances Warneford. And Miss Biden was deemed an ineligible candidate on the grounds of her father's illness—not her own—which must have been hereditary.

Miss Warneford was one of ten children, whose father, the Vicar of Ashburnham in Sussex, had died a widower in 1840 and had left them "wholly destitute". The subscribers elected her a ward a few months later but owing to "a spinal affection", which had first to be cured, she was allowed to defer her entrance and was entrusted to the care of a surgeon,

[23] The source of government assistance, related to need and rank, for the legitimate children of officers killed in action or within six months of being wounded or (lesser amounts) who died elsehow, for sons till aged 18 and for daughters till married or till aged 21, exceptions being made for "cripples, lunatics or idiots", unfit to be employed.

[24] Gregory, George, nephew and grandson of distinguished Edinburgh physicians, Physician to the Small-Pox and Vaccination Hospital, London, and Lecturer at the Windmill Street School and St Thomas's Hospital. His *Elements of the Practice of Physic*, 1820, ran to six editions.

Mr Kerrall. Mr Kerrall's treatment failed, his patient's condition grew worse; any hope that she might yet become a ward had now to be abandoned; and the Gentlemen agreed that any applicant "labouring under any strikingly apparent affection of the spine" should be disqualified.

The minutes of the meetings of the Ladies' and Gentlemen's Committees did not as a rule convey much sorrow when a ward fell sick or died. It does not follow, however, that little was felt. In the Marchioness Cornwallis Miss Warneford had found a kind friend whose initiative and help spoke louder than condolences, though not perhaps as loud as when in 1841 the virtue of her actions was proclaimed in the Annual Report, most likely again by Mr Sandilands:

The Managing Committee cannot pass over this case without adverting to the great kindness exercised by the President of the Ladies' Committee towards this afflicted girl; for the continuance of whose education at a most respectable school at Brighton, together with the application of the best means for the cure of her distortion, she undertook to provide, as manager of a subscription which was raised for the purpose, amongst her own and the orphan's friends, and to which she was the principal contributor. Nor did she allow herself to desist from the charge, which for some months she personally superintended, until the attainment of the object in view was rendered hopeless, in consequence of the change in constitution already mentioned, when the poor Orphan was restored to the care of her relations. This, indeed, is an instance of private charity which the Managing Committee would not have ventured to notice, but for the circumstance of its having arisen from the connection of that benevolent lady with the Institution; on which account they conceive it to deserve the grateful attention of the meeting, both for the credit which it obtains for the Institution itself, and the proof it affords of the tender interest taken in the welfare of its Wards by one who is so immediately and notedly engaged in its superintendence.

Almost all the wards fell ill of something—the measles or chicken-pox or scarlet fever or influenza or, for want of worse, erysipelas. About eight physicians and-or surgeons and-or apothecaries (a confused list) attended them for nothing. A change of air was often recommended, with family or friends. Dr Gregory, however, seemed to trust in wine, prescribing twelve bottles of port—42s. worth—for Martha Mayor, feeling weak after illness.

Next year Miss Mayor got small-pox, a virulent attack, vaccination appearing to have failed. The wards were collected by their alarmed friends or mothers. Miss Mayor improved. She too went home. The walls of her room were white-washed and coloured and her mattress was destroyed. The other wards returned and were again vaccinated. Miss Mayor took posts, near Bath and in London, but did not work long, for she died, most likely of consumption, at the age of 24.

Sometimes it happened that a ward who had been prescribed a change of air outstayed her leave or misused it. Anna Bishop seemed to be one,

given leave to go and convalesce with a friend, Miss Wood, in the Kent Road, but slipping away to Tenterden instead, abetted and accompanied by her mother. The Ladies complained: Miss Bishop's return was overdue; she had said not a word about a change of plan; her name would have to be deleted from the register. But all was somehow explained. The Ladies hastened to make amends, granting Miss Bishop another three weeks; ere long three more; then a holiday in Broadstairs.

A number of seniors too fell ill and had to leave their posts and abandon their careers: Ellen Jones, daughter of the Vicar of Vere in Jamaica; Gertrude Eveleigh; and Sarah Stanes; though Ellen six months later, and Sarah at once, recovered and could marry. Others died: Hannah Dowell, 24, sister of the scrofulous Betsy—the Ladies recorded their "most painful feelings"—Maria Hibbert, 25, "in a hopeless state of serious ill health"; and Anna Gray, 21, piously admired in the Annual Report of July 1839:

who, last year, to use the words of a benevolent lady making the communication, "returned home, fully qualified to become the comfort of her mother in the management of her school, it has pleased God to dispose otherwise, and to take her away by rapid consumption, under which she expired a few weeks ago. The afflicted mother", the same lady adds, "begs me to say, that her daughter spoke with the greatest affection of her friends and companions in the Institution; that during her whole illness she was an example of patience, resignation, and cheerful acquiescence in the will of God, and that her last hours were blessed with perfect peace"; and she concludes by observing, that "this communication appears to me . . . a tribute of respect and gratitude which will be kindly received, and not with entire indifference, by those who, I am sure, take a personal interest, whether in life or death of the young creatures who owe so much to their benevolence and protection". The Managing Committee, lamenting as they do this loss of a Ward who gave promise, if she had lived, of becoming a most valuable member of society, cannot but express their thanks to the lady communicating it, for the testimony she has given to the benefits resulting from an education in this Asylum; by which such young persons may be prepared, not only to live virtuous, useful, and religious lives, but, if it should please God to shorten their term of days, to die also "the death of the righteous".

The wards not expelled or incurably deformed or sick or dead, or who could not or would not learn, were each presented with a Bible and a Book of Common Prayer, then sent on their way to their first post, there "to form in others", the Committees hoped, "that character for cultivated understandings, purity of manners and strong Christian faith and devotion, by which British females of gentle and superior birth are so generally distinguished".

Dr George Murray, Bishop of Rochester and father of the makings of a classful of eleven, took Amelia Webb, daughter of a minor canon at St George's Chapel, Windsor; Sir Edward—later General—and Lady Kerri-

son, RM Lt. Williams's Caroline and Lt. Bambrick's Anne; Dr the Hon. Edward Grey,[25] Bishop of Hereford, Lt. Cumming's Jane; the Walkers of Dumfriesshire, in Boulogne and heading south for the Riviera, Eliza Preston, daughter of the Curate of Ilminster in Somerset, as nanny—she was later apprenticed to Miss Charlton, a dressmaker, in Princes Street, Hanover Square, for a fifty guineas fee, paid by the Sons of the Clergy and her school; Harriet, Countess of Sheffield,[26] Whittlesea Vicar John Pratt's Isabella (the unhappy Pratt, Elizabeth, was not her sister); Lady Elizabeth Clinton[27] asked for the services of one of the most accomplished of the wards and received Frances Rowland, daughter of the Rector of Llansantffraid, in Brecknockshire, now Clwyd; the Rev. Sir Herbert Oakley, Dean of Bocking in Essex, followed in turn by the Rev. Mr George Pretyman, a Canon of Winchester Cathedral, the Mackworths of Wiesbaden and some Edinburgh Stuarts, took RN Lt. Danford's Hannah; Sir George Arthur, Governor of Bombay, provisionally Governor-General of India and father of twelve, Laura Jewry, a brilliant, prolific, now long-forgotten writer of romantic novels and other works, under her maiden name and as Mrs Valentine—her father, Henry, Lt. RN, had been killed aboard the mail-boat *Hearty*, West Indies bound, in 1827; the Very Rev. Mr James Cotton, Dean of Bangor, Matilda, daughter of RN Lt. Thomas Taplen, drowned in the West Indies, commanding HMS *Pickle*, in 1831; the Hon. and Rev. Mr C. W. Moore, another Canon of Windsor, Cmdr Eveleigh's Gertrude; and Mr George Norman, an eminent monetary economist, the Rev. Mr Joseph Taylor's Jane Violetta.

Employers were sometimes hard to please: Lady Sarah Murray, wife of George, Bishop of Rochester, released Canon Webb's Amelia—"in consequence of a defect in Miss Webb's pronunciation"; a Mrs Hawthorne, Margaret Young, wanting someone older—Miss Young was 21 (it was her first post); and Sir Ralph and Lady Howard, Martha Mayor, after only one or two months (of her last two years or so of life), whom they found to be blessed with "attainments beyond what is required for her Pupil".

Hannah Dowell had been allowed to leave the family of Dr William Lyall, Archdeacon of Colchester, for the Sligos of Seacliffe House, at Preston Kirk, North Berwickshire, where "very great pecuniary advantages" were offered; but remained with the Lyalls till her death next year. Mr Richard Bingham, however, the Perpetual and scholarly Curate of Trinity in Gosport, could not afford to continue to employ the excellent Harriet Ryan, who after three years was transferred to the Chudleighs in Southampton, there to stay till her health appeared to suffer from the sea-and-autumn air.

25 Fifth son of Charles, first Earl.

26 Daughter of Henry Lascelles, second Earl of Harewood, and wife of George, second Earl, who lived nearby, among many others connected with the school, at 58 Portland Place.

27 Daughter of William, sixth Marquess of Lothian, and wife of Charles, nineteenth Baron.

Mrs Allgood of Tynemouth, a disappointed applicant in 1830, acquired Anne Grisdale, but returned her to the school as she was not yet "sufficiently qualified in Music". The same want lost wards their posts with Lady Kinloch of Gilmerton House, Drem, East Lothian,[28] with Schombergs and Thesigers, and with the Grants of Elchies, in what is now Morayshire. Miss Grisdale moved on: from Tynemouth to the Turners of Clapham, from Clapham to the Langtons of Liverpool, from Liverpool to the Sligos of Preston Kirk—after six months they decided not to take her with them to the Continent, her health seeming too delicate, but to drop her at the school on their way south to board the Channel ferry—from Preston Kirk to the Davises of Mortlake, from Mortlake to some Edinburgh Smiths, from Edinburgh to the Spicers of Esher Place, in Esher, and from Esher to the Youngs, No. 1, Carlton Place, Southampton, her eighth abode in about eight years.

Mothers, like employers, could be tiresome. Jessie Campbell's "conducted herself in a very disgraceful manner": the Ladies having made "the most satisfactory arrangements", she "refused to allow her Daughter to go to any Situation except at a short distance from London"; so the Gentlemen regretfully agreed with the Ladies and removed Miss Campbell's name from the senior list. Elizabeth Eades found her name deleted too, having changed her post without the school's consent, thus forfeiting her claim to its protection, which wards enjoyed if they were shabbily treated or uncomfortably lodged.

The school which, it seems, Casanova's daughter founded, was now aged 22. It had enrolled 188 wards, 54 of the Clergy, 67 of the Army and another 67 either Naval or Marine. Forty seniors remained. Juniors numbered 33. Miss Hervey had retired; Earl Manvers, however, continued to head the Managing Committee, where Mr Rowley Lascelles and Mr James Mure still served. Illness often raged. And girls might misbehave. But their knowledge and demeanour impressed visiting examiners. Expenditure had fallen and receipts had increased. Adelaide, Queen Dowager, had agreed to add her patronage to that of Queen Victoria and the Duchess of Gloucester; this was good news, as the Committee explained in its Report to the Subscribers:

The sanction . . . of so illustrious and at the same time so justly venerated a personnage, bespeaks for the Institution the approbation and support of all who would follow, at however humble a distance, in the same track of well-considered *benevolence.*

It looked as if success would continue to succeed. But that was not to be. Support began to falter and in the next thirty-five years or so the rising spiral of success would be reversed.

[28] Eleanor, wife of Sir David, ninth baronet.

Chapter Three

1842–1870

In April 1842 the Committees appointed a new Lady Governess; "Miss Horden" was all that they recorded of her name and all that their minutes reveal about her family is that her nephew attended the Philological School[1] at 228 Marylebone Road, nearby, and was allowed to visit her in her rooms at 11 St Andrew's Place—eleven years old, too young to be the kind of nuisance they would fear.

As "a good German scholar" Miss Horden introduced her subject to the wards, teaching literature as well as language, including works by Lessing, Goethe, Schiller, and by authors now forgotten. Dr Charles Longley, still Bishop of Ripon, returned as examiner in 1843, when the Duke of Cambridge[2] "most condescendingly" assisted him with the German and the French. They "were pleased to express themselves highly satisfied with the result": evidence that the wards had been well trained and were "peculiarly well qualified to impart sound and solid instruction, in both religious and general knowledge, to those who might hereafter be committed to their charge".

The next examination in German was postponed, no one being present who appeared to be qualified to conduct it. Dr Adolphus Bernays, however, then agreed to come and help, Professor in the subject at King's College, London,[3] "who commended the proficiency which the pupils had made in the grammar and their pronunciation of the language", for which they were "wholly indebted" to the Lady Governess.

Mr Blomfield continued as Visitor. He questioned the wards on "the Doctrines of our Holy Religion" and "the History of our own Country", and admired their reading, and translation into English, of Latin, Italian and French, and their understanding of the rules of grammar. His manner, though "searching", was "yet most kind".

Other clergy followed him: Dr Samuel Wilberforce, Bishop of Oxford,

[1] Originally the Philological Society, founded in Mary (now Stanhope) Street in 1792 "for Educating and Clothing the Sons of Clergymen, Naval and Military Officers, Professional Men, Merchants, Manufacturers, Clerks in Public Offices and the Higher Order of Tradesmen in Reduced Circumstances", fees £9 a year and beating forbidden. It moved to the Marylebone Road in 1827; in 1908, when the London County Council helped fund it, it became St Marylebone Grammar School; and in 1981 it had to close. Its old boys call themselves the Old Philologians.

[2] Adolphus Frederick, King George III's tenth child, seventh son, and husband of Princess Augusta of Hesse-Cassel; he had studied at the University of Göttingen; served as Major-General under General Walmoden in the campaign of 1794–95; and was Colonel-in-Chief of the King's German Legion.

[3] Founded in 1828, entry at 16; now King's College, Wimbledon.

Miss Horden about 1852

11 St Andrew's Place, 1853. Top left the Colosseum.

called "Soapy Sam" by those who found his eloquence equivocal; Dr Edward Denison, Bishop of Salisbury, an intolerant theologian, even for his day; his friend and once his curate,[4] then episcopal successor, Dr Walter Kerr-Hamilton, holding views controversially high; the Dean of Westminster, the Very Rev. Mr Richard Chenevix Trench, poet, and future Archbishop of Dublin; the Rev. Mr Charles Phipps-Eyre, Rector of St Marylebone,[5] helped by Mr Edwin Abbott,[6] Mr Abbott from the age of 19 and for forty-five years headmaster of Miss Horden's nephew's school, then its secretary for another ten, his life's last; Dr John Lonsdale, Bishop of Lichfield,[7] and in the late sixties Dr Herbert Kynaston, High Master of St Paul's,[8] and Dr Samuel Waldegrave, Bishop of Carlisle. Bishops Waldegrave and Lonsdale were Managing Gentlemen, and Sophia Lonsdale, Jane Waldegrave and two other bishops' wives, Caroline Longley[9] and Dorothy Blomfield, served with the Ladies. Dr Archibald Tait came twice, for thirteen years Mr Blomfield's successor,[10] returning as Archbishop of Canterbury in 1869. The new Bishop of London, Dr John Jackson, another father of eleven (ten daughters and a son) and author of many published sermons, most notably a series called *The Sinfulness of Little Sins*, took his place as Visitor. Members of the Committees and sometimes a local clergyman examined the younger classes, II and III. Quarterly examinations, begun in about 1833, appear to have lapsed by 1869, when the Gentlemen called upon the Ladies to form a sub-committee to ensure that they continued, which they perhaps did, for at the most eight years, till twice a year seemed usual.

Illustrious patrons began to show less interest: the Duchess of Gloucester had paid eight visits by 1849, the Duchess of Kent three; after 1854 no other member of their family attended the examinations till Princess Mary of Cambridge, Duchess of Teck[11] came in 1865—in 1869

[4] At St Peter in the East, Queen's Lane, Oxford. St Edmund Hall absorbed it for a library (un-deconsecrated) in 1971.

[5] The parish church in the Marylebone Road, built in 1817 and heavily Victorianised in 1883. In 1846 Robert Browning and Elizabeth Barrett were secretly married there.

[6] Author of English and Latin grammars and in 1875 of a *Complete Concordance to the Works of Alexander Pope*. Dr Edwin Abbott, Headmaster of University College School, 1865–82, was his son.

[7] Principal of King's College, London, 1839–42. The best scholar his headmaster at Eton, Dr Goodall, could recall. Elected to be Provost there in 1840, he declined the appointment. Richard Garnett, DNB: "a perfect model of justice, kindness, humility and shrewd sense".

[8] From 1834, aged 28, to 1872. Eminent composer of hymns and Latin verse and a near miss for the Oxford Chair of Poetry.

[9] The first Lord Congleton's eldest child.

[10] Headmaster of Rugby after Arnold; bereft of five of the first seven children of his nine, when from March to April, 1856, they died of scarlet fever; then Bishop of London within five months.

[11] Mary Adelaide, youngest daughter of the Duke of Cambridge and Princess Augusta of Hesse-Cassel, the wife of Prince Francis of Teck, and mother of Mary,

she returned, with "many other ladies of distinction", including Queen Victoria's third daughter, Helena, when "much satisfaction was graciously expressed".

Elections too had been losing their appeal. The Queen and Prince Albert, who in 1850 had asked to be kept informed of the results, can hardly have been impressed. Fewer young women appeared to wish to stand, the procedure had sometimes to be postponed till enough candidates had accumulated, and wards were admitted who either could not learn or were unwilling to.

Thamar[12] Kellow was one such ward, the daughter of a captain in the Royal Marines. In 1847 Mr Tyler and the Ladies found her "quite incompetent to benefit from any further residence" at the school and cited the bye-law requiring her departure. But other Gentlemen, Rear-Admiral Sir William Bowles,[13] Treasurer, Maj.-Gen. Edward Fanshawe, Lt.-Col. Sir John Hamilton,[14] and Mr John Turner, disregarded their advice and Miss Kellow was reprieved, who not once had misbehaved (and whose mother had ten more children to support, on a yearly income of only £50).

Mr Tyler now indignantly resigned his post; the Gentlemen, however, begged him to remain, for they were "keenly alive" to "the inestimable value" of his services, with which the school's best interest was "intimately blended"; Mr Tyler agreed, soothed no doubt by their "feelings of unaffected respect and gratitude" and perhaps reassured, being told that the second chance Miss Kellow had been granted "was best calculated to prepare her Mother for the event which they fully concurred with their Clerical Superintendent would ultimately be inevitable"; the Committee removed Miss Kellow; and Mr Tyler remained in office for the next three years.

The Ladies had been vindicated and must now have felt relieved. Mr Tyler's "deservedly eminent station in the Church", and "the sound views entertained by him amid the conflicting opinions of the times",[15] had earned him their respect and it seemed mistaken kindness to them to keep a

King George V's Queen Consort. "Fat Mary" to the crowd, for she is said to have weighed at least seventeen stone, a spendthrift host but a watchful mother: "A child has quite enough to do to learn obedience, and attend to her lessons, and to *grow*, without many parties and late hours, which take the freshness of childhood away, and the brightness and beauty from girlhood—and then children become intolerable. There are far too many grown-up children in the present day." C. K. Cooke, *A Memoir of Princess Mary Adelaide, Duchess of Teck*, 1909.

12 The syllables of Martha reversed.

13 Widower since 1838 of the Hon. Frances Temple, sister of Lord Palmerston; MP for Launceston; Admiral of the Blue, 1857, and of the Fleet, 1869.

14 Hamilton of Trebinshun, Charles John James, of the Scots Guards. Address: 5 Portman Square.

15 A reference to the Tractarians, with whom began the Oxford Movement, promoting Catholic or Early Christian belief and ritual within the Established Church. Queen Victoria disapproved of it and so did Mr Punch.

ward at the school "if her natural incapacity precluded all possibility of her becoming an eligible Governess, the superior education given to the wards being of too expensive a character to admit of its being bestowed on those fitted only for the inferior station of Nursery Governess". Again they had their way: a bye-law was amended and each candidate for election was now to be required to produce a certificate indicating that she could "read English accurately and fluently", was "acquainted with the Scripture History" and had been taught "the rudiments of religious knowledge", was "familiar with at least the first four rules of Arithmetic, the Outlines of History—of Geography—and of Grammar", what progress she had already made "in the Elementary parts of a liberal Education" and how able she was to complete her course of training and succeed.

Miss Horden made "unwearied efforts" to educate the wards. Their "general demeanour" could not be faulted and they mostly did their best. But in 1853 pupils remained who would not make governesses and whose progress in all subjects but Music was "so imperceptible" that it was "doubtful if there be any at all". They had not improved in 1855; and in 1856 Miss Horden still regretted their "very low rate of capacity and indolence". In 1862 they "promised fairly", once or twice they were "diligent" and in 1866 a slight improvement was observed in Classes II and III. Thus little was the praise which the wards now earned after all the glowing tributes which visiting examiners had paid them in Miss Horden's first ten years.

Quality of staff could hardly be blamed. The school stood "sufficiently in town to allow of the assistance of London Masters". A Frenchman taught French; and an Italian, Italian: Signor Gabriele Rossetti in the early 1840s, who lived at 50 Charlotte Street nearby, the father of the poet, Christina, and of Dante Gabriel, the painter—having fled from Naples in 1824, under sentence of death,[16] he was now Professor of Italian at King's College, a colleague of Dr Bernays; Mr George Harley, RA, taught drawing, a water-colourist, landscape-lithographer and master of repute;[17] Dr Timothy Essex[18] and his daughter, music (he unpaid); and following them: Mr James Turle, who stayed for twenty-two of the fifty-one years that he was Organist and Master of the Choristers at Westminster Abbey—he once gave back to the school, as "conscience money", £10 of his £130 salary, for lessons his pupils had missed when they were ill; Mr Dorrell, "of the Royal Academy of Music" (earning half a guinea an hour)—"many competent judges" had recommended him, but he only stayed two months; then Mr Hopkins (£120 a year), Organist at the Temple Church.

[16] He had belonged to a revolutionary society, the Carbonari, and had condemned in verse Ferdinand II, the tyrant King of Naples.

[17] His watercolour view of Fulham Church and Putney Old Bridge hangs at the Victoria and Albert Museum.

[18] Organist and Choirmaster of St George's Chapel, in Albemarle Street; a composer.

Who taught what else is much less clear. Ineffective staff did not stay long. Ladies were dropped and the Gentlemen were nudged.

The minutes indicate that a wide range of text-books and works of reference was supplied: Francis Walkinggame's *Compendium of Arithmetic*, John Colenso, Bishop of Natal's[19] *The Elements of Algebra*, "Euclid's Geometry" ("Euclid" for short), *The Penny Cyclopaedia* (much valued),[20] Dr John Blair's *The Chronology and History of the World from the Creation to the World of Christ*, maps of the Holy Land, historical, geographical and French dictionaries, Joseph Timothy Haydn's *A Dictionary of Dates* and *The Book of Dignities* ("rolls of the official personages of the British Empire . . . the sovereigns of Europe . . . the peerage of England and Great Britain"), James Parker's *A Glossary of Terms Used in Heraldry*, six copies of a cheap edition of Cowper's poems, Virgil's *The Iliad*, and Cicero's book about old age, *De Senectute*, the Latin entailing literature and not just proses and unseens.

Few other clues are given to curriculum and method. In 1843 the Gentlemen agreed that Mr Harley's classes be allowed to draw from solids and plaster models. The Rev. Mr Arthur Wallace, of Monks Leigh in Suffolk, gave the school a harp, for it to keep or sell, though not for less than £25. It was then sold, the Committee seeming to feel that it needed more money more than it needed more music. In 1847 a start was made on Physics, when a French text was adopted, *La Physique popularisée, ou les pourquoi et les parceque*, killing two birds with only one stone.

Some brief, informal notes in the Report of the Taunton Commission Schools' Inquiry, 1864–68, provide the only coherent account of how the school was staffed and equipped. It employed three resident teachers—the Governess (£100 a year), the English Mistress (£45), the French (£35)—and five visiting "Professors". Religious Knowledge, English Grammar, Composition, Literature, French, History, Geography, Arithmetic, "Vocal Music", Callisthenics (gymnastics promoting health and grace), Dancing and Needlework were taught to all thirty-six of the wards, sixteen of whom took Latin, sixteen Italian, ten German and twenty-five Drawing. The Library contained over 400 books, consisting of "judiciously selected works of approved authors", including Dr Johnson, and many "volumes of travels" were read, *The Saturday Magazine*,[21] *The Penny Magazine*,[22] selected articles in *The Quarterly Review*,[23] and other literary periodicals, "according to their suitableness to circumstances". Committees and "a select company" examined the top class once a year and awarded books as prizes.

19 Second wrangler at Cambridge, then Fellow of St John's; appointed by Dr Charles Longley as mathematics tutor at Harrow; uncompromising biblical scholar; translator from the Zulu; he outspokenly denounced the war against the Zulus in 1879.

20 Published by the Society for the Diffusion of Useful Knowledge, 1833–1858.

21 Published by the Society for Promoting Christian Knowledge, 1832–44.

22 A sister publication to *The Penny Cyclopaedia*, 1832–45.

23 1809–1967.

The Commission noted that girls who had entered late from other schools were generally the better prepared; but it may not have meant to criticise facilities or staff. Enrolled sows' ears had tended to remain, for whereas, from 1841 to 1852, twelve wards had had to leave who failed to learn, from 1856 to 1870 it was mostly the wayward and the sick who were discharged. Performance had declined, a less responsive intake having had to be accepted.

To attract into the school the right number of suitably qualified pupils the rules governing admission were relaxed. A daughter of a paymaster RN arrived in 1845 and in 1851 an assistant naval surgeon's; Law II was revised, so that girls would be received whose late fathers had sold their commission but had earned full pay for twenty years; also Bye-Law VIII, disqualifying those with a sister already installed, a rule which the Ladies had been anxious to keep, who, for reasons difficult to guess, mistrusted sisters more than they mistrusted other girls.

War in the Crimea helped fill the desks and beds. As the Gentlemen foresaw, at a meeting held on the 15th of June 1855, it could not fail "to make desolate the home of many a deserving Officer" if it did not soon end, and only three days later, on the fortieth anniversary of the Battle of Waterloo, their fears were confirmed: the enemy repulsed an assault launched on the Redan and, in the words of the Committee's next Report, "a fearful scene of havoc was added to the many which this brief and destructive war had witnessed".

Lt.-Col. Shadforth lay among the dead, leaving four daughters for his widow to support on a pension of £200 a year, with another £75 from the Compassionate Fund. His young Louisa, however, found "a friendly shelter" at the school; and so, next year, did Augusta Whitfeld, whose father, a chaplain at the Palace Hospital in Scutari, had died of cholera. Miss Harriette Parker did not arrive till 1862, followed by her sisters, Fanny and Augusta, three squabblesome daughters of a captain in the 77th Regiment who had also been killed in that assault. Five wards were thus enrolled, thanks to the ravages of war and plague, but in answer to their needs, rather than on merit, and only one of these, Augusta Whitfeld, would be appointed to a post from Regent's Park.

An alternative to slaughter as a means of recruiting enough young women of the right calibre had somehow to be found. The Ladies put forward two ideas: firstly, to add to "Education" in what had now become the school's full title, "The Adult Orphan Institution for the Relief and Education of the Friendless and Unprovided Orphan Daughters of Clergymen of the Established Church and of Military and Naval Officers", the words "as Governesses", thus making clearer the inducement of careers; the Gentlemen said yes; and secondly, to accept as wards the daughters of lawyers and physicians; but the Gentlemen, whose word was almost always law, said no.

Another proposal, from Capt. (later Admiral) Ryder, was rejected: that girls at the Royal Naval Female School at Richmond and the Clergy

Orphan School at St John's Wood be examined and compete to have their names listed as eligible candidates. It was agreed, however, in 1863, that the qualifying period of naval or military service be reduced from twenty years to twelve (to within three years of death), which may have sometimes helped to fill a vacancy or two.

The Royal Commissioners of the Patriotic Fund provided £40 a year for two daughters of naval and-or military officers, whom they themselves had nominated. Col. John Browne's Dora was acquired, from the Royal School for the Daughters of Officers of the Army, at Bath. And the Clergy Orphan School still presented candidates (unexamined). But they, it seems, were rather less elected than the rest, perhaps having fewer influential friends to canvas ("issue cards") on their behalf. It was a clergyman, indeed, Dr John Bull, Archdeacon of Christ Church, Oxford, who in 1850 complained about such friends. He did not succeed. The Managing Committee expressed its regret "that the Subscribers should be subjected to any inconvenience" but they pointed out that "the practice alluded to" was adopted at the elections of nearly all the metropolitan charities and that they were "not aware what steps could satisfactorily be taken to prevent the same".

Years later, in 1869, to reduce the cost of repeated canvassing—"severely felt"—and "to lessen the chance of the recurrence of these terrible and expensive disappointments", the Ladies recommended that votes polled for unsuccessful candidates be carried forward from one election to the next. The proposal had enjoyed "the cordial approval of the late lamented Chairman", Admiral (by then) Sir William Bowles, but the Gentlemen dismissed it with so little ado as to seem impatient.

The number of votes cast rose more slowly than the size of the electorate. It peaked overall in June 1869 at 7,124 (1,509 for Sophia Stace) and in December 1869 for the successful candidate, Grace Hathorn polling 1,654 (of a total of 5,900); then declined.

In 1860 the votes were mistold and Augusta Whitfeld's sister, Evelyn, was elected, who ought not to have been, edging out Emma Jane Stirling's sister, Mary; so the Gentlemen decided to admit both candidates, each the daughter of clergy—the Rev. Mr John Mayne Stirling had been Rector of Mangerville, New Brunswick, "in British North America".

The Taunton Commission's Report included notes about the diet, recreation and comfort which the wards enjoyed (but nothing else to do with health):

Four meals a day; meat daily . . . Usual washing apparatus of a bedroom in a gentleman's family, with unlimited supply of hot and cold water. Assemble at prayers 8 a.m.; retire 10 p.m. . . . Pupils walk out, accompanied by some lady in authority.

School rooms warmed and ventilated by keeping good fires, and opening all windows when not occupied. Seats, very comfortable chairs with backs.

School open all the year, except a fortnight at Christmas and two months in summer. Pupils in school about 20 hours in the week. Exercise in Park or Botanic Garden daily.

The wards had long been privileged to exercise themselves in the reserved area of Regent's Park called the Queen's Garden, near the present site of the Open Air Theatre, and breathe fresh air, or air as fresh as London offered. The Ladies had long disapproved, preferring them to keep to their own gardens in St Andrew's Place, which till 1853 were often wet and soggy, needing drains, but at least safer; to use the Park only on occasions designated special; and only then if they were properly escorted. Permission from the Royal Botanical Society for the use of its garden added "much interest and pleasure" to their exercise in and after 1845, but it did not apply to days when the rest of the public was admitted ("Exhibition and Promenade") or after 2.0 p.m.

Walking in the Park to disinfect the lungs, weather permitting, began to seem inadequate when in 1843 Mary Slade fell ill and, having lost both parents, was returned to her friends. A physician, Dr Engledue, examined her; he decided that want of recreation out of doors had undermined her health and that the health of other wards might also have been impaired.

Mr John Propert, surgeon,[24] the school's chief medical consultant, absolved the school from blame but agreed with his colleague, Dr Theodore Gordon,[25] that more fresh air and exercise were needed, and the Ladies, having thought their arrangements satisfactory, appear to have changed their minds about three months later and proposed and financed the acquisition of a big new room which allowed for callisthenics and where, by 1852, £160 worth of apparatus had been supplied, including "a beam".

In their 1844 Report, after three wards had been removed, sick, in the year just ended, and one of them had died, the Gentlemen took pains to assure the subscribers how mindful they were that prevention was better than cure and that as much had been arranged as was likely to achieve it.

The confinement to which young persons are subjected in the course of instruction, may, in some instances, be injurious to health. The importance of relaxation is always born in mind; and the Wards are accustomed to walk in the Park at a convenient hour; and are permitted, at another part of the day, to employ themselves in the Garden; the best and most healthy of all occupations out of doors, and most suitable to young persons in their condition.

. . . . .

Callisthenic exercises . . . have been introduced by the advice of the Ladies' Committee, particularly the Marchioness Cornwallis, who has

[24] Founder of the Royal Medical Benevolent College, Epsom, 1855.

[25] Inspector, retired, of Army Hospitals, he had served as Physician to the Forces with Wellington's staff in Paris.

added to her Ladyship's many instances of kind attention and liberal expenditure, the providing, at her own charge, with the kind assistance of a few friends, of a new and spacious apartment, well adapted for the purpose for which it is designed. These exercises have superseded the necessity of lessons in Dancing, which have therefore been discontinued, at the recommendation of the Ladies' Committee. The services of Mrs Wilson, the dancing mistress, have been dispensed with; and the sum of £50 annually paid to her has been transferred to Captain Michele by whom the exercises are conducted.

The Report for 1860 impressed on the subscribers how salubrious a location the school enjoyed: one "sufficiently open and healthy to afford, with God's blessing, that air and those opportunities for healthy exercise which none need more than those who are devoting more time to study than women are usually called upon to give". And in the bad year 1861–62, when so many fell ill and were kept in bed at school or at home, the Ladies assured the Gentlemen that the wards got all the exercise and fresh air needed, no lack of either have caused ill health.

Sanitation, however, left much to be desired. It had improved when the privy was put outside; but a smell still rose from the cellar; the "Long Room" filled with smoke; the kitchen floor was often damp, where the drains did not work properly; repairs were mooted but had to be postponed; and rats, "making their way into the apartments", were "a mischief" difficult to remedy.

Almost always there was something wrong with someone: a scalp verminous, teeth causing "face-ache", eyes inflamed, throat ulcerated or relaxed, swollen legs and feet, or upset stomach—suspected of disfiguring the skin—boils, whitlows, "a derangement of the Liver", the cause of Zelie Avarne's cough, "bilious headaches" or mood hysterical. Elizabeth Winckler, whose father had been Curate of Chichester, Jamaica, felt more or less all right, but walked in her sleep, alarmingly. Mild small-pox occurred in 1845, if small-pox at all, and small-pox no doubt of it in 1859, when a servant died who had not been vaccinated—the school paid for his funeral (£4)—and the wards had all to be taken home or to friends, their examinations cancelled.

At least nine honorary surgeons, physicians and apothecaries attended the sick. Mr Propert, appointed in 1828, nearly had to depart in 1832, when he proposed to charge for his services, but remained, unpaid, even for his medicines, for almost forty years, an honorary subscriber casting five votes in the election of the wards, until the day he died in 1868, when his son, Dr John Lumsden Propert,[26] continued his work. Quinine and aspirins

[26] A prosperous physician, also etcher and art critic, whose home at 112 Gloucester Place was a treasure-house of miniatures, jewelled work, porcelain and bronze.

Others gratuitously on call were Dr Archibald Billing, an authority on engraved gems and coins and perhaps the last GP to visit his patients on horseback; Sir James

were prescribed, cod-liver oil, indefinite leave, with mother or friends, and sea-side air. The wards recovering from small-pox mild stayed either with a Mrs Wishart at 40 Baker Street or somewhere in the country. Mrs Harriet Loyd-Lindsay,[27] of the Ladies' Committee, paid for Anna Lane to spend three months at the Home for Invalid Gentlewomen at St Leonard's. Mary Stirling was allowed to go and convalesce in Germany, accompanied by her sister, Emma Jane, a governess with Capt., later Rear-Admiral, the Hon. Thomas Pakenham,[28] of Holly Bank, Emsworth, who released her. Leonora Noble went to Sydney, with a cousin, Dr Pittaire, and his family, and Jemima Woolward to Madeira, they each needing sun. The Prideaux-Selbys of Swansfield, near Alnwick, took Mary Alder with them to Brussels, which may have done her good, for she lived to be 84 and, so far as we can tell, in about 1880 her daughter, Fanny Nicholson, would be the school's first old girl's daughter.

About a quarter of the junior wards fell ill and had to leave the Institution, almost a twelfth more than with Miss Hervey, which may either mean that more candidates should have been disqualified before they were elected or that illness was rifer or that wards elected were more readily removed if it looked as if their imperfect health might shorten their careers and waste the support of donors and subscribers and the efforts of the Ladies' and Gentlemen's Committees and the staff. Miss Grace Martin was invalided out, the daughter of a senior vicar at Lincoln Cathedral; Anna Elgee; Mary Ryan, after a long sick-leave in Alderney; Julia Bardin, daughter of the Rector of Derryloran, Armagh; Sarah Johnson, who died, 17; Henrietta Boor; Cordelia Cuming, who needed to escape from London's cold and damp and fog and sailed to join her brother and his family in the Bahamas; Catharine Davidson; Emily Pott, who had wintered in vain at her mother's home in Devon; and Ellen Clayton, her strength outgrown. Mrs Wardell wished to reclaim her daughter, Jane Wilson, "on account of her delicate state of health", but Mr Propert reported that Miss Wilson was "in as good a state of health as any young lady can well be". The Committee refused to consent to her release but Mrs Wardell withdrew her all the same and reimbursed by instalments, under Bye-Law XII, and with much exchange of letters, what ought to have been about £40 for her daughter's tuition and board but somehow amounted to only £13–8s. Augusta Lawrence died, 17—"painful intelligence" for the Ladies—and Mary Amey, 20, the daughter of a paymaster in the 6th

Alderson, President of the College of Physicians and later the Queen's Physician Extraordinary; and Sir John Tomes, whose methods, inventions and success won dentistry esteem.

[27] Daughter of the first Lord Overstone and wife of Robert, Lt.-Col., V.C., Conservative MP for Berkshire from 1865 till in 1885 he became the first and last Lord Wantage.

[28] Third son of the second Earl of Longford and Sophia, daughter of Sir Tatton Sykes (q.v.).

Battalion of the King's German Legion,[29] at home with her mother in Bath; Elizabeth Shannon had to leave in 1849; then all at once, next year, Elizabeth Clayton, sister of Ellen; Emma Haswell; Elizabeth Tuson; Sophia Hammill, with a tumour growing on her spleen; and her sister, Frances; but Frances was later readmitted. Mary Wallace died at the school, a girl, it was said, of outstanding quality and promise. The Committee paid warm tribute to her doctors, especially to Mr Propert, for his skill and care, and to Miss Horden and the Matron, Miss Davis, "whose assiduity and tender watchfulness were beyond all praise". The will of God would have to be accepted but grief so overwhelmed the wards that examinations could not take place. Others fallen ill remained at home or with friends: Laura Cowell; Henrietta Dukes; Eliza Myers; Sophia Jenkins; Margaret Persse; Emma Grange, 16, daughter of Edmund, British Chaplain at Bad Ems, in the Duchy of Nassau, she returning to her mother in Ireland, there to die; and Jane Barlee. Priscilla Lyster died at the school, unmourned however, in the minutes and Report—her sister, Emma, was admitted in her stead. Maria Sweny had to leave; Harriet Burges, 20, epileptic, who at 35 would be placed at the Royal Hospital for Incurables; Johanna Mullen; Clara Burton; Annie Hunt; and Louisa Gore. Three other wards died, from 1858 to 1860, who had long lain ill: Mary Newman, daughter of a surgeon RN; Elizabeth Hewett, whose father had captained the *Fairy* and perished with its crew in the cold North Sea, in November 1840; and Catherine Parr, daughter of the Rector of Stonton Wyville in Leicestershire. Ellen Collins was withdrawn in 1859, followed by Georgina Presgrave, one of the nine children of William, Curate of Knockholt, in Kent, and Headmaster of Queen Elizabeth's Grammar School, at Sevenoaks, nearby;[30] Amelia Booth; Evelyn Whitfeld, the miselected; Georgiana Francis; Mary Jones and Maria Ancell, who died within three weeks of one another in 1862; and about two years later Alicia Lawrance and Mary Jane Rose.

On the 7th of August 1865, Mrs Newbury, an army paymaster's widow, of Medina Cottage, Mall, Newport, Isle of Wight, wrote a letter to the Patriotic Fund which the Fund passed to the Gentlemen's Committee. She had two complaints. Her daughter, Mary, had been kept back in her studies, music having been taught her by a lady—Miss Manwell—and drawing not at all. Much worse: the school had neglected her health, her survival was at best precarious and all that now remained of what had once been "a healthy blooming girl" was "a sad wreck".

The Ladies, whom the Gentlemen now supported, could not accept these accusations. Mrs Newbury's daughter's music was not sufficiently advanced for her to receive instruction from Mr Turle. They had found Miss Manwell "very indefatigable in the discharge of her duties" and it was

[29] A force in British pay, intended to relieve Hanover, threatened in 1803 by the advancing French. Colonel-in-Chief: Adolphus, Duke of Cambridge.

[30] Called Sevenoaks School since 1877. Mr Presgrave started badly there in 1843, declared bankrupt the day before taking up his duties and his property sequestered, but remaining headmaster till his death in 1854.

"not usual for any of the Young Ladies in the lowest Class to have instruction from the Drawing Master", Mr Harley. Mary's falling ill did not bespeak neglect and when she left the Institution on the 19th of June 1865, bound for the Isle of Wight, she enjoyed good health, fully cured of what the Committee understood to be rheumatic fever.

Be that as it may, only nine and a half weeks later, on the 24th of August, Mary Newbury died and, whatever sorrow they may have felt, the Ladies and the Gentlemen recorded not a word of it.

Now twelve girls had died among Miss Horden's few. Mary Trench was the last in 1868. And another eight were to leave, all invalids: Anne Berrey, who twice returned after epileptic fits, left early, but taught as a governess for at least ten years; Helen Archdall; Ellen Swann; Julia Storey; Sophia Penfold; Mary Johnson; Edith Hughes, with one or both of her legs in irons; Elizabeth Thompson, the daughter of a lieutenant in the Gold Coast Artillery; and Mary Maxwell, whose father had been Vicar of St Paul's, Wellington, New Zealand.

At least nine seniors fell ill but later returned to their posts, including Frances Nott, one of the eleven children of a captain RN, and two with the Marchioness Cornwallis and her daughter Elizabeth: Frances Anwyl Roberts, daughter of the Curate of St Germaine's, Llanrwst, Denbigh, and Caroline Lammin, whose clergyman father, Thomas, had been Master of the Free Grammar School, Tamworth.[31] Lucy Philips, daughter of an Indian Army lieutenant, had to leave Malta and Admiral the Hon. Sir Montagu[32] and Lady Stopford, and return to her aunt, Mrs Corby, in Pimlico, but recovered, and was employed by Mr Murray Gladstone, son of William Ewart's eldest brother, Sir Thomas, at Broughton near Manchester, where her debts mounted and her health improved.

Others fallen ill (and most of them still young) had to end their careers: the Rev. Mr Cyrus Perkins's Mary, "inmate of a Lunatic Asylum"—"confirmed lunacy"—whose lack of music had lost her an appointment; Jemima Jones, sister of Ellen; Matilda Boger, having taught the young Cornwallises; Anne Hunter, "mentally deranged"—"aberration of intellect"; Margaret Bogle, sent home to her mother in Edinburgh, and Amelia Jones, already going blind—but a good school was found for her in Hanover, where her English conversation earned her board and lodging. Martha Mayor had died in 1843 and was followed to the grave by Louisa Smith; Julia Thompson; Emily Acton; Elizabeth Hayden, daughter of the Chaplain to the Birmingham Workhouse and Asylum; and Adela Church, one of a family of nine, who had lost not only her father but two brothers,

[31] Founded in 1588 as "the Free Grammar School of Elizabeth Queen of England in Tamworth". It had lost all its pupils by 1827, so the headship was a sinecure. When under Mr Lammin, till 1836, it had from thirty to forty day-boys and about eight fee-paying boarders. In 1979, combined with another school, it became Queen Elizabeth's Mercian Comprehensive.

[32] Admiral Superintendent there and heavily decorated for his services in the war against Russia in the Black Sea.

when HMS *Thais* sank in 1833, and who, as a junior, had survived mild small-pox and also, thanks to Admiral Bowles's support, the Marchioness Cornwallis's proposal to remove her; only one of these was over 25 years old.

Misbehaviour took its toll, satisfied though Miss Horden almost always was, with all or almost all her wards, when she reported to the Ladies. Another twenty-eight and a letter-smuggling servant were expelled, at an average rate of exactly one a year, three absconded, and the names of another three seniors were ignominiously struck from the list.

Disgraceful, however, though dismissal may have been for the dismissed, behaviour entailing it was seldom incorrigibly naughty. When in 1843 Elizabeth Maclean, 19, "clandestinely left the Institution whilst the Family were at breakfast and returned to her Mother's house at Gosport", the Committee recognised that "the fault was in some degree alleviated by the occasion which led to it, the sudden return of her brother from India", and also by her having gone directly to her mother's house, not stopping on the way. But rules once published had still to be obeyed and enforced, and precedents carefully established and observed, for the good of all. That was policy. Elizabeth's mother's letter of entreaty failed, the Committee feeling "bound, by a strong sense of duty, to refuse a re-admission, as an instance of wholesome discipline and as a warning to others".

Mrs E. B. Pim, a naval lieutenant's widow, did not wait for her daughter, Amelia, to abscond but descended on Miss Horden and "violently demanded" her release from the school. Miss Horden resisted her for two whole hours, urging Mrs Pim to adhere to the rules and first obtain the sanction of the Gentlemen's Committee, but failed. Thus the law whereby the mother paid a fine ("an additional contribution") if she withdrew her daughter arbitrarily or, if pleading illness, she did not return her with a medical certificate, was flouted. Three mothers honoured it in 1859. Lady Sarah Nicolas,[33] however, widow of Nelson's biographer, Sir Nicholas Harris Nicolas, Lt. RN,[34] and mother of Helen, and Mrs Hewett, mother of Ann (and Elizabeth), preferred to keep their daughters at the school when their request to take them home had been refused. We hear no more of Helen. Ann Hewett took posts in Kent, Somerset and Wales and in 1850, having married, wrote and thanked the Institution for all the benefits which she had there enjoyed.

Disharmony arose in 1844 between the two Committees. It began in June when the Gentlemen accused Miss Horden of installing a stove in her room, having failed to ask for their permission. Miss Horden rejected the charge. The Ladies sprang to her defence: Miss Horden's word could be

33 A direct descendant of William Davison, Secretary of State to Queen Elizabeth.

34 He had joined the Royal Navy aged 9; at 16 became a lieutenant; then retired a year later on half pay. A none too active barrister but a jovially combative, antiquarian writer. His seven volumes of *The Dispatches and Letters of Vice-Admiral Lord Nelson* appeared from 1844 to 1846. He died in Boulogne, aged 49, leaving eight children for his widow to support on an income of £304 a year, later supplemented by a civil list pension of £100.

trusted. The Gentlemen half-heartedly apologised, seeming not convinced. And a fortnight later, when they again met, they upset the Marchioness, resolving that her Ladyship be asked to repay, into the general funds, £20 of a £50 donation entrusted to her by Col. Edward Douglas-Pennant[35] and which she had set aside to buy a chimney for the new playroom (mainly paid for by herself). The Ladies, all, were most displeased. A criticism had been implied against their much respected President which was totally unjust, her Ladyship felt "deeply hurt and wounded", her health had suffered, and they called upon the Gentlemen to erase from their books "the objectionable resolution".

The Gentlemen ignored their request. They assured the Marchioness of their unwavering esteem but their resolution stood. Her Ladyship riposted: refusing to surrender the £20, she instead paid Col. Pennant the £10–4s. which the Gentlemen had deducted from the General Fund toward the cost of the playroom. This appeared to score a hit. The Gentlemen declared their debt of gratitude for her Ladyship's "unremitting and zealous devotedness to the best interests of the Institution" and within two months an external chimney to the new room had been erected "under the direction of the Marchioness Cornwallis"—"agreeably to her desire"—the Commissioners of Woods and Forests all approving.

Unpleasantness recurred a week or two later when Emily Hughes, a clergyman's daughter, back from Paris, with improved French, would not accept the posts that she was offered. Miss Hughes wrote to the Gentlemen, complaining that the Ladies had dismissed her from the school on an unfounded charge of disrespectful conduct. The Ladies explained: Miss Hughes had refused to stand and wait and listen to a reprimand; announced that she would herself delete her name from the senior list; then promptly did so. The Committee, Col. Fanshawe—as he then still was—and the Rev. Mr Thomas Bowdler,[36] just the two, took note but left no comment.

The peace had been restored but it did not last more than about three months. A ward, Susan Mott, had had to be removed, whose conduct before her admission nine months earlier was at last revealed to have been unsatisfactory. Miss Mott complained that she was wrongfully dismissed; her mother egged her on; together they retaliated and the Ladies and the

[35] Husband of Louisa, youngest daughter of the fifth Duke of Grafton; Honorary Colonel of the Scots Fusilier Guards; and Conservative MP for Carnarvonshire from 1841 till in 1866 he was created Baron Penrhyn.

[36] Secretary of the Church Building Society, Chaplain of St Katharine's Hospital and writer of many published sermons. Of his nine children seven died young, when "the bereaved parents were left alone, still uncomplaining, blessing the Hand that smote them" (*The Gentleman's Magazine*, 1857). A bigoted Anglican, he would not meet or have anything more to do with friends gone over to the Church of Rome, lest he seem to condone what he felt to be their treachery. The Bowdler, also Thomas, who had edited—bowdlerised—Shakespeare in such a way that families could read him together and aloud without blushing, was not his brother, as the above obituary states, but his uncle.

Gentlemen were dismayed to discover "that a pamphlet had been put into very general circulation [the subscribers were referred to], containing various unfounded statements affecting the Institution itself and unsparingly charging the President of the Ladies' Committee with harshness and unfairness".

The Duke of Cambridge and the Duchess of Gloucester investigated and rejected the complaints: Miss Mott's removal had been justified. The Gentlemen, in their Annual Report, dismissed as "unmerited calumnies" the accusations made against the Marchioness Cornwallis, "a Lady not more exalted by her rank than by her high religious and moral principles"; and Miss Horden too was not to be reproached, whose character the pamphlets had impugned, for they were well satisfied that the discipline Miss Horden imposed was not only firm but kind and understanding.

Louisa, Marchioness Cornwallis, died in 1850, having served as President of the Ladies' Committee for more than twenty years. The Gentlemen paid tribute to her work: she had been "zealous and unwearied" in her effort to promote the school's best interest, her kindness to its officers and inmates was "undeviating", her care to secure the most suitable and advantageous appointments for the wards "considerate and anxious", and every year she had contributed to the school "a large measure of pecuniary assistance". A sum of £34 was spent on mourning for the wards and resident staff. Lady Mary Ross, daughter of the Marchioness, and wife of Mr Charles Ross, formerly MP,[37] became the Ladies' President, and her sister, Lady Elizabeth Cornwallis, joined her Committee.

The lot of the wards had continued to improve. Decoration, and the periodical emptying of drains and cesspools, had made holidays more than ever "the usual", which in the summer of 1843 meant mostly with mother or friends or both, and for some of the wards a house in Tunbridge Wells with Miss Horden and a servant or two. The longer it took the paint to dry and the smell of it to clear, the longer did they last, from four weeks to six, or even twelve if need arose, until in 1854 a new regulation was published, declaring summer holidays to be more or less compulsory: "that during the vacation, which usually occurs in the course of the Summer, the friends of the Wards are required to provide for their removal". For the next eighteen years the holidays would last from five to eleven weeks (Taunton's "two months"). Within that time Miss Horden would report to the Ladies' Committee that each of the wards had returned home safely.

At Christmas, from two weeks to four, and at Easter for a few days, lessons were suspended, but the wards had still to remain at school. The Rev. Mr Henry Burrows,[38] Clerical Superintendent, disapproved and in

[37] For St Germans first and then for Northampton. A close friend of the second Earl Cornwallis, whose correspondence he edited in 1859.

[38] Vicar of Christ Church in Albany Street, St Pancras; "a true shepherd of his flock", his memorial tablet there (unpunctuated) reads: "watchful single-minded eminent in humility and love of truth ever sedulous for others careless for self". The Rossettis remained his life-long friends; they worshipped in his church. Christina, the

1864 he proposed that they all be allowed to spend their Christmases at home. The Ladies opposed him; the two Committees met and voted; Mr Burrows had his way. But another motion followed, which Lady Mary Ross proposed: that the change of rule should be postponed for one whole year lest the writer of "a certain anonymous letter" be encouraged to suppose "that the said objectionable document had influenced the Committees"; the friends and mothers would have to be informed; and they should each one of them be made to understand that anonymous letters would always be treated with the contempt which they deserved. The Gentlemen concurred: the rule should be relaxed, but not while the offending correspondent might still feel gratified.

The school itself offered changes of scene: worship at St Katharine's Chapel,[39] in reserved seats; and confirmation at St Mary's, Bryanston Square,[40] or Holy Trinity, in the Marylebone Road, just round the corner, or at Christ Church in Albany Street, with Mr Burrows. A visit here and there was arranged. Six of the wards were invited to a concert in 1844 at Mr Turner's home at 2 North Bank, and seven years later Eleanor, Duchess of Northumberland,[41] gave tickets enabling them to view her stately home[42] on a day when it was closed to the public. But that was the sum, for all we read, of their eventful releases till in March 1863 as many wards as had mothers or friends in town were given leave of absence from the Friday to the Wednesday to enable them to witness "the public rejoicings" that would greet the arrival in London, by ship, of the Prince of Wales's bride, Princess Alexandra of Denmark, and her departure with the Prince for St George's Chapel, Windsor.

How many wards had mothers or friends in town or near it we cannot tell. It is likely, however, that most saw little of their next of kin, unless they had fallen ill and were allowed to go and convalesce; not all could travel home for Christmas—eight had to stay behind in 1868 and five next year; and the less they were scholars the more they must have felt how little else there was to life but school. Had they rebelled or badly misbehaved, it would not have been surprising. They often broke rules. But where did the fault mostly lie? With the rules or with the ruled?

It had come to light in 1843 that Emily Brock, who had left six months

poet, was his District Visitor in Old Robert Street nearby and would have written his life had illness not prevented her.

39 Built at the same time as 11 St Andrew's Place, damaged in World War II, then restored, in 1952 it became the Danish Church in London.

40 A much criticised "pepper-box" church, built in 1823 by Sir Robert Smirke.

41 Wife of Algernon, sixth Duke. Charlotte, Duchess Dowager, 3 Portman Square, who served with her on the Committee, had been governess to the Queen when the Queen was Princess Victoria.

42 Built in 1605; partly destroyed by fire in 1868; and in 1874 compulsorily acquired and demolished by the Metropolitan Board of Works for the building of a new street, Northumberland Avenue, connecting Charing Cross with the Victoria Embankment.

ago for a post with the family of the Rev. Mr John Bramston, of Witham in Essex, used to get and send clandestine letters. The Ladies were displeased ("very improper conduct"), they refused to recommend her to another employer and proposed that "in future, any Ward who shall be detected in receiving, or forwarding, Letters or Parcels through an improper Channel, shall, upon the offence being satisfactorily proved to the Committee, be subject to immediate dismissal". The public would otherwise lose all confidence in the school; and the Gentlemen agreed.

It was a dire warning. But rules about letters were difficult to enforce and it must have been obvious how often they were flouted when in 1846 the Dead Letter Office returned to Mary Ann (not Mary) Jones, then absent, ill, a letter posted half a year before to an address in Canada. Miss Davis, Matron, or Miss Horden, intercepted it; Mary Ann was exposed; another ten wards, Mary Amey (she would die within three years), Mary Beckwith, Mary Clarke, Maria Garrett, Ann Hill, Philippa Lys, Horatia Mathias, Frances Nott, Victoria Parker, whom staff found tiresome anyway, and Jane Wilson all admitted to illicit—private—correspondence; Amelia McEwen and Olivia Fry, seniors, and Miss Pitcher, who had once taught at the school, had been "accessory to violation of the Rules"; and Mrs Jones told Miss Davis that "the transmission of letters by the Wards was a circumstance of frequent occurrence".

The Ladies acknowledged the candour of the ten but denied them visitors for about eight weeks. Mary Ann was removed.

Letters may have tended to undermine authority, like the two which Miss Horden withheld from Fanny Prattent, in 1851, from an uncle and a brother, "in consequence of certain expressions contained therein disrespectful to herself". But the rule was harsh, it did not accord with information published in the Taunton Committee Report: "Pupils never punished; reproof and admonition only resorted to when needed", for punishment was what removal must have felt like to its victim.

Lady Harriet Carbery,[43] of Laxton Hall, Wansford, near Stamford, wrote in 1855 complaining about the inspection of wards' letters to and from their parents. The Ladies prevaricated: their attention had often been directed to the rule; it was "expedient", however, "to retain the Power thereby conferred", exercised though it was "with every possible consideration and frequently relaxed as circumstances may warrant".

Mary Ann's removal may have worked, as an example, or Miss Horden and Miss Davis have aged, with impaired faculties, or the letter-smugglers took more care; it was twenty years before another illicit correspondent was exposed: Belinda Tottenham, aged 20, who had kept in touch with a gentleman whom she had met over Christmas, "during a five days' visit". She had lost both parents, her father, Curate of St Nicholas, Cork, having died when she was ten, and her mother a few days later, so depended on her friends, and to her friends she had to pack her bags and travel.

[43] Wife of George, seventh Baron.

The Gentlemen had objected when the Ladies had proposed that anyone visiting a ward for the first time should sign an undertaking to observe the rules. Miss Tottenham's removal seemed to put them on their guard: the rules about visits should be tightened lest "a similar event" bring the school discredit. But the Ladies convinced them that the rules were already tight enough (visits from grandfathers had had to be curtailed in 1847 to only one a quarter) and the Gentlemen agreed, instead, that each new ward be asked to copy out the rules and forward them to her mother or her friends.

A clandestine correspondent, Mary Clarke, took her first post, with the family of Praed, at Wadenhoe near Oundle; but left pleading injury, the result of a fall at the house of Mr James Mure, father or son, which Miss Catherine Mure then said had never happened. Her name was deleted from the senior list. Selina, daughter of the Rev. Mr James Cooper, Curate of Ugley-cum-Berden in Essex, was removed, having failed her examinations, and so, a year later, in 1848, was Matilda Burges, a sister of the epileptic Harriet, found "guilty", Miss Horden told the Ladies, "of great insubordination, which she had found it necessary to reprove, but without producing any amendment". Victoria Ffinney got a second chance, whom the Ladies had wished to expel, she having "practised imposition by painting her face" (impersonating someone?) and then told lies, but she did not respond, so after five months the Ladies had their way (or as the Gentlemen chose to put it: her election was not confirmed—if the word election applied, for in April 1853 Victoria and four others were admitted unopposed, when vacancies outnumbered the eligible candidates).

Miss Maclean had absconded, others followed, unhappy or naughty or in love. Elizabeth Stanes, 18, a sister of the ailing Sarah, ran home to her stepmother, "in a very unsettled state"; Alice Coghlan, 17, took lodgings, pursuing "an attachment"—in vain did their mothers and Miss Coghlan's uncle plead; Frances Hamett, 18, daughter of Sir John, Deputy Inspector of Fleets and Hospitals, had to leave, who had gone and stayed with her friend, Mrs Holl, in Pimlico; and in May 1857 Ellen Fennell, 19, skipped morning prayers and married Mr Curwen, or Kirwen, Salmon, "of Gray's Inn",[44] with whom for the last four months she had "obtained interviews" not only at the Botanical Gardens in Regent's Park but also at the Colosseum.

The two Committees, who met as one, could do nothing at all about Miss Fennell, eloped and newly wed. Mr John Lawrell, Clerical Superintendent,[45] agreed to severely admonish those who had known about her plan and had failed to report it. Frances Osborn, daughter of David, Island Curate of St George's, Jamaica, had already slipped away, upset, returning to her mother, and Emily Hall was at home too, celebrating her coming of

[44] No one of either name appears in the Society's admission records at about this time or in its pension books. It looks as if it was where he had his lodgings.

[45] Perpetual Curate of St Matthew's, Berkeley Crescent, built in 1848 and destroyed by bombs in 1940.

age that very day and in the first week of the one month's leave each ward now enjoyed before her first engagement. But Emma Lyster could be summoned to appear—sister of the Priscilla who had died at the school, and of Elizabeth to follow—Elizabeth Richmond and Julia Nunn. Mr Lawrell warned all three that their complicity in Miss Fennell's conduct would be reported to any lady who might think of appointing them to a post; the sisters Cornwallis and Ross, three other of the Ladies, Earl Manvers, John Lonsdale, Bishop of Lichfield, Vice-Admiral (then) Sir William Bowles, Maj.-Gen. Horatio Broke, called Horace, Mr James Mure, son of James, and Lady Mary's son-in-law, Mr James Whatman, MP for Maidstone, a formidable eleven, still present and supportive, resolved that he be thanked for his "very kind but faithful reproof"; and they all hoped that the words which he had spoken would help to bring about "a deep sense of the offence committed and . . . improved conduct in future".

Mme Emary or Emery, French governess probationer, must also have disgraced herself, for she lost her post. Mr Lawrell wrote to Mrs Fennell and Mrs Osborn, seeking payment of fines under Bye-Law XII. Mrs Osborn expressed "her utter inability to meet the demand" and did not consider herself "justly liable, as her Daughter's departure . . . was without her knowledge or consent and . . . she deeply regretted the step her Daughter had taken". Mrs Fennell did not reply. Emma and Elizabeth in turn completed their course; the Beachcrofts of Harrow-on-the-Hill took Elizabeth; the Wildeses of Elm Bank, Manchester, Emma; but to Emily's one month's holiday were added seven months of unemployment before a Mrs Baugh of Exeter accepted her. And Julia Nunn, absent nursing her sick mother, was forbidden to return when she was not quite 21, the Ladies being slow to forget, if they ever would, that she had known all along about Miss Fennell's assignations.

The Gentlemen tended more to relent than did the Ladies, when mischief was exposed, were less defensive, being more detached from the day-to-day running of the school, embroiled themselves less in its internal disputes, and belike more readily searched their hearts and heads if the right number of intelligent, law-abiding pupils eluded them or if the school was criticised.

On the 2nd of January 1864 it was criticised severely. A letter headed "Female Education" appeared in *The York Herald*.[46] Addressed to the editors, it read:

Gentlemen, I feel sure that you will find a place in your columns for the insertion of the following statement concerning the "Adult Orphan Institution", near Regent's Park, London, as I really think that it is a case on which your powerful influence ought to bear. The state of the case is this:- Girls, after being once entered, are not permitted, according to the society's published rule (bye-law No. xii), to leave the school without the permission of the "committees", in accordance with an engagement

[46] 1790–1889; as *The Yorkshire Herald*: 1890–1954.

entered into before they are admitted, by which, if they do leave without this permission, their mothers or guardians are liable to be fined twenty pounds for every year during which their daughters or wards have been inmates of the institution. Now, though at first sight it may appear that even if the fine were enforced, £20 a year is a small sum to pay for a first-class education, yet when it is considered that some, not to say many of the girls' mothers are in a state bordering on destitution, it must be seen that such a fine (in addition to £12 a year paid, in any case, during the girl's residence), might be an impossibility for a mother to pay, and might therefore positively preclude her from removing her daughter from the school, under any circumstances. But this is not the worst part of the system. The hours of work begin at nine a.m. and end at half-past eight p.m., during which time the only moments supposed to be allowed for relaxation are three-quarters of an hour for dinner, half an hour for tea, and an hour for walking, from which last is deducted the time taken up in getting ready for the walk, and the time again required for getting ready for the lessons.

This might not seem so very short a time for relaxation, if wholly applied to that purpose; yet, as I understand, there is so much work to be prepared during the day, that only those of supernatural abilities are able to prepare it during actual school hours, whilst those of moderate abilities are obliged to intrench upon their hours of recreation so as to make up their required work, and thus it generally happens that, the weaker girls are in mind and body, the less healthy exercise they are allowed to have. It would appear then that it is not without a cause that a heavy fine is imposed on guardians removing their wards, for if the system were less severe it would be very improbable that girls would be removed before the expiration of their term from a school where they could obtain a first-class education at a comparatively little cost. As I have no personal interest in this matter, I should not have troubled you with this letter, had I not ascertained, both from personal knowledge and information which I have received, that the health of the girls does, in too many instances, suffer under this absurdly severe system. In fact, the system seems something like that of the ancient Spartans, calculated only for the very robust and strong.

I am, Gentlemen, yours obediently,
Dec. 29th, 1863 Scrutator

The Ladies noted "the aspersions on the Institution" which Scrutator's letter cast. Admiral Sir William Bowles, however, Chairman, and another three of the Managing Gentlemen, resolved that to reply was "not expedient".

Dismayed they may have felt, but hardly surprised. In 1860, when Committees had been formed, a Naval and a Clerical, "to confer with kindred establishments in the same professions, and by a diligent investigation into the position of the Institution, to propose such reforms as might be deemed necessary for its improvement", they had clearly suspected that

something was amiss, with the school and-or with its image, and the findings of the Committee RN, early next year, "that an opinion existed in some quarters to the effect that the Wards in the Institution were treated with unnecessary restraint and severity, and that young persons were unwilling to become candidates for admission", must have deepened their misgivings.

The naval officers were divided, and the Admiral worried least, but Mrs Dorothy Blomfield, the bishop's wife, Capt. Charles Egerton, RN, Treasurer, and Mrs Egerton, did not doubt that the school was now unpopular, Mrs Egerton quoting from a letter from an unnamed friend who had complained about Miss Horden's treatment of the ward, Emma Grange, who had returned to her mother's care in Ireland, and had died there, in 1852.

A joint conference of the two Committees was therefore convened, from which another Sub-Committee of two Ladies and three Gentlemen emerged, including Lady Mary Ross and the Admiral, to investigate and report on Mrs Egerton's friend's complaint against Miss Horden; but with due regard, the Admiral insisted, to Miss Horden's "high character", her many years of loyal service, her strong claim "to the fairest and most impartial enquiry" and the need to ensure that no charges against her would be brought which did not rest upon a strict compliance with the Rules of Evidence or which relied on "vague reports or hearsay accusations" (this presumably referring to the "not forthcoming letter" from the unnamed friend of Mrs Egerton).

The senior wards who had left the school in the last seven years were circularised, their mothers and friends, also Miss Martha Roberts, who had taught them English for fourteen years, and their opinions were invited on the way in which the wards and their work had been supervised. Again Miss Horden was vindicated and in 1861 the findings of the enquiry were published in the Annual Report.

The answers received to those enquiries form a body of evidence of the most conclusive nature, and which cannot fail to be satisfactory to every friend of the Institution.

The letters written were to the number of twenty-two, and, without a single exception, the writers of them, from distant and different parts of the country, bore unanimous and grateful testimony to the kindness and maternal care they had experienced while under the tuition of the present Governess; many of them affirming that they looked back to the years passed in the Institution as the happiest of their lives, and expressing a deep sense of gratitude for the blessings which they are at present enjoying, and which they owe to the good fortune of having been Wards of the Adult Orphan Institution.

It must be added that this testimony was not confined to that elicited by the letters sent from the Committee. Before that step was taken, the fact of the enquiry having become known, voluntary letters flowed in from the

same former pupils of the Governess, couched in terms of the warmest affection, and even indignation, that she should have been the object of such unfounded aspersions.

The senior wards and other former pupils were also invited "to pronounce generally, from their own experience, their opinion of the existing Rules, and to suggest such changes in them as might appear beneficial".

To this enquiry many replied, that whatever might have been their opinion during their residence as Pupils, the experience they have acquired as Teachers had convinced them that the Rules had been wisely framed to promote the best interests of the Wards, and were admirably calculated to further the soundest views of education.

The Ladies and the Gentlemen now met and unanimously resolved that Miss Horden "be assured in the strongest terms of the undiminished confidence and regard of both Committees, and of their sincerest regret" that she had been subjected to "enquiries inevitably painful to her feelings". They did not, however, doubt that "her purest consolation" would derive from "the universal testimony" she had received "of the regard and affection of her former pupils and of the warm and lasting gratitude" with which they looked back on "her maternal care and solicitude for their welfare". And next term the Gentlemen authorised her "to obtain a Supply of Wine for her own use, the Ladies' Committee having represented that her health requires the occasional use of it".

Departed wards made clear to Miss Horden how they felt by making her a gift of a handsome silver tea-pot, presenting it to her at the end-of-year examination of the top class, and they wrote to her as follows:

Dear Miss Horden,

Will you accept this mark of our affection towards you, and of our gratitude for all your kindness to us, both while we were in the Institution, and since we have left it. We know that we can never repay all you have done for us; but we have long wished to give you some little token of our grateful love, and feel the present a suitable occasion for doing so, now that you are entering upon your twentieth year at the Institution.

We remain, dear Miss Horden,
Your affectionate Friends.

And four years later a mother unnamed paid tribute to the school in a letter addressed to the Patriotic Fund:[47]

[47] Established in 1803 by Sir Francis Baring and John Julius Angerstein, each of Lloyd's, to assist disabled soldiers and sailors and the widows of the fallen. Sir Francis, of German descent, founded Baring Bros. Angerstein, born Russian, died in 1823. In 1824 the government bought his collection of pictures, in effect launching the National Gallery and enabling it to develop. The Fund has been known as the Lloyd's Patriotic since 1854.

The extreme kindness and motherly attention which she has uniformly received from the several heads of the Institution are most highly appreciated by me and my child.

No doubt support was welcome. A year hardly ever passed when nothing acrimonious developed. The Grand Inquiry had run its anxious course. But something would upset what little now remained of Miss Horden's work and life: the presence, at the school, of the sisters Parker, whose father had been killed in the Crimean War, in the assault on the Redan: Harriette, the eldest, Fanny next, with whom she "quarrelled so much . . . as to prove a disturbance and great annoyance to the other wards", then the youngest, Augusta. Augusta and Fanny each suffered from "delicacy of constitution", Harriette's and Augusta's tonsils were enlarged and Fanny had neuralgia. Worse for everybody else, they had sharp and wagging tongues.

Harriette was removed from the senior list; she had refused a post, then accepted another, without the school's consent. Augusta took her place. "Misconduct" being proved against Fanny, Mrs Parker wrote that she would readily take her away, if allowed to do so of her own free will. The Gentlemen agreed, thus avoiding an upset. Mrs Parker could be difficult. A statement was produced, which seventeen junior wards had signed, complaining of her conduct. The Gentlemen resolved that Mrs Parker should now be excluded from the house; a Mrs Douglas Crawford would be permitted to call on her behalf and see Augusta. Augusta too was loud and shrill. The Ladies earnestly wished that she depart, it being "most objectionable . . . that any Member of Mrs Parker's family should remain in the Institution or even enter its doors". Admiral Bowles resisted their pleas; it was useless, they decided, to persist. But still they seemed to bristle. On the 5th of February 1869 the minutes of their meeting were signed, not by one on their behalf, but by them all: Ladies Mary Ross and Elizabeth Cornwallis, Miss Catherine Mure,[48] Miss Sarah Hildyard—a ward of 18 in 1829, now 58, royal governess retired—Louisa, Countess Dowager of Lichfield,[49] her name vehemently underlined, Miss Mary Heberden[50] and Anne, Marchioness of Thomond.

In the end they got their way, but not before Augusta had spent five months at home, after two of summer holiday, with "a very severe cough", her mother wrote to explain, when the Gentlemen transferred her to

48 Sister of James, son of Treasurer James, and from 1839 to 1872 a revered member of the Ladies' Committee.

49 Widow of Thomas, first Earl (Postmaster General, 1835–41, when he introduced the penny post), she was well-known for nearly forty years as a leader of fashion.

50 Thought to be one of the nine children of Dr William Heberden the younger, an eminent Physician in Ordinary to George III. A biblical and classical scholar, it was he who composed the inscription on Addison's monument in Westminster Abbey. A Charles Heberden served for two years with the Managing Gentlemen.

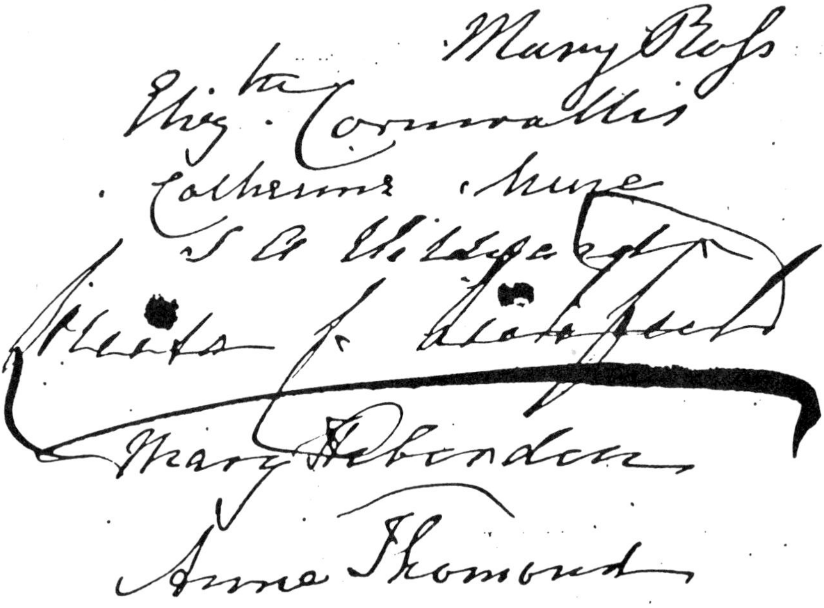

another school, helped again by a grant from the Patriotic Fund, which had supported all three Parkers.

Harriette, meanwhile, had not lain low. A letter she had written to Sir John Anson,[51] complaining about Miss Horden, was discussed by each of the Committees. Yet another investigation followed. The wards resident with Harriette were written to and consulted; twenty-eight of them replied; rallying to their Governess, they again testified to her many benefits and kindness; Emma Swan (Mrs Tudor Craig), sister of Ellen (and of Mary), called Harriette's accusations false; and the Gentlemen, agreeing, increased Miss Horden's salary from £100 a year to £150, "as a willing (though inadequate) proof of their esteem and satisfaction".

We do not know what the "statements" were, "respecting Mrs Lindsay", which the Ladies referred to in 1868. Mrs Lindsay's daughter, Anne, had been accepted as a candidate on condition that her mother would "in no way interfere with her" and that her aunt guaranteed to keep her out of reach of her mother in the holidays. What the Ladies were most likely to have feared, however, from the contact of a mother with her child, was her misguiding love, the premature departure of a pupil and an embarrassing and lamentable waste of subscriptions and donations.

[51] One of the Managing Gentlemen and son of the first baronet, General Sir William, he would die from injury when in 1873 an accident occurred at the Wigan junction of the London and North-Western Railway.

Another ward had to leave at about this time: Margaret Goodchild, aged 16, who in 1868 had almost polled a record vote. The sisters Parker had talked too much; Miss Goodchild, in her first-and-last six months, "notwithstanding many remonstrances was obstinately silent".

By May 1852 at least 295 wards had been elected or admitted, rather more than the register includes, thirty-nine of them juniors; another four were about to be enrolled; and thirty-four were employed seniors in touch with the school. The overall total in 1870 must have risen to about 450.

Demand for governesses continued to exceed supply and appointments with "families of the highest respectability" appear to have been more easily arranged. Jane Forbes, daughter of John, Lt. RN, was "placed out" with Archbishop Howley, presumably to teach his grandchildren, but left after four years, too continually ill to be of use, Dr Howley by then aged 81. Mr George Stoddart, British Consul in Madeira, took Army Capt. John Smith's Margaret, sister of the doomed Louisa, the Ladies recording in their minutes that her ship had safely arrived. It was the ninth of fourteen posts that she would occupy, including a spell in Nice. In St Petersburg she worked for a Mrs Carr, from whom she was transferred to a Prince and Princess Volkonsky;[52] had to leave Russia when war broke out in the Crimea ("The Czar[53] having commanded the Prince Volkonsky to part with Miss Smith, she is to return to England as soon as possible"); but reclaimed her post once peace had been restored. The Blaauws (*sic*) of Beechfield, Uckfield, Sussex, employed Sarah Tucker, home from Paris; Lt. Thomas Egan's Ellen, a governess from 1841 to 1876, spent four months with the family of Sir Tatton Sykes, of Sledmore near Malton, a well-known boxer, sheep and race-horse breeder, jockey (orange-and-purple-clad), master of foxhounds, and five years with Dr Longley, teaching Caroline (till she married) and her sister, Rosamond—after Caroline, their mother, was three months dead—he within that time Bishop of Durham, Archbishop of York, then Primate; the Delmé-Radcliffes, of Hitchin Priory (it stands intact but is a home no more), took Ramsgate Harbour-Master,

[52] Prince Sergei Volkonsky, 1860–1943, in *My Reminiscences*, translated from the Russian by A. E. Chamot, 1924: "Pictures of my childhood rise up before me. I am three years old. On the stone steps of the portico an old Englishwoman—Miss Smith—a former governess of my aunts, my mother's cousins, is sitting showing me how to twist my fingers so as to form a house; the forefinger is lowered and represents a counter, the little finger is the shopkeeper and the two thumbs are customers."

The place is the home of his family, Schloss Fall, on the sea-shore near Reval, in Estonia. Elisabeth, his mother, was herself born Volkonsky. Volkonsky, Sophia, the wife of Elisabeth's brother's son, Peter, in *The Way of Bitterness: Soviet Russia 1920*, dedicated to Princess Helena's daughter, Marie Louise, and published by Methuen in 1931, records how in 1918 the Red Army took over the house and destroyed it, with all its treasure.

Which one of the Volkonskys employed Miss Smith we cannot tell. Dominic Lieven, *Russia's Rulers Under The Old Régime*, Yale, 1989: "attempting to trace relationships in the huge Volkonsky family is a nightmare."

[53] Nicholas I.

Cmdr John Woolward's Jemima; the Earl[54] and Countess of Clarendon, Philippa Lys, clandestine correspondence notwithstanding, a daughter of John, Perpetual Curate of the Island of Alderney—at Dublin Castle, their Lord Lieutenant's home, she suffered "a severe accident", but recovered, going on to other posts, in Cornwall, Italy and France; Sir Thomas[55] and Lady Buchan-Hepburn, in Geneva, Ann, daughter of Lt. Mordaunt Hill, RN, clandestine correspondent 1846, who travelled on, recommended by the Hepburns, to "Count" Bronkhorst[56] and his family in Como, but without the school's consent, so her name was deleted; the Rodds of Trebartha, Launceston, Cornwall, Charlotte Richmond, daughter of Christopher, Rector of Six Hills, Legsby, and of Ludford Magna, in Lincolnshire, sister of the Elizabeth who abetted Ellen Fennell—her next nine posts were as governess to Lady Julia Cornwallis,[57] with the Hon. and Very Rev. Dr Henry Howard, Dean of Lichfield,[58] her mother who ran a school in Folkestone, Lord[59] and Lady Dorchester, the Earl[60] and Lady Nelson, Trafalgar House, in Salisbury, and at four vicarages or rectories, till in 1867, aged 39 and still a senior ward, she was allowed to sail for Canada and visit her brother; the Duke of Newcastle,[61] two years divorced, took the Rev. Mr Luke Ripley's Sarah, a governess with nine families in about as many years and one of those who had to move when her pupil fell ill and died; the Rev. Mr Henry Gosse, of Redhill, Surrey, Quartermaster Collins's Mary, sister of Ellen, who could not be accepted as a ward till doubt had been dispelled that her principles were those of a true Protestant; Mr Robertson Gladstone, of Court Hey, Broad Green, Liverpool, the future Prime Minister's brother, the second of Sir John's four sons—tallest (6′7″) and fattest—the Rev. Mr William Nunn's Marianne, who had pleaded in vain for her sister, Julia, after Julia had helped Ellen Fennell to elope—Miss Nunn stayed with the Gladstones for thirteen years; Sir David Brewster, Kt, of Edinburgh, inventor of the kaleidoscope, Lt.-Col. James Bogle's Margaret, who lived with her Edinburgh mother, too delicate to be a

[54] George Villiers, fourth Earl. He would be Foreign Secretary, 1853–58, 1865–66 and 1868–70. In 1880 his daughter, Constance—Philippa's pupil—joined the Ladies' Committee.

[55] Third baronet, MP for Haddington, 1838–47.

[56] Ludolph van Bronkhorst, 1813–82, minuted as Count, but a Jonkheer, not a Graaf, a titular colonel and intendant at the Royal Palace near Apeldoorn, then on holiday, it seems, with his wife, Clara, and their daughters, Sophie, 10, and Suzanna, 7. Their family died out in 1923.

[57] Orphan daughter of James, fifth and last Cornwallis Earl. In 1862 she married William, Viscount Holmesdale, who in 1886, three years after Julia's death, became the third Earl Amherst.

[58] Youngest of the seven children of the fifth Earl of Carlisle (of Castle Howard).

[59] Guy, third Baron, whose vicious racing stallion, Cruiser, killed several of his grooms.

[60] The second, Thomas.

[61] Henry, fifth Duke, Secretary for the Colonies, under Lord Aberdeen, then War Secretary in the Crimean War.

governess but allowed to tutor Sir David's grandchildren and a Princess Gauromma of Coorg;[62] Lord[63] and Lady Saltoun, Ness Castle, Inverness,[64] Isabella Armstrong, daughter of Andrew, a surgeon in the Grenadier Guards; Sir George Brown, Kt (with his orphan niece), anon General and Lord Raglan's second-in-command in the Crimea, Gladstone himself—William Ewart[65]—and Mr James Johnstone, of the Hanging Shaw, Selkirk, MP for Clackmannan and Kinross, RN Lt. Edward Scott's Elizabeth;[66] Sir Arthur Kennedy, Governor of Western Australia,[67] RN Lt. Andrew Munro's Charlotte; Laura, Countess of Antrim,[68] RN Capt. Henry Drury's Alice, but only for a week and a half—she was not sufficiently advanced in French; Lord[69] and Lady Fermoy of Cork, the Rev. Mr Henry Stevenson's Rosa, who did as they advised and spent two months in Heidelberg in 1864, improving her German—with Charlotte Richmond, as it happened or was planned, the Nelsons either patient or approving—then returned to her pupils for three more years, making eight—RN Lt. Cater's Clarissa Jacyntha had sabbaticaled in Dresden; Sir Henry Brand, Parliamentary Secretary to the Treasury and a future Speaker of the House of Commons,[70] there revered, took Charlotte's sister, Elizabeth; Dr William Budd, the famed authority on zymotic diseases in folk and cattle, Celeste Hall, sister of Emily; the Hon. and Rev. Mr Latimer Neville, Master of Magdalene College, Cambridge,[71] the Rev. Mr William Faulkner's Rose; Lady Margaret Mansfield,[72] the Rev. Mr John Dodd's Ellen, till in 1865 she had to sail with her children for India and her husband there, the haughty and quarrelsome Sir William, C.-in-C.,[73] and the Whartons of Skelton ("the

[62] A province of Southern India, east of Mysore.

[63] Alexander, seventeenth Lord Saltoun, of the Frasers of Philorth.

[64] A mansion, built in 1840, near the little remaining of the Borlum Castle which in 1760 a Mr Simon Fraser had bought and then called Ness. It is today the Culloden Park Hotel.

[65] While or soon after he was Chancellor of the Exchequer, 1852–55, in Aberdeen's coalition.

[66] The never-praising governess in *Mary Gladstone (Mrs Drew), Her Diaries and Letters*, edited by Lucy Masterton, 1930, arrived later, teaching Mary aged 10 till 17.

[67] 1855–62. The convicts he imported there helped raise the birth-rate and develop the economy. His Chinese servants felt less welcome than the convicts, but they kept their jobs, he refusing to appease the native unemployed.

[68] Widow of Hugh, fourth Earl.

[69] Edmund, first Baron. MP for Marylebone, 1859–65.

[70] A Liberal MP, first for Lewes, then for Cambridgeshire. Created first Viscount Hampden in 1884 and twenty-third Baron Dacre in 1890.

[71] Son of Jane, Lady Braybrooke, daughter of Louisa, Marchioness Cornwallis, the Ladies' Committee President; in his last two years of life sixth Baron Braybrooke; for five years a Fellow of his College, then its Master for fifty, till his death in 1904; and from 1859 to 61 Vice-Chancellor of the University.

[72] A staunch Liberal who, in the last six of her sixteen years of widowhood, would prominently support Mr Gladstone and his policies, not least Home Rule.

[73] Created first Lord Sandhurst in 1871.

Crazy") Castle,[74] Sarah, daughter of the Rev. Mr William Smith, of Hinderwell in Yorkshire.

Overlapping with almost all these appointments, more prestigious and therefore most helpful to the school, had been and would remain Sarah Hildyard's, which Miss Hildyard had reported in a letter addressed to the Marchioness Cornwallis, at the time still President.

Dear Madam,

The kindness I have ever received from you, both during my residence in the Institution and since I left it, induces me to take an early opportunity of informing you that Her Majesty has graciously appointed me Governess to the Royal children under Lady Lyttelton.[75]

I need scarcely say that this has been totally unsought for on my part, but the recommendation of Lady Pembroke,[76] *then applied to, caused my name to be brought before the Queen.*

I passed some days at Osborne, and had the honour of a presentation—this was followed by the appointment which arrived this morning.

I cannot conclude without offering my truly grateful thanks to your Ladyship and the Committee in general, to whose Patronage and care I am so deeply indebted.

Believe me to remain, Dear Madam,
Your sincerely obliged
Sarah Anne Hildyard
Bromley College, 7th of January 1847

Two years later she sent ten guineas to her "former happy home"—words likely to have much reassured Miss Horden and the President.

It could surprise no one that Miss Hildyard was appointed. Her late father, the Rev. Mr John Hildyard, was a friend of Baron Christian Friedrich Stockmar, the trusted adviser of Prince Albert and the Queen,[77] who had each responded to her modesty, gentleness, ideals and sense of humour. Her interest in botany appealed to the Prince. Tilla to the children, she continued as their governess till in 1864 her health began to fail. In 1865 the Ladies elected her to their Committee, where she served devotedly for fifteen years.

[74] A fifteenth-century half ruin which John Hall-Stevenson, 1718–85, inherited and his grandson and namesake restored. Hall-Stevenson was a life-long friend of Laurence Sterne, author of *Tristram Shandy*, and founder and host of a "club of demoniacks", reputedly obscene.

[75] Sarah, daughter of George, second Earl Spencer, wife of William Henry, third Baron Lyttelton of the second creation, Lady of the Bedchamber, 1838–42, and Governess to the Queen's children, 1842–50.

[76] Catherine, daughter of Count Woronzoff, Russian Ambassador in London, and wife of George, eleventh Earl.

[77] Earlier Physician and Secretary to Leopold, King of the Belgians, Queen Victoria's uncle, then Counsellor to Prince Albert in Coburg, it was he who on the Government's behalf arranged their marriage.

Not all Miss Horden's seniors took posts with families. At least nine of them ran or helped run schools: the sisters Cleeve, Charlotte and Janet, who established "a very respectable one" in Tooting, which Sarah and Elizabeth Ripley would acquire, Hannah Danford, the much travelled, Charlotte Richmond, Frances Fenwick, Philippa Lys (in Jersey) and Harriet Allen. It is likely that each had first faced a class while still at school, or between jobs, when staff were absent, ill. Katherine Browne, 23, taught English to her juniors. Her salary was low, only £45 a year, but her mother was allowed to spend Christmas at the school with her in 1862, "as an act of kindness" (a very exceptional concession), and eight years later the Gentlemen agreed to the Ladies' request that her salary rise from £45 a year to £60, inconsistent though it seemed with their own rules, it being still £20 less than she could have earned elsewhere.

Miss Laura Jewry, come home from her post in India in 1844, had set to work on the first of the seventy books that she would write or contribute to. *The Vassal: a Story of Old Normandy* appeared in 1850, an account where King Henry I, a rascal, and the evil de Beauchamp contend with saintly others, Norman-French; it was "humbly dedicated with the most profound loyalty and respect, by Her Majesty's devoted subject and servant", "to the Queen's Most Excellent Majesty (by Her Majesty's Gracious Permission)"; the proceeds from its sale were devoted to the school: £136–5s., less £44–8s.–10d. for the printer, together with the copyright; and Miss Jewry and Mr Newby, her publisher, who also took no payment, were awarded two votes each in the elections.

Another of her books came out that year, *The Forest and the Fortress*: a three-volume, Hungarian romance, about Vanda, the foundling; Kara George, the strong brave chieftain; the beautiful Shirine; and Milan, the stalwart peasant chief, with heart pure gold. A reviewer in *The Athenaeum*[78] suspected that Miss Jewry did not know Hungary, but her scenery was picturesque, and her sentiments were genuine. "Miss Jewry, moreover, delineates her male characters better than some among the female romancers who never seem to get nearer the real images of a hero than did Madame Tussaud. But the tale, as one of the last of an exhausted line, cannot hope for a long life or a large audience."

Miss Jewry's name[79] could no longer be included in the Annual Report. More names were removed as wards either married, fell sick, grew old, or died. Five wards out of eight removed in 1862 had settled overseas, two in Australia, two in Canada, and one in South Africa. The list still grew, so had often to be pruned, and in 1870 a new regulation appeared, excluding any ward out of touch with the Ladies' Committee for the last five years.

Remaining on the list meant subjection to control, but also protection,

[78] A literary and critical journal, 1828–1921.

[79] After April 1853 she wrote as Mrs Valentine: for thirteen months wife of Richard, Vicar of Holy Trinity, Portsea (which Portsmouth has absorbed), then for forty-six years his widow.

as Miss Emilie Kentish must have understood, better than most, who in 1844 returned from Mrs Vernon at Harrow on the Hill, with a good reference, only marred by adverse comments on her religious beliefs. Mr Tyler explored the beliefs and he approved. Her way thus cleared, she took another post, with the Rev. Mr Charles Holme Sumner, Rector of Ringwoud in Kent. The Committee struck off her name when she left the Sumners independently, but it must have been restored, for in 1849 they transferred her to the Wegnelins, of Goldings near Hertford, and two years later she wrote to them a letter of thanks, giving news of her betrothal to a local clergyman, who, it seems, had accepted her credentials.

Removal was by no means automatic if a ward deserted her employer. Ann Chambers was deemed fully justified when, for reasons undisclosed, she left Miss Plowden. And removal could always be annulled, as for Edith Adcock, who in 1860 abandoned Mr Gladstone's eldest brother, Sir Thomas,[80] of Fasque, Laurencekirk, North Berwick, but showed "deep penitence", reinforced by her mother's pleading, and was transferred—if not exiled—to Mr S. W. Ruyssenaers, Netherlands Consul-General in Alexandria.

A junior ward might spend up to seven years at the school, then keep in touch with it for up to twice as long and sometimes more. Staff often stayed only a term or two, or even less if they were French governesses. But many remained almost all their working life: Mr Jesse, first clerk then secretary, for thirty-four years; Ann Russell, a parlour-maid for twenty-six, who retired with failing health, when the Gentlemen agreed to the Ladies' request for an allowance to be given her of £5 a year, to be supplied by a deduction of the same amount from the pay of her successor, whom Matron was then "in treaty for"; and Mr Harley, the drawing-master, from about 1827 till early in the year of his death, 1871—aged 80 or almost, he would not leave before the Ladies supported by the Gentlemen had asked him to: "a most painful duty . . . Mr Harley is very poor, and has attended the Institution for about forty-four years." And Signor Rossetti had outstayed his prime, "too old" in 1843 "to give his lessons with his accustomed punctuality"—he was then 60—but another three years passed before he was replaced, "almost incapable of conducting the Italian instruction", going blind.

Signora, called also Mademoiselle, Berrurier to the Ladies, to the Gentlemen Barrurière, taught Italian next, with French, "a Protestant Lady" and highly recommended. Earl Manvers, Bishop Lonsdale and Col. Fanshawe expressed regret that she had "been suffered" by Miss Horden "to take up her abode in the house before her appointment had taken place", but they appeared to be consoled, not having to employ a master instead, "especially with regard to the present state of the finances". Mrs Byrn, Callisthenics and Dancing, replaced Capt. Michele, who had

[80] Conservative MP, 1830–37, for Queensborough first, then Portarlington, then Leicester. His famous brother had fagged for him at Eton.

been dropped having asked for better pay. Mr Edwin Abbott, Philological School Headmaster and once the wards' examiner, taught Latin; he received a salary of forty guineas a year, having at first made no charge; but need to economise interrupted his services and would later delay the arrival of Mr Moore, a member of his staff, who would probably have had to wait longer had Lady Elizabeth Cornwallis not paid his first term's fees.

The women, called teachers, got little shrift if their results disappointed. But results might not be everything, as an assistant governess discovered: "The Ladies find that the Irish accent possessed by Miss Hill does not diminish and therefore propose to dispense with her services at Lady Day next." Another Miss Hill was found to take her place, "a highly accomplished Lady, both as regards Music and French", spoken English satisfactory.

Mlle Bourdin arrived in 1845, recommended by Lady Jane Peel, sister-in-law of the statesman, Robert, and by Dr Michael Luscombe, from his Scottish Episcopal bishopric in Paris,[81] where she lived. The school paid half her fare, the rest to be withheld till after one whole year of service, a good idea. She was so highly qualified, and so effective was her work, that old Monsieur Grégoire could be retired. Unhappily, however, she resigned—her year complete but only just—complaining that her English-with-Arithmetic colleague, Miss Silke, had spoken about her to the wards (and about the rules) "in very disrespectful terms". Miss Horden "made public enquiry into the affair" and Miss Silke, who "could not disprove the assertion", left the house at once, pre-empting her dismissal.

It was difficult to replace Miss Silke, "so few Ladies being able to teach the higher branches of Arithmetic". The Miss Lauder (or Lander) who followed her was cheap but she had soon to be removed, "not equal to her duties".

Monsieur Enot taught French for seven years before retiring, ill. Mlle Stenson was appointed, then resigned, and Mlle Millot asked for her pay to be increased and instead was told to leave, all within a year. The Committees begged Monsieur Enot to return, so he did, and was employed for as long a time again. Disappointment followed, with Monsieur Puyo: "The French Master's want of personal cleanliness is so great that the Wards go to his classes with undisguised reluctance", the Ladies complained, so his year had to end with three months' notice. Monsieur Haslé, took his place, recommended by Matron Miss Davis's sister, and he stayed until 1869, the school having paid for his journey from Paris, at once and in full.

French assistant governesses, who almost all seemed "perfectly satisfactory" at interview, were employed mostly for a term or two, then left of their own free will or whim or had to go—twenty-one all told in Miss Horden's time.

[81] In 1834 he had a church built for him in the rue d'Aguesseau and as Chaplain at the British Embassy in 1836 wed Isabella Shawe to William Makepeace Thackeray.

. . . the Ladies' Committee being dissatisfied with Mme Coussediere's[82] *sudden desire to return to France, where she had already been spending some little time during the summer holidays, recommend that her services, valuable as they had proved whilst uninterrupted, should be dispensed with altogether.*

Mlle, if not Signora, Barrurière (or Berrurier) lasted three years, then left unhappy about some of the rules to which the wards were subject. Mlle de Joux was relieved of her post, "from indifferent health" and "unequal to the task of accompanying the Wards in their walking exercise", as were Mlle Duvernay, on trial, who "did not sufficiently advance her pupils", and four appointments later Mlle O'Reilly.[83]

Mrs Hunt, Matron when Miss Horden had arrived, resigned in 1843. Warm tribute had been paid to her in the Annual Report. It at once seemed premature. Various irregularities had already been disclosed. Mrs Hunt had allowed Maria Garrett to be visited by her brother on two Saturdays in a row, against the rules; invited gentlemen to the house for tea; "wholly supplied" Martha Mayor (dying) and her friends with food from the school's larder; deposited at Martha's house Jane Forbes and Sarah Ripley, whom she had taken to the oculist and who did not return till after 9.0 p.m., escorted by a servant; and had been too much absent from the premises. It also appears that she had argued with Miss Horden over rank and sphere, for the Ladies now made clear that, although Matron kept house, appointed servants, nursed the sick and had custody of letters addressed to the Committees, the Lady Governess stood overall in charge.

Miss Davis, an assistant governess for three years, worked as matron for the next fourteen. Her pious tact earned praise: "The Ladies desire to express their approbation of the mode adopted . . . in the disposal of several mutilated and very old Bibles and Prayer Books." Were they decently interred? She died in 1857, "in a state of great prostration", when the Gentlemen recorded with "unfeigned regret" their sense of "the unceasing assiduity and strict integrity" with which she had discharged her duties. Her funeral cost them rather more—£21–15s.–6d.—than a year's wages for the cook or for a chambermaid.

Mrs Neville followed. She also died in office, which "naturally affected the whole household". Miss Matilda Whitfield took her place, and stayed ten years, but like Mrs Hunt she left unhappy, pursued by enquiries about goods that she had bought for the school from the unauthorised sale of its dripping and about nineteen articles of missing plate, most of it belonging to wards either present or departed.

Miss Horden meanwhile had fallen much too ill to supervise her staff, let alone the plate and the dripping. Miss Katherine Browne, senior ward and teacher underpaid, now 31, took over, with Mlle Marmey (in whom

[82] Coussedière? Cassadiere in the Report. Cassadière?

[83] Recommended by Lady Lucy Seaford when Lord Seaford was employed as Minister Plenipotentiary in Brussels.

Miss Horden foresaw "a valuable acquisition"). Mrs Bond, next matron, had only a term in which to find her feet. A difficult six months began, ending when on the 30th of August 1870 Miss Horden died, after twenty-eight years as Lady Governess.

The tributes were renewed: to her humanity and judgement, as well as to her scholarship:

A still more valuable service of the late Governess consisted in that nice discrimination of character, which enabled her to manage with success the widely differing dispositions with which she had to deal, and to mould them . . . by that moral training which would best prepare them in their turn to form the minds of the young children whose education they would be called upon to direct.

Mrs Nisbet Lodge, widow of the Rector of Duncormick, County Wexford, wrote to say how happy her daughter, Katherine, had been with Miss Horden. They and others may have felt that a chapter had closed. If it had, it was slowly. Much continued undisturbed. Or so it could have seemed. The same long list of patrons headed the Reports. It began with the Queen and other Royal Highnesses, a President Archbishop followed, the Bishop of London as Visitor, then Duke, Marquess, Earl, Viscount (Palmerston), Lord Bishop, Lord, Admiral and General, Vice-Presidents, and from page to page it travelled, to a lonely Esquire, James Mure, the son of James, most useful of them all, once Auditor, now Chairman of the Managing Committee and from 1831 till his death in 1876 the longest serving of about a dozen Mures. (Princess Alexandra had also been approached but she did not feel that she could offer her name without a donation, which she could not yet afford, so many other claims being made upon her charity.) Their status reassured. But administrative gaps appeared and widened. The gentlemen who managed began to lose their grip. Half were inactive, little seen or heard. In August, when quarterly bills fell due to be scrutinised and paid, most of them took their holidays. The clergy, as a rule, set a good example. Lord Kenyon,[84] however, Lord Teignmouth,[85] and the two Bosanquets, Samuel and Charles, had been so much missed by 1842 that, politely being told so, they graciously resigned, all but Lord Kenyon, still Trustee, who did not resign or in any way respond. Only one member was present at a meeting called in 1848, Bishop Lonsdale—the Ladies' attendance was seldom if at all better—and in November 1859 not a Gentleman arrived, even of the church.

The Rev. Mr Thomas Bowdler had served as the last Honorary Secretary in 1843, then remained on the Committee, but resigned after six years, "on account of other important avocations". Earl Manvers, Chairman since 1823, died in 1860, "that estimable Nobleman", whose

[84] George, second Baron, a bencher of the Middle Temple.

[85] Charles, second Baron, MP for Marylebone, 1838–41, and President of Mr Abbott's School, the Philological.

good example of the Christian life had shone and was proclaimed. A new Committee member was elected at about that time, a Col. Lindsay, but without his knowledge, for he wrote and complained that he had never been approached. Admiral Bowles took over from the Earl. The year before, he had resigned as Treasurer, but not from the Committee, when appointed to the Chief Command at Portsmouth.[86] Now 79 years old, he was to die, still Chairman, in 1869, in his ninetieth year of life and in his thirty-ninth of service to the school, a friend to all the Ladies, whose "dear familiar face they would never again behold", and whose "boundless liberality, unwearied exertions and never failing kindness and courtesy upon all occasions" they would always remember.

The Gentlemen continued their work as hitherto, saying yes or no, but almost always yes, when the Ladies asked for chintz or dimity or calico or damask, Brussels carpet, Russian towelling, snuffers for candlesticks, hot-water tins for the warming of beds, chairs (durable, convenient and cheap), or new chair-bottoms, finger-plates for doors, the clock with alarum, butter-boats, fish-kettle, bottle-jack, a filtering-stone, the coffee percolator, a knife-cleaning machine, chains for scrapers in the forecourt and Fortnum and Company's brandy; they paid the bills for the West Middlesex Water Company's water and the Imperial Gas Company's gas, the gas being introduced in 1856 to feed the lamps, but not into the bedrooms, where the Ladies considered it "very objectionable", so that candles there remained and oil; had the zinc, blown-down chimney-pot replaced by one of galvanised iron; and provided the wards with baths in 1870 ("which Mr Propert considers it quite necessary that they should have").

Through their secretary, Mr Jesse, they continued to drive hard bargains. The butterman was replaced, now Teversham, then Cutbush, now Benning, and the baker, Mr Bruce—flour unsatisfactory—the green-grocer, "inattentive and high in his prices", the butcher, the laundry—they tried among others the London Female Penitentiary at Pentonville,[87] the Marchioness Cornwallis undertaking to meet what extra cost it might entail, and the Ranelagh in Camden, where linen was often ruined or lost—the coal merchant: Pope or Jones as before, also Richmond and Silkstone—Mr Richmond's coal was small and dusty—and the chimney-sweep, Ramoneur Patent, about whose men complaints were made, unspecified. They sampled the beer and did not enjoy it. The brewer who supplied the

[86] *The Times* obituary, 3.7.1869: "which he resigned . . . owing to something like a reprimand . . . from the Admiralty for his apparent want of judgement in allowing an unseemly *émeute* to break out in one of Her Majesty's Ships which had just returned from a foreign station."

[87] A charity "intended to save those whom vanity, idleness and the treachery of man have led astray . . . their earnings at needlework and washing go far to maintain the institution . . . blessed must be those who step forward to rescue poor women like these who are willing to repent, but who are by poverty drifted irresistibly down the black river to the inevitable grave." Walter Thornbury, *London Old and New*, 1879–85.

ingredients was warned that something "of a better description" was required; he did not respond; so no more orders were placed for malt and hops but for "the best beer" that the school could buy "at about the present cost". More than twice as much went on beer as on gas, and almost as much as on vegetables and fruit, but only half as much as on bread and flour and a quarter as much as was spent on meat.

The liberality of donors had to be acknowledged. Among much else it provided six pianos, Lady Julia Cornwallis giving one, two clergymen one each. The clergy were awarded honorary votes, and Messrs Broadwood earned six more, who had repaired a piano free of charge, which would have made fourteen, had their first allocation not been overlooked.

It appears from the accounts, in the four decades beginning in the thirties, that revenue held steady at about £2,600 a year. Fees paid for the wards by their mothers or their friends—"wards' contributions"—made up about a sixth of it. Though "an accidental feature of the system", they were considered advantageous, having "tended to excite the energies of the Pupils in order to profit by an education that was not altogether without cost to their families" and "given to parental influence a degree of power over the Institution itself", whereby the Institution had had to be, "in some degree, sensible to the approbation and alive to the criticism of the natural parents and guardians of its Wards".

Donations brought in rather less; the subscriptions at least a third—"regular income"; and the other third or so consisted of fees paid by the Commissioners of the Patriotic Fund, legacies, receipts from the sale of consols and Exchequer bills accumulated earlier and from concerts and bazaars.

A failure to increase revenue or reduce expenditure caused "serious alarm" and there was talk of accepting fewer wards, and even of closure, if the drain on invested capital remained unchecked. "Is an Institution, proved to be practically useful", the subscribers were asked in 1859, "to be allowed to languish, to wither and to die?"

"Unto every one that hath shall be given . . ." But the Managing Committee may have doubted it. Success, if it implied an aim fulfilled, could make subscriptions and donations appear unnecessary:

The original supporters of an institution die out—the gloss of novelty wears off—new institutions arise—public liberality is diverted into new channels—what is old is supposed to be well supported, or to be able to support itself. Because a building is well placed, and an institution well conducted, it is supposed to be well known and well endowed. It is taken for granted that what has existed so long is sure to continue.

A wrong impression had now to be corrected. Advertisements were placed in *The Times*, *Morning Herald*,[88] *The Morning Post*[89] and *The*

[88] 1780–1869.
[89] 1772–1937; then absorbed by *The Daily Telegraph*.

Standard.[90] A notice-board would have helped ("an efficient means of attracting pecuniary support") but "the Woods and Forests" allowed no kind of advertisement to be displayed in Regent's Park, however discreetly. In 1858 the Commissioners withdrew their grant of £50, halving the ground rent which they charged. Admiral Sir William Bowles, then Treasurer, conferred with Disraeli, Chancellor of the Exchequer under Derby, but the grant was not restored. The Church, the Army and the Navy were circularised, to publicise the school and win support. Approaches to the Worshipful Companies of Ironmongers, Mercers, Skinners and Fishmongers "were not attended with a beneficial result"—all said no; the Goldsmiths responded, the Drapers, Clothworkers, Grocers, Merchant Taylors (years later the Brewers, Cordwainers, Tallow Chandlers, but not the Salters or Leatherworkers; the Central London Dwellings Improvement Company;[91] the London Labourers' Dwellings Society;[92] and the Committee of the Society for the Discharge and Relief of Persons Imprisoned for Small Debts.[93] The Scots Fusilier Guards had raised £30, earning one vote "in perpetuity", to be cast on their behalf by their Lieutenant-Colonel in command, and the Rev. Dr George Boudier, a fellow of King's College, Cambridge, £27–11s. (one vote) and the Rev. Mr James Wallace £6–6s. (no vote), the amounts being moieties of offertory sacramental collections they had made in the Crimea, where they served as chaplains. Bishop Wilberforce, appealed to by the Duke of Cambridge, had "powerfully advocated the cause of the Institution" in a sermon preached in the Grosvenor Chapel,[94] raising £113–2s.–1d. Bishops Denison and Kerr-Hamilton of Salisbury, Dr Thomas Short, of St Asaph, and Dr Walter Trower, late of Glasgow, preached in other fashionable London churches, where within ten years £1,200 or so was collected. A Fancy Bazaar, organised by the Admiral and his Committee and "holden in June" 1857,

[90] 1827–1916; since then *The Evening Standard*.

[91] Formed in 1861 by gentlemen chiefly of Lincoln's Inn, "to try for themselves whether a company might not get a fair profit out of weekly property [yielding weekly rents], and yet deal considerately with the tenants . . . It has . . . been obliged to turn out most of the occupants, in order to clean and repair the houses; but it has received back many of them, and deals with the very lowest class of industrious poor—Covent Garden porters, labourers and others. The rents average 4s. for two rooms, and 2s.–9d. for one . . . The dividend paid . . . has varied between 3 and 4 per cent. The company provides accommodation for about 180 families, some taking single rooms . . . others two . . ." C. B. P. Bosanquet, one of two of its honorary secretaries, *London: Some Account of its Growth, Charitable Agencies and Wants*, 1868.

[92] Founded by Dr William Greenhill, physician and scholar, in the same year. It too bought old and insanitary dwellings, repaired and improved them, paying dividends as high as 5%.

[93] Established in 1772 by a group of London philanthropists. It had by now begun to divert its funds to other worthy causes. In 1965 it changed its name to the Debtors' Relief Funds Charity.

[94] South Audley Street, 1730.

at the Rooms in Hanover Square,[95] which the Queen attended with Prince Albert and "the rest of the Royal Family", raised another £1,000 and more, providing three pianos and some carpets. Mr Joshua Boord, responding to an appeal published in *The Times*, offered ten guineas a year for the next four years and to make it fifty a year if twenty-four subscribers agreed to do the same. But his lead failed. In the words of the Report of 1859: "This liberal offer has been repeatedly advertised, but at present only three other offers have been made to meet it."

What else could be done? Hardly anything. In 1863 the Committee brought forward the publication of its Report to early March, "when the wealthy and charitable inhabitants of the Metropolis had not yet left for their country residences or travels"; and where they could they economised; did not replace dilapidated text-books, which had served for twenty years; asked (but in vain) to be relieved of their subscription to the Park Gardens (as well they might, being a Charity—they already got water at a nominal rent of only two shillings a year); and encouraged Miss Whitfield to exercise economy, on whose "meritorious vigilance" they so much depended, there being no word yet about the dripping or the plate. A concert, arranged by the Countess Dowager of Lichfield, performed by the Society of the Wandering Minstrels,[96] attended by the Queen and the Prince and Princess of Wales, produced £270. The Bank of England advanced £500. Another appeal was launched, "special and urgent", in 1866. Dr William Carey, Bishop of St Asaph,[97] twenty-one years dead, indirectly bequeathed £844–0s.–3d. worth of consols—his niece was awarded seventeen votes—and the Rev. Mr George Bosanquet, son of Charles, handed over to the treasurer a yearly £130, the dividends on his shares in the Dwellings Society and the Improvement Company.

The Report of 1866 reads like a prospectus, wherein are extolled the benefits a ward enjoyed, transported from penury or the threat of it to a home where comforts were restored and fears dispelled:

Well boarded and lodged in an excellent house, she passes her time under maternal protection and care, and in the society of persons of her own age, receiving a religious and intellectual education attainable only by the children of the wealthier classes.

[95] Karl Friedrich Abel, Johann Christian Bach and a Swiss, Giovanni Gallini, had them built in 1775, on the east side of the Square, where they remained used as concert-rooms till 1874.

[96] An amateur orchestra, founded in 1860, presided over and conducted by the Hon. Seymour J. G. Egerton (future fourth Earl of Wilton), it met at the house of Lord Gerald Fitzgerald and supported charities.

[97] Scholar, Captain and, aged 33, Headmaster of Westminster; Bishop of Exeter and then of St Asaph (Llanelli), its cathedral the smallest in England and Wales but wealthier than Exeter.

A school like that deserved to survive. But still the invested capital declined. Heavy amounts of bills and bonds were being sold. Arrears of decoration accumulated. The outside walls of the house were grubby and would need to be stripped and coated with Portland cement, or they would not accept the paint which the Commissioners of Woods and Forests insisted on, their lessors. It all cost money. The plaster was dropping from the ceiling in the lower gallery and in the dining-room. The end kept seeming nigh.

Chapter Four

1870–1882

Lady Mary Ross retired in 1872, for forty years a member of the Ladies' Committee, its President in the last twenty-one. Her sister, Lady Elizabeth Cornwallis, took her place, but died two years later. To the school she bequeathed £2,000, £15 of which the Gentlemen set aside so that treats might continue which Lady Mary had provided for the wards: at Christmas "a Treat and Dinner" and after the examinations "Tea and Supper". The treats had had "an excellent effect . . . in increasing their energy in the studies, as well as creating a kindly feeling between the Wards and the Committees", and would help to keep alive the memory of the Marchioness Cornwallis; her daughters, Ladies Mary and Elizabeth; Alexander Ross, MP,[1] Treasurer, son of Charles, MP, and Lady Mary; Alexander's wife, Juliana;[2] his sisters, Louisa—Mrs Whatman— and Jemima, anon the Ladies' Vice-President; and Charlotte Richmond's orphan pupil, Lady Julia Holmesdale, Cornwallis born, who had provided "a valuable piano".

Elizabeth's bequest was the last of her many benefactions, which had included fees paid for the Latin master, to keep his subject taught; linen; and a nurse and other help for the late Miss Horden.

In 1874 a new President of the Ladies' Committee was installed: HRH Princess Helena, fifth child, third daughter, of Prince Albert and the Queen; 28 years old; and a patron of the school since 1868. She would leave no diaries or memoirs or private letters. We have no history of her adult life. A sparkling account of her childhood appeared in 1980: Chapter V of Mrs Daphne Bennett's *Queen Victoria's Children*, almost half of all that we know of her worth knowing. Some footnotes here and there about others royal or famed offer glimpses of a stable, quietly benign, intelligent woman, with a mind autocratically her own. Obituaries list her achievements. But the only life-like portrait to be found of her mature self is the one which her first daughter, Princess Marie Louise, draws in her memoirs:[3]

She was very lovely, with wavy brown hair, a beautiful little straight nose, and lovely amber-coloured eyes. I cannot describe them in any other way . . . they were amber—not brown, not blue, not grey, not green—just amber. She was very talented: played the piano exquisitely, had a distinct gift for drawing and painting in water-colours, and she had a very clear, though not very strong, soprano voice. Her outstanding gift was her

[1] Barrister; Conservative MP for Maidstone, 1880–88.

[2] Born Moseley, daughter of William, of Leaton Hall in Staffordshire. The house, taken over by the Air Ministry in 1943, was in 1981 bought by Unifurnaces Ltd.

[3] *My Memories of Six Reigns*, Evans Bros, 1956.

Princess Helena

Fifth child, third daughter, of Prince Albert and Queen Victoria

loyalty to her friends, whatever happened and whatever they might do. She was brilliantly clever, had a wonderful head for business, and, indeed, she was truly a daughter of Queen Victoria.

Among my mother's many great qualities was one I must not omit to mention, as I think it will help you to understand what a very remarkable character she possessed. If a situation or matter of urgency arose and was brought to her notice as needing her sound and accurate judgement or opinion as well as help, she set herself the task of dealing with it forthwith, and invariably overcame all the difficulties and obstacles that might ensue.

Here is an incident which illustrates what I am trying to convey. During the First World War, the wife of one of the gamekeepers in Windsor Park came to her in great distress. Her daughter had—as it was delicately expressed in those days—"got into trouble". The complication was as follows: the young couple were going to be married but, alas, the bridegroom in question had been whisked off to France with his unit before the marriage could take place. The interesting event was rather imminent and no time could be lost to make everything correct. The distracted mother appealed to my mother for help.

"Leave it to me and I will deal with it," was my mother's reply. Then, as my sister and I used to say, "When Mother puts on her bonnet and shawl, we know that something is up"—and something was *up. Mother motored up to London, went direct to the War Office and, with her most beguiling smile, asked to see Sir John Cowans, who was then Quartermaster-General and happened to be a great friend of ours. She then*

informed him that Private X, serving in such and such a battalion, must have forty-eight hours' compassionate leave, and be brought home at once in order to marry his young lady. In vain did Sir John explain that it was impossible to withdraw Private X from his unit, which happened to be holding a very important sector in the trenches opposite the enemy. "No matter", said my mother—and the argument continued. Then, believe it or not, Private X was *brought back home, was given his forty-eight hours' compassionate leave so that he could marry his young lady, and all was well.*

My mother was very direct in the way she expressed her opinions, and here is an instance of this characteristic. It was at the time of one of the big dock-strikes, and the Archbishop of Canterbury had composed a special prayer of intercession to be said in all the churches, that the strike might be settled. On the Sunday we went as usual to the little chapel in Windsor Park, and leaflets with this special prayer were lying in our pews. My mother took one up, scrutinised it very carefully through her glasses and then—in what we used to describe as the penetrating Royal Family whisper, which carried farther than any megaphone—remarked: "that prayer won't settle any strike", and put the leaflet down! I think the passage she objected to was a rather long-winded one mentioning that we were to pray for a fuller realisation of our brotherhood.

To her mother especially Princess Helena was loyal, for not till she had lost her, in 1901, did she at last leave Cumberland Lodge in Windsor Great Park and make a new home for her family in London. Her father she adored, who approved of her love of horses and the countryside and encouraged her interest in machinery. His early death, when she was only fifteen, left her deeply bruised and may have quickened her sympathy with those of about her age at the school in Regent's Park, which her great aunt, Augusta, had helped to found and which the Queen had patronised since 1838.

On the 5th of July 1866, in the private chapel at Windsor, Princess Helena married Prince Christian of Schleswig-Holstein, Sonderburg-Augustenburg. (So Princess Christian became her official name but Helena she remained, at home and for the school.) The Queen approved, whose plan thus took effect, but not the Prince of Wales, King Edward VII to be, or his wife, Alexandra, a Dane, who could only see in Prince Christian a man whose family had sided with Prussia, which had defeated Austria at Königgrätz only two days before the wedding, and had then absorbed both Holstein and Schleswig.

The Prince was an amiable, rather uncommunicative man,[4] with few

[4] But Marie Louise would not forget his "German lessons by means of German fairy-tales" and other "wonderful stories". "Papa, do tell us your ghost story." He was "extremely handsome"—"my old knight"—"with a pointed white beard, clear blue eyes, and a very aristocratic face". "It was he who taught us and gave me my love of literature." (ibid.)

friends and even fewer enemies. Unlike his wife he was not an outstanding public servant or even a busy one. His inactivity, though more or less enforced, and his twenty-four cigars a day, annoyed the Queen. They found him a post in Windsor Park, where as Range Warden he successfully abated a plague of frogs, having sought and taken a naturalist's advice and introduced more ducks. But he was not so much remembered for the plague that he abated as he was for his collection of glass eyes, replacements for the one that he had lost in a shooting accident,[5] including a watery and rather bloodshot specimen he wore to match the other, when he ran a heavy cold, and which he passed about among his guests at dinner, to revive conversation.

If the young Princess had had her way, or perhaps if her father had lived, she would have trained to be a nurse at one of the London hospitals. A certificate of proficiency in nursing was all that they allowed her to acquire instead. But she had married young, and soon there would be children, two boys,[6] two girls,[7] and whatever she might have accomplished as a nurse could hardly have compared with the service that she gave to nursing as its patron, or to the many charities that she launched, helped run, and to some of which she gave her married name.

As President of the Ladies' Committee Princess Helena was businesslike. She insisted on agendas, which her deputy was asked to prepare, took the chair and signed the minutes. What helped much more, she bestirred others into action (who may anyway have jumped to do her royal will). Facilities improved. Gaslight was installed in Matron's room and, in the library, a gas-lit chandelier. The library, the "Long Room" and Matron's received new carpets, tiles replaced floor-cloth in the corridor and front hall, the kitchen got coconut matting. New curtains were hung—red damask for Matron and Governess—and walls whitewashed and coloured. A clock on the landing and the candlesticks upstairs were replaced—the candlesticks as well as the clocks "worn out"—and so was the tradesman, whose clocks did not keep proper time. Running water was supplied to the first floor; and bottled, to drink, put in each bedroom. Nine hip-baths had appeared. Water-cans were painted and they and the doors all numbered, the numbers on the doors matching those on the cans and pails. In no other period after 1824 had the school acquired so much new equipment and furniture as in Princess Helena's first few years.

Lord Braybrooke[8] gave tickets for the nearby zoo, which improved Christmas for wards who could not travel home to their mothers or friends.

[5] Princess Helena's brother, Prince Arthur, was to blame, Duke of Connaught and Strathearn, an army officer, who fifteen years before, in 1876, had been put in charge of the 1st Battalion, the Rifle Brigade.

[6] Christian Victor and Albert—a third followed, who died aged 8, and a fourth, still-born.

[7] Helena Victoria and Marie Louise.

[8] Charles Cornwallis Neville, fifth Baron, who in 1849 married Florence Cornwallis Maude.

Miss Georgina Bramston made everyone a sponge-bag. A Miss Hamilton sent a hamper full of apples. *The Times* opened windows to the world outside for them in 1870, as did later *The Illustrated London News*. Visits were paid to the Grosvenor Art Gallery and the United Services Museum. Dr John Festing,[9] now Clerical Superintendent, showed them Westminster Abbey. They listened to a Miss Scott, who lectured on English Literature—"A few Copies of Chaucer's 'Prologue' are requested in order that the Wards may more readily understand"—and served as their guide to the Lambeth Palace library and other "objects of interest". Admiral Sir Erasmus[10] and Lady Mary Ommanney got them seats for a lecture at the Society of Arts.[11] The Dowager Countess of Lichfield treated them to an evening with Mr Samuel Brandram,[12] who recited from *The Tempest*—he also performed to them from *Hamlet*, somewhere, and from *The Merchant of Venice*, at the home of the Marquess of Salisbury,[13] raising funds for the school. They attended concerts at the Exeter Hall[14] and the St George's,[15] an Anton Rubinstein[16] at most likely the St James's,[17] with tickets from the Rosses Alexander and Jemima—the French governess was allowed to take two of them there for the "Saturday popular concerts" ("Saturday Pops"), orchestra seats recommended, a shilling each, Amusement Fund permitting—a recital at the Royal Academy[18] and a performance of "the Passion Music" at St Anne's in Soho Square.[19] After 1872 they regularly celebrated the Prince of Wales's birthday with a holiday for all, a feast, and with sometimes a visit to the Kensington Museum, and by 1878 they enjoyed a free half day for Princess Helena's. The two-week Easter holiday

[9] Vicar of Christ Church after Mr Burrows. Appointed Bishop of St Albans in 1890, he could not occupy his palace at Dansbury, near Chelmsford, his predecessor there refusing to vacate it, so chose to live in Endsleigh Street instead, conveniently near to the main-line stations and the school in Regent's Park.

[10] Retired from an exciting career, world-wide, and notably active in the Crimean War, blockading first Archangel, then Riga.

[11] Founded in 1754 as "The Society for the Encouragement of Arts, Manufactures and Commerce", it did not become "The Royal" till 1908.

[12] He had practised as a barrister for twenty-six years but could now earn more reciting Shakespeare, often whole plays.

[13] From 1782 to 1919 at Arlington House, Arlington Street, Piccadilly. In 1936 a dreary block of flats replaced it, the work of Mr M. Rosenauer.

[14] Oratorios were performed there from 1831 till the YMCA acquired it in 1880, a body which frowned upon "oratorios for amusement" and on those who were said to live a life not always as holy as the words they sang from holy writ. It was pulled down in 1907. The Strand Palace Hotel now occupies the site.

[15] In Langham Place from 1867 till fire-bombs destroyed it in 1941.

[16] A Russian-Jewish pianist; his technique was acclaimed, his taste not always.

[17] St James's in Regent Street, 1858–1905—2,127 seats—London's most echo-proof and best-known concert-hall.

[18] In Tenterden Street, off Hanover Square, where it had opened in 1823.

[19] A Wren church of 1685. Bombing destroyed the body of it in 1940, leaving only the tower of 1803.

could now be spent with friends. But Holy Week itself meant church instead of morning lessons.

Her Royal Highness had been President of the Ladies' Committee for about four years. Its other members, the Duchess—now Dowager Duchess—of Northumberland, the Marchioness of Thomond, the Countesses of Dalkeith,[20] Manvers,[21] Amherst,[22] the Countess Dowager of Lichfield, the Ladies Alexander Russell,[23] Annora Williams-Wynn,[24] Louisa Rolle,[25] and Katherine Hulse,[26] the Hon. Mrs Loyd-Lindsay, Miss Bramston, the sponge-bag maker, Mrs Georgina Broke,[27] Mrs Harriet FitzHugh,[28] Miss Sarah Hildyard, a Mrs Emmeline Porcher, who would help to pay the French master his salary, Miss Ross and Mrs Scrivener,[29] had mostly served much longer. No doubt they were eager to please. But sometimes, at least, they must have felt that they knew better than the young princess.

In April 1875, when a grand piano had to be replaced, and Helena, President, offered to enquire whether Stuttgart could meet their requirements, they did not, it seems, respond. Three months elapsed. The absent Princess had got no answer from anyone in or on behalf of Stuttgart, a piano had had to be hired for a concert to be given by the wards, and the Ladies "being advised"—or Mrs FitzHugh and Mrs Porcher reporting—"that the German pianos do not last", the Gentlemen agreed that Mr

[20] Louisa, daughter of James Hamilton, first Duke of Abercorn, and wife of William, the future sixth Duke of Buccleugh.

[21] Georgiana, daughter of Augustin, Duke of Coigny, and wife of Sidney, Conservative MP for South Notts, 1852–60, third Earl, who from profits drawn from the coal beneath his land built Thoresby Hall, the great Victorian treasure-house in Sherwood Forest. The National Coal Board bought the house in 1980, with its 12,000 acres of land, and in 1989 sold it to Roo Management, of Australia, for conversion into a luxury hotel, Sotheby's having auctioned and dispersed its contents.

[22] Dr Hugh Percy, Bishop of Carlisle's daughter, Mary, second wife of William, second Earl, and mother-in-law of Julia, Viscountess Holmesdale, the one surviving child of the fifth and last Cornwallis Earl, Charlotte Richmond's pupil.

[23] Born Worsley, Anne Emily, daughter of Sir Leonard Worsley Holmes, ninth baronet and last, and wife of General Alexander George Russell, sixth Duke of Bedford's seventh son.

[24] Daughter of Charles, second Earl Manvers, and wife of Charles Watkin Williams-Wynn, Conservative MP for Montgomery.

[25] Younger daughter of Robert Trefusis, sixteenth Lord Clinton, and widow of John, the first Lord Rolle.

[26] Daughter of the Rev. Mr Henry Hamilton, the wealthy, generous, mathematically gifted Dean of Salisbury, and widow of Sir Edward, a Fellow of All Souls, Oxford, of Breamore, near Salisbury, and 47 Portland Place.

[27] Widow, now, of Managing Gentleman Horatio called Horace, Major-General.

[28] Daughter of the younger James Mure by his first wife, also a Harriet, who had died aged 26.

[29] Most likely Anne, born Blofeld, wife of Dr Frederick Scrivener, then Vicar of Hendon, an eminent biblical scholar.

Charles Hallé[30] be asked to choose one of Messrs Broadwood and Co.'s, their old supplier and benefactor's, No. 9 on the list, price £115–10s. or (cash) £81–14s.

HRH had missed three meetings, and would miss another four, and not until February 1876 did she and her Ladies reunite. But then more than ever she as President took charge. A member of the Committee now visited the school each month, whosever turn it was, instructed to inform the President immediately if she could not appear. Then month by month Visitor, Vice-President and Lady Governess laid before her their report.

The Ladies were at last allowed to see and comment on the household accounts. But the Gentlemen still managed. The Ladies asked for and got their electro-plated tea-spoons, kamptulicon,[31] a basket with padlocks for the conveyance of linen, chest-expanders, poles for the dancers, medicinal wine, medicinal sherry, medicinal port, medicinal brandy and non-medicinal beer. But none could authorise expenditure or veto it.

A lot of argument arose about how much beer the staff were entitled to. The Ladies thought it "objectionable" that the gardener got any and the Gentlemen agreed. And was the cook entitled to her daily gallon? The gardener, the cook and the house and kitchen-maids all lost theirs, the women however getting "beer-money" instead, 2s. a week, and the maids 1s.–6d. A year later their beer was restored but not the gardener's. The Governess, meanwhile, had kept her porter, Matron her Guinness's bottled stout and the invalids their wine.

Marshal and Snelgrove delivered the carpets and all kinds of things appeared from the Civil Service Supply Association and the Oxford Street Co-operative. A poro-plastic jacket was ordered for Major John McQueen's Lucy, and another dessert-spoon, which, General Spencer Stanhope, Mr Roger Kynaston, father of Herbert of St Paul's, and Rear-Admiral Sir Edward Sotheby[32] decided, should replace the one which Fanny Millery had lost. Suppliers were changed as hitherto, about one each term, a chimney-sweep or a laundry—the Discharged Prisoners' Aid Society's Westminster Memorial Refuge's[33] for that of the Refuge for the Destitute[34]—the butterman—Mr Scott of Burbage in Wiltshire for Perelli Rocco, Greek Street, Soho Square—or the butcher—selling meat in 1871 "pronounced by a competent judge to be quite unwholesome"—the

30 Pianist, conductor, and founder in 1857 of the orchestra bearing his name.

31 A floor-covering. Invented by Elijah Galloway and used in Barry's Houses of Parliament, it foreran linoleum.

32 Chairman, for many years, of the Institute for the Blind in Tottenham Court Road.

33 Women convicts whose character appeared to have enough improved were employed at a refuge (home) within nine months of their conditional release. The Westminster, at Streatham, was for Protestants, while Catholics had theirs at Finchley.

34 A workhouse.

Committee dropped the butcher (cheapest tenderer) almost as often as the French assistant governess dropped French.

Both staff and food cost more in the seventies, especially from 1875 to 1877, when heavy bills had also to be met for improvements and repairs. The cook and the parlour-maid each earned £18 a year in 1873, the upper housemaid £16 and the kitchen and under housemaid each £10. Within the next five years the under housemaid's wage had increased to £13 and the cook's to £20.

This in itself was not too worrying. In the early years, however, of the 1870s, and again in the late, income fell short of expenditure; subscriptions ("regular") fell in all but two; and legacies and donations ("adventitious") continued to vary unreliably. Exchequer bills and railway stock took the strain but as the decade closed they were heavily depleted.

Economies had to be made. A servant would now clean the wards' boots only three times a week; Mrs Rowland White, Matron, was not to be allowed to bring her two little boys into the house once a week for supper—the Ladies had suggested once a fortnight, but the Gentlemen still said no; if a ward died, her mother or friends would have to pay for her funeral; iron bedsteads were ordered without white curtains or brass knobs, old wooden ones were used as fuel—the firewood sold by the Association for the Blind could no longer be afforded; and a very cheap and varnishable paper had to serve in the bedrooms. A parlour-maid, however, Miss Rose Todd, was allowed to marry from the Institution and there enjoy a wedding breakfast.

Dr John Mackarness, Bishop of Oxford,[35] Mr Thomas Legh Claughton, Bishop of Rochester,[36] and others, preached more sermons, in London and in Hove. A spelling bee was held, now a fashionable pastime, when the Gentlemen agreed to provide an audience and to help "as interrogators or referees". Princess Helena arranged for a concert to be given at the Earl of Dudley's home in Park Lane,[37] raising £400. And classes, advertised in *The Times*, *The Standard* and *The Telegraph*, were given at the school, which ladies in the neighbourhood attended for a fee, in English Literature and History, with Prof. Henry Morley,[38] and in French and Drawing.[39]

It helped but not enough. The Gentlemen's Report, 1877, contained dire warning and, to those whom the Lord had favoured, this appeal:

[35] 1870–88.

[36] 1867–77, then Bishop of St Albans till 1890, high church but not extreme. It was he who, refusing to vacate Dansbury Palace, had excluded Dr Festing.

[37] Dudley House, where the Lane meets Upper Brook Street. In 1940 it was bombed and wrecked.

[38] Professor of English Language and Literature at King's, University and Queen's Colleges, London, he lectured far and wide and his kindly enthusiasm drew big crowds.

[39] Perhaps inspired by but not otherwise connected with the University Teaching Extension schemes.

It would not be easy to find those who have a greater claim on the sympathy of the public than the Wards of this Institution. They are the orphan daughters of clergymen who have served their generation, and of military and naval officers, men who at the call of duty were ever ready to expose their lives either in action or to the not less deadly effects of climate. In most cases it was not possible for the father to make any provision for his family, and thus, many a young lady who at the outset of life had sustained the double blow of bereavement and adversity, would have had little or no education, and would thus have been unable to fight the battle of life, had not this Institution, in carrying out its noble mission, rendered her the most valuable of all assistance, viz. the power to help herself. Nor is it a small boon to those parents who wish to educate their children at home, to know where to turn for governesses, gently born, and religiously and highly educated, who can teach, train and become the friends and companions of their pupils.

. . . . .

The Committee cannot close their report without commending the Adult Orphan Institution to the protection of Almighty God, with an earnest prayer that He may be pleased to pour out a blessing upon the work of mercy in which they are engaged.

Another 450 appeals were printed and distributed, which yielded some result, including a subscription (£5 a year) from a senior ward, Lilla West Blyth, now 24, who thus became a voter. But the gloom only thickened. The Gentlemen thanked God for the mercies which another year had brought, humbly praying that His mercies would continue. But they still felt bound to impress upon their public "the lamentable inadequacy of the regular income" and the extent to which the Institution depended upon "the chance of donations or legacies, and other precarious sources of supply".

The dearth of eligible candidates persisted. It seemed to reflect more absence of publicity than absence of distress. Advertisements were renewed in *The Times* and *The Morning Post* and appeared in gazettes or magazines, clerical, naval, military and charitable. The daughters were considered, not only of "Clergymen of the Established Church of England", but also of "the Episcopal Churches of Scotland and Ireland", and of Civil Servants too, if "of the First Class or of equal or superior rank". A naval architect did not, however, count. Nor did a master in the Bengal Pilot Service. Miss Gregory had to be disqualified, whose mother was insane, and so did Miss Finley, a pupil at St Mary's Hall in Brighton, who had only "some little knowledge of Music and Singing" and was already 18½ years old; though other candidates were now accepted over age, two, 18 and 17, from the Royal School for Daughters of Officers of the Army at Bath, and Beatrice Swinburne, whose father had been Curate of St Giles in the Fields. From 1879 the ballot papers included the advice of the Committees, with against each candidate's name either "very strong claims" or "strong

claims" or merely "claims", the claims however resting more on need—"painful circumstances"—than on merit.

Ill health was reported much as hitherto. Mary Lacey, daughter of George, late Rev. Headmaster of Colfe's Grammar School in Lewisham,[40] had "congestion of the liver"; and "rheumatism in the eyes" afflicted Mary Warren, who was "ordered not to use them". The Medical Officers continued to esteem the restorative effect of port and sherry, which may not have helped to decongest the liver. Dr Lumsden Propert recommended baths but hip-baths were all that the school could yet afford. A sick-room was provided, "so that no Young Lady . . . obliged to keep her bed for even one day should have any others sleeping in the room". No doubt this improved on sheets hung from the ceiling, steeped in disinfectant. The kitchen was thoroughly cleaned but many of the rooms were still too cold and damp for either comfort or health.

In April 1876 Henrietta Ringwood, one of four Ringwood wards, was sent to convalesce at a nursing-home in Eastbourne; Princess Helena paid for the first week's board and treatment, Mrs Porcher and Mrs FitzHugh for the next fortnight's. Accommodation was select: "At Eastbourne", the Ladies' meeting minutes read, "there are private rooms so that on payment of a weekly sum patients of a superior class are able to benefit by the Hospital without mixing with the other patients." Henrietta recovered and survived, four years later took her first post with the Hankeys of Southsea, met a Surgeon-Major O'Dwyer, asked to be allowed to teach in Watford for her mother, and perhaps did, but within seven months had become the surgeon-major's wife; their daughter, Joyce, would be enrolled a pupil in 1902. Her sisters were Caroline: having lost a post through lack of music, with a Col. Edward Grain, she took her next with Florence, Countess of Erne,[41] at her lakeside home, Crom Castle, in Fermanagh—a boat brought her to the same church on Sundays where her father had been Curate; Ellen, who was excused music, having made no effort; and Emily, HS83:[42] a governess with Mrs Lushington, sister of Sir Stafford Northcote, Earl of Iddesleigh, in England and Madeira; then secretary: choosing not to be employed at her old school, she worked for Mrs Ryle, the Bishop of Winchester's wife, who found her indispensable; had to leave and nurse her mother, as daughters were expected to; and would be last reported, fifty-five years old, with a friend in Hampshire, where without the help of men she ran a farm.

Another twelve juniors were invalided out in these twelve years—the last—of the school in Regent's Park: Amy Flora Armstrong, daughter of a

[40] Founded in 1652. Voluntarily aided from 1952 till in 1977, as Colfe's School, it reclaimed its independence.

[41] The fourth Earl's wife: a daughter of William, third Earl of Enniskillen, by his first wife, Jane.

[42] Here and to follow: HS for Head of School (Head Girl) with the last two digits of her final year.

captain in the East Indian Army, removed in her first term, "too delicate"; Maj.-Gen. Robert Shortrede's Mary, restored to her mother, at 10 Pagoda Villas, Lee, not only too near-sighted but also too high church; Mary du Val, daughter of a missionary at Channel Port-aux-Basques, Newfoundland, who died, 19, consumptive; Army Capt. Hamilton's Elinor, health "extremely delicate", though she did teach, for a mother and friend in Whitby (light work, low pay); Lt.-Col. Hamilton's "very delicate" Augusta; the Rector of Wymington, Bedfordshire, the Rev. Mr Abel Lendon's Annie—inflamed eyes; Army Capt. Rainier's Florence, who could not dance, "on account of a weak action of the heart"—Laura, her sister, had also to leave: "It is doubtful if she would ever have been fit to take a first-class Situation . . . her height being against her" (whether lack or excess of it is not made clear)—she was allowed to take a job instead as a Post Office clerk; Ethel Reed, who died aged 20, daughter of the Vicar of Twynnells cum Warren, Pembrokeshire; another Laura, the Rev. Mr William Sprigge's, from Brockley in Suffolk, she complaining of neuralgia, rheumatism, a frightful ear-ache and two abscesses; Constance Murray, daughter of a captain in the 2nd West India Regiment, whom the Ladies had kindly sent to Worthing to enjoy a change of air, but who had later to return home with her mother, Mrs Roche, to 4 Hastings Terrace, St Helen's, Jersey; Maj.-Gen. Henry Turner's Emmeline, a victim of "brain-fag", thought likely to recur; and Major William Castle's Florence de Meuron, who had started late, from the Royal School at Bath: "she would never be fit to study"—with a weak heart—"and she cannot take the exercise required of a Governess." Annie Crawford too looked likely to have to depart, owing to a speech defect, but HRH sent her to a Mr Thomas Smith of Stratford Place, who was "very clever in such cases", her friends agreeing to pay.

More seniors fell ill and gave up posts: Elizabeth Hamilton, sister of Elinor, whose mother and ten children had been left "totally unprovided for"—22 when she died; Margaret Halton; Isabel Wilcox; and two who left the country seeking better health: Anna Smith for the Cape of Good Hope and Isabella Keighly for her brother in India, where her father had served in the Bengal Native Infantry.

Inability to learn, more than illness, now cost wards their careers. Fourteen were removed, "incompetent to remain": one "on Account of her Deficiency in Power of Attaining Knowledge", two "very backward and unlikely to improve sufficiently to fit themselves for governesses", and one said not to have so much as what it took to be a nanny. The weakest often did their best. Arithmetic, however, took a heavy toll.

Fanny Millery had to leave, she "having imbibed Roman Catholic views" and intending to defect, whom the high command had allowed another spoon. Mary Barker could be difficult—"continued disregard of all rules, particularly in her Bedroom"—but it was fifteen months before the school dismissed her. Constance Daniell followed, who did not, it seemed, understand what the purpose was of the education that the school offered,

her mother having said that she did not in the least intend to allow her to be a governess and "her example and influence in the house" being "likely to be productive of much harm to the junior wards". Julia, daughter of the Rev. Mr George Percival, of the Society for the Propagation of the Gospel, Tamatave, Madagascar, ran away to her grandfather's house at Audlem in Cheshire, for reasons no one at the school could understand or guess, and Annie Cunnick defied the two Committees and went and helped her mother run a school at Roath, a village then, near Cardiff, now a suburb.

The Ladies had begun to allow the wards more freedom, voting 7–3 with Princess Helena to ease the rule about letters, exempting from inspection those to or from a mother or a guardian, if they did not feel that they had cause to intervene. Eva Moynihan, HS82—sister of the future surgeon baron[43]—enjoyed an extra visit from her uncle, due to sail for Africa, and Hannah Symmons, daughter of the Rev. Principal of the Hebrew Missionary College, Cambridge Heath, two days away from school to be a bridesmaid;[44] her friends, however, "going only as spectators", had had to be excluded. Army medical purveyor Lonsdale's Mabel was refused a visit from her brother. Brothers continued to be mistrusted: unaccompanied by mother they were not allowed to step inside the door. The school knew best. And it also disappointed Capt. Rainier's Edith, whose mother had asked that she be given two days' leave to attend "some sports". "Resolved", the minutes enigmatically read, "that such absence be not allowed except in very urgent cases."

The wards did not wear uniform, but standards were prescribed, attention being drawn to inappropriate coiffure, and in 1872 a circular was published, which the wards had all to take home with them, intended to discourage vulgarity and promote good taste:

undesirable deviations from the original simplicity of attire having gradually been made, the Ladies would beg Mothers and Friends to remember that the plainest and most inexpensive style is most becoming to young ladies in their position. It should be neat, plain without flounces, frills or trimmings. Plain linen collars may be worn instead of the muslin kerchiefs now in use. No ornaments are allowed but plain gold rings may be worn in the ears. The bonnet should be neither feathers, flowers or streamers, in short it should be as quiet as possible.

Attendance began to grow more lax. Fines were imposed on the friends or mothers of wards who, returning late, did not bring back with them a medical certificate. Mrs Castle was rebuked, when her Florence de Meuron

[43] Berkeley, George Andrew, Lord Moynihan of Leeds. As retired President of the Royal College of Surgeons, in 1934 and in his last two years of life, he would join the Board of Governors.

[44] Nine months later, aged 16, she would leave school, abandoning her career, and go and nurse her mother.

overstayed her leave, and so, for the same reason, was Edith Kelly's grandfather. But behaviour on the whole appears to have improved. In 1873 it either was or seemed to be particularly good, the wards being "uniformly attentive and well-behaved" in February; in March "industrious" and "amiable and lady-like"; in April "all that can be desired"; in June "very desirous of learning and very attentive"; and in February 1878 the classes were "in excellent working order", despite still poor arithmetic.

Not always were they taught as the best of them deserved. John Parker[45] failed to please, the Gentlemen agreeing with the Ladies that he go. He changed their minds—"The Ladies are happy to say that the dissatisfaction caused by Mr Parker's teaching arose from his having been led into a very mistaken notion that the great object was to get up drawings for show"—but was removed, unsatisfactory, some two years later. Henry Moseley,[46] his successor, taught less: "so continually unpunctual that a third of his time is wasted". He too would have to leave. And so would Mr Hopkins, whose method and choice of music the Ladies felt to be "decidedly too old-fashioned". Might it help to soothe his feelings if the Gentlemen offered him some honorary votes? They did not appear to think so, for he left given none, vacating posts which Dr Günther, Miss Burgess and Miss Katie Rivaz, all three, were now appointed to.

Mr Moore, Arithmetic and Latin, earned respect, but had to stop coming, once installed as Head at his school, the Philological. A colleague, Mr Dolleymore, replaced him. The Rev. Mr Edwin Boger, Headmaster of Queen Elizabeth's School, Southwark, the examiner, taught history unpaid. Wards in the top form, called mothers, took junior classes, even German and Latin. Prof. Joseph Payne, England's first Professor of Education,[47] showed them how—"Lessoning not Lecturing" his motto—till he died, 68, followed by Mr John Meikeljohn,[48] who stayed till in 1876 St Andrew's University offered him its first chair in the same subject, and then by the Rev. Mr James Hannum, Curate of the new church of St Stephen's in South Kensington.[49]

When gentlemen taught, in or out of holy orders, the attendance of one of the ladies of the house was deemed to be "imperative".

More women were employed, replacing men, whom the school could less and less afford. December 1870: "it would be very desirable that a Young Lady should be substituted for the present Italian Master"—Signor

[45] Successful in London in and after 1867. His water-colours were often displayed at the Royal Academy and in other galleries.

[46] A portraitist. The Academy hung twenty-four of his works.

[47] Elected as such by the College of Preceptors in 1872.

[48] A prolific writer. Translator of Kant's *Kritik der reinen Vernunft*. War correspondent in the Danish–German war of 1864; mistaken for a spy there and arrested.

[49] Built in 1867, where a tablet now records that for twenty-five years T. S. Eliot, poet and dramatist, served in it as warden.

Magrini—"as at present the Wards do not converse in Italian, and a saving might also be thereby effected." The women tended not to stay. A teacher of English lasted only two months—"Miss Deane's style . . . is different to any that has hitherto been followed in the Institution." Madame Bizet-Michau, however, remained twelve years. Dancing, with or without light poles, and Callisthenics were her subjects. It was thanks to her that chest expanders were introduced into each bedroom, 6s.–6d. a set, "covered" (so as not to pinch?) and of the best quality; they later found their way onto the clothing-list.

Italian stopped, Mrs or Madame (but not Signora) Lega Fletcher, though cheap, being given two months' notice, so that French might benefit. Signor F. de Asarta restored and taught it a few years more; it then expired. But German developed, which Princess Helena no doubt found sensible. "A Hanoverian Lady", Fräulein Hagmann (or Haymann) was appointed, the first of a long line of resident German governesses, 1878–1914.

Six copies had been ordered of some "Polyglot Bibles", perhaps to advance the French, German, Italian and Divinity all at once. Dr Festing used a book called *Steps to the Altar*, including, it seems, an indelicate appendix, which he agreed to ignore. English was taught from "Mason's Public School Grammar".[50] The school already thought or would soon like to think itself "public school". Subscriptions to Rolandi's and Mudie's lending libraries—and later, instead, to the London—eked out the supply of texts. Geography ran short of maps. The library had quickly to be improved, which Miss Penfold, Governess Superintendent, found "defective". It contained no history reference book or encyclopaedia. Theological works appear to have predominated, which tended to survive, unblemished and intact, their pages hardly if at all disturbed. A geographical dictionary bore the date 1812. More books were needed and many and more useful were acquired, mainly history, geography and French, and old ones bound. Queen Victoria gave a copy of her *Leaves from my Journal*; Princess Helena, books of family prayer; and Miss Hildyard, E. H. Hudson's *The Life and Times of Louisa, Queen of Prussia*. They would in time disappear—*sic transit*, whether furniture or books, *gloria*—all but the Hudson Vol. II.

The 1st Class *viva voce* petered out but "an Examination of the Wards" took place in 1874. A few days later Princess Helena gave away the prizes and "a distinguished assembly of the Nobility and Gentry"—"supporters of the Institution"—then at last returned. The Committees deemed the prizes "a most useful encouragement". Recitals vocal and instrumental were performed. HRH was "pleased to express her approbation of the proficiency exhibited"—a good sign, for Music had languished, about a year had passed since most of the pianos were "in too bad a condition for

[50] There appears to be no such title. Most likely C. P. Mason's *English Grammar, including the Principles of Grammatical Analysis*, 1858.

profitable practice", so could only be scrapped, and less than a year since the masters had complained about a lack of standard works which their pupils might consult.

Prize-Giving again lapsed in 1875. Word had been awaited from Princess Helena about the choice of day. It was already June. Term ended, nothing heard. The Stuttgart piano may have been to blame. Next year the event was restored, when Princess Mary, Duchess of Teck, deputised for the "unavoidably prevented" Royal President, giving out the first, also last, Princess Helena Essay Prize; then lapsed once more, due to illness in the house.

The publicly examined wards took posts. Some were unlucky. A Mrs Hancock rejected Gertrude Brown;[51] a Mrs Herbert, Lucy Porter—they had found them each too young, aged 21, too inexperienced; and a Mrs Church, Maj.-Gen. Nedham's Edith, deficient in Music and Latin, who would later, however, teach women how to teach, at Bishop Otter's College, Chichester.[52]

Ruth Hathorn, daughter of James, a major in the Bengal Royal Artillery, and sister of Grace, was allowed to interrupt her career and spend six months "abroad". Lilla West Blyth, the rejected Lucy and Gertrude, and Marian Firman, studied German in Germany, Lilla and Gertrude in Hanover and Marian with a Frau Matthieu, in Cassel.[53] The same Lucy, Caroline Fox and Louisa Howard studied French in France, Caroline *au pair* with a Mme Robin, a clergyman's wife, in Paris,[54] later settling in New Zealand, and Louisa teaching English in return for lessons in German and drawing, as well as in French—the Committees warmly approved of her "plan for self-improvement"—then travelling on to a Mr T. T. Smither, Avenida da Boavista, Fonte da Moura, in Porto.

Employed wards had now to pay 10s.–6d. a year for their names to be kept on the books. Their numbers fell, perhaps as a result, from fifty-four to forty-six, but recovered and increased until by 1878 they stood at sixty-one, among them Frances Nott—reprieved clandestine correspondent—Charlotte Richmond and Marianne Nunn, each in her early fifties, Caroline Crosthwaite, daughter of the Rector of Drimoleague in County Cork, and governess now to her brother's children in India (£120 a year), Charlotte Cranney, a schoolteacher in Cape Town, her place of birth, and Katherine Major, whom Lady Louisa Egerton had appointed, at Holker Hall, Cark-in-Cartmel, in Lancashire, the favourite, sumptuous, delightfully

[51] Daughter of the Rev. Mr James Layton Brown, Vicar of Holbeck in Yorkshire, who had died in 1855, leaving a widow with thirteen children to support, "five . . . entirely and some of the others partly", on an income of £70 a year from charities.

[52] A teacher-training college for men in and after 1832, for women after 1872 and for both since 1960.

[53] Königstrasse 31, a 1720 house attached to the Royal Theatre, on a site now occupied by a store.

[54] No. 24 rue Clavel.

gardened home of her father, William Cavendish, seventh Duke of Devonshire.[55]

The Hon. Mrs Katherine Cholmondeley,[56] of Abbots Moss Hall in Cheshire, employed Ethel Chambers,[57] and was much impressed, as a letter explains, which she addressed to the Ladies:

I gladly take this opportunity of expressing to you how extremely satisfied we are with Miss Chambers and how completely she comes up to the high character you gave of her. She has entirely gained the confidence of her pupils and I feel that I can leave home quite comfortably knowing how happy they are with her and how well and steadily the lessons will go on.

The same year Ethel's elder sister, Evelyn, already employed by the Emsworth Pakenhams, had passed the Cambridge Higher Local Examination for Women and obtained a scholarship for a year's course at Cambridge University. In 1880, aged 30, she became Headmistress of the High School in York. And a year later Miss Alice Zimmern, 26, although not a pupil but a very part-time teacher of Latin and German, was proclaimed a success, having won herself a scholarship to Girton, there to read the Classical Tripos.[58]

It was in 1863, experimentally, then nation-wide in 1864, that girls were first allowed to sit the Cambridge University Local Examinations. "The most curious development", it had seemed to *The Saturday Review*.[59] "The idea almost takes one's breath away." Pretty faces would succeed; the plain would stand no chance.[60] And a gibe ran, from club to common-room and from common-room to club, that half the young women in the land would contract brain fever or end in a lunatic asylum, if they decided to attempt Mathematics and persevered with it.

The belief that women's brains were as inferior to men's as was their brawn died hard but it was doomed. Mrs Williams's school had long ago ceased to be unique. Queen's College for Women had been founded in

[55] Chancellor of Cambridge University, to whom it owes the laboratory called after him. The Duchess, Blanche, had died in 1840, aged 28. Louisa, their daughter, and wife of Rear-Admiral the Hon. Sir Francis Egerton, was mistress of the house.

[56] Daughter of the Sir Tatton Sykes, jockey, who had employed Ellen Egan, and wife of Thomas, son of the first Lord Delamere.

[57] Daughter of the Rev. Mr James Chambers, of All Souls College, Oxford, and Headmaster of the High School, the Island of St Helena, in the South Atlantic, where Ethel was born. The school was soon to close, aged 60, in 1885.

[58] A founder and editor of *The Girton Review*. Played the Chorus Leader in Sophocles's *Electra*, the first Greek play in Greek which the College had performed. A travelled, versatile and lucid writer. Among her books: *Renaissance of Girls' Education in England*, 1898, and *Women's Suffrage in Many Lands*, 1910. She bequeathed £150 to Girton, so establishing the Alice Zimmern Memorial Prize for Classics there in 1939.

[59] *The Saturday Review of Politics, Literature, Science and Art*, 1855–1938.

[60] "Feminine Wranglers", 23.7.1864.

Harley Street in 1848, from the pupils of which emerged Miss Buss, thence the North London Collegiate School for Ladies, model day, and Miss Beale, thence Cheltenham Ladies' College, model board. Miss Emily Davies had published *The Higher Education of Women* in 1866, to whom had been due the inclusion of girls' schools in the work of the Schools Inquiry Commission and the establishment in Hitchin in 1869 of the College which originated Girton. Her campaign for an education and examinations for girls the same as for boys would slowly succeed. Mrs Maria Grey formed the Girls' Public Day School Company (now Trust) in 1872; a women's teacher-training college would bear her name. And St Leonard's School for Girls was founded in St Andrews in 1877.

The Ladies and Gentlemen can hardly have remained unaware of what had happened and was still happening or have failed to understand what it implied: how urgently necessary it was to expand and progress, competing to survive.

Development depended on finance, finance on development, and the only way out which they could see from the impasse was to launch yet another appeal, which, God at last willing, would enable them to modify and enlarge the premises and accommodate the daughters of gentlemen "of the class required". They need not, the subscribers were informed, be orphans but "preferably belonging to the professions for whose benefit the Institution is maintained". Remunerative charges would be made—"this feature is commonly found in the principal Colleges and Schools in the country"—£81 a year for senior boarders 13 years old to 16 and £102 for those 17 to 21, the fees at Girton being quoted as a guide, and six guineas a term, "as at Queen's", for the day-girl juniors aged 6 to 14—the junior classes would help the wards to learn to teach small children and not just those at the Christ Church Sunday School nearby. Advertisements for pupils appeared in *The Times*, *The Morning Post*, *The Daily News*,[61] *The Globe*,[62] *The Guardian*,[63] *John Bull*,[64] *The Spectator*, *The Academy*,[65] *The Broad Arrow*,[66] *The Pall Mall Gazette*[67] and *The Civilian*.[68] At last it seemed that, in any sense, the school meant business.

A new wing on the north side of the house would provide classrooms for about a hundred pupils. The Commissioners of Woods and Forests felt uneasy about the ornamental terrace garden on a flat roof, "the Roof to be

[61] 1846–1930; merged in 1930 with *The News Chronicle* and in 1960 with *The Daily Mail*.

[62] 1804–22, continuing as *The Globe and Traveller* till in 1921 *The Pall Mall Gazette* incorporated it.

[63] The 1846–1951.

[64] The 1820–92.

[65] A scholarly review, 1869–1902 and under other titles till 1915.

[66] A combined naval and military gazette, 1868–1917.

[67] From 1865 till in 1923 it was absorbed by *The Evening Standard*.

[68] "The accredited organ of the Civil Service", 1869–1926; then as *New Civilian*, 1926–28.

covered with lead, with pugging or thatching underneath", but allowed it, so long as the design was their idea of good, the walls to be finished in Portland cement and the whole to stand no higher than 14 feet.

Perhaps royal influence told. In 1879 the Committees had elected Princess Helena their President overall. "The Adult Orphan Institution" took the name of "The Princess Helena College for Young Ladies" (senior boarders) "and High School for Girls" (day juniors).[69]

It was Vice-Admiral Sir Alfred Ryder who had urged and proposed the more important changes: an expert in light-houses, fuel economy and navigation, with special reference to hurricanes, Commander-in-Chief, China, from 1874 to 1877, and now at Portsmouth (like Admiral Bowles, only younger—59), in the next few years he would publish a paper titled *Purity and the Prevention of the Degradation of Women and Children*, then drown in the Thames near Vauxhall Pier, on his way to meet his brother. He, more than anyone, had been eager to abandon the school's original name. It was "objectionable, misleading and unintelligible" as to the sex and social status of its pupils. His Committee agreed.

The new title was cumbersome, but "High School for Girls" lapsed, the rest first shrank to its first three words and then to the initials, PHC.[70]

Having two separate committees unequally in charge seeming "very complicated and embarrassing" to the Princess and her Admiral Ryder and enough others, the subscribers were now to elect a governing council instead, of at least ten ladies and at least ten gentlemen. The gentlemen kept to themselves a sub-committee of building and finance, where, it is clear, they did not yet feel that ladies could be trusted, but only for as long as they still had plans to enlarge the school at 11 St Andrew's Place.

Of the members of the old committees only five ladies, two gentlemen, remained: Mrs FitzHugh; Mrs Lucy Goschen, wife of George, then Liberal MP for Ripon and future Chancellor of the Exchequer;[71] Georgina, Marchioness of Salisbury, wife of the just outgone Foreign Secretary and future Prime Minister;[72] Lady Constance Stanley, the President's nominee,[73] who had Philippa Lys as her governess in Dublin; her widowed

[69] The Helena ("Heleena") School in Darlington, Australia, an independent primary, is said to have been founded in 1888 by a clergyman's widow, Mrs Jessie Jones, born Loade, as a preparatory school for boys. Her daughter, Jessica, took it over in 1928 and named it Helena, her mother having taught at the school in Regent's Park. But we find no record of anyone called Loade.

[70] Mr Reginald (the latest) Mure, son of James the younger, by his second wife, Anna, August 1880: "When do the P.H.C. holidays begin?"

[71] 1886–92. A founder of the Liberal Unionist Party and architect of its alliance with the Conservatives. An expansionist First Lord of the Admiralty, 1895–1900, and Lord Salisbury's successor as Chancellor of Oxford University.

[72] 1885–86, 86–92, 95–1900, 1900–02.

[73] Daughter of George Villiers, fourth Earl of Clarendon, since 1864 the wife of the sixteenth Earl of Derby, he a minister under Disraeli and Salisbury, and Governor-General of Canada, 1888–93.

sister-in-law, formerly the Hon. Mrs John Stanley, become Mrs Francis Jeune;[74] Francis himself;[75] and Mr G. T.—T for Trout—Bartley.[76] Miss Hildyard, aged 70, had left, as had Admirals Ryder, Sotheby, Oliver, and General Sir Edward Walker. Mr Mure, the Duke of Edinburgh[77] and Prince Christian took their place, with Julia, Marchioness of Tweeddale, Mrs Jeune's sister; Charlotte, the Countess Spencer;[78] Lady Olivia Ardilaun;[79] Sir Edward Scott;[80] Sir William Anson, Warden of All Souls, Oxford;[81] Madame Lind-Goldschmidt, Princess Helena's dear friend, whom the public had known as the singer, Jenny Lind, "the Swedish Nightingale"—she now took over as the school's Musical Director;[82] Admiral Sir William Houston Stewart; Maj.-Gen. Sir Frederick Roberts—not yet Field Marshal and Lord; Mr Charles Phipps-Eyre; Sir Thomas Brassey, MP for Hastings;[83] Colonel—later General—Sir Reginald Gipps; the Rev. Mr W. Page-Roberts; and a Rev. Mr Henry White.[84] From among this Council Princess Helena assembled an Executive Committee: Lady Constance, Mrs Jeune, Mrs Goschen, Mrs FitzHugh, Prince Christian and Mr Bartley, a manageable six. Mr Bartley served as her Chairman and Treasurer, more Treasurer than Chairman. The Hon. Henry Brand[85] soon joined them, MP

[74] Born Stewart-Mackenzie, Susan *Mary* Elizabeth, widow of Lt.-Col. the Hon. John Constantine Stanley, by 1891 Lady Jeune, and Lady St Helier by 1905, the eminent society hostess. From 1892 to 1907 almost all the Council and Committee meetings were held at her home at 79 Harley Street. A member of the Council till her death in 1931 and a Lady-in-Waiting to Princess Helena.

[75] A Fellow of Hertford College, Oxford, and future QC, knight, judge, peer. A rabbi-like figure as cartooned by "Stuff", in the *Vanity Fair* of 1891, hook-nosed and with black beard and moustache.

[76] Author of much about social problems, among it *The Educational Condition and Requirements of One Square Mile in the East End of London*, 1870, and *Schools for the People*, 1871; co-editor, 1873–82, of the journal of the Women's Educational Union; advocate of thrift and of thrift-based pensions—in 1875 he founded the National Penny Bank—and of poor-law reform, hence many publications, including—that year—*The Seven Ages of a Village Pauper*; Conservative MP for Islington, 1885–1906; in 1891 he opposed his party's free education bill but was knighted Sir George in 1902.

[77] Queen Victoria's second son, Alfred, 1844–1900. In 1874 he had married the Grand Duchess Marie Alexandrovna, the only daughter of Alexander II, Czar of Russia. Admiral by 1887 and Commander-in-Chief, Mediterranean Fleet. A violinist.

[78] Wife of John, Liberal MP for South Northants, 1857, fifth Earl, and Lord Lieutenant of Ireland, 1868–74.

[79] Daughter of the third Earl of Bantry and wife of the first Baron (till 1880 Sir Arthur Guinness).

[80] A wealthy London banker.

[81] Vice-Chancellor of Oxford University by 1898 and in 1899 elected its MP.

[82] After three years, Otto, her Jewish husband, took her place: composer, pianist and by 1876 first conductor of the newly-formed Bach Choir.

[83] Civil Lord of the Admiralty, then its Parliamentary Secretary, in Gladstone's second administration, 1880–85. Created Earl Brassey in 1911.

[84] One of six Whites, Henry, listed clergy C. of E. that year.

[85] Son of the Henry, Speaker of the House of Commons, who had employed Elizabeth Richmond. Future second Viscount Hampden, twenty-fourth Baron Dacre.

for Stroud, later Governor of New South Wales,[86] and Sir Stafford Northcote, Disraeli's Chancellor of the Exchequer, 1874–80, who in 1886 would briefly serve as Lord Salisbury's Foreign Secretary.[87]

An honorary secretary had now to be found for the Executive Committee. Mrs FitzHugh wanted "some lady of high rank". The Royal President and the rest of her team disagreed. A lady of high rank was none the less appointed: Mrs Jeune.

Late in December 1880 the Council asked Princess Helena to continue as President; she resigned seventeen days later, explanation unrecorded, but letters were exchanged and she returned. In her first four years, when the Ladies sat alone, she had attended nine of thirty-four meetings; in her last forty, when so many good causes had enlisted her support, thirty-seven of 400 were all that she could grace. In the years between, 1878–82, busy standing the school upon its feet, she presided over seventy of 118, an impressive three in five.

It was HRH who chose the day and hour when the new Committee met; proposed the new curriculum; signed letters thanking benefactors, and testimonials for departing staff; advised on the appointment of "Masters and Teachers"—"teachers" still meant women but "mistress" too was sometimes said—and decided how much the ladies of the neighbourhood should be charged who came to Prof. Morley's lectures and whether to postpone his visits till after "sun-burners"—gas-lamps—had been installed in the dormitories and the wards could all return. Her "unwavering interest in the details of management", in the words of the Report of 1880 on the previous year, was not an idle tribute. She functioned in effect as her own Chairman of the Governing Council and Committee and in some ways also as her own, long-range, Headmistress-Bursar, with a Lady Superintendent on the spot, as her Right-Hand Woman.

Elections continued. Almost all the thousand or so donors and subscribers had votes to cast, 3,275 all told, Queen Victoria, 115, the Prince of Wales, 30, Princess Helena, 11, the Duke of Edinburgh, 5, the Duchess of Cambridge[88], 10, the Duke, her son,[89] 8, the Trustees of the Cholmondeley Charities, the Worshipful Companies of Brewers, Clothworkers, Drapers, Fishmongers, Goldsmiths, Grocers, Mercers, Merchant Taylors and Salters together, 42. The Cordwainers, however, Ironmongers and Skinners, the Society for the Discharge and Relief of Persons Imprisoned for Small Debts, umpteen Dukes and Admirals and such, and the Archbishop of Canterbury, who had each donated or subscribed monies, had for some or other reason not a vote.

[86] 1895–99.

[87] Created Earl of Iddesleigh in 1885, he died next year on the day that he resigned.

[88] Augusta of Hesse-Cassel, widow of Adolphus.

[89] George, Field Marshal and by 1887 Commander-in-Chief of the Army. His wife was Mrs Fitzgeorge, of Queen Street, Mayfair, the actress Louise Fairbrother, whom he had married in 1847, disregarding the Royal Marriage Act.

Candidates for wardships could now include the daughter of a deceased civil servant of the first class or who had held appointments "of equal or superior rank". They were admitted younger—Eva Abbot was only 12—each one of them supported by two referees, testifying that she and her mother were respectable, and vouching for her ability to read and write and for her knowledge of Grammar, the Elementary Rules of Arithmetic, including Vulgar Fractions, of the outlines of Geography, History, Bible History and Christian Faith. Moreover, to ensure that no mistake was made: before she could graduate, aged 17, from the Lower Division of the school into the Upper, she had first to be examined and acquire a certificate of worth (a) moral: knowledge of Scripture and of the truths deduced therefrom, in accordance with the teaching of the English Church; tact, conscientiousness, good temper, kindness to juniors; and (b) intellectual: ability to learn and teach English, French, German, Latin, Music and Mathematics. Thereupon she was allowed to remain as a pupil till the age of 21.

Queen Victoria's subscriptions provided two scholarships. Princess Helena, the Hon. Mrs Loyd-Lindsay, the Mrs Stanley not yet Mrs Jeune, Miss Eleanor Mure,[90] Admiral Sir Hastings Yelverton[91] and General Spencer Stanhope, then Chairman, founded more. The wards got most, who in time were shown to have least deserved them. The President signed letters to the Tallow Chandlers, Goldsmiths and other worshipful companies, asking them for "scholarships and funds". The Goldsmiths gave her £50.

Teachers would be hired, the best whom "a reasonable outlay" could obtain, "the most experienced in examining the ladies' schools, such as Tutors or Professors from the Universities of Oxford, Cambridge and London, or from King's College". Prof. Thomas Huxley, the famous biologist[92] and a close friend of the Jeunes, agreed to recommend a lady who could lecture on "Physical Science". A Miss Halcrow took the post. The Committee, however, was rather disappointed. "Physiography"—Geography, more or less—was what it had meant and it now got Chemistry.

The list of prizes grew, including one for General Excellence, the Rev. Mr William Cadman's "for Biblical Knowledge", and Admiral Ryder's, "of the value of One Year's School Fees, viz. £13–13s.", for scholarship and virtue. (Mr Cadman, whose extraordinary memorial[93] many thousands of

[90] A sister of James the son of James.

[91] Married since 1845 to Barbara, Baroness Grey de Ruthyn, widow of George, second Marquess of Hastings, he had changed his surname from Henry to Yelverton by Royal Sign Manual in 1849.

[92] Educationalist also: an original member of the School Board for London.

[93] A stone pulpit attached to the outside wall to the left of the south door of Holy Trinity, Marylebone, headquarters now of the Society for the Propagation of Christian Knowledge, where as Rector of the Parish, 1859–91, Mr Cadman "with unfaltering fidelity, unfailing sympathy and unwearied zeal preached the gospel of *Jesus Christ* and adorned the doctrine he taught by a life of saintliness spent in communing with

Londoners a day either see or overlook, was now one of two clerical superintendents, Dr Festing the other.)

Some complicated rules governed Admiral Ryder's award. The names of "those *three* Young Ladies" who had scored the highest marks in their midsummer examination were to be written on a board, alphabetically, and each other young lady, who had attended the College for at least three months, and was not then "under the censure of the Ladies' Committee" (still functioning), was to vote for the one of the three "whom she most esteemed, as possessing, in the highest degree, in her opinion, the qualifications which go to make up a *high-principled, kind, considerate character*", provided that she had not yet won and decided to accept the Yelverton Memorial Exhibition. The three names and the examination marks were not to be disclosed "until the instant of election" and the voters were not to be allowed to confer with one another till the votes had been cast. Other rules followed. Should two girls tie or perhaps all three . . . The Admiral did not leave anything to chance.

Each top-form leaver would receive, if she deserved it, a parchment Diploma, either 1st or 2nd Class, which Princess Helena as President of the Council, or her Vice-President, the Lady Superintendent and the Examiners had all signed, attesting her proficiency in each subject. Bye-Law XXIII: "Such Diplomas will be of great service to the Wards when wishing to obtain situations, and will also prevent disappointment to employers and discredit to the College."

Alterations to the house had continued. Upstairs was rearranged, so that ten fee-paying boarders could join the thirty wards. A chest of drawers and a basket for linen went underneath each bed, next to which either stood or was planned a pipe-and-tap-fed wash-hand basin, with towel-rod in reach, coat-pegs, chair, all privately cubicled with curtain and rail. The sun-burner gas-lamps gave better light. Walls were papered up to 6 ft high in varnished "oak" then distempered at the top. Fire-places had been added to three cold bedrooms. A Boyd's stove[94] kept the dining-room warm and it and the kitchen were properly ventilated. New lamp-globes appeared in the "Long Room" and the library—where a drugget could not be afforded and a second-hand carpet had to serve instead—desks were acquired, which Mr George Lawson, an ophthalmic surgeon,[95] No. 12 Harley Street, gratuitously vetted, an enamelled-iron umbrella-trough was ordered for the entrance hall, where stood another stove—a Gurney's[96] from Mrs Ross—a drying-room installed, another hip-bath, a flat-bath and a foot-tub.

Expenditure still exceeded income, in 1879 by about £1,300. More

his Lord. He died May 12th 1891. He being dead yet speaketh. Heb. xi. 4." He had drawn big crowds.

[94] As supplied by Alexander Boyd and Son.

[95] In 1886 appointed Surgeon-Oculist to Queen Victoria.

[96] A stove fed by a tubular boiler, as in the old House of Commons, invented by Sir Goldsworthy Gurney, 1793–1875.

and more of the invested funds were sold. The crisis deepened. "If nothing be done," the Gentlemen warned, "the Institution will probably have to be closed in a very few years, as the Committees can suggest no other alternative than extrusion—both as to accommodation and numbers"; only thus, and "under God's blessing", could it continue its useful work, "with a higher standard of education, renewed energy and enhanced success".

A new collector was appointed (commission 10% on donations and on first-year subscriptions; on other payments 5%). Mr Brandram's recital at Arlington House brought in £131. Pilasters, cornices, dados were trimmed from the proposed new wing; asphalt instead of York stone had to do for the basement. But only £2,000 could be raised or guaranteed of the £4,380–10s. that the classrooms would cost, intended to house the seventy or so day-girls whose fees might save the school.

Princess Helena asked her brother, the Prince of Wales, to speak at a fund-raising dinner; he agreed; and it was held at Willis's Rooms[97] in King Street on the 22nd of May 1880. A hundred and fifty guests attended it, among them the Duke of Cambridge, Earls Sydney[98] and of Cork,[99] Admirals Egerton, Duncombe, Oliver and Buckle, Generals Walker, Macdonald, Daubeney and Wilbraham, and many other worthies, political and clerical. Lord Sydney spoke, followed by the Duke of Cambridge for the Army, its Commander-in-Chief, and by Admiral Duncombe[100] for the Navy, the Church unrepresented. Then rose the Prince of Wales, his purpose to rally the guests and to appeal for their support for his sister's ailing school and rescue it.

I must now beg you to charge your glasses and to drink this toast in bumpers. It is one which will, I know, readily commend itself to your notice, for it is "prosperity to the Princess Helena College". [Cheers]

At many of the dinners at which I have the pleasure of taking the chair the charities in support of which they are given require more words to bring them to the notice of those who attend than the present one does. But though the specific nature of this institution relieves me from the necessity of entering upon any lengthened advocacy of its claims, it is not the less deserving of your hearty support in every respect. [Cheers]

As you are aware, the Princess Helena College was formerly called The Adult Orphan Institution and it has for its object the bringing up of daughters of officers of the Army and Navy and of Clergymen.

[97] Originally Almack's, 1765–1843, with a galleried dining-room and a ballroom accommodating 1,700 dancers (at a pinch). The building, next to St James's Theatre, was destroyed in an air-raid in 1944.

[98] John, third Viscount, first Earl, and grandson of the Elizabeth, Dowager Viscountess, who had lodged Mrs Williams.

[99] Richard, ninth Earl, who would be Aide-de-Camp to Queen Victoria and a Deputy Speaker of the House of Lords.

[100] Arthur, fourth son of the first Baron Feversham.

Its first meeting took place as far back as 1818, and in 1820 the institution was built. As Lord Sydney told you, it originated with a relative of his own.[101] *It was founded by her and by my great-aunt, Princess Augusta of Gloucester. King George IV also took great interest in its welfare, allotting the plot of ground in the Regent's Park where the College now stands.*

The Prince here touched upon the building in the Park, which was still to be enlarged, the need to increase receipts and remove pecuniary difficulties. He continued:

I am informed that a distinguished naval officer is acting as steward here tonight in gratitude for the benefit his daughters have derived in their education from a governess who was brought up at the Princess Helena College.[102] *[Cheers] I have mentioned before that the Queen is its Patron. Her Majesty subscribes £50 a year to its funds and on this special occasion she presents one hundred guineas. [Cheers] The interest taken by my sister, the Princess Helena, in its welfare I have alluded to before, so I will not refer to it again; but I will, in conclusion, again ask you to let me feel by the liberality of your contributions that I have not failed in my duty as your Chairman. [Loud cheers]*

A list was then read of donations and subscriptions which, including those from the Queen and another hundred guineas from the Prince of Wales himself, amounted to £2,060.

It did not suffice, after costs had been deducted from receipts. Members of the Council were prepared to lend only £900. Alterations to the house were incomplete; no fee-paying boarders could yet be received. A fourth storey was proposed, a smaller wing, each discussed and rejected. Instead the house and grounds were sold, for £11,550 gross—£10,224 net—rather less than someone had offered in 1869 when they were not for sale and when the Gentlemen had thought that they would fetch much more; a new site was bought in Ealing, Mr Winter's meadows, at the top of Eaton Rise, costing £6,000; Princess Helena had preferred it to Harrow and said that the Queen had approved; the balance from the sale was deposited with Mr Bartley's National Penny Bank; and the College moved into temporary quarters, for a rent of £250 a year—no liability for damage—at Normand House in Fulham Fields, an "Asylum", hitherto, "for Insane Young Ladies".

The list of senior wards was now abolished. "The idea that whenever a Governess who has been trained at the College is out of employment she

[101] This cannot be. John Taylor would have seen it as the product of another of Mrs Williams's deceits.

[102] Rear-Admiral Sir Francis Egerton, whose wife, Louisa, daughter of the seventh Duke of Devonshire, had appointed Katherine Major, daughter of John, late Curate of Boughton Aluph, Kent.

shall apply to the Committee to find her occupation, tends to prevent the growth of independence and reliance on self which is essential to success."

Teachers and servants were given three months' notice to leave, but at least their salaries were at once paid, unlike the tradesmen's bills, settlement of which was postponed; a few were reinstated, and they all got testimonials, which Princess Helena had signed. Dr Propert was to vaccinate the pupils, then resign, and Mrs Clatsworthy's job, that of Matron now called Housekeeper, was to be absorbed by the Governess now called Lady Superintendent.

The Rev. Mr Francis Holland must have welcomed the news that the College was to move. He had written to Admiral Ryder, proposing that the school in Regent's Park and his newly founded one in Baker Street[103] adopt a common policy on wages, fees, hours, terms, holidays and religious teaching, "in order to avoid the appearance of rivalry". The Council declined his offer but its challenge was removed, his school survived and today still thrives.

On the 17th of December 1881 HRH Prince Leopold, Duke of Albany,[104] laid the foundation stone for the new abode, accompanied by his sister, Princess Helena (in honour of whom a banner was displayed on a nearby house: "God bless the Princess!"); Prince Christian; Marchionesses Georgina, of Salisbury, and Julia, of Tweeddale; and other members of the Council. A tent had been raised, which nearly collapsed under heavy rain and began to leak, an organ was hired for 15s., a band played, supplied by the children of an industrial school,[105] who earned their school two guineas, and a choir from somewhere sang a New National Part-Song written and composed by Mr Harold Stidolph,[106] about England's throne, her bulwarks, her good Queen's pride, her sons, her princes, the welkin to be rung, her daughters, who were gracious in look and word and deed, eager to soothe a bleeding heart, their royal mother's joy and stay and holding sway in every bosom, and the wives and husbands who came from other lands, all welcome. Mr Stidolph's offer to arrange the music for the opening ceremony next year was politely declined.

The new Lady Superintendent had now to be appointed. Hardly anyone had stayed for long, following Miss Horden's illness and retirement. Mlle Marmey and Miss Browne having deputised, an Acting Gover-

[103] Built there in 1878 and now in Clarence Gate, the first of the two Francis Holland schools. The other, launched in 1881, in Coleshill Street (today called Eaton Terrace), now stands in Graham Street. Their motto, *Filiae Nostrae Angeli Incisi Similitudine Templi*, is drawn from Psalm cxliv, v. 12: "that our daughters may be as the polished corners of the temple".

[104] Eighth of Queen Victoria's nine children; her most scholarly and musical; the first of the royal haemophiliacs, he would die, aged 30, little more than two years later.

[105] A school where children found vagrant or neglected were trained for work.

[106] As a child, aged 8, organist at a church in Tonbridge or Tunbridge Wells, and from 1880, of Christ Church, Ealing, till in 1884 he settled in Johannesburg.

ness, Miss Robinson, was found. Miss Robinson fell out with the matron, Mrs Bond, or Mrs Bond with Miss Robinson and others. Miss Robinson reported Mrs Bond to Lady Mary Ross, then Mrs Bond complained, it seems to Lady Mary:

What her charges are, I am at a loss to know, as I have ever studied all in the Establishment to the utmost of my power. In accepting the situation of Matron here, I expected to be treated as a Lady and regret to say I have met with much insult from those in power. If I am to retain my situation, I beg that my duties may be more distinctly allotted to me; however, I . . . am willing to resign if such is your wish, altho' it would be a serious matter to me with three children to support.

Mrs Bond's offer was accepted, and Miss Robinson fell ill, so only stayed a year. Another five months passed. Miss Pugh followed but resigned after six months' trial, "with great respect" and, for reasons undisclosed, "in many ways deep sorrow". Advertisements appeared in *The Times* and *The Morning Post*. Miss Cresswell came next—also on trial—but started late, "having met with a severe accident on her journey". A kind soul, she herself paid for the hire of a harmonium on which the wards could practise. A year or two later the Rev. Mr Thomas Fearne, Archdeacon of Pietermaritzburg, who and whose wife had founded Natal's first boarding-school for girls, St Mary's College, Richmond,[107] appointed Miss Cresswell its headmistress, the Gentlemen having written to assure him that she had not been summarily dismissed. Miss Penfold took Miss Cresswell's place, her subject music. She asked to be allowed a copying-press, called a phonograph—"There are many letters of which it would be desirable to retain a copy, which is at present impossible on account of time and labour"—and the Gentlemen agreed, so long as it did not cost more than 30s.—also wine instead of beer.

In December 1873 Miss Penfold received and passed to the Ladies' Committee a letter from a parent, Mrs Shortrede, whose daughter, Mary, had been half removed, half invalided out, alleging that Miss Cresswell had imported high church practices. Recrimination must have somehow then ensued. Miss Penfold's own beliefs were challenged. The Ladies enquired and reported to the Gentlemen that the Lady Governess held no "extreme religious views" and that it was only her "anxiety to control the High Church tendencies which had crept in under Miss Cresswell that had made her desirous that Miss Shortrede should not return, as she was the ringleader of these opinions". This cleared Miss Penfold but the findings blurred the truth about Mary, as to where she had stood and about her failing eyesight as the cause of her departure.

[107] It had attracted pupils from as far away as the Transvaal and the Orange Free State. But numbers had fallen from thirty-five to five, and it was £400 in debt, when Miss Cresswell left it. She had by then founded another school, St Anne's, which lasted two years. St Mary's closed in 1882, aged 10. Now only a brick-and-concrete garden seat of it remains.

Renewed fears about high church practices induced the Committee to withdraw the wards from evensong at the Church of the Holy Trinity, just round the corner, and send them instead to Christ Church in Albany Street, the lower, it seems, of two high or highish churches; which anyway made sense, the pews at Holy Trinity being mostly rented and occupied and the rest taken up by the poor, whereas the Christ Church seats were rent-free and the wards could sit together in a side-aisle, properly supervised. But they were still to attend Holy Trinity for communion, at least in the summer; which, till matins at St Katharine's lapsed, meant three Sunday services at three different churches, or two in the winter for those with a chill or a bad cough, who were excused evensong, but evensong only, and the walk to and from it in the cold air of the night.

A low instead of high church fright arose a few years later, when it looked as if Lucy McQueen was a congregationalist. The alarm was false. Lucy had been recommended by the Patriotic Fund and was genuinely Anglican.

Mrs Egley, "a Widow Lady",[108] followed Miss Penfold in 1877, whom the Ladies had proposed, Princess Helena had interviewed and (at that time) the Gentlemen alone might appoint. The first "Lady Superintendent", she would not teach (hence a low salary of £100 a year, two-thirds or so of the full amount, though within three months she taught Italian) but was "fully competent to judge of the efficiency of the instruction given" and would "make herself acquainted with the characters and dispositions of the Wards . . . and endeavour to make the A.O.I. [as it then still was] a Home and not merely a school". There she succeeded, winning praise for matching wards to posts and posts to wards. Next year she fell ill and had to resign, then suffered an accident—she too—so could not depart, and for two months had to stay in bed, attended by the learned Mr Prescott Gardner Hewett,[109] Serjeant-Surgeon-Extraordinary to the Queen, and nursed by the matron, Mrs Fleen, and an attendant—the Dowager Countess of Lichfield paid—while her post was being advertised in all the better-known newspapers and in *The Court Journal*,[110] a lady being sought whose duties would include "general supervision" and "the usual correspondence".

The Ladies now interviewed two candidates. One was "over age", being forty-seven years old, and "had never taught at all". The other, Mme Clémentine d'Arenberg, whom Princess Helena and the Ladies preferred, "English by birth and the daughter of a clergyman", had worked as a governess for twenty years at home and abroad. She decided not to teach, so could only earn £100 a year, conversant though she was, not only with Italian, but with German and French.

108 Wife, perhaps, of the late William Egley, painter of miniatures. Dr Propert is likely to have known him and collected his work and may well have recommended Mrs Egley for the post.

109 Created a baronet in 1883.

110 "A record of manners, literature, science, art and fashion", 1829–1925.

Mme d'Arenberg remained five months. Miss Walker followed, aged 32, another born of clergy, who after five years with the two daughters of Duke Frederick of Schleswig-Holstein[111] and three with the one of a Princess Lapoukhine,[112] had returned to England when the English in Russia had become unpopular and her position there uncomfortable. A high salary was agreed, £200 a year. But she could not take up her post at once, having first to complete a course of study for a "Cambridge Diploma" at "the College in Skinner Street".[113] Miss Yardley took charge. Seven months later Miss Walker came and stayed two years. Again the post was advertised. Miss Emily Eddes agreed to serve. As well as being Lady Superintendent she would take "the Mathematical Classes" (for the time being) and arrange at her discretion "the visits of the Wards to Institutions and places of Educational recreation". To her salary of £100 a year there would be added a capitation fee of £1–10s. for each of over twenty pupils and £2 for each of over forty, with free residence and in term free board.

She too was soon to go. Margaret Ibbetson, 18, daughter of the Vicar of St John's, Adelaide, and winner of the royal and other prizes, wrote a letter of complaint about Miss Eddes which Mrs Jeune, Lady Stanley and Mr Bartley were asked to investigate. It then appeared that at 10.15 p.m. or so on the 31st of May, 1881, Miss Eddes had left the College and come back about three-quarters of an hour later with a bottle of brandy. The housekeeper,[114] Mrs Rose, and all the servants, "either by some strange accident or intent", had gone to bed and Miss Eddes had found herself locked out. The brandy, as always, was medicinal but at that late hour it had aroused suspicion. Furthermore it was revealed that a Mrs Thompson, who had visited Miss Eddes when Miss Eddes was ill in bed, had told her sister, Beatrice Davies, a ward, 16, that Miss Eddes had criticised Margaret Ibbetson and that Margaret, upset, had felt it only right that she inform the Committee that Beatrice had said that her sister had said that Miss Eddes overdrank.

Margaret Ibbetson was supported by three other wards, one of them Catherine Crabbe, called Kate, 18, a naval surgeon's daughter and winner of the Admiral Yelverton £12 Memorial Exhibition, "who persisted in treating the whole thing as a joke"—indeed "her manner in so serious an investigation was extremely unbecoming"—and by Mrs Rose, whose

[111] Auguste—future wife of Kaiser Wilhelm II, who herself would appoint as governess a Princess Helena girl—and Caroline.

[112] "Lapuschio" in the committee meeting minutes must be wrong. Lapoukhine, also spelt Lopoukhine, is the only possibility. But which princess it was, thus named, it is impossible to say.

[113] Founded in 1878 by the Teachers' Training Registration Society; known also as the Bishopsgate, where it stood nine years; and from 1888 as the Maria Grey; till in 1976, merging with the Borough Road College of Education and the Chiswick Polytechnic, it became the West London Institute of Higher Education.

[114] As HRH now wanted Matron to be called.

conduct was open to "very grave censure", undermining as it did her superior's authority.

Mrs Thompson was sent for; her statements, made in the presence of the wards concerned, "absolutely contradicted the evidence of her sister and showed on what a groundless foundation the whole case rested". Mr Turner, the surgeon, gave witness too: he "emphatically stated that there was not the least shadow of reason for the accusation against Miss Eddes and that he had distinctly ordered her on the day in question to take either Port Wine or Brandy as absolutely necessary to her condition of health".

Other staff were interviewed. Margaret Ibbetson was then suspended for a month and Mr Bartley proposed that Her Royal Highness be informed that the conduct of Mrs Rose "in connection with the conspiracy against Miss Eddes" was such that it was "absolutely necessary that she leave at once". Mrs Rose again appeared and was formally dismissed, with "one month's wages, lodging money and board", but not before she had accused Miss Eddes of inviting her to her room, there to drink gin and water. And so it all dragged on. The Committee found that the gin and water too had been medicinal but considered Miss Eddes's conduct to have been "foolish and undignified". Margaret Ibbetson asked, unsuccessfully, for a testimonial, so had already decided to stay away for good; yet a week later, when a letter was read which she had written to the French governess, its tone was such that the Committee decided to forbid her to return. And Mrs Owen Davies, of Highland Villa, Brent Road, Shooter's Hill, withdrew her Beatrice.

Miss Eddes resigned,[115] without due notice, so without due pay. Miss Rand, called Senior Mistress, took her place, but only for as long as the school was housed in Fulham; and so much did she resent being passed over, when the new premises in Ealing were complete and another Lady Superintendent was appointed, that the Committee agreed to deny her any post, Princess Helena approving.

A headmistress was looked for now—a "Lady Superintendent of the College and Head Mistress of the High School"—who had "passed the examination of some recognised Examining Body", or had successfully helped others pass theirs, and who would capably organise the new and bigger school in its new and bigger home and there maintain a "firm but kindly discipline".

About a hundred women applied, including a Madame Valero, who was told rather guardedly that it was "probably unlikely" that a foreigner would be chosen, and from whom twenty-four were short-listed, then seven, then two, from two girls' high schools, Miss Jurgensen—despite the

[115] She would in turn be Headmistress of the University College for Ladies, Avenue Road, St John's Wood; Superintendent of the Girls' Schools of the Maharajah of Vizianagram, then in Madras and now in Andhra Pradesh; and in 1889 Principal of Trinity College Hostel, a House of Residence for Women Students of Melbourne University, now Janet Clarke Hall.

name—from Norwich, and Miss Margaret Williamson, of 29 Blenheim Crescent, Notting Hill.

Miss Williamson was offered the post and accepted it. Her "great experience" had impressed the Executive Committee and "a rapid extension of the College" was expected, "under her superintendence, both in numbers and the efficiency of the education". She would not be known as Lady Superintendent or Head Mistress but as Principal, at her own request and with Princess Helena's consent. Salary: £250 a year with a capitation fee of £1–10s. for each pupil above 100, up to 200, and of £2 for each above 200, up to 300, making £600 with luck, residence free, free board in term, subject to one term's notice on either side.

From 1872 to 1882 twelve headmistresses or their substitutes had been employed, following Miss Horden. Miss Williamson would stay for twenty years.

Main stairs — Queen's bust

Great Hall

Resident Staff

Margaret Williamson and Helen Roberts

Billy and Bobby

Library — Form VI HQ

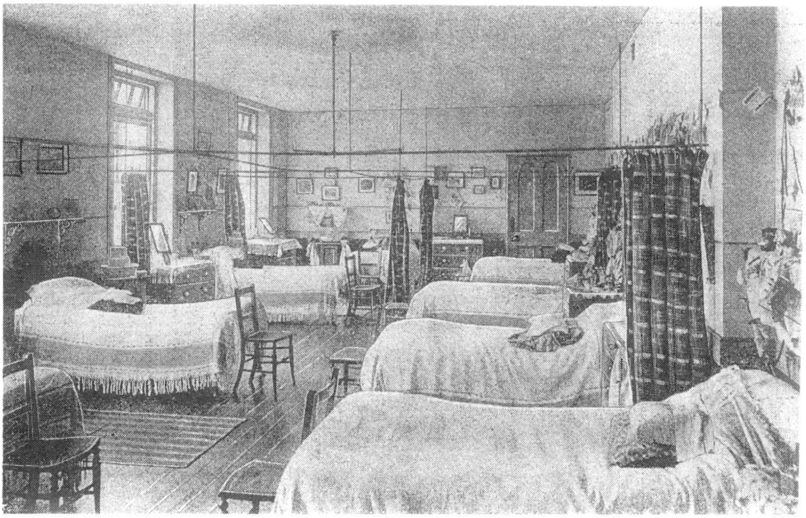

Dormitory 1896 — beds bared

1894 or 95

1896

Above: Miss Winlaw, Mlle Lava, Miss Clarke, Miss David, Miss Ryle, Miss Nicholson, Miss Adolphsen, Miss Sheerson. Below: Miss Campbell, Mrs Taylor, Miss Williamson, Miss Roberts and Fräulein Kleberger.

Winter hockey on the cowfield

Summer tennis tea

Tennis 1900 or so

Cricket in about 1900 . . .

. . . played in the shadow of St Peter's Church

Miss Roberts, coach, with XIs

A later 1st wears white

Chapter Five

1882–1902

On the 11th of July 1882 the new school house was formally opened by the Prince and Princess of Wales, accompanied by Princess Helena and Prince Christian. *The Middlesex County Times* excitedly reported the event. It had for weeks past been "the all-absorbing topic of conversation" in the town and was to "count among the important records in the annals of the past".

Henceforth Ealing will not be obscured in the minds of Englishmen but will live in their memories as one of the towns which have been raised to fame by the condescension of the heir apparent to pay a special visit and its being the locality of an historic education establishment founded by royal bounty and opened with much pomp by the future King of England.

The flags and banners hung limp with rain on the morning of the day, but sun followed and they dried and fluttered in the wind "like a perfect forest". Sightseers local and from nearby villages and towns flocked into the street, "their loyal hearts burning with enthusiasm". A Mr Culberry brought the old ladies of St Saviour's Home in a van specially fitted for their comfort by a kind Mr Sanders, to see the passing show. The wards arrived from Fulham; it would be six more weeks before their term began. Princess Helena stood waiting at the College for her brother's arrival. The west wing and the hall were adorned with palm and greenhouse plants, all the way upstairs to the suite of rooms reserved for the most important guests, where furniture had been introduced "of the most elegant description", with valuable carpets hired and borrowed, and a grand epergne occupied the tea-room, spectacularly dressed with lilies, cornflowers and choice exotics.

The royal party drove into the town, "heartily cheered by the assembled multitude"; the bells of St Mary's Church rang forth, signifying "rapture", the newspaper explained; Messrs Jones Bros, Ironmongers, fired a "royal salute" or "anvil salvo" from the rear of their premises; the 8th Middlesex Volunteers under Captain Tyrrell formed a guard of honour; their band played; and on a stand erected in the grounds a thousand elementary schoolchildren trained and conducted by Mr Harold E. Stidolph—so there he was after all—stood and sang "God Save the Queen".

Having first inspected the building and admired it, the chief guests passed through a breached wall and into a pavilion, where the Marchioness of Tweeddale, Prof. Huxley and other "influential" visitors sat waiting on a dais, overhung with a canopy of crimson cloth and strewn with stonecrop

yellow and roses red. All stood. Princesses and Princes took their seats. The National Anthem was again played, only now by the Band of the 2nd Lifeguards. A Miss Nelson in her satin dress and hat, daughter of someone locally important, stepped forward, bearing rare orchids and other flowers, for Princess Alexandra (wearing plum), all in the Danish national colours, with a satin and swansdown holder trimmed with Spanish lace. The Royal President outlined the history and aims of her College and foresaw the benefits to the girls of "the society of more numerous companions and the stimulus of increased competition". A Miss Maud Hutchinson, enhancingly announced as Admiral Sir Richard Collinson's[1] niece, then presented her with a bouquet of gardenias, Maréchal Neil roses[2] and maidenhair fern.

An illuminated address of civic welcome, engrossed on vellum, leather-bound, was handed to the Prince; the Chairman of the Council, Mr Bartley, dropped a rather heavy brick, referring to "the late Miss Eleanor Mure", who was not yet late and wrote to him to say so, touching rather sorely on the subject of the £300 that she had sent to the College; and Dr John Mackarness, Bishop of Oxford, thanked Their Royal Highnesses and spoke about the need for teaching girls to teach (referring to the wards and to someone mathematical, who had taught untrained and had tried and failed to teach him mathematics). The Prince and Princess retired into the wings. Minutes later they returned. Children on the stand sang "God Bless the Prince of Wales" (their singing was "most hearty", like their appetite for tea). Messrs Wilkinson had taken photographs, half of the profits from the sale of which they would pass to the school. The visit then complete, a horse-drawn carriage drove the royal couple home, "amidst the greatest enthusiasm and demonstration of loyalty", and "the cheers of the elated spectators were continuously maintained" along the moor and common.

A reception had been planned for Princess Helena and Prince Christian but HRH declined it and insisted that the money it would have cost be spent instead on the funding of a scholarship to assist a local girl ("someone connected with Ealing"). She was known for her common sense.

Only one thing, aside from Mr Bartley's gaffe, had marred the occasion. A carpenter, Mr Rixon, who was helping to erect an Arch of Triumph near the Station Bridge, had fallen from his ladder and broken a leg. But Princess Helena did her best to make amends, the Chairman writing thus on her behalf to the man's employer:

[1] Retired in Ealing; to be buried next year in Perivale nearby, which then comprised only seven houses.

[2] Among Queen Victoria's favourites, climber or shrub, with deep yellow, tea-scented blooms.

St Margaret's House, Victoria Street, Westminster
11th of July 1882

Dear Sir,

Her Royal Highness, Princess Christian, hears with deep regret and sorrow that one of your carpenters broke his leg this morning in doing the decorations. Her Royal Highness wishes me to ask after the sufferer and will be very glad to hear from him how he is. Enclosed also is £2 which her Royal Highness hopes will be of use in assisting to the expenses which the poor man may be put to.

Yours truly,
G. C. T. Bartley

The red-brick building, dressed in stone, stood in nine acres of land on the north side of the town, commanding views over undisfigured countryside to Windsor, the Crystal Palace, Highgate and "the pleasant village of Harrow". It had cost £17,398. Mortgage: £9,000. A handsome wide oak stairway (for visitors and staff and, later or already, for senior pupils) led up into the hall, with its long galleries and domed glass roof, classrooms below, dormitories above—parquetry floors almost everywhere—all of them "warmed with hot water". But the heat was erratic. Miss Williamson feared that the classrooms and bigger dormitories would be much too cold in winter, where the "nice glow" had failed to penetrate. After six months Princess Helena found the classrooms overheated, so had bills printed and displayed, ordering that all the windows be opened before and after each lesson. The dormitories also would be deemed too hot; the corridors, too cold. But in 1882 the Committee ventured to think that its new school was "not surpassed in adaptability for its purpose by any similar institution in the country".

The girls collected money with which to buy engravings and beautify their form-rooms—Franz Hals's *The Laughing Cavalier* would survive—and their own paintings were framed and hung in the great new hall. The Committee decided not to buy a donkey. But a playground was laid out, equipped with a trapeze swing and a giant's stride—the boarders accused the day-girls of hogging the swing. Saplings were planted, including lime, which years later would shade an almost half-mile walk, and lawns and flower-beds arranged. Girls kept their own garden plots and watered them from ginger-beer bottles. A cottage was built, with a ground-floor flat for the gardener and his wife, sanatorium above, and a Sedan chair stood ready, for infectious patients needing to be fetched. The school had always insured itself against fire, first with the Palladium, then for most of its life with the Phoenix, and now with the Palatine, but not until 1900 did fire-escapes appear, with drill once a term, when a roped, wood-rung ladder would be loosed from the sanatorium and a canvas chute—great fun and fright—from the top floor of the dormitories.

A prospectus declared the Committee's good intent: to remedy the defects in "middle-class female education" which the Schools Inquiry

Commission had exposed in 1867: "its want of thoroughness and foundation; want of system; slovenliness and showy superficiality". Schools for boys had been found to be generally bad. The girls were offered worse:

as a rule, a very small amount of professional skill, an inferior set of schoolbooks, a vast deal of dry, uninteresting task-work, rules put into the memory with no explanation of their principles, no system of examination worthy of the name, a very false estimate of the relative value of the several kinds of acquirement, a reference to effect rather than to solid worth, a tendency to fill or adorn rather than strengthen the mind . . .

Accomplishments had been given too much time, particularly music, which, to little avail, was as prominent in girls' schools as was classics in the boys'; and so had modern languages, where, none the less, the standard achieved was usually wretched. The teaching of arithmetic was meagre and almost always unintelligent. As for what they called their science, "few things are sadder", Mr Joshua Fitch[3] reported, "they . . . think they are learning astronomy when they are twisting a globe round and round and solving a few problems in latitude and longitude." "The lack of all physical training" was deplored and so were attempts made "to combine exercise and instruction, e.g. by repeating French verbs when out walking".

To ensure high standards the College now appointed a special Education Committee to advise it. The Rev. Mr G. C. Bell, Master of Marlborough College, agreed to serve; Mrs G. P. Bidder;[4] Mr H. W. Eve, Headmaster of University College School; the said Mr Fitch; Lord George Hamilton, the local MP;[5] Prof. William Hudson, a mathematician and Fellow of King's College, London;[6] Prof. Huxley, keener on science and handicraft than on the classics; the Rev. Mr William Jowitt, Rector of Stevenage, first Headmaster of the Cowper Street Schools[7] and the Girls' Public Day School Company's own Inspector, now retired; Miss Eleanor Smith, of the University Museum, Oxford;[8] Miss Roma Westmacott, Headmistress of the second Church of England High School for Girls (now Francis Holland—the one in Graham Terrace); and the Very Rev. Mr

[3] Sir Joshua by 1896; Inspector of Schools. In 1867 he helped to found the College for Women at Hitchin which in 1874 became Girton College, Cambridge, the year in which he also helped to found the Girls' Public Day School Company, now Trust.

[4] Daughter-in-law of the Bidder, George, a railway engineer, whose father had withdrawn him from school to tour the country as a "calculating phenomenon". His mental arithmetic, thought to be unique, was inherited by his son and grandchildren.

[5] Son of the first Lord Abercorn; Conservative MP first for Middlesex, then Ealing; Secretary of State for India, 1895–1903; and a Governor of Harrow School.

[6] Also Fellow of St John's College, Cambridge. Third wrangler there in 1861.

[7] Founded in 1867 by the Rev. Mr William Rogers and his Middle Class Schools Corporation.

[8] Sister of Henry, the museum's keeper. A Governor of Bedford College, London. Alice Cooke (DNB): "a woman of exceptional ability and judgement, whose main energies were devoted to philanthropic and educational objects".

George Bradley, Dean of Wesminster.[9] Princess Helena sometimes took the chair. Miss Frances Buss[10] and Miss Dorothea Beale[11] wished not to involve themselves.

From 1889 to 1917 the Executive Committee found well-informed advice more readily available, Miss Mary Gurney[12] having joined it, who despite the title of her book, *Are We to Have Education for Our Middle-Class Girls?*,[13] advocated schools that were socially inclusive, as well as non-sectarian, and where girls and boys enjoyed equal opportunities.

A clothing-list was published in 1882, comprising 1 garden hat, 2 outdoor hats or bonnets, 1 shawl, 1 ulster, 1 outdoor jacket, 3 dresses, 2 pairs of outdoor boots, 1 pair of indoor boots, 1 pair of dancing shoes, 1 pair of galoshes, 1 umbrella, 6 pairs of stockings, 8 collars, 6 pairs of cuffs, 18 pocket handkerchiefs and "a proper supply of the ordinary underlinen required"; to all of which were to be added in the next few years more detail: bags, for linen, shoes, including tennis-shoes, and comb and brush, tuckers for evening wear; nightdresses; a reminder that boots had to have strong soles and not need mending; stays; and a chest expander. With the list went rules:

Memorandum
April 1886

It is the earnest desire of Her Royal Highness the President, as of the other Governors, that the work of the College should inculcate and develop simple womanly habits, and that the utmost neatness and simplicity of attire should prevail among the Pupils.

The quantity of clothing stated in the list is quite sufficient for school wear, and it is very important that no unnecessary articles of clothing or of jewellery should be brought to school.

It is equally important that all the clothing—underlinen as well as outer garments—should be neatly and simply made, of good but not tight fit, and in thorough repair; also that every article, including gloves, shoes and umbrella, should be marked in full; *a fine of one penny is exacted for every article found unmarked.*

So much has been said of late as to the injurious effect of high pointed heels on the young growing spine, that nothing further need be urged than

[9] A distinguished scholar and teacher, in turn a housemaster at Rugby, his old school, Master of Marlborough and of University College, Oxford.

[10] Founder and Headmistress of the North London Collegiate School.

[11] Founder and Principal of Cheltenham Ladies' College.

Miss Buss and Miss Beale
Cupid's darts do not feel.
How different from us,
Miss Beale and Miss Buss.
Anon.

[12] A principal founder of the Girls' Public Day School Trust.

[13] *Or the History of the Camden Collegiate Schools*, 1872.

the simple request that house shoes and boots should have either very flat heels or none.

As there are regular hours for mending and needlework, it is specially requested that Pupils be provided with a full quantity of sewing materials and one piece of plain work.

Each Pupil must be provided with the following:

Small box for bedroom, with good lock.
Pencil box and penwiper and ruler.
General atlas.
French Dictionary.

Nothing remains in print about uniform. But games required it: an ample, dark-green dress, known or to be known as the cally, from neck to wrist and to ankle or calf long, gathered to the waist with a wide, yellow-gold sash, tied at the back into a huge, long-tailed bow, and perhaps, as a photograph suggests, a yellow-gold-bobbled tam-o'-shanter. It became, or in summer was exchanged for, a gold-braided, sailor-collar dress. A flat and broad-brimmed boater sat lightly on the head.

Notices and other rules were published, addressed as much to parents as to girls:

1: No places can be kept on or after *the first day of Term or Half Term. Pupils absenting themselves on either of these days must take the risk of there being no vacancy in their Form, and will further be required to pay a fine of 10s.-6d. if Boarders, or 2s.-6d. if Day Pupils, unless a doctor's certificate justifying such absence be forwarded to the Lady Principal on the first day.*
2: School hours are: Morning, 9.15 to 1.30, with an interval of 25 minutes at 11.30 for Lunch. Afternoon Preparation, 2.30 to 5 (Optional). Dinner is provided at 1.45 for those who wish to remain the whole day. Tickets can be obtained from the Matron at 1s. each, or 11s.-6d. per dozen.
3: In the afternoon preparation of lessons is superintended by the Mistresses, and Pupils who are backward, or find some difficulty in their work, should attend, that they may have the benefit of this help.

. . . . .

6: No excuse, except illness, can be accepted for unprepared work. Such excuse must be in writing, and signed by the Parent or Guardian. Returned lessons and unsatisfactory work will be reported to the Parents every week, with a request that the Pupil will return on Friday afternoon to revise it.
7: Any Pupil who does not attend regularly, or who is, in the judgement of the Lady Principal, unable or unwilling to profit by the educational advantages offered, will, after reasonable notice . . . be requested to withdraw at the end of the current term.
8: Any Pupil who, in the judgement of the Lady Principal, is insubordinate, or exercises an injurious influence on her companions, will be required to withdraw at once.

. . . . .

11: No Jewellery is allowed except such as is absolutely necessary.

. . . . . .

14: No lending or borrowing of even the smallest trifle is allowed.
15: No Story Books must be brought to School, nor any thing be given away without express permission from the Lady Principal.

By 1890 a parent registering his daughter had to sign an undertaking, "I hereby agree to abide by the Rules of the College as at present in force."

The year was divided into three terms, each of up to thirteen weeks, with two weeks of holiday at Easter, about seven at Midsummer and at Christmas up to five. Mistresses escorted boarders to Victoria and Paddington main-line stations when term ended and met them there returning on the eve of the first full working day. A girl could be visited by parents or guardians between 2.30 and 4.30 p.m. on Saturdays (by others once a month; and the rule still stood: brothers only if with mothers), but could not then step outside the gates unless she had the Principal's written consent—in Fulham, it appears, the reins were held more loosely—and only "under specially urgent circumstances" could she travel home in term. Miss Williamson was available for parents once a week and allowed (or was allowed to allow) them to sit and watch the callisthenics class on Fridays.

The Committee did its best to keep boarders and day-girls apart. Even when senior day-girls were enrolled, it assured parents that "the most complete separation between the two Classes of Pupils" was enforced, "except during the actual lessons"; they would not allow boarders to visit day-girls' homes; assigned day-girls to their own wash-rooms and loos; and excluded them, till 1891, from the Cricket 1st XI.

When the school opened on the 25th of September, 1882, sixty-four pupils were expected: twenty-one wards, other boarders eight, with day-girls thirty-five. The total increased almost year by year, to 146, 186, 185, 206 . . . By December 1891 269 pupils were received, thirty fewer than was planned, but everyone's idea of a big school. Three years later the total fell to 220. It recovered, helped by a description of the school placed in *The St James's Budget*.[14] But the number of boarders, including wards, peaked at only sixty-one.

Ages ranged widely within each form: in II from 8 to 12½, in Lower III from 10 to 14⅓, in IV from 12 to 16½, in V Remove from 15 to 19; 19 was the average of the sixteen girls in VI. The proposed ratio of one teacher to every twenty pupils would have satisfied Lord Taunton's Inquiry Commission, which had found that schools for girls tended to be much too small, with sometimes only two or three pupils to a class. The Committee could easily maintain it, shedding staff "without assigning cause", if intake fell—more readily, no doubt, now that staff were mostly women—at the end of any

[14] A weekly edition of *The St James's Gazette*, 1880–1911. In 1905 the gazette, a record and review of news, was incorporated with *The Evening Standard*.

term, giving one month's notice; or without notice, paying three months' salary instead.

In her first end-of-term report to Princess Helena Miss Williamson was pleased with "the excellent spirit and high morale" prevailing.

Of the wards I cannot speak too warmly—they have identified themselves with so much enthusiasm with all that has been done that, if in after years this Institution become, as we trust it will under your gracious patronage, one of the first in our kingdom, we shall look back with a feeling of gratitude to those who in its early days so materially helped by their loyalty and docility to give it a firm and sure basis.

In many subjects the wards had been "well and carefully taught". Their "general information, spelling and neatness", however, would have to be improved; "in good deportment and carriage" they were "sadly lacking"; "a low state of physique" had been reported by the doctor, "requiring attention and generous diet"; and the clothing of some had urgently to be repaired or replaced.

I should be glad if calico could, in some way, be purchased, to make where we cannot mend—Violet Stewart, Georgie Hopper, the Irwins, the Symmonses are specially in need—we have a needlwork hour four times a week, one of which is devoted to a regular lesson in Sewing by Mademoiselle.

A few weeks later the Symmonses had been allowed to leave, Frances and perhaps Hannah to emigrate to Australia with their sick mother (she had applied for the post of Lady Principal), and in 1884 Georgie—Georgiana—Hopper, who had no parents and whose sister, Florence, had settled in New Zealand, became a nurse at the Addenbrooke's in Cambridge, going on to the London St Mary's.

Election by donors and subscribers had now been discontinued. The published guidance as to which candidates had claims "very strong" or "strong" or merely "claims" to their support did little to help the more deserving, especially if they had few if any influential friends canvassing on their behalf or were found to have a private income. An applicant for a place had still to intend to be a governess and might be asked to declare so in writing. Certificates had still to be produced as to her conduct, mental capacity and health; and "the respectability and character of the Mother, or, if she be dead, of the Guardians or friends with whom the Orphan may reside"; together with "a satisfactory guarantee for the payment of the fees each term in advance". Examinations followed, not always as competitive as they were meant to be, in Scripture—as the English Church understood and taught it, even though clergymen fathers had no longer to be of that denomination—English, French—not German—Arithmetic, Geography, History, and Music if already studied. If then the Committee accepted her, it would review her progress after one term and yearly withdraw or renew

her scholarship, and if all went well she would leave aged 21, with her Diploma 1st or 2nd Class and the offer of a post which the College had procured.

Wards had become more difficult to recruit and keep. At best they numbered twenty. Mrs Jeune had wanted more. Was it not for them that the College had been founded? In 1885 the Committee offered two "free scholarships" for daughters of officers killed in the Egyptian War. It was the year of Gordon of Khartoum. Fanny Adeline Watkins, aged 12, took one: daughter of Alfred, Lieutenant, who lost his life in the first battle of El Teb, when his Egyptian troops threw down their guns and fled; Lucy Eastmead, 13, the other: her father, Quartermaster Charles, was killed at Suakin not seven weeks later. But Fanny had to leave after a year (unsatisfactory work) and Lucy after two (misconduct). Lady Fannie Morris[15] was forced to withdraw her Gwendolen, having kept her at home for reasons which the Committee could not accept and having failed to apologise. In time, however, wards tended more to stay, including Cissie and Mabel Every, orphans, whose father, Oswald,[16] had governed Dartmoor Convict Prison; and three who had arrived aged 10: Catherine Welsh-Kellner, daughter of Sir George, Paymaster of the High Courts of Chancery; Martha Carter, born of Richard, Rear-Admiral, who had died when Martha was still a babe in arms; and Major F. S. W. Raikes's Alice called Grace, bereaved in 1897, when Kitchener waged war in the Sudan. The Boer War followed; many fell; but it did not provide any Boer War wards.

Daughters of clergy, clergy dead or alive, took places left unfilled, at a reduced fee. Two were refused: one with an "alive but insane" father and one with parents found to be divorced—"There is no hope", the Committee's minutes read, "of her being accepted." But children whose families did not adhere to the teaching of the English church, or of any other, in or out of communion with it, were received. The Chapman sisters were Jews, morning prayers they would attend, but Scripture they could miss, and although Miss Howard, a Jewish boarder, had to go to church on Sundays, the Committee allowed her to absent herself from school to attend religious festivals.

A bank-clerk enrolled his niece in 1889. An application next year "for admission as Boarders of Hotel Keepers"—of the Telegraph Hotel in Shepherd's Bush—was considered and rejected. "The Crown", Westerham in Kent, whence Mabel Ford, and "The South Western", in Southampton,

[15] Wife of Sir Evan, a solicitor.

[16] Brother of Henry, tenth baronet, of Egginton Hall, near Derby; and of Edward, whose had died storming the Redan in 1855, with Lt.-Col. Shadforth and Capt. Parker. Lady Mary, guardian aunt, income not disclosed to the Committee, paid what fee was asked. Soldiers, who in World War II had occupied the house, turned on all the taps and flooded it when in 1945 they left; Wyatt ceilings collapsed. In 1954 the family decided to demolish what stood, then move into the stables.

whence Ida Rand, may have seemed to provide a better clientele. The Pupils' Register, 1896–1902, lists mainly professions; but garments, furniture, antiques, nets, coal, iron, houses, seeds, hops, tea, victuals, meat, poultry, wine and beer all sprinkled it.

In January 1887 a kindergarten class was established for boys and girls from four to six years old, who mostly sang and played, from 9.30 a.m. till 12.30 p.m., afternoons optional. By March, however, "only five little people" had appeared, "probably owing to the wintry weather"; the appointment of a trained mistress was therefore deferred.

The more the pupils' parents paid full fees, the less did they hesitate to complain: Mr Squire, that a mistress had been unkind to his Florence—he withheld payment until payment was enforced; Mr Richards, that his daughter suffered from too much prep. Mrs FitzHugh disapproved of the heating and sanitation; was placated; had a mind to withdraw her Mildred and Muriel;[17] decided not to; but resigned from the Executive Committee; withdrew them after all; then gave £100 to start a library, commemorating her aunt, the late, now definitely late, Miss Eleanor Mure. Delusion and melancholy had begun to overtake her. In 1889 she was certified insane and spent her last eleven years at Ticehurst House, an asylum in Tunbridge Wells, but remained listed as a Councillor till 1891.

Reports could give offence, which parents now received each end of term. It was not, however, true, Miss Williamson explained, that they included expressions like "no great ability" or "very little ability" or "no idea of work or discipline" or "very little mental power" or "inattentive and rude" or "no mental capacity or energy" or "sometimes mutinous": these comments had only been supplied "for the guidance of the Council".

The mothers and guardians of wards, who least contributed to the full cost of the pupil's education, were least of all indulged. It was to them that the rule mainly applied, or even entirely, that parents would be fined whose daughters failed to return on time or, if overdue, with a medical certificate. An army captain's widow, Mrs Russwurm, of 3 West Street, Stratford-upon-Avon, had it brought to her notice. Her Veronica did not come back to school at all, but married instead, becoming Mrs Butler. The other daughter, Emily, arrived eight days late. Mrs Russwurm refused to pay the £4 fine, however—eight days x 10s. a day—and withdrew Emily on the eve of Summer Term.

An end-of-term party was frowned upon, though chiefly perhaps because the Committee had not sanctioned it, from whom alone such blessings could legitimately flow, and a matron was dismissed who had allowed "people" to dance in the hall while Miss Williamson was away. But the school itself was homelier. From seven to nine of the teachers, about one in three, lived in the house. Miss Williamson was known as Billy to the girls and saw herself as mother; the boarders filed into her room at bed-time, when she kissed them all goodnight; her deputy, Miss Helen

[17] Two of her ten children.

Roberts, LLA,[18] they knew as Bobby. And whereas the Executive Committee meeting minutes made the school sound austere, in the College Magazine it seemed to bubble.

The Magazine first appeared in the Spring Term, 1885. Alice Atkinson and Armine Mathias edited it, Miss Roberts their guide, who in a preface to it wrote that she hoped that it would serve "as a bond of union and medium of intercourse between pupils past and present . . . No pains will be spared to make the Magazine worthy of the College and of our Royal President."

A plea was made on behalf of Alice in "The Editor's Corner" of November 1887: "She wishes to take charge of some Indian or other young children. Address: Victoria House, Great Cheverell, West Lavington, near Devizes, Wiltshire." The wish was fulfilled as to children "other" and "young", as Princess Helena explained, distributing the prizes the Christmas after next:

It will give the company great pleasure to hear that one of our wards who was educated here is at the moment governess to the Emperor of Germany's four little boys,[19] and I learn that she is doing extremely well and is giving great satisfaction.

In 1921 Miss Williamson, retired, paid tribute to the "great tact and ability" Miss Atkinson had displayed at the imperial court, and reported her death aboard ship, as she returned from South Africa, 55 to 56 years old, where she had gone to nurse a sister.

The College Magazine could be sentimental; exciting—lunatics and ghosts; edifying—Octavia, sister of Augustus, was "a specimen of the noblest type of womanhood which the ancient world could present . . . a character of so varied and striking excellence that it deserves to be imitated, as well as esteemed, by all succeeding generations"; cautionary—"A girl never describes herself as faithfully as when she is describing another girl's character"; patriotic—Nora Duncan and the prolific Mary A. Roberts wrote well-turned odes to Queen Victoria; scholarly—Mr Grimson on famous composers for the strings and a masterly translation by Eva Moynihan, now a young old girl, from Schiller's *Wallenstein*; critical—Winifred Austin wrote how feeble the singing was at morning prayers; and happily supplied with riddles, buried names, "puzzledom", howlers, comic verse and sometimes jokes.

Little boy. Pair of skates.
Hole in ice! Golden gates!

[18] Lady Literate in Arts. A diploma awarded by the University of St Andrews, 1877–1931, and intended to bestow on women the status which degrees gave men. Examinations for it could be sat anywhere in the world, if supervised by a clergyman or headmaster.

[19] There would be six boys and a girl. Queen Victoria was their great-grandmother; Princess Helena, their great-aunt. The Emperor had been Crown Prince when Alice was appointed, about a year before, as governess to Prince William, his eldest son.

Little girl. Box of paints.
Sucked the brush! Joined the saints!

"Have you been much at sea?" "Why no, not exactly; but my brother married an admiral's daughter."

"Were you ever abroad?" "No, not exactly; but my mother's maiden name was French."

In the Summer Term of 1886 a two-day bazaar in aid of St Andrew's Church and an outing to Windsor had been much looked forward to:

(i)

for some days . . . the chief topic of conversation was the Bazaar, and the absorbing interest, how to make most things with least trouble, and to make, too, such things as would sell. The contributions were many and varied, including all the pretty or useful articles which are generally to be seen at bazaars. Among the features of the College stall was a fish-pond, ingeniously constructed out of a bath, whose severe outline was concealed by draperies and bunches of grass. The "fishes" were of a highly miscellaneous character, ranging from pen-wipers and pin-cushions to unwearable babies' shoes and unpresentable dolls . . . the Lyric Hall looked very bright and pretty with its gaily-hung stalls and tasteful wares displayed by the shopwomen in their fresh summer dresses . . . a gaily-clad gipsy stood in the doors of her tent, ready to tell fortunes, good, bad, or indifferent, for the sum of sixpence. Close by was a green bower, shading a well—of lemonade, cool glasses of which were in great request among the thirty pleasure-seekers . . . and our famous fishpond . . . was largely frequented by small boys, whose feelings on opening the parcels, laboriously fished out with a bent hook suspended from a home-made line, defy description. The largest and most inviting-looking packets proved to contain dolls, needle-books, and other articles equally interesting and pleasing to the male mind. Music was not wanting to soothe such breasts as might be savage, for throughout the two days a band stationed on the stage kept up a brisk succession of popular airs, and from time to time concerts were held in an upper part of the building. Among these was one given by Mr Forrester, our musical professor. The manager of the refreshment stall appeared to be doing a brisk trade, especially in ices, strawberries and cream, and other seasonable luxuries.

Perhaps it is scarcely to be wondered at that after so many similar bazaars, a certain reluctance to buy should be visible on the part of the visitors. Certain it is that on this occasion the only means of disposing of the more expensive wares seemed to be a persevering, if somewhat monotonous, system of raffling—in which the College girls joined with zeal, and with, on the whole, a more than average proportion of success.

[Unsigned]

(ii)

During our last Exeat, a delightful proposal was made, namely, that all those who did not go away for their two or three days' holiday should drive down to Windsor, and there spend a nice long day.

The day fixed for our expedition was Whit-Tuesday, and, as may be expected, the sky was viewed with anxious eyes for some time previously. The early part of Tuesday was dark and stormy, but about 10 o'clock the weather seemed more favourable, and it was decided that we should start. On these occasions the vehicles are invariably late, and ours were no exception to the general rule, but at length the first carriage arrived, into which most of us were packed. After a short delay, caused by the late arrival of the smaller carriage, we started off in high glee. Some of the youthful members of the party had provided themselves with balls, and as soon as we got a little way into the country these were produced, and a game of "catch" within very narrow limits began. For some time all went smoothly, till a too vigorous throw sent the ball into the dusty road beneath. This interesting episode was repeated two or three times, on each occasion the ball being picked up by the inmates of the carriage behind. But even their patience would not last for ever, and our luckless balls were consigned once more to their resting-place at the bottom of the carriage.

As we drove through Hanwell, great excitement arose among some of our party at the sight of the unfortunate lunatics. A few of the juvenile members were much astonished that such beings were capable of work; and as we passed through several villages, considerably removed from Hanwell, which were inhabited by very ordinary people, and still the question, "Are those *lunatics?", was repeated, the subject was tabooed.*

It was decided that we should drive by way of Datchet, and on arriving at that delightful riverside village, some of us alighted in order to visit the pretty church. No words can adequately describe the beauty of the scenery between Datchet and Windsor, especially the magnificent view of the Castle from Datchet Bridge, looking up the river. It is bounded on one side by the fine trees of Windsor Old Park, and on the other by fields which seemed as if they could never change their brilliant hue.

Passing over the bridge we came in sight of the Castle on our left, and a "distant prospect of Eton College" on our right. On arriving at Windsor some delay was caused by the search for a place in which we could have tea, and meanwhile we became a mark for the scorn and derision of some of the scholars of the said illustrious College, who politely designated us as a "cartload of rubbish", much to our disgust. After these ribald insults we started off on our voyage of discovery . . .

They climbed the many steps to the Castle; admired the Memorial Chapel; toiled and groaned their way to the Round Tower, two hundred steps more; waited patiently their turn to be conducted "by severe officials" through the state apartments; had to wait till the service in St George's Chapel ended; beheld the tomb of the Princess Charlotte, where "a golden

and glorified light" from the stained glass window overspread the statue and the figures weeping at its feet; then made their way towards Eton.

The place which had been decided upon as convenient for our picnic meal was by no means aristocratic, being nothing more nor less than a bowling-green. We immediately began the unpacking of our interesting-looking hampers, and the tables were soon covered, but long as they were, they hardly sufficed for our numerous party, and so the younger members contentedly seated themselves on the grass, where they were supplied with good things.

After we were somewhat rested, we devoted ourselves to games on the bowling-green, which was surrounded by trees and overhanging shrubs, thus making a very pleasant playground.

. . . . .

We had a quiet drive home, the only incident worthy of note occurring at a little wayside inn, at which we stopped for the horses to be refreshed. The worthy host assured us he had a beautiful dancing-saloon, and invited us to take advantage of it, seeming much surprised that we did not comply with his request.

We drove through Hounslow and Brentford, but finding the latter place in a too holiday condition for our enjoyment, we turned off into a side road, and arrived at the College about nine, after having spent a most enjoyable day.

Katie Walker

The town of Ealing could still be told from London and the girls and staff knew or would come to know it as "the village". But it still had to share the London fog, which on the day of the Christmas concert, in 1888, was especially unwelcome:

the morning awoke in a white mist, which only deepened as the day wore on. Anxious faces peered out of the windows from time to time, to see if any hope might be cherished of the visit of friends . . .

The whole afternoon poor Mr Peppercorn, the piano tuner, was twang-twanging away, to his own and everybody else's despair, to get two miserable pianos to forget the atmosphere and agree . . . At last the persuasive power of the screw seemed successful, and he departed with a dolorous sigh, vaguely hinting at discords to come, which the event but too surely realized. The hour approached and the fog grew denser; but, to our great joy and thankfulness, one kind friend after another . . . arrived to gladden our hearts . . .

[Unsigned]

The fog had almost won, "the poor pianos were still at fatal enmity", but the audience was "kind and ready to appreciate", and Miss Aldridge, newly-appointed singing-mistress, put "the thrilling pathos of her rich voice" into Cowen's "The Better Land" and sang the less well known "The

Arrow and the Song" by Otto Goldschmidt, "of whose wife [Jenny Lind] she was the favourite pupil". "The pretty little duet performed by Florence and Jessie Hughes gave great pleasure. Their little hands went dancing over the keys as if they thoroughly enjoyed the performance, and were determined others should enjoy it too." And the orchestra pleased.

A Sports Day had been held in 1885, perhaps the first, when cricket was played, interrupted by rain, followed by tennis, the three-legged and other races, interrupted by tea, then "an egg and spoon race, dance, and also high-jumping, those who had won no prizes being the competitors. The prizes were very varied, being chosen with great taste by Miss Johnson." By 1889 "Sports" read "Tournament" and for almost fifty years that Day would be the most looked-forward-to event in the school calendar.

A games afternoon was arranged with other schools: cricket against the Ashford Royal Welsh[20] and tennis against the Baker Street High (Francis Holland):

the Ashford School were our superiors . . . obtaining first prize. We hope, however, that this will prove a stimulant to further exertions on the part of our eleven. In tennis, after a fierce contest, we defeated our adversaries, though the latter, as a reward for their steady resistance, obtained second prizes. The first prizes were awarded to Chattie and Maude Cooper, whose splendid play well sustained the honour of the College.

In 1887 new heroines emerged, pursuing glory, and again the fortunes of battle ebbed and flowed:

some of our number accepted an invitation to Ashford, to a tennis match, which was to be played by two champions, chosen from each school. We had as our champions Ella Skipworth[21] *and Bertha Griffiths. The Ashford champions came off victorious. The following Saturday the return match was played at the College. At first our champions seemed to be gaining, but in the end the Ashford girls were again victors. We hope, however, another year to retrieve our honour.*

Another year soon followed. Having lost against Sutton High School,[22] they defeated "the Belgravia",[23] then Ashford twice. And in 1891 results would have been "capital" had players anticipated shots and hit the ball

[20] Founded in Clerkenwell by the London Welsh Society in 1716; boys only till in 1758 it also took girls; moved to Gray's Inn Road in 1772; in 1857 to Ashford, Middlesex; St David's School for Girls since 1870.

[21] Like Sarah Hildyard, daughter of a Vicar of Bonby in Lincolnshire. Her mother too was dead.

[22] Founded in 1884 by the Girls' Public Day School Company, now Trust.

[23] Most likely the "Belgrave College, School for Ladies", included in Vol. II of Frederick de Carteret-Bisson's *Our Schools and Colleges*, 1884: in Buckingham Palace Road; Headmistress: Miss R. Brake. In Kelly's *Directory*: at No. 120 ("Miss Rebecca Brake, school for girls")—also at 134 Warwick Street—after 22 Upper Belgrave Place, 1867–68. In 1888, when the teams last met, the entry disappeared.

with less panache, more care, or had racquets not collided in the doubles, girls collapsing, "as strength and energy were excellent on both sides".

Dorothea Douglass had by now become a pupil, who as Mrs Lambert-Chambers would for seven years, in and after 1903, find fame as the Women's World Lawn Tennis Champion; but she cannot have yet stood out, for she did not, in 1891, with a tennis prize, whether racquet or silver clasp or pencil, when already or almost seventeen years old. It was her father at home in Ealing who taught her best, or so she would claim, in "Some Personal Reminiscences" included in her book, *Lawn Tennis for Ladies*, in 1910.

There was not much chance of improving at school, because nobody took the trouble to have the court or net of the right dimensions. The rules of the game were not even known. Every ball that touched the line was given out. I remember a very heated argument I had with a mistress who was umpiring a match for me, the result of which was that I was given lines for impertinence!

When in 1888 the tennis pairs did better, the Cricket XI mostly lost:

versus *Ealing Butterfly Club. College victorious . . . Daphne Club. Daphne victorious . . . Notting Hill High School. Notting Hill victorious. Return match with Daphne Club. Daphne victorious.*

Though cricket was a game more team and public school than tennis, and more strictly meant for boys, the girls feminised and enjoyed it:

Midsummer Term
1889

The all-absorbing topic this term has been Cricket. We have had altogether five matches and have been successful in three. The first took place on May 31st between the Worcester Park[24] *school eleven and the College eleven, on the College ground, when we scored a glorious victory . . . This match was a very pretty sight. The Worcester Park costume is white flannel faced with red, and red caps, which made a nice contrast to our own green and gold. The running was pronounced very graceful on both sides.*

At least three local gentlemen supported the team: Colonel Augustus Le Messurier,[25] father of Maud and of her sisters listed L. and D., the self-styled, Honorary Umpire of the Princess Helena College Cricket Club, who left for Calcutta in 1887 and from there sent home to it "a large box of delicious Indian fruits and preserves"; Mr Norton—"Uncle John"—who liked to watch the girls' XI play and took them to Lords to see matches as important as Cambridge University v. the MCC, Middlesex v. Surrey, and players as famous as Ranji; and—father of Ethel?—Mr Veal.

[24] Founded in 1814, in 1908 it moved to Westgate on Sea, where in 1924 it changed its address and became Ledge Point. In 1931 or 32 it closed.

[25] 16 Mount Avenue.

Entries from the Colonel's diary, headed "Contrasts from Calcutta", appeared (not thought too gruesome) in the College Magazine:

23rd July, 1887. Dentist at 10. Princess Helena College 4–7. Cricket match against High School, Notting Hill; Notting Hill won 55 to 48! Isabel missed a catch, and someone else tumbled over because her frock was too tight!

15th October, 1887. Started on horseback at 8 a.m. through Bokhara city. Streets full; man being executed in front of the palace; simply cut his head off. Troops marched past, 6,000 in all. Dr Heyfelder and Engineer Hugovitch came to dinner. (True extracts from the diary of the H.U.P.H.C.L.C.C.)*

(*Solution in our next issue and possibly a prize for best guess!)

The cricket club (like the tennis) was self-financing, therefore rather short of funds, but in 1891 "two prizes were given, of which the first, a gold bangle, was gained by M. Holding, and the second, a brooch, by M. Allen", who had "excelled greatly in batting and fielding". Margaret Dobson,[26] called Daisy, and Mary Deacon deserved "honourable mention for their bowling" and Gertrude Roberts and Dorothy Dobson[27] "were exceptionally good catches". Elsie Martin made "a very capable captain" and the whole team was commended "for the enthusiastic and vigorous way" it "universally contested for the honour of the Princess Helena College". Collegians played against Oppidans, as on the playing-fields of Eton, Collegian however meaning any kind of boarder and Oppidan a day-girl.

In 1896 the 1st XI won seven of its matches and lost only one:

batting was the chief feature, many girls having made exceptionally good scores. There is still much room for improvement on the field, where the girls are apt to get sleepy and slack, and leave the difficult work to their more energetic companions.

Perhaps the bad fielding, which is most marked this season, is partially due to the interference of the hats (would there were no such trivial hindrances!) which generally fly off at the critical moment, and in the circumstances it is difficult to determine whether the fielder will capture the ball or the hat. Preference seems generally to be given to the latter.

Another good year was 1899. A Mr Rolf coached. The College won six matches but it lost against "Miss Carter's XI (Eton)"[28] and a new and up-and-coming school called Wycombe Abbey.

[26–27] Two of five sisters Dobson attending the school, the daughters of the scholar and poet, Henry Austin Dobson, 1840–1921, who also had five sons. Mr Dobson worked at the Board of Trade, with at least three other men of letters, including Sir Edmund Gosse. Their department was there described as "a nest of singing birds", which no doubt was kindly meant, though some thought that the birds concentrated too much on "singing", and not enough on trade, to be really efficient.

[28] Most likely a daughter of Thomas Carter, a revered housemaster, with other daughters and wives of Eton staff.

In the autumn of 1888 cricket had given way to hockey. Hockey then made sense. Autumn cricketers had either stood and waited in the cold or stood and sat in it and watched. A team was chosen. It lost against an Atlanta Club. Little more is recorded of the game. In 1896 it was to share the Lower Field with the College butcher, Mr Gosney, who grazed his cows there twice a week, his rent unchanged. Kathleen O'Flaherty, who left in 1903, must have flourished in the mire: only one year later she would play the game for Ireland.

A Callisthenics and Duelling Mistress was about to be appointed in 1882 but did not, it seems, arrive. No more was heard about duels. Girls rode horses; they swam in a local pool; and croquet was played on the lawn, but not encouraged. Dancing continued, with Mme de Hayes-George. Mme George was also meant to be teaching callisthenics. Yet in 1887, when she found herself replaced, the Magazine reported it as a new and bright idea:

We hope to have a valuable addition to our curriculum of subjects next term, namely a Callisthenics class, open to the whole school. It is proposed that Miss Vincent, whose charming exercises are so well known, and who has the support of many of our leading medical authorities, should conduct this class. The fee, which will include the use of all impedimenta (skipping-ropes, balls, clubs, etc.) will be 10s. per term. The Lady Principal will be glad to receive the names of those wishing to attend the class.

The response was good: 120 pupils enrolled. But the charming activity did not last long. In 1901 Callisthenics and Miss Vincent—now Mrs Vincent Glass—made room for Fröken Gertzell and her Swedish Physical Culture. But the cally endured, the green with gold, which in time would become the all-day uniform some loved, some hated.

Attention had been drawn to "the home comforts" which everyone enjoyed, "the spacious grounds, the bracing air and general healthfulness of the neighbourhood". The parents undertook not to bring or send any "eatables or sweets". A balanced diet was provided. It excluded beer. Princess Helena and three of her Committee had agreed that the pupils moving out of Regent's Park should not be allowed it (the servants to be given £4 a year instead; the governesses, however, "what sort of beer they like"). The school kept hens and grew its own vegetables and fruit, including strawberries, and fed the girls on beef bought from the butcher, Mr Carter if it was not still Mr Gosney, whose cows it had supplied with its own well-trampled grass. The purpose of the school, which was to train its pupils not only to be cultured and refined but also healthy, may thus have been fulfilled.

An honorary physician and four honorary surgeons could be called upon when girls fell sick, not quite as many as in Regent's Park—and the same physician or another advised when a parent complained about the length or timing of the lunch-hour. A nurse began her duties in 1894. The matrons had not been medically qualified. Parents of the sick had to pay an

extra fee. Some were difficult. The Drews withdrew either Annie or Ethel or them both, objecting to the use of allo(not homeo)pathic medicine. As "allo" was as now the usual kind, they ought to have expected it.

In the period 1884 to 1887 another five girls died: Eva Abbot, a ward (15), at the College, Mary Hardy (age not shown), Maud Stocken (17), Emily Gadsden (16) and Maud Grice (13). The year 1890 was happier for all, when Miss Williamson reported that no one (boarder?) had fallen ill (contagiously?). But 1892 began and ended bad. Influenza delayed the start of the Spring Term (and shortened the Easter holidays) by from ten days to a fortnight. In September Theodora Meakin, a ward, got scarlet fever and was sent to the isolation hospital.

The Lady Principal gave instructions to the doctor that the child should be placed in a separate room as the symptoms were so slight as to be doubtful—and the public ward had five cases in it from the poorest part of Ealing.

The fever began to spread among the boarders. A few, who could, went home. Others, who remained, were kept apart and nursed.

The most prompt measures . . . were adopted. The Council took two houses, and there the Day School was carried on as a separate establishment. The quarters were cramped and the arrangements for so large a number were in some cases very trying; but the utmost good feeling and good conduct prevailed, and all went smoothly. In three weeks we were able to present a clean bill of health, and work at the College was resumed by the half-term.

Fourteen pupils were removed, ill-behaved, in the twenty years that Miss Williamson ruled; Gertrude Robinson was suspended, "in consequence of her hair not being in a proper state",[29] then returned; and six more were in effect sent home for good when the Committee decided to terminate their scholarships. Either all or almost all had been wards, who may have felt interned, and had little to rebel against but school, whereas day-girls and other boarders had each two parents.

What it meant for a pupil to become so tiresome that she had to be expelled became less clear. Lucy Eastmead had been "withdrawn by consent of the Council" after writing "a letter of very improper character" to her mother, who lived and taught in Paris; Rosina Hopkins ran away,[30] reprimanded after "grave acts of disobedience", Lucy abetting her, and was not allowed back; but Violet Holbroke was reprieved "on promise through her father of good behaviour", having overstayed her Easter holiday by three days (without her father's knowledge).

[29] The Committee then ruled "that the Matron must give attention to the hair and general habits of every Pupil as soon after the reassembling each Term as possible".

[30] Most likely to her guardian in Dulwich. Her mother lived out of touch, perhaps in West Africa, where her husband, David, had been Consul.

From 1885 to 1887 misconduct came repeatedly to light. It culminated in the removal of wards and a letter to Miss Williamson, which the Chairman, Mr Bartley, had drafted and Mrs Jeune had signed.

Dear Miss Williamson,

The Council have had under their very careful consideration the recent incidents which have happened in the College and have thought it right to request me to bring several points before you.

From the enquiry that was made and from the evidence which you yourself gave, it is clear that you not only had some suspicion as to something not being right in the middle of last year but that such suspicions were more or less confirmed before the meeting of the Council when the Wards' Scholarships were renewed.

The Council cannot but regret that you did not then fully inform them of these facts, for, had you done so, grave danger to the pupils would have been removed, and that without the unpleasantness and possibility of publicity which all regretted.

While alluding to the subject, the Council do not feel quite satisfied that strict supervision is exercised with all the pupils and especially the Boarders, for, had this been the case, the Council cannot but think that this particular incident could not have spread as it did to four or five of the pupils but must have been detected in its earlier stages of mischief.

The Council are desirous of knowing whether in consequence of these occurrences you have framed any special rules to obviate such a thing happening again and if so they would like to have a copy of them so that the Committee may ascertain whether in their judgement they are strict enough to meet with the approval of the Council.

The Council are aware that you have on more than one occasion urged the necessity for an increase of the Staff of Resident Teachers in order to secure greater and stricter supervision, a step which the Council have not seen their way to agree to; I would, however, point out to you that at present, besides yourself, there are seven Resident Teachers and a Matron, in addition to other Teachers, two of whom devote practically the whole day to the work of the College.

With efficient organization this, the Council consider, should suffice, and it is quite as much as the fees of the students justify.

Further than this it would seem possible and very desirable that some of this supervision should be entrusted to the elder girls, especially those who intend to become teachers themselves, so that, by giving them a greater sense of responsibility in School, they may be the sooner and more efficiently prepared for that responsibility which must come upon them as soon as they enter into practical life.[31]

By arranging a rota of the Teachers for play time and preparation time you would be able to render it very difficult if not impossible for any evil-

[31] But the whole VIth Form had been designated prefects.

disposed pupil to have the opportunity of doing mischief without its being readily discovered.

The Council are alive to the fact that the College has been so successful under your management that they speak thus freely to you feeling sure that you would wish them to be quite candid.

The great aim of all education, especially in such a College as this, must be to develop a sense of responsibility.

While maintaining then yourself a firm and decided hold over every detail as well as directing the broad outlines of the system of the College, it should be your aim as Lady Principal to throw as much responsibility on each member of the staff as is possible. In this way, the Council is convinced, the best and highest results can most surely be secured.

About three weeks later Miss Williamson replied:

Dear Madam,

Were it not that I am fully aware how little the Council know, 1: of the difficulties grappled with in organizing the threefold scheme[32] *of the Princess Helena College; 2: of the actual organization during the four and a half years in which I have had the direction of it; and 3: of the character and abilities of the wards elected during those years, I should have been painfully surprised at the want of sympathy and of confidence in my work evinced by your letter of the 9th of February. In response to the request therein expressed I submit, for the inspection and criticism of the Council, copies of our table of organization and the rules and regulations at present in force. They have been framed in correspondence with the gradual growth of the College: they are the result of twenty years' devotion to and study of the work of education and are in my opinion as strict as is good for the healthy development of our girls.*

With regard to the two charges in your letter, 1: that I last year knew, but refrained from reporting, definite misconduct bearing on the occurrence of last term, and 2: that, had the supervision been strict enough, the incident would have been detected in its earlier stages of mischief, I would beg to remind the Council how slight the whole evidence was. With the exception of the occurrence of last term, it was entirely based on a few circumstances so slight, and taking place at such long intervals, that, had the supervision not been most careful and watchful, they would never have been detected; and had they not all occurred in connection with a clique of girls already recognized as vulgar and untrustworthy, could have excited no suspicion.

It is impossible that every little irregularity should be treated as indication of grave mischief and it is well known to those experienced in training the young that, however perfect the supervision, one evil spirit can do a great deal of harm in a large school in the very simplest way.

I would beg to draw the attention of the Council to my reports on the

[32] College (boarders), High School (day-girls) and Kindergarten.

girls in question from 1885 onwards. The majority of the Wards elected during the past four years have been, not merely of no intellectual ability whatever, but of a very low moral tone, and I have always reported exactly as we found them.

Knowing as I do the difficulties and dangers which beset a scheme such as ours, I would most respectfully implore the Council to adhere as rigidly to the Bye-Laws relating to the admission of Wards as they used to do in old days when every Ward was interviewed and examined before being admitted.

In the case of girls whose parentage is of such doubtful character as O. Mansergh,[33] *M. Macarthy*[34] *and L. Stewart,*[35] *who was expelled two years ago, I feel that special enquiry should be made and that, if admitted, they should be distinctly on trial for one term.*

From the Registry of the Old Wards it would seem that this was frequently done, and there are most urgent reasons why we should be more careful in all admissions of resident pupils than was necessary in former times, the most important being the large number of young children who enter as full paying boarders.

I am, dear Madam,
Your Obedient Servant,
Margaret Williamson

No more was said or at least no more was recorded in the minutes. The inspector was encouraging in 1889, who visited the school and was impressed by its discipline and moral tone, and conduct must have improved still further after 1893, when Kathleen Shortt, a ward, "the very mutinous and insubordinate daughter" of a colonel, was expelled, having stolen from other girls and even from mistresses. Amy Locke had also then to leave, after "aggravated disobedience". Her late father had been Principal of the Government School of Arts in Calcutta.

It seems that Miss Williamson's powers were ill-defined and rather contradictory. The Committee appointed and dismissed staff, but consulted the Lady Principal and may have chiefly relied on her advice; reprimanded her when she advertised the need to find a ward a post, without their consent; allowed her to decide the earliest age at which pupils were accepted; invited her to revise, as she thought fit, a special prospectus for Ealing only, which she had not felt happy about; but rebuked her for arranging Saturday morning detention for girls whose work had been

[33] Olive de Burgh Mansergh, daughter of a civil servant—and three-legged race prize-winner—was removed, troublesome, aged 12.

[34] Madeline, daughter of Charles, a physician, who had left home in 1873 and nine years later was presumed to have died. She was accepted as a special case but removed, aged 11, having failed to respond to a warning that her scholarship would not be renewed if she was not "more careful and tidy".

[35] Elizabeth Ruby Alicia Georgina, called Lily, daughter of Allan (*sic*), a captain in the 82nd Regiment; excluded from the drawing-class in 1882, having failed to benefit; and removed, aged 17, "by request of the Council", in 1884.

unsatisfactory; then undermined her authority by exempting those whose parents disapproved of it.

Her duties included the bursarial, as when estimates were needed for a stove in the sick-wing; sinks, either lead or zinc, for the scullery; a drainpipe and trap; bedding, chairs and crockery, as numbers rose; when tenders were invited for the use of the Lower Field as pasture; for the supply of groceries and meat; and when details had to be produced, of the reduced mortgage, for the auditor's balance-sheet and report. "Mr Jowitt enquired whether the Lady Principal was not too fully occupied with details of domestic arrangement." However:

It appeared that though Miss Williamson did a good deal in this way . . . she was usually from 9 o'clock till one in the College instructing and superintending the teachers especially and teaching herself . . . the house duties did not in any way detract from her more important work of Head-mistress . . . regularly twice a term she had a meeting of the class teachers to consider modes of teaching and other general matters and other meetings as occasion required.

In 1894 Miss Veal—young Ethel?—accepted the post which Emily Ringwood had declined, her salary £60 a year, living in—they had offered Emily £10 less—and was allowed to continue in it, married, living out, for £100, and "with such meals as intervened during her working hours". Miss Williamson, however, was still her own assistant and, although the Committee now agreed to consider her "petition" for help, another six months would pass before they granted it.

The Executive Committee, acting for the Council, held most of the reins. Not only did it vet each penny spent, as the Gentlemen had done in Regent's Park: it fixed the dates of holidays; ruled which if any girl might travel home by an earlier train; agreed that cricket and tennis matches be arranged against other schools; chose which other schools; adopted the leather cricket-ball (Princess Helena, Prince Christian, Mr Bartley, Mrs Jeune); examined the medical book; wanted to be told if a girl in church had fainted; and decided when to let anyone return whom they had allowed Miss Williamson to suspend.

Only once did the school make a profit; its deficits varied from £29 to £999; but never did crisis develop or treasurer despair. As ever the staff cost most: £1,835–7s.–1d. for teachers in 1885 and £357–8s.–9d. for servants. The market for labour was free: £70 a year, with lodging and board, had not at first attracted the right mistress for French in 1884; Mme de Costa Tallon was then appointed, an extra £10 being promised her in her second year; yet ten years later Mlle Lava—"Dip. Off. Belg."—took the same post, who had been offered £60.

Men still earned twice as much as women for the same workload—the drawing master 12s.–6d. a lesson in 1871, the Italian mistress and the German only 5s. each. Arrangements were sometimes complicated: Miss Hatton, who taught the piano, was offered £1–11s.–6d. for twelve lessons,

each of twenty minutes, £2–2s. for the next twelve, each of half an hour, which was somewhat less, and for every seventh pupil nothing.

Subscriptions and donations, which in 1880 stood at £975, steadily fell to only twelve guineas in 1916, and in 1924 to only one. The College depended almost entirely on fees: £21–£24 a term for board, seniors paying more than juniors, and more again if they occupied a single room or remained at school in the holidays and were then taken out into the country or to the seaside.

As in Regent's Park, resources continued to be husbanded. Pianos, worn out, could be converted into tables or exchanged for a cupboard. And economy was enjoined when boarders added too much linen to the wash.

Princess Helena still chaired meetings; offered to enquire when a parent defaulted over fees, as parents often did; and undertook to find a teacher of music when a post fell vacant. She did not lose touch. But her role tended to become more decorative than managerial, now that the school was set on course.

Flags and evergreen decked the hall when in 1887 she gave away the prizes. A greeting ran above the stage, "Welcome to the Royal President", and on the far wall, opposite, the motto Miss Williamson had found in Dean Stanley's[36] *Memorials of Canterbury Cathedral* (1854), a piously embroidered and rather insipid translation of Edward, the Black Prince's *Hoch Mut — Ich Dien*: "High Spirit, Reverent Service". About four hundred parents and friends occupied the hall. The girls watched from the galleries above. Orchestra and choir performed. The Princess appeared and, as the National Anthem was played and sung, Meg Leslie, youngest child, gave her yellow roses and maidenhair fern (the colours of the school) in a basket tied with ribbon to match. A camera-man took photographs (charging half a crown each); Miss Williamson read her report; more singing followed. The Royal President then gave a short address:

I have been asked to say a few words to you on this occasion, being the first of my giving away the prizes in this College. It is needless for me to say that it affords me great pleasure to be here among you, and to distribute the well-earned rewards to the successful students. In congratulating you on having obtained them, I would express the hope that you will not be content with your success, but rather that you will be stimulated and urged on to future effort. And as for you who have been less fortunate, let me beg of you not to be discouraged, but only to work the harder, so that in your turn you may succeed in attaining the same honours.

You know the history of this College; how it has been built upon foundations laid many years ago; how, to meet the requirements of the times, much had to be changed; yet you know, too, how gratefully we remember the labours of those who are no longer among us. Therefore, I look to you, its inmates, to carry out my earnest hope, and that of all

[36] Arthur Penrhyn Stanley, 1815–81, Dean of Westminster, much of whom, as a boy, Thomas Hughes portrays as Arthur in *Tom Brown's Schooldays*, 1856.

interested in it, that this College may stand forth and take the highest place among educational institutions in the country, with regard not only to its intellectual attainments, but to its moral tone. You have a Lady Principal, in whose praise I cannot say too much. You have governesses, who are unwearied in following her lead, and you have masters who devote talent and trouble to your education. But all this of little avail unless you yourselves cordially co-operate with them. Your standard cannot be too high. Remember the influence for good or for evil which one girl can have upon another, and the great responsibility which therefore rests with each one of you.

And now let me wish you God speed, a joyful Christmas and a happy New Year.

Some young old girls were presented, who had come from Fulham when the College in Ealing opened: Eva Moynihan, Edith Rainier, Emily Ringwood, Georgiana—Georgie—Hough, daughter of a Chaplain to the Millbank Prison,[37] and Amy Potter. Displays followed, needlework and art, then callisthenics in the entrance hall, first for the President, who was much pleased, then for all the other guests.

Princess Helena returned next year and, as the second verse ended of "God Save the Queen", Muriel Burwood and Jessie, sister of Meg, stepped forward, bringing with them a bouquet of gold chrysanthemums.

The two children, in their white "Liberty" dresses, looked very sweet, and solemnly responsible as they bore along their little burden; and the kindly and gracious smile of the Princess as she received it from them made them very happy, though Jessie did remark, afterwards, that she thought "Princesses always *wore long trains!"*

The school was but one of many interests which HRH pursued and one of many causes that she served. In 1884 appeared her translation, into English, of commentaries in German by a Dane, Dr Carl Sell, on letters written by her sister, Alice, Grand Duchess of Hesse-Darmstadt;[38] in 1888 that of letters from the Margravine of Bayreuth, sister of Frederick the Great; and of those, in French, which Frederick himself had written to Voltaire. Her work on behalf of nurses, their training and terms of employment, took more and more of her energy and time. But as late as 1891 the Committee could still repeat and mean what it had said twelve years earlier, how "unwavering" her interest was "in the details of management and the general progress of the College"—"the President . . . has spared no pains in promoting all measures necessary for the comfort and well-being of the Pupils"; it often sought her approval and advice; and her private influence and public encouragement remained.

[37] Part of the land where it stood (1799–1890) is now occupied by the Tate Gallery.

[38] Queen Victoria's third child, second daughter; the wife of Ludwig XIV; benefactress; translator into German of some of Octavia Hill's essays, *On the Homes of the London Poor*; she had died of diphtheria in 1878, aged 35.

In 1886 a petition which Princess Helena had signed, with her brother, Alfred, Duke of Edinburgh, and others, was laid upon the table of the House of Commons and a Royal Charter was thus obtained, warranted under the sign manual of Queen Victoria. "We declare it", it read, "to be our will and pleasure that We and Our Successors should for ever be the Patrons of the said College."

The Charter empowered the Council to enact bye-laws, so it made one right away: a Seal was authorised, bearing the arms of HRH Princess Christian of Schleswig-Holstein (Princess Helena of Great Britain), to wit a St George's cross, flanked by two red roses. But this was a mistake. The Council had exceeded its powers: the arms, being royal, should not have been transferred; so the Seal was not displayed.

A replica was acquired, next, of the Queen's white marble bust, included in the Royal Academy Exhibition in 1887, costing 150 guineas, the work of her private sculptor, Mr Francis Williamson. It occupied a niche, half way up the main stairway, where it could best be admired.

The royal connection meant more to the girls than charter and bust. A fancy dress ball was allowed them in 1886 to celebrate the birthday of the Prince of Wales; the Queen's silver jubilee brought three extra days of holiday; the Duke of York's and Princess Mary of Teck's wedding, one; the Queen's diamond jubilee, a bumper nine (four in June and five in July); and the coronation in 1902 of the Prince of Wales as King, three more.

In 1891, when Princess Helena celebrated her silver wedding, a handsome embossed silver bowl was purchased, four smaller ones to match, and photographs assembled "of every part of the College", in an album green and gold, gifts from all the Council, Staff and Girls, which a party of seven was invited to deliver and present: Miss Williamson; Leonora Collett, Mabel Nash, Lina Robinson, called Linie, and Daisy Dutton, monitresses in the four higher forms; the two girls who had been longest at the school, Edith Popham and Margaret Dobson; and Mary Crabbe, old girl (sister of the Catherine who had seemed to think the Miss Eddes enquiry funny). Mabel Nash's impressions were published six months later in the College Magazine:

THE VISIT TO BUCKINGHAM PALACE
(ON THE OCCASION OF THE SILVER WEDDING
OF H.R.H. PRINCESS CHRISTIAN)

It is my pleasant duty (having been an eye-witness) to recount, or rather remind you (for you have often heard it before), of this, the most interesting event of the Midsummer Term.

. . . . .

On June 25th (Thursday), at 11 a.m., we started for the Palace, in two landaus, amidst a burst of clapping from the girls, which at any less momentous time would have been thought sheer madness, as it frightened the horses and endangered our lives.

However, nothing happened, and all went smoothly. In due time we arrived at the Palace. I don't know how my companions felt; but for myself I never felt so absurdly self-conscious and shy in my life as we waited for Lady Jeune, who was going to present us. (It is bad enough to walk up the College Hall before the mistresses on music examination days, but this was ten times worse.)

Well, we put the present on the table of the room into which we were shown, and waited for Lady Jeune. Soon after she had arrived, and just as we—that is I—were beginning to feel a little better, a sound was heard which caused a curious beating of the heart; it was but the handle turning in the door, but under the circumstances it seemed so loud and awful. The door opened, and we were in the presence of Royalty.

I really don't know what happened next. I believe I caught a glimpse of somebody bobbing a curtsey, and tried to do the same. There was no occasion for this alarm, for what did Her Royal Highness do but graciously shake hands all round, and say "How do you do?" like any other lady, and this kind action put us at our ease at once.

Our Princess was very pleased with the present, and begged Miss Williamson to "thank all the girls very much for the beautiful gift". Then, with her usual kind thoughtfulness, she took us through all the State apartments, and showed us the plate.

After once more shaking hands, we made our curious little "bobs", and said good-bye. Thus the awful ceremony was gone through, and we drove to 79 Harley Street, where Lady Jeune had kindly invited us to lunch.

It was now about three o'clock, so we started for home, having spent a most exciting and never-to-be-forgotten day in the annals of our school life.

Two weeks later all but a day Miss Williamson was invited to a Garden Party at Cumberland Lodge, Windsor, an event which the same issue of the Magazine reported. She too felt awed.

My Dear Girls,

I am sure you will be glad to have some account of my visit to Cumberland Lodge in July. Perhaps you would like to know what form the invitation took. It is indeed something to be very proud of that your *College was so honoured among all the schools of England, and I give it to you in full.*

To have the honour of meeting
HER MAJESTY THE QUEEN
and
Their Imperial Majesties the German Emperor and German Empress.

The Equerry-in-Waiting is desired by
Their Royal Highnesses the Prince and Princess Christian
To invite Miss Williamson
To a Garden Party at Cumberland Lodge
On Wednesday, July 8th.

3.30 to 7 o'clock.

I left the College early, accompanied by Fräulein Lebrun,[39] *who was to wait for me in Windsor to try to get a glimpse if possible of her beloved Emperor and Empress.*

We drove together through the beautiful park, and I left her under a tree at the top of the Long Walk, where she made the acquaintance of a charming old lady, who whiled the time away with sweet stories of our dear Princess's goodness, and where she had her heart's desire, and more, in a most gracious Imperial recognition all to herself.

The Royal borough was gaily decorated, for, as you know, on the Monday previously, the second daughter of our beloved Princess, Princess Louise,[40] *had been wedded to the husband of her choice, Prince Aribert.*[41]

Among the many mottoes expressing the devotion of the people to the Royal Family, one I thought beautiful: "May you be as much beloved in your new home as your Royal Mother is in hers."

On arriving at Cumberland Lodge, as I passed through the gates my name was entered in a book. I walked up the long lawn towards the large gathering grouped at the farther end. A gentleman met me, and asked my name. On hearing it, he said, "The Princess is expecting you, and will be so glad you have come." You can imagine, my dear children, how this removed all that seemed formidable in entering those sacred precincts, and made me feel quite at home.

He directed me to a long plank, along which each guest passed, to be received by T.R.H. the Prince and Princess Christian.

The Princess came forward to meet me very kindly and warmly, and thanked me for the beautiful gift the College had presented to her on her silver wedding, and asked me to tell you how much pleasure it had given her and her husband.

She then presented me to the Prince, and I walked away to listen to some beautiful music, and to watch a cricket match, in which one of the captains was a Royal Prince.

The silver wedding gifts and the wedding gifts were on view in the house, conspicuous among the former being the flower bowls from the College, with a card attached in the Princess's own handwriting.

Soon after my arrival a slight stir and movement forward indicated the approach of some distinguished guests, and we soon saw the blue outriders of the Emperor's carriage. I was quite in front, and had a lovely view. It was a sight indeed never to be forgotten—the Royal bearing of the walk to and fro along that narrow footway—the mutual grace and dignity of the Imperial reception.

[39] Teacher of Music and German since 1889, one of four staff who had resigned early that term, three of whom felt underpaid, including perhaps herself, earning £40 a year with it seems free board.

[40] Marie Louise, the youngest of Princess Helena's four children.

[41] Prince of the North German Duchy of Anhalt. Nine years later his father, the Duke, exercising his feudal prerogative, annulled the marriage.

After spending an hour in most genial conversation, and then adjourning to the house for tea, the Emperor and Empress departed; but as one constellation set and left us gazing sadly after departed glories, another brighter and dearer to our hearts arose. The message flew round, "The Queen is coming, and the Princess desires all her friends to assemble to receive her at the front entrance." But alas! for the wishes of even Royal Princesses, and for the enthusiasm of devoted hearts, the rain, which had been threatening all day, came splash! splash! in huge heavy drops as we all hastened forward, pouring down in a perfect deluge as we reached the house. There was a general rush for shelter, only a few braving the elements. These went on, gladly risking the results, and were rewarded by seeing how daintily and with what dignity Her Majesty alighted from her carriage and walked to the pavilion under so unusual a clouding of "Queen's weather".

The rain poured on pitilessly, and from attendants, outriders and horses perfect rivers of water ran as they hastened to shelter.

In a short time, however, the clouds cleared away, the Queen came out attended by the Prince and Princess Christian, and the guests were presented to her one by one. She smiled so graciously as the Princess mentioned my name, I wondered if she were thinking, with her tender mother's heart, of all the children whom I represented, and I made my curtsey for you all, thanking her with the deepest feelings of love and reverence for the honour she had done us. I then wended my way to the paddock to get my carriage, and picking up Fräulein Lebrun in Windsor, returned home.

In July 1892 HRH proposed that a commemoration and prize-giving day be held, each year, on her birthday, the 25th of May. By 1899 or sooner it had lapsed, but the royal birthday remained on the school calendar, together with Miss Williamson's.

Another two ornaments lent the school their lustre: the first in 1893, when a lodge-keeper or gate-porter was appointed, wearing uniform (pay: 26s.–6d. a week, with rent, coal and gas-light free)—he also served as boilerman (in 1909 his name would be Sergeant Stokes); and the next in 1897, which Miss Roberts foretold, editing the Magazine:

the College . . . still stands and flourishes. There is not much to record as to the building itself, except that the Council have arranged that during the summer months we are to have electric light installed. This, we think, we shall all find delightful in many ways, and it will certainly add very considerably to our prestige. Imagine the glory of some 400 brilliant lights.

A time-table, called "Day's Work", headed with a version of the words of Macbeth, contemplating murder, "If 'twere done when 'tis done, then 'twere well 'twere done quickly", was printed and displayed. It ran from breakfast at eight to "dinner" at three and on to "tea" at seven. So the hours had changed. Classes began at 9.30 a.m. and ended at 1.30 (later 1.15) p.m. The curriculum consisted of Divinity; English: Grammar, Dictation

and Literature; Latin (optional), French and German (each compulsory); Arithmetic; Mathematics (optional): "Euclid and Algebra"; Music; Model Drawing; Needlework; Laws of Health; Dancing and Callisthenics. Or so it began. The Education Committee deleted Laws of Health, adding "one or more branches of Physical Science", perhaps including Botany, which Economics, called Political Economy, replaced in it seems the top two forms. The teaching of Greek began in 1890 (and continued till at least 1905).

The school was inspected and the girls were examined, from 1886 to 1891 by the London University Board; then by the Oxford and Cambridge; and from 1901 by the Oxford only. A mixture of other examinations intervened: the Cambridge Locals, London Matriculation, the College of Preceptors, the Froebel Union, the Royal Academy and Trinity College of Music, the South Kensington Science and Art and the Royal College of Drawing. The first reports of the university examiners appeared in January 1887. Mr Edward Pinches[42] and two of his colleagues had set the written questions; Miss Williamson and her staff were left to mark the scripts ("and I gladly bear testimony", Mr Pinches wrote, "to the exceedingly judicious and perfectly impartial way in which this wearisome and difficult task was performed.") Results were mixed, especially in English. Form I, who understood and recited expressively their memorised poetry, showed promise; the reading in II was "not so bright, the falling inflection being given . . . in a dull, listless manner"; Upper III made curious grammatical blunders; IV and Lower V excelled. Papers on *Coriolanus*, from V Remove, were mostly "almost worthless" (the attempt had been premature), but next year, having learnt by heart and paraphrased from Henry V, Part I, they impressed using language "clear and terse". The seniors wrote "in a clear, bold hand, easily legible". In IV the words were less distinct: "increased thickness" was needed "in the downstroke".

Mr Pinches criticised parents and their "want of sympathetic co-operation":

An inspection of the "attendances book" showed an unusually large number of absences recorded, and until the great importance of regular attendance is recognized a larger proportion of thoroughly good work can hardly be looked for.

At Prize-Giving three months later Miss Williamson too addressed herself to parents, whom she urged to insist that their daughters persevere with subjects they did not yet like or had not yet grasped.

There is a tendency, in the present day, to put aside everything that is not of some definite utility. There is a still graver tendency to remove every difficulty and cross out of a child's life, and consequently we are appealed to to excuse even such a subject as Arithmetic, on the ground either that the child will never need to use it or that she does not like it! Difficulties

[42] Treasurer of the College of Preceptors and a member of the Royal (Bryce) Commission Report on Secondary Education, 1894–95.

have their educational value and a child can only become really healthy-minded and strong, and fit for the after-struggle with the world, by being left to conquer its own difficulties as they come, and allowed, with Tom Brown, to learn "the joy so dear to an Englishman of standing out against something and not giving in". Often the subject or work most distasteful to a child offers just the discipline and training she most needs, and mathematics and classics have a special value in developing the mind quite apart from their precise utility. The young mind is often utterly incapable of carrying out a process of reasoning, however simple, and much future usefulness and happiness may depend on its being trained to see the logical conclusions of things. Life is made up of small emergencies, calling for the exercise of common sense, and what is common sense but the power of rapid reasoning about common practical things? I would, therefore, beg of the parents to leave the education of their children in our hands, and to allow them to fight their own battles. It is very rarely that a pupil works better, in any one subject, for being excused another, and in point of fact it is not *the hard-working pupils for whom excuses are requested. I am not, of course, now alluding to the exceptional cases, which must occur in every school, for which a good and sufficient cause may demand some modification of the school course. Really delicate health, defective elementary education or, after a certain age, special tastes or some special aim—for each of these cases we are always ready, to our utmost power, to sympathise and to help.*

The examiners approved of the status enjoyed by Modern Languages and in these subjects the girls did best. Mr James Beuzemaker,[43] assisting Mr Pinches, found little to criticise in 1887. Results in French were "uniformly good" in the middle forms and pronunciation in Lower III was "unusually correct for such young children". For that, no doubt, they could partly thank Miss Glatz, or Mademoiselle, who also taught them Needlework. She resigned two years later but word of her was minuted in 1895. "The Proposed Prospectus of Miss Glatz for a French Boarding House [it appears that this meant weekly board] was approved with certain alterations." An article about the school, published in July next year in a magazine, *Church Bells*,[44] indicates that the plan was fulfilled:

One special feature . . . which is probably unique, is the establishment of a French boarding-house in connexion with it, where a girl can receive the same advantages for acquiring the language as if she was living in a family in France, while at the same time she is able to carry on her English education. This is, of course, a most exceptional advantage, and deserves to be more widely known.

The choice of uninteresting poetry in German, which the higher forms had had to learn by heart, Mr Beuzemaker found to be "disastrous". "To make the teaching of a language thoroughly successful it must be

[43] A contributor to Blackie's Modern Language Series.
[44] "An illustrated weekly paper for church folk everywhere", 1871–1906.

interesting, and that is not difficult with advanced pupils." But standards were high and had not stopped rising.

Results in Arithmetic and Mathematics varied widely within and between forms. Presentation could be "exceedingly neat and accurate . . . deserving the highest praise". In 1888 not one pupil in Upper V and VI was arithmetically weak. Mary Dobson, Ella Skipworth and Emily Lewis all shone, Ella the brightest, admonished though she was for "mutinous conduct" and "indifference to her work"—she also excelled at games. But some girls depended "more upon memory than upon a clear understanding of the reasoning employed".

Dr Richard Weymouth, Baptist and scholar, retired Headmaster of Mill Hill School, followed Mr Pinches. He did not approve of the attempt to write blank verse ("The writing of poetry in the form of prose should not be tolerated") and, although not surprised that only two girls in Lower V could spell "ichthyology", it disturbed him to find that "mischievous" defeated two of them in three. Spelling, in 1890, was "a weak point throughout the school".

Latin, though optional, was taught to about sixty pupils. Too little time had been devoted to it, with results almost worthless. But it soon improved. Translation from the first book of the Odes of Horace, in the top division of VI, was "remarkably correct" and Mary Dobson's prose composition "highly creditable".

The girls knew how to read maps. Dr Weymouth felt "pleased with the readiness with which Florrie Hill could assign reasons why Edinburgh should be the capital of Scotland rather than Glasgow", when Glasgow was so much bigger. But more reference was needed to changes of boundary in Africa and the claims thereto of Europeans. No fault could be found with the economists. "Six pupils of the Upper Vth have studied carefully Mrs Fawcett's excellent little work,[45] and have mastered the elementary principles of this important subject." The Spaldings, like the Dobsons, excelled, Ethel especially, HS90, who in her Cambridge Highers for Women next year got 1st Class Honours in English, Anglo-Saxon, Latin, French and German. Upper V knew about Ascham, Lyly, Sidney, Spenser, Hooker and Milton, quoted accurately from *Paradise Lost*, and had read and mastered a demanding text in French: Molière's *Le Misanthrope*. Science now included Mechanics, Hydrostatics, Heat and Light. Emily Lewis again stood out, whose answers "were of considerable merit", and "a good average was obtained". So much for the idea that female heads would not withstand the strain. And discipline, behaviour, morale, deserved to be admired:

the excellent order and good temper everywhere exhibited could not . . . be surpassed . . . the School, as a whole, seems to be in a thoroughly

[45] *Political Economy for Beginners*, 1870. Millicent Fawcett, born Garrett, later Dame, 1847–1929, championed women's rights. Philippa, her daughter, topped all in Mathematics at Cambridge in 1890 but could not, as a woman, be awarded her BA.

healthy condition. There is evidence in every department of high aims, intelligent choice of methods and unwearying energy in working on those methods. Point de zèle *is not the principle here acted on. And I am persuaded that the girls who are educated in this College will hereafter congratulate themselves on having been placed at so important a period in their lives under the able and conscientious care of Miss Williamson and the highly competent colleagues by whom she is supported.*

I have the honour to be,
My Lords and Gentlemen,
Your faithful Servant,
R. F. Weymouth, D.Litt., M.A.
Acton, December 10th 1890

His Lords and Gentlemen were the Chancellor, Vice-Chancellor and Senate of the University of London. The report then had to go to Princess Helena.

The Rev. Mr J. P. Fannthorpe[46] came next. On the whole he left satisfied. "I have worked through the Latin papers with much pleasure, even the poorest show some sound knowledge, and of Latin it may certainly be said that 'a little knowledge' is *not* 'a dangerous thing'." Most pupils in History "did good papers, some answers being above the average", but there was "a good deal of guessing" by the weaker, "some romance and not a little anachronism". Recitation, whether English, French or German was at times "mere gabble . . . too fast, thin and hurried". They did best in Scripture, where he enjoyed their "brightness, readiness and reverence".

The College has achieved much, but it is fitted to become still greater, and if the parents will give their children the stimulus they need in their home-work, they will not only develop the intellectual faculties of the children, but they will help the College in attaining the position which is its object, namely, that of being recognised as a very high, a very grand, and also a very holy means of education in Ealing.

Monsieur de la Lande examined the French: the girls spoke "too low" (*trop bas*?) but Form VI had studied the historical grammar, which delighted and impressed him, and had "a fair knowledge of the Literature of the *Siècle Louis XIV*". "I addressed the Senior Pupils . . . and they answered me readily in that tongue without the stupid shyness common to schoolgirls." His wife took the juniors: "the written work was excellent . . . the College . . . much to be congratulated". And a colleague, Miss Birch, praised Music: the standard reached was "exceptionally high".

Mr Herbert Courthope Bowen,[47] who arrived with the first of the

[46] Principal of Whitelands (Teacher-Training) College (now part of the Roehampton Institute of Higher Education), 1874–1907.

[47] First Headmaster, 1876–81, of the Grocers' School (by 1904 called Hackney Downs), where the boys' winter cap and summer boater displayed the Grocers' crest:

Oxford and Cambridge Board in 1892, found grammatical analysis in IV "too bookish and not enough the work of the girls' own observation and thought". Some in IV Remove were "completely silent", Lower V "seemed afraid to speak out" and V Remove "rather uncommunicative". Most of Upper V understood their Shakespeare, "though one or two . . . seemed hardly to appreciate what they read, or the meaning of the plays they had studied".

Mr Bowen liked the building, which was "well adapted to its purpose", the classrooms, "of a good size and well ventilated", the library, "large and pleasant",[48] the dormitories, "large, airy and cheerful", the playground, "ample", the games, "evidently followed with zest and success", producing "an excellent effect both moral and physical" and giving "ample opportunity for corporate enthusiasm and that devotion of self to the good of the whole which are of so great moral and social value—a value not yet universally recognised in girls' schools". The girls had their own gardens, which they kept "in a very satisfactory state", the classes were "orderly and cheerful", everything seemed to be done to make the pupils happy, "without any undue worry over examination results", and "the vivacity and friendliness" of Lower III made his work "real pleasure".

In 1895 Dr Schüddekopf enjoyed what he read and heard in German. "Nearly all the girls write . . . with so much grammatical correctness that the result is highly creditable to teacher and pupils alike. The German of some even deserves to be called idiomatic." Mr Bowen reported that English Grammar as taught in Lower IV was "rather formal and stiff". Algebra disappointed Mr Blaikie, "the answering . . . inaccurate . . . the principles apparently not understood". So did Botany. "The work leaves a good deal to be desired. The questions were answered often very carelessly, points asked for not being given and a great deal being written about matters not set at all. The grass flower was not properly described by anyone, though all attempted it." Work in other subjects pleased. Mr Bowen summed up: "The School seemed to . . . be working efficiently and happily . . . producing very satisfactory results. The cheerfulness and friendliness of everyone form a very noticeable feature, due in no small measure . . . to the excellent use made of the excellent playground." "The playground and the pupils' gardens were as delightful as ever", he had already said, interrupting his report on English.

Answers were good next year in the Higher Certificate *Macbeth* and Bacon's *Essays*, weak in *A Midsummer Night's Dream*, the girls wrote well on Corneille and Sandeau, their French composition was the best the

a camel bearing spices. Principal of Finsbury Training-College for Teachers, 1882–86, and Lecturer on Education at Cambridge, 1884–98.

[48] Miss Roberts, Magazine, took pride in it. "It already contains 600 volumes and we hope, as years go on, to possess such a library as is rarely found in a school." It included the twenty-five volumes of the 1875 *Encyclopaedia Britannica*, price £24, half bound in calf and lavishly gold-tooled, and was beautifully catalogued.

examiner had ever marked, accurate and colloquial, translations into English were "of a high class, some being brilliant. Only two candidates obtained less than 70 per cent." German and Arithmetic were good; Algebra and Euclid weak. Botanical specimens, for a lower form, had suffered in the post but work thereon was still satisfactory.

In 1899 the Rev. Dr H. W. P. Stevens, of Downing College,[49] Cambridge, "could not help noticing the uniform neatness of the work as well as the legibility of the writing" and "was very favourably impressed by the excellent discipline, and by the cheerful and willing attention to school rules, both in the school and in the playground." He saw the kindergarten (five boys, two girls—four pupils absent), their arithmetic, geography, drawing, paper-folding, sewing, embroidery, mat-plaiting and upright writing with pencil and ink. "A song with action was sung by all . . . but the little ones did not seem to be very familiar with it." "There is a tendency", he wrote, "at some schools to overdo the work in Kindergartens, and to put too great a strain on the brain at a very tender age. I think this danger has been foreseen at this school." Upper III knew its English History, but answered rather slowly, perhaps as a result of "the excessive heat". The Lower Certificate Shakespeare and Macaulay was "very creditable and sometimes excellent"; Higher Spenser "excellent in style . . . free from the diffusiveness which often spoils answers . . . exceptionally good"; Lower Old Testament History earned praise, where questions were set on Zerubbabel, Ezra, Nehemiah and Joshua's speech at Shechem; Prof. Victor Spiers[50] enjoyed the Higher French: "Six copies of the Dictation were very good, A. M. Fiddian being first with *no mistake*"; Una Bird, HS02, got 97 in Lower Arithmetic, Hilda Berry 99; five girls did "really capital work" in Higher Mathematics and B. E. Sparks excelled in Statics and Dynamics.

The examining inspectors did not report on all the subjects taught. Music and Art they tended to neglect. "Technical subjects" escaped comment: the "Course of Training in the Domestic Arts and Sciences and other practical subjects for Ladies over the age of 17", optional extras, at an extra charge, comprising Dressmaking, Millinery, Plain Needlework and Cutting-out, Clear Starching and Laundry Work, Hygiene and Nursing, Household Management, Cookery—Miss Williamson noted that everyone had survived who had eaten the puddings which other girls had cooked—Book-keeping and Shorthand. Yet Needlework seemed to be thought important, for it was heavily staffed. In 1894 Mlle Lava taught it with French, Fräulein Kleberger with German and Miss Adolphsen "of Copenhagen" with Piano. The inspectors, men, may not have understood it.

A Debating Society met at least twice in 1899 and perhaps earlier. It

49 An honorary canon there and writer of its history, for eleven years an assistant master at Barnet Grammar School and for the next fifty-six or so Vicar of Tadlow with East Hatley, near Royston, Hertfordshire.

50 Fellow, and late Professor of French, of King's College, London, for thirty-seven years, till 1926.

decided not to admire Oliver Cromwell but narrowly agreed that women were suited to a medical career. *Tableaux vivants* were performed and *Mrs Jarley's Waxworks*.[51] But drama like debate developed late and slowly. A cantata was allowed in 1885. The Committee had approved of it to help raise funds for St Andrew's Church. It was called *La Gitana*. Ada Roberts's mother, it seems, wrote the words, to music specially composed for the College by Joseph Roeckel,[52] well known to the Victorians for his drawing-room songs. "The stage was . . . tastefully decorated by the inmates . . . the effect . . . extremely pretty . . . the light dresses . . . showed to the best advantage among the foliage . . . the audience was most encouraging" and "the Gypsies' Chorus, with tambourine accompaniment", was "specially admired".

Pretty though it was, the Committee had firmly laid it down "that no costumes or dressing up could be permitted and that this was to be a distinct and invariable rule of the College and that Miss Williamson be so informed". As late as 1899, when a garden fête took place to help finance the building of a Mission Hall, and the elocution class acted scenes from *A Midsummer Night's Dream*, "in a pretty corner of the cricket field", and the choir sang, and the orchestra "seated under the trees . . . played Mendelssohn's lovely strains with such effect that . . . many friends living opposite, who had been prevented from coming, opened their windows to enjoy the music", it was so reviewed as tacitly to indicate that Gladys Dare, playing Bottom the Weaver, did not wear costume, let alone a donkey's head, and that the fairies wore no wings. But within two years the rule distinct and invariable appears to have lapsed.

In the Autumn Term Töpfer's *Der Dichter und der Page* was performed in German and Molière's *Le Médecin Malgré Lui* in French, each a comedy. E. Frampton—E. for Ethel—did a colonel in the one and a peasant in the other.

The mistresses too acted. A girl unnamed reviewed their production in 1897 of Lord Lytton's *Money*. They had secretly rehearsed it, intending a surprise.

It was late in the Michaelmas Term, and, to our great consternation, we could not discover any symptoms of dramatic mania among the mistresses. Morning after morning they came down with their usual severe and noble air, with no signs of a new experiment in hair-dressing, or of rouge or paint about them, symptoms which, in former years, coupled with a sudden and overwhelming interest in the costumes worn by our great-grandfather or our great-grandmother in the portrait, had enabled us to diagnose with

[51] A series of sketches by G. B. Bartlett, 1873–89, where, after hours, wax figures come to life and entertain. Mrs Jarley, a travelling Mme Tussaud, had first appeared in Charles Dickens's *The Old Curiosity Shop* in 1841.

[52] Joseph Leopold, son of Joseph Augustus, the singer and producer of operas. His brother, Augustus, conducted opera in Dresden with Richard Wagner. Brother Edward played and composed for the piano.

unfailing accuracy the Mistresses' play. Now, all that we could assert of the staff was that it was seized with a virulent form of cacoethes docendi, *which, as the Upper Fifth knows, means a desire to instruct. Did we at breakfast, in our most cajoling tones, inform one of the Staff that Anstey's "Vice Versa", or Dickens's "Christmas Carol", would be easy to dramatise, or that Mrs Malaprop would be a suitable part for Fräulein, we were promptly informed, to quote the former, that such remarks did not become a young woman, and before we knew it, the conversation had assumed the form of an* argumentum ad hominem,[53] *which the Upper Third know is the Latin for turning the tables, and we were made to feel that if we* would *write such long essays, and with such careful and abstruse mathematical calculations, the Staff could not possibly give a thought to the dramatic possibilities of Scrooge, or Little Nell or Alice in Wonderland.*

Perchance the bolder among us ventured to remark that the Staff had given plays in former years; but this was met by the unassailable and, as the boys, and sometimes the cricket eleven, say, squashing remark that it was a pleasure *to teach our predecessors. I leave the rest of you to draw the inference. Moreover, to make matters worse, it really was getting near examination time. Problem: Could the Staff set examination papers, correct them, keep us in order, and undertake the staging of a play at the same time? Happy thought! The fittest would survive, and that, of course, would be the play.*

Fräulein Kleberger was Graves, "a melancholy but good-hearted widower"; Miss Roberts, Lady Franklin—"gay dress and powdered hair"; and Mlle Lava, Stout.

The fun of the evening was, needless to say, principally supplied by Fräulein and Miss Roberts, who together sang "The Merry Peasant", that ditty which is so well known in the region of No. 13 and which has so often wakened the mistresses in the dewy morn . . . the collection was very satisfactory, so the charity treasurer was able to congratulate herself. We did have examinations as well, such is the energy of the staff.

The mistresses were spinsters; unlike the school secretary, if they married they retired. Mme Mathis, "Dip. Off. German, Pupil of Liszt", and Mrs A. Arnold either were or should have been widows. Mrs Arnold taught the harp; Miss Mason, with others, the piano. In 1895, when Miss Mason was listed as "Miss E. Mason (Mrs Arnold)", still piano, with *Miss* A. Arnold, harp, the Committee dismissed Mrs Arnold (thus named) "forthwith without assigning cause" and a few weeks later called a special meeting, "information having been received from Germany respecting her husband". The meeting began at 10.30 a.m. Sir Joseph Savory,[54] now Chairman, and Miss Williamson, were then instructed at once to consult

[53] An argument addressed to someone's prejudice or an attack upon his character.

[54] Alderman of the City of London, in 1891 Lord Mayor; and Conservative MP, 1892–1900, for Appleby in Westmoreland.

Sir George Lewis, of Lewis and Lewis, Holborn, Solicitors, and act as he advised. Clearly they lost no time. "An interview was obtained at 11.30", a deleted minute reads. "He considers the information authentic and advised that it should be used to warn the parents whose daughters are being allowed to visit at the house, but that it is not expedient at present to take further action." Miss Arnold the harpist also withdrew. Exactly what it meant and to what risk Mrs Arnold's pupils might have been exposed is not revealed.

Masters were still appointed. Dr Günther retired as "Head Professor of Music". W. Crowther Alwyn was then preferred to Mr Stidolph. F. Everard Hulton quickly followed. Mr Millard, Professor at the Royal College of Music, taught elocution. In 1890 Mr Millard and Mr Cliffe-Forrester were listed as Visiting Mistresses but were Masters again by 1891. Mr Frank Quatremayne, Mr Phayre Loch and Mr Evetts, who was oddly and repeatedly designated "Pupil of Shakespeare", all taught singing. In Music men still ruled, where women mainly helped. But women taught everything else, most of the science and the entire mathematics.

Miss Williamson spoke warmly or hopefully of all but one of her staff, Miss Sugden, who wielded "no influence or authority in the house", lacking "force of character and originality". "Being also a dissenter", she could not fully share in "Advanced Work" (unexplained) and could not be trusted to teach divinity or even history.[55] So pupils might be Jews but teachers not dissent. The Chairman, Mr Bartley, was asked to review her appointment and a few months later he dismissed her.

Distinctions were somewhat blurred between pupils past and present and the staff. Wards, the more capable, took classes, but received no salary; Mary Crabbe came back and stood in for Miss Roberts, away six weeks; and in 1890 a committee of former day-girls helped establish at the school a centre for the London Society for the Extension of (Cambridge, London and Oxford) University Teaching,[56] where ladies living near could sit at the feet of "eminent professors". Magazine: "Another very important addition to our work, and one of which we are justly proud . . . we think we may now hold our own with the first educational establishments in the land. We have a University Lecturer"—Mr John Churton Collins,[57] on Shakespeare

[55] These were not the subjects that she offered: "English, Latin and Euclid" had been named.

[56] Evening courses, which Cambridge pioneered in 1867, then properly organised in 1873, followed by London (in London only) and by Oxford. The participants tended to be middle-class women, more prompted than were most by interest or need, and who could better afford the time and fees.

[57] A combative scholar; though refused a post at Oxford, he successfully agitated till the final honours school of English was established there in 1893; friend of the poet Swinburne; a would-be Sherlock Holmes, collaborating once with Sir Arthur Conan Doyle; and a well-known visiting lecturer at many schools for girls. In 1908, having taken drugs enabling him to sleep, he fell into a dyke at Oulton Broad, thus drowning.

and his times—"as well as Science, Greek and Elocution Classes." Elocution, Greek and Science had been added to the girls' own curriculum, the Science Mr G. S. Newth's Chemistry, his "numerous and beautiful experiments"; the Greek Miss Allnutt's: "and we hope some day that a P.H.C. girl will go from us to one of the colleges at Cambridge or Oxford, and will reflect as much credit on her school as Miss Agnata Ramsay[58] did on hers." Human Physiology was offered too, Astronomy and Music. And a Holiday Sketching Club was formed, where neighbours and old girls won almost every prize.

Pupils won many handsome books, leather-bound, gold-tooled: the Princess Helena, for Advanced Pianoforte, the Evelyn Hilliard, for Scripture and Church Teaching, the Alfred Barrett, for Advanced Mathematics . . . Parent-poet Austin Dobson awarded his, for English Composition. In 1888 he set an essay, titled "No man has less reason to be ignorant of the Science of Geography than the modern Englishman", and a story had also to be told about a Bank of England £5 note. The prize was "a very beautiful book of Illustrated Lays and Lyrics". Frances Lane won. Her Englishmen were restless, they roved the world, desired riches, promoted trade, and therefore peace, which they loved; as soldiers they needed to know about geography, "in order to gain power for themselves and for England"; and they also displayed the "Coolness, Intrepidity and Perseverance" without which it was impossible to travel. A "Sunshine Prize", awarded by Dr Charles Reuben Hale, Bishop Coadjutor of Cairo, Illinois, was presented to the girl with (a) "a sunny disposition and unselfish ways", and who (b) commanded a majority of the combined votes of mistresses and pupils. The girls top of the class earned silver Winchester crosses, if they also avoided order marks all term, and were allowed to keep them if they behaved themselves all year and missed no lessons. And honours boards appeared, one for the names of the first four Heads of School in Ealing, leaving room for many more, the other for those of the more successful scholars.

Field Marshal Lord Roberts, a member of the Council, gave away the prizes on the 8th of November 1899, in a crowded hall bedight with bunting, red, white and blue. Arriving "with military punctuality" he mounted the platform and was greeted with hearty applause and the singing by the girls of "Soldiers of the Queen". Chairman Sir Joshua Savory paid tribute both to him, "great soldier", who had come that day "in the midst of his arduous labours for his Queen and his country", and to all his troops, "those gallant men [they called him Bobs] . . . fighting in England's cause" in South Africa. The war there had broken out in October; within two months Mr Balfour would ask Lord Roberts to conduct it. Sixty-seven years old, he had faced death many a time in India, where a leather pouch

[58] The only candidate placed in the 1st Division of the 1st Class of the Classical Tripos at Cambridge in 1887. Women had been allowed to sit the tripos examinations since 1880 but could not receive the degrees which they had earned till 1948, even later than at Oxford.

between a bullet and his spine had saved his life; and in Afghanistan; but he approached his present task rather anxiously.

I must confess I felt considerable diffidence . . . for although I may consider myself fairly competent as a judge of military proficiency, the training of young ladies is a novel and somewhat perplexing subject, and a Ladies' College is an altogether new sphere of action for me to enter upon. So unequal did I feel myself to the position that I am afraid I should have refused outright were it not that, only a few months ago, a young lady in whom I was interested was admitted by my request to this institution, and I felt that it behoved me to pull myself together and face the ordeal, out of gratitude for the favour accorded to the young lady in question and myself.

Having consented to take part in this interesting ceremony, I thought before I ventured to do so that it would be advisable to learn something more about the Helena College[59] *than could be gained by reading the annual reports. And, being only a man, I deemed that it would be wise to have the opinion of an expert in young ladies' training before committing myself to an expression of my views as to the merits of the establishment. I therefore proposed to the Lady Principal that Lady Roberts and I should pay her a visit. Miss Williamson was good enough to agree, and on our arrival here she most kindly shewed us over the whole place.*

We were greatly pleased with all we saw. The comfort and completeness of the arrangements impressed us most favourably, and, so far as we could judge, the system of education seemed thoroughly practical and useful. We were also gratified to find that, while every attention is paid to intellectual development, the development of the body is not neglected. For, although I am not an admirer of the "new woman", and am old-fashioned enough to consider intellectual and domestic training of supreme importance to young ladies, I quite think that physical training and out-of-doors recreation—which in strengthening the body strengthen the mind as well—are as essential for girls as they are for boys.

The best tests of a system of education are the characters, acquirements and manners of those who have been trained under it. Lady Roberts and I have met many ladies in India who have had the advantage of being educated at the Helena College, and one and all do it the greatest credit.

. . . . .

I am quite sure that you young ladies do not expect me to make you a speech . . . But, perhaps, you will not mind my giving you a very few words of advice . . . more especially to the elder girls—to those amongst you who are about to leave . . . Do not think when your school days are at an end that your education is finished. The more you have learnt here, the better able you will be to appreciate the fact, that your education has only been

[59] A printer's error? An original, still listed, albeit inactive member of the Council, he was no more likely to forget the school's full name than was the school to let the error stand.

begun. Every day you live ought to add to your store of knowledge. And then, the great lesson of life has to be learnt. I earnestly hope that, while strengthening your characters, and developing all that is best in your natures, the teachings of this lesson may be gentle, the discipline not too severe. And I sincerely trust that to each and all of you the future may bring many prizes, and no failures.

Col. Henry St Leger, father of Lilian, proposed a vote of thanks, which Col. Wyndham Hughes-Hallett, father of Emma, seconded. He was sure that the recipients of the prizes would value them a hundredfold more for having received them at Lord Roberts's hands. His Lordship replied:

I came here in some trepidation. I thought the ordeal would be a very severe one, and I am going away delighted and pleased with what I have seen. I shall remember this afternoon as one of the brightest afternoons I have spent for a long time.

Nora Stransom[60] won the prize which he had offered for a patriotic essay, the title to be either "They Never Fail who Die in a Good Cause" or "What Constitutes National Greatness?", a copy of his book, *Forty-One Years in India*—"a prize indeed", the magazine editor wrote, ". . . very eagerly we prepared for it". And the girls were duly stirred, singing more patriotic songs for the benefit of the widows and orphans of the slain and knitting helmets and tam-o'shanters for the men still fighting.

The supply of comforts for the troops was one of many good causes which enjoyed their support. In 1886 they had collected their own money for the local unemployed; and a Dorcas[61] Society, as in many a church, began in 1887 and would last for almost ninety years. Magazine: "At Christmas we had a very interesting distribution of the garments made" and "those most deserving help . . . were each invited to come up to the College for a cup of coffee and their bundle of things." The Royal President, whom the London East End poor were said to see so often as to call her "our Princess", encouraged the Society, which the boarders, at least, wholeheartedly supported, and its work impressed her when in 1888 she gave away more prizes.

The Dorcas Society is in a thriving condition, a larger number of garments of a larger size *having been made last term than ever before. These garments were exhibited . . . The Princess was so delighted with them that she expressed a wish to have some of them for her district in Windsor. Accordingly a box of the nicest things was packed and sent to H.R.H. Miss Williamson received a very kind letter from H.R.H., acknowledging them, to which she says: "I am delighted with the contents of the parcel, and*

[60] Daughter of Stransom, Archer William, Hatter, Tailor and Hosier, Uxbridge, Middlesex.

[61] Dorcas (Greek for the Aramaic *tabitha*, gazelle), *Acts of the Apostles*, ix: 36, made clothing for the poor.

thank you so many times.[62] *It would be most kind if the girls would work for my district. Big and small garments will be most useful. It is very nice of the girls to wish to do something for me. I need not tell you how constantly the college takes up my most anxious thoughts, and how earnestly I pray for its entire success."*

She was pleased too with some embroidered pillow-slips which the girls had made for her own use. "They are beautiful and a real joy to me."

More and more clothing was sewn and sent to the royal home in Windsor Park, or to the East End by way of Lady[63] Jeune, the Marylebone Infirmary and the Kilburn Orphanage. Another orphanage, or the same, got second-hand. The day-girls tended not to do their share. Miss Williamson's "Report on the Charitable Work", Christmas 1891:

The . . . clothing has nearly all been made by the boarders. We think that if the day girls would each bring us one garment a year we might do much for the thousands of ragged, almost naked, fellow-creatures to be found in every district of our great city.

Money was collected for a Children's Holiday Fund, which Lady Jeune had founded and ran—"Will you please thank the students . . . for their kind donation . . . I cannot employ it better than by sending away to the country a poor little boy of eight years old . . . pining for want of fresh air and change"—a Cyprus Society and the St Peter's Church Building Fund. The school helped launch the United Girls Schools' Mission in 1886 and provided a hall for it in Culmington Road in Camberwell, where forty-seven years later a memorial plaque was unveiled, honouring Miss Williamson.

It was factory girls, who lived "such a miserable, uncared-for existence", that the Mission sought to rescue:

They have a club where they meet for instruction, entertainment and callisthenics. When Mrs Veazey [the missioner's wife] visited the College last term she spoke to us about these girls and their dreary lives and asked whether some of us would not write to them, as a letter from a lady and the feeling that someone cared for them was a great help in their struggle to do right.

Some doubt the compassion of the better fed and housed and as the verb "to slum" suggests, newly defined in 1884 as "to visit slums for charitable or philanthropic purposes, or out of curiosity, especially as a fashionable pursuit" (*OED*), the concern of the middle-to-upper class may have sometimes fallen short of the best and purest. But the helped accepted help of their own free will and even welcomed it.

An Association of Old Girls began in 1897. It too supported charities:

[62] The English here, "thank you . . . many times", echoes German idiom.

[63] Since 1891.

the Mission to Seamen, St Agnes's Mission to Young Girls, All Saints' Church at Mile End, the Aged Women's Home at Ealing, the Essex Cottage Homes; and provided the school with a "Science Hall and Gymnasium", commemorating the twentieth anniversary of its Ealing abode. It adopted a hat-band for its own straw hat, which combined "true blue" with the College green and gold, price a shilling. After hats and bands came ties and belts.

The College Magazine included their news. Only seventeen of its first twenty-four issues have survived. Scissors have removed what are likely to have been the more interesting passages. From 1885 to 1890 it appeared each term; till 1899 at best once a year; and more than once its future lay in doubt.

Christmas Number, 1891 *Price 9d.*

Notice to Subscribers

The Editor and Sub-Editors beg to call your attention to the fact that the Magazine does not receive the support it desires or deserves, either in money or manuscript, the former being the more important. It is a farce to call it "The Princess Helena College Magazine" if it is to be the unaided work of two or three of the members. Let us summon up a little esprit de corps, *and not allow ourselves to be beaten by other schools, where the girls manage the magazine entirely themselves. Perhaps you silent and modest people look upon the "unaided members" as "fools" who rush (in this case, into print) where you, dear "angels, fear to tread". Be that as it may, if this lack of interest and money continues, we most solemnly assure you that this number will be the conclusion of the whole matter—an event we should greatly deplore, as the Magazine not only forms a link between girls past and present, but is an interesting record for us to hand down to posterity, thus leaving behind us "footprints on the sands of time".*[64]

Footprints remain, a more faithful record than inspectors could provide, of the school as a family, its warmth, eagerness and seeming innocence, teams, picnics and bazaars. Knowledge it pursued but friendship meant more to the girls than knowledge. Examination honours were aspired to and extolled but they endeared no one to anybody and could seldom guarantee a means of self-support, if needed, bridging school and marriage.

Career opportunities were few. Schools, hospitals, church missions, offered most of the best, before the first world war. The Post Office, other goverment services and banks needed "lady clerks" and "lady typewriters"; department stores: assistants; parents: day-governesses, nannies, bicycle chaperones, at home and on the continent, and walkers-out of dogs—from 18d. an hour to as much as 2s. A living could be scraped from the spinning

[64] Henry Wadsworth Longfellow: "A Psalm of Life", included in his *Voices of the Night*, 1839.

and weaving of silk, millinery, art needlework, the making of pillow-lace, lamp-shades, jewellery, engraving, lithography, heraldic designing, illustrations for children's books, book-binding and repair, woodcarving, table decoration, cookery and the teaching of it, the writing of articles for magazines, correction of proofs, indexing, translation of business letters, the work of secretary or clerk; also music.

Eva Moynihan, governess for a while to the children of Sir Henry Maxwell-Lyte,[65] 3 Portman Square, lived for twenty years in Norway, there translating Bjørnson's prose and verse; came back to England when war broke out; worked as a War Office censor; and wrote and sold a "War-Time Litany" in aid of the Red Cross. In the one year, 1888, Melba Rix, a musician, got a place at the Royal Holloway College;[66] an Arnott Scholarship took Emily Lewis to Bedford College[67] (the only candidate but a worthy mathematician)—BSc. Division I, she would return as staff then teach at the Cape of Good Hope; and Lucy Mitchell, HS88, began to read for her BA at Cheltenham College, Oxford, now St Hilda's. More girls than hitherto studied German or music, or both, in Germany, or French or painting, or both, in France. Gwynne McQueen[68] chose Leipzig, and Violet Conway-Gordon, Mabel Every, May Hilliard and Gertrude Taylor went to Cassel, where most of them or all stayed with Fräulein Jagst, who had lately taught them German and piano and had there established a school and home for English girls, a *Pensionat*, where the comforts and diet were supplied which the English expected, costing "Sixty Guineas a year. Music, Painting, Dancing, extras". The year was divided into three terms: "Christmas, Easter and July".

Impressions of a girl's five months in Cassel were recorded in the Magazine, perhaps by Violet or May. Her Sundays there were jollier than at home. At home she had attended church, morning and evening; and in the afternoon had written letters or read and, if the weather was fine enough, had walked. In Germany theatres and concert-halls opened, the best of plays and operas were performed, evenings were often devoted to a ball, and once, when "a fearful cold on my chest" had kept the writer indoors, Fräulein took the others to an *Eisfest* at the Wilhelmshöhe, the estate in the hills, where stand two castles, then a mile and a half or so outside town.

They drove there in two sledges, and after skating on the lake till it was dark, had café *with another* Pension *in one of the many restaurants there. After dark the lake was illuminated—but as some of the people were rather rough, Fräulein would not let "her girls" skate then. They came home*

[65] Author of histories of Eton College and Oxford University and an original member of the British Academy; his grandfather was the Henry Francis Lyte whose many hymns include "Abide with me" and "Praise, my soul, the King of Heaven".

[66–67] Since 1985 the Royal Holloway and Bedford New, still at Egham, which in 1886 Queen Victoria had opened.

[68] The McQueens Lucy and Gwynne were not sisters.

about ten. Sometimes one of the military bands played, and that heightened the enjoyment; it is so delicious, skating in time to music, especially valses. The fashionable one was "Don Caesar".[69]

. . . . .

We enjoyed our classes very much, and were fortunate enough to get amusing masters and mistresses. Fräulein L., our German mistress, was nice. She knew English very well, grammatically, and could understand anything she read, but her pronunciation of some words was very funny, for instance moustache, mùstache—with the accent on the first syllable, and shoulder, shawlder. Our drawing master was an ex-artillery officer, but greatly preferred being called a "Maître" to a "Hauptmann"; he was one of the most learned and well read I have ever met.

We went very often to the theatre and to concerts. The acting was very good indeed, marvellous good for such a small town as Cassel. It seemed to us so strange that girls should be allowed to go alone to the theatre, and they were just as surprised when told that English girls never went unattended. "Oh!", they exclaimed, "why, if we waited for someone to take us, we should never go at all." The plays and operas began at 6 or 6.30, and were generally over at 9.30; in this way it was much more convenient than in England.

Maud Emerson chose Dresden; Edith Barratt, Berlin; E. N.[70] Rawle, Hanover, then Paris, where Evelyn Michell had stayed with Lina Robinson at it chanced the same *pension*. Ada Roberts taught English at the Kaiserin Augusta Stiftung, Charlottenburg, Berlin, producing *La Gitana* for the Empress[71] and her Court, to their "great satisfaction", with Rumanian pupils dressed in national costume, "thus very prettily representing the Gypsies".

Katie Walker, who had written about the outing to Windsor, left school soon after and was straightaway appointed to a post as junior mistress at Sheffield High School, where her aunt taught scripture, history and English, and then to another, at the Queen's School, Chester, at the same time as the same aunt installed herself as Head—subject: "musical drill"; Elizabeth Coleby, called Lizzie, took a post for a year at the Clergy Daughters' School at Casterton, which had enrolled the sisters Brontë; Isabella, her sister, governessed in Troyes, on the Seine; and the mutinous, idle Ella Skipworth, intelligent and gamesy, was taught how to teach, at the

69 In the German: *Don Cesar*, a comic operetta by Rudolph Dellinger, 1857–1910, including walzes; it was acclaimed at the Carl Schulze Theater, Hamburg, in 1885, then flopped on Broadway.

70 N for Nelson, by which manly name she was familiarly known.

71 Augusta, Princess of Saxe-Weimar, consort of Wilhelm I. She had established the school in 1872 for the daughters of German officers killed in the Franco-Prussian War. The girls wore blue. In 1902 the school moved to Potsdam, Albrechtstrasse 20–24, and there remained till in 1945 the Russians commandeered it.

Cambridge Training College for Women,[72] but left or had to leave after only four terms.

Amy Potter worked in Cyprus, "training native nurses to assist her", was claimed to be the youngest hospital matron in the British Empire, left Cyprus for Jamaica, having now become a judge's wife, then sailed for Singapore, where she continued to do "good work among the natives". Edith Rainier served as a dispenser at the Warneford Hospital, Leamington. By 1891 she had bought herself a farm at Belmont, Manitoba, in Canada. Old Girls' News:

Edith Rainier is leading a most happy and peaceful life . . . She has become a most expert sportswoman, and told us that during the summer months her dinner is generally shot and cooked by her own hands. During the long winter, sleighing, skating and tobogganing take up much of the time.

Rachel Paterson distinguished herself as a hospital matron in Central Africa. Irene Coghill, a Thurso Scot from the Isle of Wight, graduated in Medicine at Edinburgh in 1897; then practised it in Liverpool; in Liverpool she died, aged 32.

Mary, HS90, eldest of the Dobson sisters five and in her last year of school, composed the tune of the hymn sung at the wedding of the Hon. Maud Ernestine Rendel[73] and Henry, Prime Minister Gladstone's third son—an anonymous prize-winning entry—had her father known?—he himself had done the words; wrote songs; in 1896 became London University's second woman Bachelor of Music; then sailed for India, where she stayed for twenty-three years as Warden of the Missionary Settlement for University Women in Bombay, helping to Christianise the women there, Parsees,[74] combating the plague and nursing the sick. Letter to Miss Williamson, 1899:

Plague still goes on here, and it is a rather bad type; at Poona the suffering is awful. I wish it would get better; one gets quite sick at heart with all the suffering. The Parsi doctor under whom I worked two years ago is very friendly towards us. I visit his wife pretty often; they are such a nice family. It was he who gave me permission to distribute anything I liked in the way of Christian literature in Arthur Road Hospital.

Her sister, Margaret, called Daisy, HS93, became an ophthalmologist; Dorothy, HS95, a housemistress at Cheltenham Ladies' College, then Principal in 1920 of the school in Casterton which had taught the Brontës and employed Elizabeth Coleby; Mildred, MA, BSc., BD, Ph.D,

[72] Founded in 1885, the first residential college in England for women intending to teach in secondary schools, Hughes Hall since 1949, an Approved Society of the University of Cambridge, and since 1973 teaching virtually all subjects, to both women and men, including graduates.

[73] Second daughter of the first and last Baron Rendel.

[74] Descendants of Zoroastrian Persians who had fled to India from Moslem persecution in the seventh and eighth centuries.

HS97, served for twenty-five years as Warden of University Hall, St Andrew's; and among these four stood Grace: a gifted writer and painter, who put aside all else to nurse her mother, in her mother's last four years of life.

"Editor's Corner", Easter 1890, gave news of seven girls who had sailed from England for "India's sunny strand", including Jessie Reid. "We have heard a rumour that Jessie, although but sweet seventeen, is engaged to be married." Amy Barnett, another, a civil servant's wife, eased famine there, "with advances of money and grain".

It is a curious sight . . . the people eating their doles of food by the camp fires, and the white-robed landlords . . . making their complaints and having justice dispensed. I travel about on an elephant over jungles and fields, through dried-up rivers, and enjoy the novelty of this life immensely.

Australia took Bessie Gillbanks; Hamilton in Canada, May Baker; Jamaica, Cissie Todd; Johannesburg, Alice Roberts—wives and mothers; and California, a Ramsay called Czarina.

The Dobsons numbered five, as did the Chapmans and the Muddocks. Mrs Muddock, Joyce, pen-name Dick Donovan, poured out detective stories, but still found it hard to pay reduced school fees. And the Spaldings were eleven, a set of seven, then one of four, all of the same and local clan, including May, HS87; Ethel, HS90, extremely bright, who after learning how to teach, with mutinous Ella, became a lecturer in History at Goldsmith's, writing text-books, then Principal of the Bingley Teachers' Training College; Hilda, Headmistress of Queen's Gate School in London, there nicknamed "Spee"—she appointed to the staff a Spalding, Olive; and Muriel, Vice-President of the Dartmouth College of Physical Education, which in 1903 took Emma Hughes-Hallett. But the longest College line was that of Anketell: twenty-one pupils long, from about 1894, with Lucy and Norah, to Jackson, Caroline, in 1979.

Rose McAndrew, HS86, a governess with the Rev. Mr Robert Godfrey-Faussett, Vicar of Cassington,[75] cared for children almost all her working life, but still found time to paint, in her own style and reproducing Turner; Nellie Bulkley made her name with landscapes and church interiors; each posted news from India; Christina Kellner earned a living from her portraits, in London and Paris; Winifred Lawrence exhibited at the Royal Academy; as did Joan Bloxham, who illustrated her own book, *Walks Around London*—she returned to the school and taught there in the two world wars—her sister, Dorothy, was by 1940 Head of the Hansard Office in Whitehall; Dora Sainsbury stained glass windows. Cicely Faussett-Osborne played her violin with an orchestra at the Crystal Palace. Connie Hemsley got her LRAM. Information thins. Allen, M., reads a ledger, left in 1894: the brooch-winning cricketer, thus named, or the Allen, M for

[75] But chiefly employed as a lecturer in Mathematics at Oxford, nearby, where he also lived.

Mary, who would go to gaol three times as a suffragette, establish the Women's Police and Auxiliary Service, campaign for Sir Oswald Mosley's British Union of Fascists, visit Hitler and worship him.

A lonelier eccentric than Mary Allen appeared among Miss Williamson's flock, news of whom was published in 1897:

We had a visit from Ethel Chawner during the Christmas holidays. She is as much interested in her "beasts" as she terms them as ever. Her collection then consisted of two tame owls, a cuckoo, which she had kept all the winter, canaries, thrushes, and many other pets. She has contributed papers to the magazines on natural history, and has presented a beetle to the South Kensington Museum, which has been named the "Chawner" beetle.

Eleven years had now gone by since Ethel had left school or at least since she had dwelt in rhyming verse, *à la* Thomas Hood, upon her little room there, its well-made bed, the cards carefully pinned in patterns on the wall, the pipes "filled with hot air", the cupboard where shoes had to be hunted for, compulsory walks, "each with a dear friend, two and two"—"what a chatter we did make!"—piano practice, decimals, and the wait, "as though on thorns", to hear her place read out in class, "those awful Monday morns". Last verse:

I remember, I remember,
The monitress's round,
The tapping at each bedroom door
To silence ev'ry sound.
Ah, well, it was a happy time,
And now it gives me pain,
To think, however long I live,
It ne'er can come again!
Chawner

The story which unfolded in the College Magazine told of laughter and success; it could no more speak for those who yearned for home or found work boring or too difficult than did the old Annual Report or the new Prospectus. Ethel Chawner seemed to think that her schooldays had been happy; Helena Lowenfeld, a weekly-boarding *externe* in Miss Glatz's hostel, felt wretched, rebelled, and years later, in 1922, when she wrote to her mother from Peking, what she thought she had endured still rankled.

7.6.1922

At 11 I was sent to Ealing, to that unspeakable Miss Glatz. How poisonously I loathed that woman, and everything to do with her disgusting little house, there aren't violent enough words in the language to describe. I learnt nothing during that time, my energies were too fully taken up with active misery. The only thing I lived for were Friday afternoons, and then, for the first time you, as you, had a really definite value, you represented escape from the horrors of the week—do you remember my beseeching you

not to send me back? Ugh—don't let's talk about that beastly time, even now it makes me shudder.

The luxuries of home, at 31 Lowndes Square, may have spoilt Helena. It surprised her to learn that other girls' parents employed no butler, Miss Glatz's meals tasted not at all as good as those prepared by the family cook and, when she misbehaved, she did not enjoy being made to sleep alone in a room on the top floor, out of reach of those who might follow her and stray. But when she changed from weekly board to full her lot improved.

When I went into the College all was different. There for the first time I felt my power, and really enjoyed myself. It was a glorious discovery to find that I was stronger than most people there, and could make the other girls do as I liked. Of course my undisciplined, erratic childhood bore fruit, and I was absolutely unruly . . .

The letters which she wrote in her last two years of three clamour less for release than for one garment or another which someone has forgotten to pack, or is better suited to the weather or events, or needs to be washed or mended or replaced. Staff are unfair; her innocence feels injured. A request has been refused, so will her "own little darling" mother please drop all and intervene. She dismisses doubts about her social class. Animosity persists, but she tinges it with glee, and in her last term the thought of being sent to another school, even to Miss Beale's Cheltenham, becomes for a while unbearable.

2.12.1900

Oh! *the reception last night, I almost died when my turn came to play, I made frantic mistakes but it is all over now, thank goodness.*

Please don't forget to send my white dress as soon as possible . . . and also the bazaar things, them also as soon as you can get them, we must *make this old bazaar a success.*

Please also send me a pair of white silk gloves and one of cotton as we are supposed to have gloves for prizegiving, and also white apparels,[76] *so they* must *come before next Saturday.*

27.1.1901

The sweets came this morning and—worse luck—I had to give them up.

. . . . .

My room looks much nicer with the shelf on the wall, could you send a few long scraggly calendars?

It is frantically *windy here today, our hats were nearly blown away this morn, my long feather had a fine time of it!*

Now darling goodbye with very very best love.

Ellie

P.S. I should very much like to see the Queen's funeral!!!!!

[76] A collar, not unlike the ornamental cloth worn by a celebrant priest, overlapping the neck and shoulders of a dress.

28.1.1901

My own little darling,

Of course I should like to come home very much indeed, but M.W. won't let me the—oh dear how wild *I am, do write and see if you can persuade her, say you must have me to get some mourning and go to a theatre or* some*thing very important, oh* do.

. . . . . .

It is absolutely against C.S.[77] *to do my exercises, I'm quite strait [*sic*] now so please say I needn't.*

[No date]

M.W. won't give me my sweets although I did give them up, some others had theirs today but I didn't have mine, please will you either send some more or write and ask why I haven't had these, as I didn't bring any back, and she said I could have them, she is a mean old thing and we do *want them so badly, so you will, won't you, darling, oh do because this is downright* mean.

31.1.1901

Please send the carriage for us at 3.30 so I shall be home in time for tea.

. . . . . .

I am trying to keep accounts as you asked me to but good gracious they are muddling. What with having holes in my pocket! to lose 6d. bits through and paying for odd things my brain gets fairly addled.

Tell Baby[78] *I am bringing her knife, I brought it here by mistake, have mine come back from being ground yet?*

. . . . . .

The hockey pitch is like playing on a mud pudding, we sink in mud, and when we move we carry half the field with us.

We miss the girls who have left very much.

In 1900 her father, Henry,[79] a Jew from Austria's share of Poland, had had the Apollo Theatre built in Shaftesbury Avenue, which he now owned and where he got to know the actresses.

3.2.1901

Oh! how I wish Papa had never built the Theatre, one of my friends has of course got the idea that you and Pups are not ladies or proper people, and she has been told not to get very intimate with me, this naturally aggravates me, her people don't in the least object to me, *they object to the*

77 Her mother was a Christian Scientist.

78 Margaret, her younger sister, who became a child psychiatrist, founded the Institute of Child Psychology in London and devised play therapy and diagnostic tests for disturbed children, which Dr Margaret Mead, the American anthropologist, then borrowed and adapted.

79 Originally Heinz Löwenfeld. In 1891 he had invented, and sold, a beer free of alcohol, Kop's Ale.

Belle of Bohemia and all that, comprenez-vous, please don't say anything about this to M.W. will you.

. . . . . .

The curate from St Peter's is coming next Saturday to give us some lectures on early Church History, interesting*!!! Happily they will be in the dark, so we can doze.*

. . . . . .

Four girls have measles now and perhaps more soon.

. . . . . .

M.W. has given me to do this afternoon, instead of reading, to answer some questions on "Stories and Teaching on the Litany", what *a lot of good it'll do me, how* little *people understand me.*

7.2.1901

I left my precious black tie at home, please will you send it, and I did bring home my fox fur because I can't find it anywhere.

On Tuesday when the snow was thick we were allowed to go out and have a snow fight, it was lovely fun, only our hands got rather cold.

. . . . . .

Please will you write to Bryanston Street and ask why they haven't sent me any "Sentinels"[80] *yet?*

. . . . . .

Eda Dalton is a little fool and Fräulein[81] *(here) is a small fat* brute, *how I loathe her.*

. . . . . .

Please will you send me a few China ornaments, mine are all getting broken, I like the figures with China lace on them.

[10.2.1901?]

My dear Mumie I do not want *any painting lessons, they are not the least necessary, please darling need I have them? Now I have asked very nicely and really I don't want them at all, because in the first place they won't teach painting unless the girls can draw and as I can't draw any more than I can fly, and another thing I should have to have it on Saturday morning, and then I should never have time to do my prep, or practice or anything, so now I hope you see how* horrible *it would be, only the Upper V do painting and then have to know about perspective. None of the little ones do, so please need I have them, oh* do *say no.*

When you send the boa please will you send the fox fur too, I miss it these cold days.

. . . . . .

80 *The Christian Science Sentinel*, published since 1898.

81 Fräulein Lähne, who had produced the German play.

I hope you won't be angry about the painting, I want to please you but you choose the most impossible things.

. . . . .

I am going in for both violin and piano exams, and will fail in them both.

14.2.1901

My own little darling,

Thanks awfully for the perfectly angelic *little Valentine you sent me, it* is *sweet, I have stuck it in my room.*

Hurrah no painting lessons!

I have got my yellow fur but not the black one. Auntie Bea hasn't got my glasses, *it's my black woollen gloves I want, the silk ones are so thin, and they'll get worn out in no time if I have to wear them every day.*

. . . . .

*Yesterday some of the girls went to see "Twelfth Night", they (Bobby) wouldn't take me because they said I had extra holidays—*rot!

Might she take a party of friends to the Apollo? Miss Williamson and Miss Roberts would have to be included. She has asked her mother to write them each a letter.

17.2.1901

My own little darling,

I have told the 10 girls and they are nearly off their heads; it must *come off, have you written to M.W. yet, oh* do *and tell her, she* must *let us come, coax or kiss her, or do what you like.*

. . . . .

Just now it started snowing violently, but now like an idiot it has stopped.

Write soon.
Love by the ton,
Ellie
Please send some stamps.

24.2.1901

My own little darling,

Have you received "the detailed account of my conduct" yet? If you have I hope you have enjoyed it.

. . . . .

Yesterday morning when I was in the middle of dressing to come to the Theatre, in comes a mistress (of course I was in someone else's room) and informed me that I was to go downstairs, when I got down I went into the Teachers Sitting-room to find a whole array of mistresses and five other girls there, M.W. was sitting at the head of the table surrounded by books;

she (M.W.) then starting, jawing me about C.M.s,[82] *general conduct, Insubordination, etc. etc. etc., and came to the conclusion that I was excited; after this the other girls were sent out, leaving me alone with them! Billy said I would have to apologise to every blessed one of them (I thought promptly that 9 apologies would be rather a business) then she (Billy) bunked and I had to apologise to them: I first went up and made a handsome apology to Greggles*[83] *and was told at the end I hadn't given her any trouble (that was damping) and then I went round the lot, my eye! it was tedious, they all had something to say, Maddy*[84] *couldn't see the seriousness of it, and was quite jubilant, as she told me how many C.M.s she had bestowed on my luckless head.*

And all that after I had been trying not to get any. What *a lot of good it is!!! That jawing almost squashed all desire for no C.M.s out of my head and made me despise the mistresses. They have no more idea how to make me better than the people at home have. Heigh ho, I suppose I'll die some day.*

Miss Glatz is here but we haven't looked at each other at all.

. . . . .

You needn't write me a jawing letter, because it won't do any good. I've had my full share, and really I have not been any worse than usual.

28.2.1901

Needless to say I am in another row! but not so very serious. Flossie[85] *and I lagged behind the others in the walk this afternoon, and lo and behold there were M.W. and M.R. [Miss Roberts?] taking a little stroll, naturally they were rather excited, and told Moses*[86] *(who was taking the walk) to put us each down 3 C.M.s.*

When we got in both of us and Eda Dalton who had also been fooling, were called out and told not to mix with the others today, so we all separated to do our prep, etc., and this evening will be Amen to it most probably.

There is a most awful animal *here who calls herself a mistress, namely Miss Moseley, this morning before all the day girls she absolutely forgot herself and her position, and downright insulted me, she said* she *would*

[82] (Bad) Conduct Marks.

[83] Miss Florence Gregory, who left in 1906 to be headmistress of four fee-paying schools all at once, a Froebel kindergarten, a Lower School, an Upper Commercial and a girls' secondary, attached to and helping to support the Whitelands Teacher-Training College. The girls' secondary has survived, as Lady Margaret, at Parson's Green in Fulham. Miss Gregory's gift to her Ealing colleagues and the girls: an oak arm-chair so girl-proof robust that it has yet to be destroyed or structurally damaged.

[84] Miss Mabel Madden, were it not that she had left in 1898. It could be, what at times happened, that someone else had inherited her nickname.

[85] Florence von Keudell, HS06. Helena and Flossie once walked out of a class and complained to Miss Williamson that their teacher could not teach.

[86] Miss Mildred Moseley, there on trial, in her second and last term.

expel me and that I was like a board school child. She had no right at all *to say such things, and especially before the day girls.*

I decline to come back next term if she is here, I can't help it darling, and I mean *it, I* won't *stand her, the whole school hates her like poison, she absolutely goes too far, I think she gave me 6 C.M.s this morning for positively* nothing.

You can't imagine what a d—. she is, how she is loathed, my eye!

Miss Glatz is all right, she came up to my room before she went and I had to kiss her 3 times, it was pretty bad.

. . . . . .

My dear Mama we don't indulge in red marks for conduct and if we did I shouldn't ever get any, with that brute Moses in existence, she trys [sic] *to give as many as she can.*

7.3.1901

Thanks for your letter, but you did not send any stamps.

. . . . . .

I think I must be getting quite good, I have only had 2 C.M.s this week and both silly ones, last week I had 9.

It is all right about my friend now, we have talked it over, and she is quite all right and is very fond of me.

The San is quite full now, I wonder how many more will get it?

I don't think I shall pass in my piano exam but there is just a ghost of a chance, and I hope I shall in the fiddle.

Don't you think it is funny how children quarrel and think it is going to be kept up for years, and the next day it is quite all right again?

I am making new friends and I think more girls like me than used to.

You will be pleased to hear, that I wear my glasses much less now, the journals have had a good effect on me, and since this last bust-up I think I have been better altogether, anyhow *I* feel *much gooder since I have heard of science!!!!*

. . . . . .

P.S. How old shall I be when I am presented to the King!!!

24.3.1901

Last night Miss Roberts gave a lecture on the Queen's Funeral and the Opening of Parliament, illustrated with photographic lantern slides.

On Tuesday we are going to have a lacrosse match of Oxford and Cambridge, of course I am Oxford and I hope you are too.

31.3.1901

Love to all, including the stuffed dog.

28.4.1901

My own little darling,

Well here I am settled again. How are you? glad to get rid of naughty Ellie, eh?

. . . . . .

28.4.1901

Our new form-mistress[87] *is rather nice, one good thing is that she is pretty strict, which is much better than a slip-shod person—I am next to her so far at meals.*

[2.5.1901?]

Nothing has happened except a cricket match between day girls and boarders, we won and beat the day girls into fits.

. . . . . .

My dear how on earth am I going to wear a hat with a blue bow on it with a bright flame colour dress? it would *look charming! I suppose the proper white one will arrive in course of time.*

. . . . . .

Can you send me 6 tennis balls please (like last year) (they needn't be the very best ones) and please can they be blackly marked with my name in full.

9.5.1901

Please will you send me these ties (I don't seem to have any), a yellow one (which Baby has), a pink, light mauve, and navy blue, I shall want them very soon for the blouses and they only cost 1/1½.

. . . . . .

This week I was 11th in class, not so bad, I hope to be read out before long.

. . . . . .

My eyes are getting bad, I am trying to use the glasses less but they are very necessary.

11.5.1901

No don't waste any more money on my eyes, if I have to be blind in the course of life I will.

16.5.1901

The other night I surpassed myself in cricket, I made 15 runs!! (My top score before was 1.)

19.5.1901

So you are "at it again", you raised my hopes saying "stamps enclosed" and lo and behold when I go to look for them . . .

. . . . . .

It's just my luck, last week, of course as I didn't want any C.M.s I had 'em by the ton, the week before when I didn't care much I scarcely had any, really I think it pays most not to try.

The girls don't go by tram they go by train, they are stuck in at this end, then someone meets them at the other end . . .

. . . . . .

[87] Miss G. H. Fisher, BA, who followed "Moses".

Nothing has happened, the balls and racket have come and they are ripping, thanks awfully.

23.5.1901

For pity's sake send the carriage early, we have tons of shopping to do.

[Misdated]

Can you get 2 tickets for "The Only Way"? In the dress circle, please, I want them for Bobby and Billy . . . Bobby wants to go so much, of course she hasn't asked for them.

Duckie I am afraid I must *have some more money, because a new subscription was arranged yesterday, and there is still Miss W.'s birthday and the flowers for the form to come. Shall I ask M.W. for it or will you send it?*

Also will you send my camera, with a fresh set of plates, I want it very badly.

6.6.1901

The Gymnasium Fund is going to be started and we are all to give as much as possible. At the end of term we are all going to be given a card to collect, and we have to get as much as we possibly can, you and Pups will help won't you? We absolutely must *have the Gym.*

. . . . .

Miss Roberts has begun to produce *As You Like It.*

I am still Touchstone and probably shall be in the end, you are going to make up a huge *party to come and see it because that is going to be the nucleus of the fund.*

Next week we are going to see "As you like it" at the Botanical Gardens, don't forget.

9.6.1901

Tomorrow is a large reception for all the day girls and boarders under 14, I am playing, I don't care a hang, but I am thankful it's not the fiddle (so are all the others!!!)

20.6.1901

I know Miss Roberts is perfectly ripping. I think she still believes I have a heart after all (a thing which very *few people do) but she says that I must* show *that I am ashamed of myself, but that's the worst part, I* cannot *show it and never shall be able to. I am so used to bottling up my feelings that I can't get out of it.*

23.6.1901

Nothing has happened. I hope we are going to the baths tomorrow, it is time.

27.6.1901

My own little darling,

We have very little time to write as we have just come back from a bazaar in aid of the church or something, we had great fun, I asked M.W. for 3/-. I hope you don't mind, I am now utterly bankrupt not possessing a single sou, please send some, and you will be pleased to hear that in obedience to your injunction had only half an ice!

1.7.1901

Tomorrow we are going to have a fire-practice, isn't it lovely, they are *such fun, especially going down the shoot.*

. . . . .

We went to the baths today, they were very nice indeed.

4.7.1901

My own little darling,

Thank you for your letter, I am glad you liked the things, but I did not work the mat, I bought it at the bazaar.

This afternoon we had a match with Wycombe Abbey and beat *them by 18 runs, we are now the cock of the cricket playing schools, being almost the only ones to have ever beaten them, isn't it awfully nice, Wyndham Hughes-Hallett made 35, and another girl 22, good scores for girls.*

. . . . .

I went in for the tennis tournament, I let myself be beaten by a small kid, but I gave her the games because it made her happy, . . it is not so bad as being properly beaten.

7.7.1901

I am now going to make a request bang out, I want to stay here and not to leave!! I know I have been a disgrace to the Col. and to the family, but it has done me a great deal of good and it would be very ungrateful to Miss Roberts and M.W. after they have taken such a lot of trouble and sacrificed themselves for me, if I left after their allowing me to stay, Miss Roberts is an absolute angel, *you don't* know *how nice she is and how she has helped me; and another thing, anyhow you will have to pay for next term as you haven't given notice and to pay for two schools would be arrant waste; Cheltenham will cost more than here probably and there I shall be just a unit among several hundreds while here both the heads are interested in me and do their best for my welfare, let me have next term as another trial, I don't deserve it but "therefore Jew though justice be thy plea consider this, that in the course of justice none of us shall see salvation", etc. (forget rest).*

[Misdated]

I have some good news for you, so far I have had no *C.M.s this week and don't intend to get any more.*

You must not be very *disappointed when you hear I have failed in my*

piano exam, I know it will be a disgrace, but it's my own fault, I have been an utter idiot, wasting my time like old boots, but there's nothing to do now but work very hard for the remaining days, which I am doing.

. . . . . .

Hurrah this time fortnight I shall be at home!

. . . . . .

Love by the ton
from
Ellie

[Misdated]

I suppose I am coming home on Saturday? I had better, it's no good going in the middle of the week, and I have made up my mind to leaving Miss Roberts and delay will be hard to bear, it is quite hard enough already.

. . . . . .

It is awfully good of you to let me have another chance and to send me to a place like Chel., believe me I really am grateful and will try to get on there.

She is still Touchstone in *As You Like It*.

My dress is a treat, you will laugh when you see it, but for goodness sake applaud everything, good, bad or indifferent, I do hope it will be a success, dear old Bobby has taken such an amount of trouble over it, I hope to goodness no one will forget their parts.

Only one more day to see Bobby in! I suppose I can come and see her, she is *so nice, you would like her awfully.*

. . . . . .

Do you know what house I am to be in at Chel. and what form, please tell me some particulars, I hope I shall not make a mess of that school, is Miss Beale nice?

. . . . . .

Now tata darling till Saturday.
Love by the ton
to all
from
Ellie

Cheltenham
3.11.1901

Miss Roberts promised to send me her photo (!!!!!) and it hasn't come yet.

16.3.1902

I enclose a letter that came the other day from Ealing, Mamma dear I do *want to give Bobby and Billy a nice present, if we can't afford it, let me sell something, because after all, they were awfully good to me, and I had a very good time there.*

Mrs Lowenfeld now took a house in Cheltenham, which enabled Helena to live at home. Her husband, an astute cad, having somehow proved that their marriage had not been lawfully contracted, a charge of bigamy against him failed to stick and it recoiled, as Helena explains, upon his daughters.

25.3.1902

Aunt Bea wrote saying he threatened to prove us illegitimate, nice *sort of thing to do to your children . . . It's a pity that you can't marry me and* roast *that* Devil.

Her mother too would have to suffer her rebuke. "Consider", she is told, in the letter from Peking, "what a grotesque childhood we had; until I was 13 . . . my parents were incessantly fighting, the one swearing at the other . . . nothing was secure . . . we lived incessantly on the verge of a volcano."

But school settled her—more a refuge than a cage—and having left Miss Williamson for Miss Beale when she was 14 and Miss Beale for the London Hospital School of Medicine when she was 20, she became Dr Helena Wright, the physician-missionary wife of a missionary surgeon. She wrote many books pioneering birth-control. Her first, *The Sex Factor in Marriage*, appeared in 1930, and her last, *Sex and Society*, in 1968. Eighty-five years old, and still ten short of her allotted span, she lectured in India.

Whatever the truth may have been about Miss Glatz, as it had still seemed to Dr Wright aged 34, let alone about Fräulein Lähne or Miss Moseley, as it had seemed to her aged 13, the women staff meet happily united in the College Magazine, exchanging news. It is June 1897; half a year has passed since they performed on stage. Promoted or married or employed overseas or returned from whence they came, departed colleagues remain in touch. "Fräulein Jagst", they read, "has a charming house at Lausanne for English girls . . . *Riantes Rives* . . . Madame de Rohden (Mlle Tallois) lives in Paris and has two charming boys whom she is bringing up quite in the English fashion. Fräulein Kleberger had a very interesting meeting last summer in the Black Forest with Madame Pollisson (Mlle Bertholon)." She too owned a beautiful house, in Bad Nauheim, for *Kur* guests in the summer, including Miss Williamson and Miss Roberts, and for girls in the winter, learning German and music. "Mrs Westwood (Miss Orridge) paid us a visit a few months ago, looking as bright and pretty as ever. She said she had little time for singing, except lullabies to her children, whom she is bringing up quite in accordance with the College rules." Miss Cruickshank had charge of a school in Calcutta: *La Martinière*. Mrs Boggs (Miss Winlaw) enjoyed a second honeymoon in Ireland.

Miss Heppel—English, Latin and Mathematics—was adored, and heavy must have been her luggage when she left, after only three years, with "a very handsome desk" from her colleagues, "beautifully fitted", a silver pencil inside it from Miss Williamson, and from her form the works of

Tennyson, in thirteen volumes, with a large photograph album engraved with her initials.[88]

What staff and pupils thought and felt about their Lady Principal, their writings leave unglimpsed. An article from somewhere, dated 1894, cut out and put by, makes clear that she was loved and admired:

What the College is today—a success beyond expectation—is due mainly to the influence of . . . Miss Margaret Williamson . . . It is unnecessary for us to praise her. A visit to the school, a chat with the teachers and pupils soon discover that she is not only a born organiser and a disciplinarian of high degree, but that she brightens every place with the happiness of her charming personality . . .

Yet something was amiss, for in February 1902 Miss Williamson and Miss Roberts each resigned, Miss Williamson aged only 54. Miss Roberts left Form VI her beautiful Sheraton bureau (it appears to have stood in Miss Williamson's study). Together they founded a new school, St Cuthbert's, in Southbourne near Bournemouth, which lasted thirty-five years in their and other hands. Its building, called Foxholes, next served as a guest-house for the Workers' Travel Association, till in 1983 it was demolished, making room for flats. The Council had paid Miss Williamson no recorded tribute. Sir Joseph was going to decide about a memorial fund; but nothing happened. Essay prizes continued to honour her name. In 1911 she attended an Old Girls' Week-End; in 1920 the School's One Hundredth Birthday Pageant; and in 1932, two years after her death, about fifty of her sometime pupils saw a tablet to her memory unveiled at St Peter's Church in Ealing. Miss Roberts, with whom she had come and gone, died in 1937.

[88] By 1899 she had become Headmistress of Kensington Park, a Church of England High School for Girls, when it was three years old; it then had five to go. A new Kensington Park School, unconnected with the first, began in 1988.

The young Miss Parker

Photograph retrieved from obscure cupboard.

Fire Brigade VIII — not yet XIII — in 1903

Red path, lime walk, bicycles propped where on Tournament
Day, in sun and shade, summer frocks competed.

Nellie Anderson

Flossie von Keudell

Prince

Theodora Boys

Kathleen Allen

Nellie, Theodora and Kathleen all at Newnham while in Lithuania Flossie's brilliance dimmed.

Kathleen Paget

Sybil Isaacson

Georgie Finch

Phyllis Challoner

Sybil: Secretary to Antarctic ship *Discovery*. Georgie — Georgiana — daughter of George, kept pigs and hens in Somerset. Sybil and Phyllis unwed. Phyllis in 1941 Chairman of the Catholic Feminist Society.

Violet in Fairyland, Cantata, 1906

Top left to bottom right: Mildred Dew, who wed Lord Hailsham; Gretchen Mack, from Ludwigsburg, Fairy Queen; Nina Hammond, a Bombay Cathedral bride — at Sticklepath in Devon she would run "The Rising Sun", a charming alehouse; J. Peake — Janet or Josephine — as Violet; Elsie Mogford, who danced — applause, though forbidden, raised the roof; Sylvia Campbell; and H. Brown.

Fairies wearing flowers and petal hats

Standing: Cecily Read: Principal of Bedford Physical Training College; Margaret Seymour, daughter of Sir Horace, Deputy Master of the Royal Mint. Seated: Eve Gardener; from Vancouver: Isabel Bell-Irving.

Madge Beaumont

Joan de Carlies Blackader

Mildred Dew

Bertha Burleigh

Madge: married heart and soul to her school as Bursar. Bertha: artist, war correspondent for *The Queen* and *Daily Telegraph* reporter.

Cecily Read

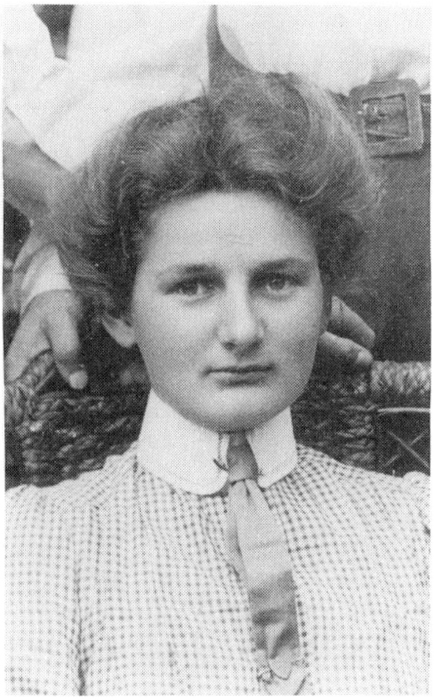

Katie Espinasse

Freda Hammond

Joyce Dennys

Katie, French at Oxford, taught at Ranchi in India; like Cecily, unwed. Joyce, artist, humorist, wrote and drew and was published till well into her nineties.

Elizabeth Brookman

Molly Mellanby

Faith Heslop

Kathleen Gamble

Elizabeth and Faith were life-long friends. Molly—with Kathleen at Newnham, like Kathleen a spinster—worked at Roedean, borstals, gaols.

Dorothy Pearson

Joan Dening

Eileen Hill

Kathleen Sissmore

Dorothy and Eileen nursed, Eileen daughter of the admiral, Hill, G.W., and clergyman's wife in Travancore. Lt.-Gen. Lewis Dening's Joan wed a major and in Kenya raised cattle, grew fruit. Kathleen Sissmore, Mrs Archer, who in MI5 initiated Sir Roger Hollis, nearly rumbled Kim Philby there, says Philby, in *My Silent War*. But rumble him she did; he was only almost right.

Joyce Rowley

Joan Rawson

Barbara Carden

Nancy Johnston

Joyce: the writer R.A. Dick; with husband to Nyasaland, where she left him for Canada and its climate, till Scotland reunited them. Joan: St Thomas's masseuse. Barbara: Dr Sharp, physician, with clergyman-missionary husband, in Iran.

Hats on a picnic — Miss Pode sits middle top

Artistic and Literary Society visits Windsor Castle

Constance Swetenham

Nancy Blankley

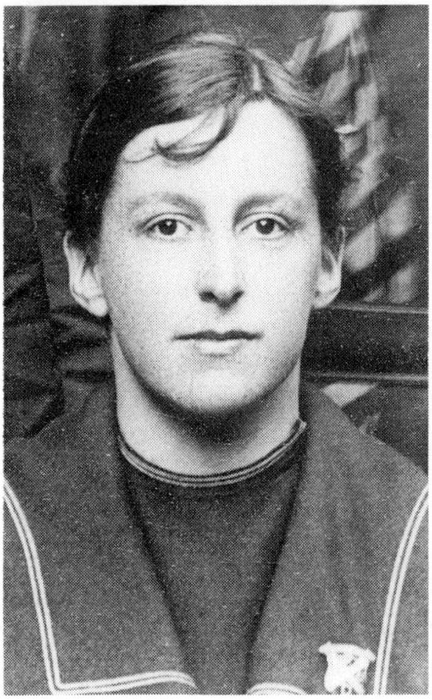

Helen Johnson

Sybil Carden

Nancy, athlete, died aged 35, after long illness. Helen, mighty batsman, MBE after thirty years with MI5 — had been interviewed there wearing school uniform — unwed, a life-long friend of Violet Baddeley, her junior at school, where Miss Parker disapproved. Sybil, from Ireland: wife of the general, Francis Rome.

Gertrude Trevelyan
Joanna Brinton
Dodo

Mary Savery
Roy
Faith Malden

Beth Ealand
Lissa Birchall-Wood
Violet Baddeley

Gertrude: scholar and novelist, killed in her bath when her house was bombed; Mary: with Gertrude at LMH, in Toronto a clergyman-headmaster's wife; Beth: music and welfare, MBE, unwed; Joanna: Eton housemaster Hubert Brinton's niece; Lissa: taught biology and violin; Dodo: a Cambridge first, Durham lecturer in French; Faith, who would fly; Violet: Barbara Allen's inseparable friend, as well as Helen's.

Left to right: Dodo, A.N. Other, Constance Henson, Beth Ealand, Sybil Carden and Gwendoline — Gubby — Witham.

Helena Appleby, Barbara Allen, Agnes Smith, Eileen — Jelly — Semple, Gubby again, May Hamilton, Marjorie Newell, with — below — Muriel Secker and Helen Swain, keeping up with the times in the 1920s.

Barbara Allen

Letter
29.11.1988

Was I — am I — the only one who from first to last loved PHC with a passionate life-time of love? Of course I was a special case because I was so unhappy at home that school became my wonderful freedom. But it was a school of such goodness . . . such idealism, such purity, with so much laughter and happiness . . . we shall never see its like again.

Rachel Powell

Veronica Philip

Lavender Norris, 1923, fairest of all whom staff could then remember. Killed, flung from a car driven by a boy-friend's friend, newly met, on the Brooklands race-track, a year after leaving school, aged 20.

Betty Stone, 1923

Margaret Summerford, 1929 — *sic transit gloria*: the cally-collar shed.

The retired Miss Parker

Portrait commissioned by her Old Girls. Went astray in Temple Dinsley. Found buried under stairs.

Miss Williams — Bill, Willy Wirtus, Crash Bang — Miss Parker in one of her hats — could be smiling? — and Miss White.

Presentation of the watch. Lady Hailsham and Miss Prain. End of chapter, end of story.

Chapter Six

1902–1931

On the 21st of March 1902 Miss Mary England Parker was appointed to replace Miss Williamson: aged only 34, the daughter of the Vicar of Wykeham, in Hampshire; educated privately, then at Newnham College, Cambridge; a historian, she had taught her subject at two High Schools for Girls: East Liverpool and Dulwich; stood bolt upright, seeming six feet tall; was intensely patriotic: awarded a ten-shilling prize for the writer of the best essay titled "Builders of the British Empire" and encouraged the girls to support the Empire League, a pen-friend link between Motherland and Colonies; mistrusted Roman Catholics, disapproved of Americans,[1] and would loathe Germans, after war had broken out, if not already, when even the daughters of the church were helped to find it difficult to love their neighbours all; worshipped her Prince, a handsome brown retriever who, if her old Old Girls do not too much exaggerate, collected dust like a rug that had gone without a shake all year; but could not stand grumblers, understanding though they found her about draughts and boiled beef and carrots.

Princess Helena decided to adopt a new school motto: *Fortis qui se vincit*—strong is she who conquers herself; and approved of the "school flower" emblem which Miss Parker now proposed: the genista or broom. Like her mother in politics, the late Queen, she might advise, warn and encourage, but seldom if at all did she interfere. Miss Parker ran the school unhindered from on high and Sir Joseph, her Chairman, gave no trouble. A secretary dealt with transport, pocket money, stationery, books . . . Miss Parker paid the servants, conferred with the architect, reported on the fabric of the building, arranged for boilers to be repaired and invited tenders for the supply of food. Her work, like Miss Williamson's before her, included much that would now fall to a bursar.

Finance caused some anxiety. The mortgage on the buildings had increased, from £6,000 to £7,600, the bank account was heavily overdrawn, and the drainage had to be improved. But a good intake of pupils was assured and, as Sir Dighton Probyn said, who kept King Edward's Privy Purse, declining to renew Queen Victoria's subscription of £50 a year, it could rely on fees.

Advertisements were published in *Paton's List of Schools*, *Broad Arrow* and other Armed Services gazettes, *Kelly's Post Office London Directory*, *The Times* and *To Ealing and Uxbridge by Tube and Car*.

[1] "They call themselves God's own country, but they are not God's people, I think."

Miss Parker, gliding, if not erect

Joyce Dennys, Mrs Evans, 1983

Boarders filled all or enough beds. But wards (whose mothers now paid nothing) appear to have become more difficult to find. Princess Helena asked Miss Parker to accept two daughters of officers who had drowned aboard the *Titanic* when it sank. Their schoolmates were asked not to question them about the sad event. But neither arrived. And only seven wards were listed in Miss Parker's first twelve years. They included Iris Sneyd, who cost her mother, of 10 Douro Place in Kensington, a 10s. fine when she missed a whole first day of term; Eileen, daughter of Hill, G. W., Rear-Admiral; and Mildred Dew, who as Mrs Lawrence would wed Lord Hailsham at Westminster Abbey in 1929, then head the Board of Governors. The fathers of other girls, all but the clergy, paid full fees: professional and businessmen of every kind; officers; and plain gentlemen who could live on unearned income.

A Mrs Wahab's daughter was refused a place, even though two weeks later Miss Parker had to work out how many fewer staff could be employed, so as to balance the accounts. But foreigners less foreign were from time to time admitted: Europeans, like the Florence von Keudell, called Flossie, whom Helena Lowenfeld had begun to lead astray, Margherita Maas, daughter of the Consul for the Netherlands, and the

sisters Mack, Margaretha, called Gretchen, and Elfrieda, from Ludwigsburg near Stuttgart.

Flossie in particular felt thoroughly at home. Though her late father was a German Baltic baron army captain, her mother was a Scot, whom Sir William Dunbar, a rich civil servant,[2] had befriended—he paid school fees for the daughter and a son. Enrolled in 1899, she boarded for most of the next eight years; became Head of School in 1906; captained all the teams; played Antonio in *The Merchant of Venice* and was Rose Queen in the pageant; excelled as a painter and in verse and prose; and composed an account of what it meant, and ought to mean, to uphold the school's new motto:

Who on power sets his aim
First must his own spirit tame;
Act, think, speak, live up to it,
Fortis qui se Vincit.

. . . . .

When the alarm goes off at morn
And lessons lie in heaps forlorn,
How cold and dismal is the dawn,
Your bed how nice, so snug and warm,
Fortis qui se Vincit.

You wish that buzzing thing would cease,
And let you sleep on still in peace.
The bedclothes round your head you crease,
While soothing dreams your prep. release,
Fortis qui se Vincit.

At last you wake and rub your eyes,
Then with a mighty spring you rise.
Your sponge and jug watch in surprise;
They've not yet learnt to realise
Fortis qui se Vincit.

First gaily to the baths you go;
The water's one degree from snow;
You shrinkingly insert a toe,
Then take a valiant plunge—oh! oh!
Fortis qui se Vincit.

At games, play like a stubborn mule;
Do all you can, keep calm and cool;
Think of the honour of your school;
Pass well, and don't forget the rule—
Fortis qui se Vincit.

[2] Second son of the seventh baronet of Mochrum, Wigtownshire, and descended from the Dunbars, Earls of Moray. Registrar-General for England 1902–09. Although married, he had no children of his own.

The Hockey Cup you long to get;
You play your best, but fail, and yet
Unflinchingly you pay your debt,
Though murmuring low, with lips tight set,
Fortis qui se Vincit.

You bitterly bemoan your loss,
But bravely conquer all remorse,
And tho' it may require some force,
Cheer your opponents till you're hoarse,
Fortis qui se Vincit.

Again, when in Lacrosse you fight,
The ball pursues its rapid flight,
Though thuds and blows rain left and right,
For no such things relax your might,
Fortis qui se Vincit.

The Shield you win, your joy is great,
But let not pride your minds elate,
Nor your own prowess over-rate;
Think of the vanquished and their fate,
Fortis qui se Vincit.

At Cricket next you try your luck;
You go in first and make a duck;
But don't despair or give it up,
Work with redoubled zeal and pluck,
Fortis qui se Vincit.

Since victory cannot always meet
Your labours, nor your work complete,
Scorn not an honourable retreat,
But bravely learn to take defeat,
Fortis qui se Vincit.

Strive hard to conquer in the fight;
Seeking thro' life all wrong to right;
And take as guide and beacon light
This motto's words emblazon'd bright,
Fortis qui se Vincit.

The College day was almost continuously organised. It started at 7.0 a.m., with the first of many bells. The girls rose, washed, gargled and dressed—gargling was compulsory; queued in the hall; filed into the dining-room; had breakfast; returned to their dormitories and made their well-aired beds. Each girl prayed. Prep followed, or an instrumental practice; the march back into hall, boarders with day-girls, in step with the music of the piano; worship; at 9.0 a.m. the day's first lesson, when the class all rose—"Good morning, Miss!"—form captain at the door to relieve their teacher of her books and lay them on her desk; milk at 11.0—some

remember it with biscuits and others with a big, round, soft, shiny and warm-from-the-oven bun; more lessons; a quarter of an hour which the girls spent walking arm in arm and round and round the hall as on board ship—noise deafening; lunch—prefects at vantage-points called cab-stands, keeping everybody silent and in line; games: out of stockings black and into stockings brown—everybody played who was fit or almost fit enough; baths; out of stockings brown and into stockings black, so that no one with cold wet feet could be overlooked—the day-girls must have then gone home; an idle ten minutes; tea; two hours of prep; supper; assembly in hall, where the Head of School gave out notices; resumed prep; mending; more prayers; an idle half hour; then, for the middle forms, a chapter of George Eliot or Charlotte Brontë or Trollope, which Miss Parker read, skipping or modifying romantic paragraphs, or so the girls believed; bedtime for most and the filling of stone water-bottles from the tap called hot; another ten minutes; and then lights out. Form VI, meanwhile, sat and listened to Miss Parker read them leading articles from *The Times*, till 10.0 p.m., when they put aside their knitting and went upstairs.

The four main dormitories, on the second floor, took the names of the four still living daughters of the Queen: Victoria, Helena, Louise and Beatrice (Alice was dead). Each bed, one of eight to a room, had its own wash-stand, pail, ewer of cold water (known to freeze), basin and chest of drawers—where only three ornaments might appear—and was each still rail-and-curtained off, as in Regent's Park, affording privacy. The VIth Form rooms were singles and sisters could occupy a double if their parents had requested one. In the corridor outside stood a "Water Palace": as it were a housmaid's cupboard, with sink and taps, where girls (each called Moab—"Moab is my washpot")[3] took turns to fetch the hot or luke-warm water in a brown enamelled jug, called a pi-can, with long spout and with handle over lid. A strip-wash was prescribed, modest and silent. The youngest girls and the prefects took a bath each day but the in-betweens got only three a week.

Form I, in Beatrice, were forbidden to talk when they rose, washed and dressed, and undressed and washed at bed-time; and girls next oldest, in Victoria, Helena and Louise, had still to keep silent for the first ten minutes after 7.0 a.m., and till the last ten minutes before lights out. Like everybody else, each had then to say her prayers and read the Bible (the Bible and the Book of Common Prayer were the only books allowed upstairs). It was left to a prefect to enforce the getting-up and bedtime rules but she may not have minded that some girls whispered to each other using only vowels—vowels, they claimed, were "not real speech".

The Vice-Principal and other staff took breakfast; Miss Parker, lunch, with sometimes her sister Dora, fat and jolly—also blunt: "What?! Sausages again, Mary? And such nesty ones too!"; and the prefects, tea and supper. Staff had supper with Miss Parker and on Saturday wore evening

[3] Psalms, lx: 6.

dress. The meals were filling. Few if any caused surprise. Breakfast meant bread and butter with golden syrup, or treacle, which in World War I turned almost black, and Canadian bacon, so salty, it was called Lot's wife; Friday lunch, always fish, as a rule cod, either fried or boiled, and called fiss-poo (it smelt), with lentils and parsnips, no potatoes; lunch on Sunday, mutton roast, then apple or apricot pie, which a senior at Miss Parker's table carved; tea, first cake, lest someone took yours—the so-called railway cake, or something better, which Cookie, the gardener's wife, had baked—then bread with either butter or jam, not both; and supper, macaroni and cheese, or toad in the hole, or fish pie and rice, with tomato sauce.

The Head of School decided who sat where, the girls moving one seat along, each meal, hoping not to start or end sitting next to staff or prefect, who would try to correct their manners or their speech, and to the next table every other week. No one was allowed to leave any food on her plate, even fat; but Prince often helped, slinking up to it discreetly; white bread might only be taken after two slices of brown; and no one asked anyone for anything but would offer it instead to someone else—who might already have it on her plate—with perhaps a hinting nudge or glance. Talk at breakfast was forbidden till after the porridge, when noise erupted; or a voluntary silence fell, "the herring hush", when bones filled mouths and lodged in teeth and gums. Juniors, whose lives the rules bound most, enjoyed one privilege: to take chipped cups outside and fling them against the ash-pit wall.

No tuck might be brought or received or kept. A birthday-cake, if sent, would be confiscated. As late as in the 1920s Norah Hanson had no idea that her grandmother had sent a big box of chocolates, till school broke up, when it appeared with Matron, who stowed it in Norah's trunk. Mary Norrington lost her stick of rock, which had been posted to her by a cousin, bad enough, who was a boy, much worse. And chocolate eggs, if Easter fell in term, what Miss Parker called "those heathen relics", were taboo anyway. But each girl might order two pennyworth of sweets, a bar of chocolate or chocolate drops or nougat or Sharp's toffee or jelly babies or acid drops or bull's eyes or peppermint creams or a whipped cream walnut or liquorice gums or other "suckies" or, what she often preferred, a mixture of four separate halfpennyworths, which an escorted delegation bought at the nearby shop, on Saturday morning, when they and everybody else's were put aside in paper bags bearing each girl's name, to be handed out next afternoon, then all devoured, Sunday being the only day of the week when the eating of sweets was allowed.

Sunday meant church, hymn-practice first, then the walk to new St Peter's, where the Rev. Mr Bertram Kite[4] conducted matins—a little too high for Miss Parker, who often took the VIth to something lower, at Christ Church or St Stephen's—on the way back she would buy herself a newspaper and tell them the news—the girls, always escorted, sat in two

[4] Dean of Hobart, Tasmania, 1897–1916.

Oh, Friday's Fish is a smart little chap,
In parsley socks and breadcrumb wrap.
He's sometimes fried and sometimes boiled
And oft in graceful folds he's coiled.

But whether in parsley or breadcrumbs dressed,
Friday's Fish is a welcome guest!

groups, one each side of the aisle—charge for the pews (in 1904): 5s. a seat a term—evensong, like matins compulsory till about 1925, all this after holy communion for those confirmed, but only once a month, half encouraged, half enforced—the Head of School called the faithful out of bed, kept a record of attendance and saw to it that each had had her milk and biscuit, so that no one would faint—the writing of letters home or to a listed friend, and after lunch Silence Hour, about an hour and a half, when the sweet-sucking juniors learnt the collect and the sweet-sucking seniors the epistle, in the hall, seated on a bench facing the wall, or on a rug, or on a deck-chair outside in the summer, for bible class on Monday.

On Monday they might suffer one or both of two ordeals: at mark-reading, after morning prayers, when girls were named whose average mark was 80% or more, Division I, the honoured, then those with 40% or

less, Division III, the disgraced, Division II being spared; and at the evening concerts where, till 1921, everyone in turn had to sing or play or dance or recite verse, as her parents might expect her to do at home, entertaining guests, while the audience knitted or sewed and most of them often felt bored, till a reel of cotton fell from somebody's lap and rolled across the floor. It amused the girls to discover, if they could, what Miss Parker would accept—"quite the most unmusical woman I have ever met", said Christabel Coles, called Peggie. Three stories have been told: that a pianist offering a Beethoven sonata could wander undetected into "Three Blind Mice" and on to a Bach fugue, ending with "Chopsticks"; that Barbara Shakespear, who could not be bothered to extend her repertoire, played the same piece twice, first as the fictitious Chariosade's "Danse Créole", and next as "The Sinking Ship" by the also fictitious Philipopolis; and that someone either nervous or scatter-brained played the tune of "Thou art the way" at morning prayers, while the rest of the school struggled vainly to support her, singing "Come, let us join our cheerful songs", unchallenged, undeterred, and whom, if she had noticed, Miss Parker alone would have dared to interrupt.

Reciters too eked out their scant resources. But Miss Parker could be kind. Faith Malden got away with Alfred Noyse's "The Highwayman" year after year after year after year.

Morning and evening prayers and the evening recitals always closed with "God save the King", the only tune Miss Parker was said to recognise; and on Empire Day, when it lasted all three verses, the Head of School, with Union Jack held high, marched everyone round the balconies in hall, to the singing of "Land of Hope and Glory".

On Thursday (why then, who knows?) the girls wrote postcards, where none but the few thought vulgar would display the words "with love". A Friday hymn was sung, *Ancient and Modern*, No. 595 (now 488)—hence "Friday fish and 595"—

Holy Father, in thy mercy
Hear our anxious prayer:
Keep our loved ones, now far distant,
'Neath thy care.

—so that girls throughout the world might glance at their clocks and watches and think of one another and of PHC. And Saturday—no lessons—brought "Eternal Father, Strong to Save", the listing of garments for the girls to repair, clean laundry to be fetched, matches, which had either to be played or watched, and dancing, girl with girl, in the hall.

Miss Parker expected young ladies to be tough; so comfort was limited. The prefects occupied the library, hence Library came to mean the prefects, known also as the heathen, for a while, they having once waged war on junior nuisances on a day when the psalmist's words were sung, "Why do the heathen so furiously rage together?"—a public room once a week, where books could be borrowed and returned—otherwise private: both

Enter Staff late for Dinner

Monday Evening Recitals. A Diversion

staff and girls knocked on the door before they entered—and a home from home with its open coal fire and a cloth spread on the table. One other sitting-room had pretty and comfortable chairs in it; out of desk and out of bed, however, most of the school could as a rule only sit on a hard wooden bench or floor, till almost the end of Miss Parker's many years. "Our flesh", said Margaret Summerford, HS29, "was mortified."

Their green serge uniform, the so-called cally, helped mortify it worse. It had now become a calf-long tunic, with fore and aft box pleats; a sailor's collar, v-shaped neck; belt, trapping the long and wide silk tie striped green and gold; sleeves long-frilled and gathered at the wrists, making roomy pockets—Mr Thompson, the gardener, would fill them with gooseberries for anyone he liked. The sailor collar, cuffs, and bloomers underneath in the same green serge, were braided with gold. On top they wore a long green cloak. A dark-green dicky kept warm the chest in winter; in summer white *piqué*. The little ones had pinafores. A red and black rosette stitched to the collar's lapel meant member of the Fire Brigade. Athletes wore a badge lettered gold over green, and the prefects theirs, a Tudor rose. Boaters remained, till some say the war and some say after, with bands green-yellow-green or with colours to distinguish boarders, teams and forms; thereto the Cricket 1st XI pinned a silver shield.

The cally survived more or less intact till about 1928, then little by little it was modified, the sailor collar shed, with the long frill, ending the sleeves, and the entire gold braid. It did not die mourned. In summer it felt too warm and itched. It could not be washed—or seldom was; and so, being worn all morning and for indoor and outdoor games all term, it smelt. Yet nothing, it is claimed, could have been more dearly prized than a cally bequeathed by a VIth Form heroine.[5]

The boarders had to be allowed their change of clothes, but it was still school uniform. It varied greatly in Miss Parker's early years. Blouses tended to be white, with frills and pleats, at least for the prefects. The skirts looked mostly the same—not all. Collars varied, high-boned or soft. Ties were allowed to come and go. Ellen Anderson, called Nellie, HS05, looked like staff. But little by little uniformity prevailed, very subject though it was to the vagaries of fashion. A navy-blue serge skirt was prescribed for after games, in winter a flannel blouse, navy with white pin-stripes, and navy ribbon tie, a felt hat, banded like the boater, with as Sunday-best a plain flannel blouse, a coat and top-coat, navy unrelieved but with hat a silver-grey, banded some think grey of another shade, others grey and navy spotted. In summer the blouse was pale blue cotton, for Sunday-best white silk, under a long white flannel costume, with white gloves and a black tie. A yellowy-cream straw hat kept the head cool; it had a white, flat-bowed band, which in 1930 a cream-white panama with broad white swathe overlapped with and replaced.

[5] Barbara Allen's, Mrs Priest's, yet to be published memoirs, *Birthdays and Bed-sitters*.

Shoes were always black, like stockings before and after games. Games ruled out gloves. Hair, well brushed, had either to be plaited and tied back with a velvet snood, like Alice's in Wonderland, green for the Hockey or Cricket 1st XI or Lacrosse 1st XII, brown for the 2nd and black for the rest of the school. Tortoise-shell hair-slides betrayed bad taste. Make-up was still unknown. Miss Parker's girls remained her ungilded lilies.

Correspondence continued to be regulated, the parents being asked to sign a list of up to twelve persons (but some say six and others five), whom their daughters wished to write to, excluding boys over 16 years old (but that sounds misremembered), and men under 60 (but some say 65 and others 70), apart from fathers and brothers—brothers might be written to twice a term—and letters addressed to anyone but parents or guardians were left unsealed and collected in a basket, so that shrewd Miss Parker could conduct spot checks. A parcel might only be unpacked with Matron watching, to see that it contained no sweets. Magazines were allowed if they enjoyed Miss Parker's blessing and books could be introduced if the fly-leaf bore her initials.

Joyce Dennys, looking back, thought that PHC had been run like a nunnery.[6] A girl was lucky if her parents came and saw her in term, when she could stroll with them up and down the drive for a quarter of an hour, or round the playing-field, but church aside, and the crocodile walk, when pitches were muddy and games had had to be cancelled, she hardly ever stepped outside the College gate.

It appears that the rule about visits was relaxed. But transport still caused difficulty. Joyce Dennys had arrived in 1909. Her mother lived in Sidmouth. Of the other boarders admitted that year, seven came from what we now call London, including Harrow; another seventeen, from Alverstoke, Chislehurst (2), Cornwall (2), Folkestone, Gerrards Cross, Harpenden, Northampton, Pewsey, Salisbury, Sevenoaks School, Shrewsbury, Swansea, Wallingford, Wantage and Wellington College; and Marjorie Johnston, a surgeon's daughter, from 1270 Beach Avenue, Vancouver.

The parents could be trusted; they could roam at will. But a son had always to be kept in sight, lest he slip away unseen. Miss Parker: "I must fly. Your son is loose among my maidens." Or so the tale was told and much repeated. Not even a brother might watch the girls play in a match. And if a boy dared come alone and ask to see his sister, the staff would either doubt his word ("How do we know that what you say is true?") or, if accepting, they would assign him to a chair outside Miss Parker's study, lest he chance upon his sister's friends and they hang upon his words. How much more sensible it therefore was, and may have seemed, to let parents with a son take their daughter out to Kew, where he as well as she could admire the trees and flowers instead and have tea somewhere afterwards.

Staff too had brothers. Mr Hunter Prain once called to see his sister,

[6] Correspondence and Chapter XV of *And Then There Was One*, 1983.

Vyvyen, and was greatly impressed when Miss Parker approached him in the drive and enquired, "My dear man, what *are* you doing in these grounds?" And so, it must have been in Miss Parker's last few years, was Doreen Goodwin's cousin: arriving from South Africa, he was allowed ten minutes in which to say hello, then little else, before goodbye, while a teacher with stop-watch in hand stood guard. It was their first meeting and would also be their last. Miss Parker enjoyed the company of fathers but mistrusted their sons and all young fellows.

The "pash" that one girl felt towards another, to be later known as "crush" and later still as "crack", she could accept; for better though it was to resist feelings which God had intended wife to offer husband, they could not be helped, or at least not much, and juniors especially would always find themselves a heroine to adore and walk round the hall with arm in arm and buy flowers for, with their Saturday pocket-money.

The girls caused no great mischief. Being naughty could mean making too much noise, and often did, or talking in the line, or arriving late for the morning roll-call or for tea. As far as is remembered, only three pupils were expelled, who had dabbled in spiritualism and upset juniors. Foul words and jokes did not yet circulate and not until the sixties did coarseness intrude, we are assured and can believe. But girls could be a pest. Sheila Bayley, hearing thunder, feigned hysteria, disturbing the class in French, and did her best to annoy Miss Green, teacher of Latin (Miss Green did not stay long), opening and shutting her umbrella when the form walked crocodile. Kate Jenkins, a Captain of Hockey, refused to wear the new panama hat—what a waste it was of her father's hard-earned income![7]—and her sister, Beryl, allowed to miss an outing and stay and do what she liked at school instead, chose to go and pick and eat Miss Parker's strawberries. The unruly sometimes ruled. "Let your mind be quiet", Miss Bryden would propose, as uproar filled the studio, "and realise the beauty of the world." Few heard and no one listened. Miss Parker restored peace, the instant she appeared, but her dog, Prince, might howl, whom she allowed into her class, or catch the eye of the girls too much, as he sat and licked his nether self, and take their mind off Scripture.

If a girl broke rules, order-marks were imposed, which were intended to disgrace her entire form, and two such order-marks could mean either "tots on Saturday" (long addition sums)—boarders only—or the learning of passages by heart from the Bible or from Shakespeare, which no one thought to be unfair on either. Detention was disfavoured and so on the whole were lines. Many a girl suffered drill, marching up and down in hall for half an hour or so, instead of having games, or was not allowed to go and watch the match—Muriel Dodds, Captain of Tennis, appointed some who misbehaved to act as ball-boys when tennis teams were coached—or they did not get sweets. Reproof could hurt and a prefect's scorn often bit deeper than staff's—or so the more smitten girls have claimed. But worse,

[7] Mr Jenkins worked as a solicitor in Swansea.

much worse, than reproof, or collecting someone's tennis balls, or "punishment gym", or learning by heart, or sums, was the shame a girl was meant to feel and often did, being told to march into hall with the babes for morning prayers and stand with them out in front; or to sit cramped with them in class, at a desk or at a table much too low, feeling inches from the floor; or in the dining-room, aware of the hush and staring eyes as she rose to her feet, clutching her plate, knife, fork and spoon, or sitting there alone, with her back turned to everybody else, which at least saved face, learning not to spill her tea or water.

In 1919 or so Miss Parker abolished formal punishments and replaced them with Saturday morning Courts of Honour, when miscreants in each year confessed their misdemeanours to their form-mistress and peers. But the policy failed. Hardened offenders did not take long to forget to mend their ways; the more the girl was sensitive, the more she desperately racked her brains to discover any foible that would earn her a rebuke; exhibitionists would invent, or luridly embroider, sins committed, or virtues neglected, with which to cause a stir; so within about a term Miss Parker abandoned it.

Another innovation succeeded and endured: charity teas, which girls in disgrace applied for at the staff-room door, confessing their misconduct to whoever answered their knock, who would then supply them with a slice of bread and a glass of some say milk and others water, to be eaten and drunk where they stood, exposed to the disdain of staff coming and going.

The blameless had often to suffer with the naughty: if a girl talked in the line going down to the dining-hall, her whole table might be made to sit silent through the meal, which did not endear her to anyone else, and was not meant to. Or if someone stayed in bed, nicely behaved, while her room-mates leapt from bed to chair and from chair to chest of drawers, full circle, and were caught, then she, like them, might not be taken out for tea next day by her parents, who in turn felt punished, being only allowed to see her in the school or grounds.

Discipline was strict and girls might feel sorry for themselves. But many of its victims felt grateful in after years.

Inspections continued. A scholar unnamed visited the College in 1910, examining the girls *viva voce*. "The recitations"—in English, French, German and Latin—"were wonderfully accurate. No girl was neglected . . . the interest of all the pupils was equally cared for . . . the tone was very high, the discipline admirable, and the whole, and not one side, of each pupil's capacity, was developed."

It sounded like the Rev. Mr Henry Hall, a retired grammar-school headmaster, who next year paid similarly glowing tributes to Miss Parker and her staff:

The bearing, discipline, clear, quick answering of the girls were worthy of the College and evidently the artistic environment of their everyday lives, and the direct interest the Principal herself takes in the development of all

that is best in each individual girl, render the College admirably adapted to attain right ideals in the education of English gentlemen and gentlewomen.

In 1912 Mr Hall or his successor was happily impressed:

the girls of all ages answered up well and brightly . . . knew their work . . . made few mistakes . . . the knowledge of the text and subject matter of the literature was excellent [Shakespeare and Tennyson] and an intelligent grasp was shown of plot and character . . . In French and German . . . recitations from all the pupils . . . were excellent throughout. In accent and punctuation, the results—with rare exceptions—were very good . . . The poetical pieces were recited with clearness of intonation, and with intelligent delivery and, where the nature of the piece lent itself to dramatic action, this was forthcoming, with vigour, appropriateness, and obviously with enjoyment.

And so, more or less, the examiner's reports glowed on until the war-time first and last, which was also the last which the College Magazine made public.

Miss Williamson's curriculum had not much changed. Latin was entrenched; and if a girl dropped it she was said to feel despised. But French now overshadowed German. Molière was performed—*L'Avare*; and Racine—*Iphigénie* (dignified emotions)—on the same night as an unattributed farce, *Embrassons-Nous, Folleville*. Messrs Bouvier and Montépic, Mme Guérin and Mlles d'Orliac and Barbier came and talked in French and, it is claimed, were understood, on France, its history and literature—Mlle Barbier on famous French women of the sixteenth and seventeenth centuries, including (*sic*) "Madame de Maintenant".

Miss Paget-Kemp taught art, who displayed her pupils' work at the Franco-British Exhibition, Shepherd's Bush, in 1908, and then in India. Her Sketching Club found cottages to draw, with overhanging eaves and rose-smothered walls; Denham, even Uxbridge, still unspoilt, with its mill-pond and red-roofed barn (tea following, at the Windsor Café); the Thames at Runnymede; Strand-on-the-Green, with its barges and willows; mummies, frescoes and scarabs—dung-beetles—at the British Museum, if outside was wet and cold; stuffed beasts, at the Museum of Natural History, South Kensington; and brocade and lace at the Victoria and Albert. The girls much enjoyed an Exhibition of Fair Women, at the New Gallery in Regent Street, where everyone agreed that Lady Marjorie Manners[8] was the fairest of them all.

A Kodak Club or Photographic Society or Camera Club was launched; it waxed and it waned: "a melancholy falling-off in photographic enthusiasm" was reported in 1907; recovered and survived; awarded prizes: landscape, portrait, animal and one from the Bishop of Kensington[9]

[8] Eldest daughter of Violet, Duchess of Rutland, whose dark and melting eyes were everywhere admired.

[9] Dr Frederic Ridgeway till in 1911 he was appointed Bishop of Salisbury.

for "the best photograph of wild birds taken in their natural surroundings in the College grounds"; elected Kathleen Gamble its Keeper of the Photographic Album; was to droop in World War I, "owing partly to the expense of chemicals . . . but largely to the slackness of some of its members"; responded to the stimulus of gas-light printing in the Summer Term of 1920; then expired.

An Artistic and Literary Society began in 1906 with 110 girl members and eight staff, its visits overlapping with the Sketching Club's to museums, exhibitions and art galleries: the National, the Tate, Burlington House—tea at the Blenheim Café—the Grafton—more tea, at a restaurant in Bond Street—the Wallace Collection—tea at Lyons—and the Dulwich. Not all its activities were literary or artistic. But all, it seems, whether in or out of doors, included tea.

Windsor to Maidenhead

1907

We left Ealing early in the afternoon and, when we reached Windsor, a short walk round the Castle brought us to the river, where we found a steam launch awaiting us. There was certainly not much room to spare when everyone had got on board, but this only added to our enjoyment.

We had a very fine view of Eton College as we left Windsor, and everyone admired the exceedingly beautiful gardens which we passed on the way. Tea, which we had on the launch, was a varied entertainment, as everyone brought her own and ate someone else's provisions.

M.E.W.[10]

Blackwater Park

1908

The weather was perfect; the time spent in roaming through the woods, or sketching the lake, or exploring adjacent fields and hedges for foxgloves, wild roses, and honeysuckle, passed all too quickly, and in the cool of the evening we returned, after a lovely drive to Langley in our half-dozen brakes, having thoroughly enjoyed the day. One or two adventures added excitement . . . having manfully surmounted a barbed-wire fence in search of foxgloves, some of us were ignominiously put to flight by being informed, in no measured terms, that we were trespassing on forbidden ground!

E. Isaacson

Picnic in Richmond Park

1915

. . . we set out directly after lunch with large baskets of strawberries and cakes and, after a delightful blow on the top of the 'bus, reached Richmond

[10] Margaret Evelyn Walker, 18, of Woodlands, Acton, whom the sisters Bear would employ to teach lacrosse at Alexandra House and who in 1959, a widow of 70, would wed Sir Alfred Holland, then almost 81, Chief Master, retired, of the Chancery Division.

Margaret Waite: from "Library Lunacies" 1916 to the Slade then Wycombe Abbey.

Above: Miss Pode. Below: Miss Stocks, if it is not Miss Prain.

L.L.
NO ?
VOL. '0042
XMAS 1917.

The Joys of Drill. Top left: Janet Sawers, the world-famous acrobat, in her best form.

Giant's Stride . . .

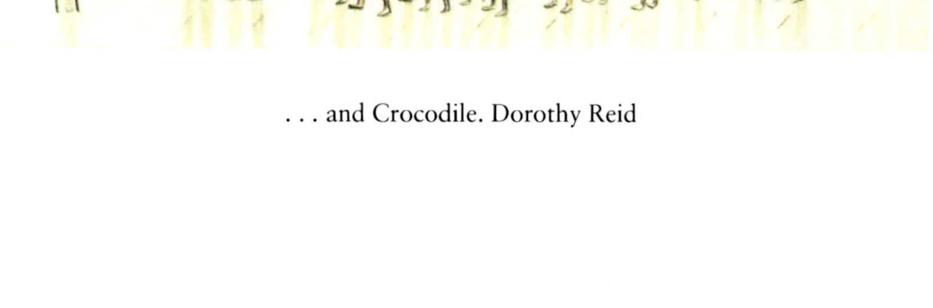

. . . and Crocodile. Dorothy Reid

A Miss Milvain View of School

Dorothy Reid

The Library send
Good luck without end
To our team that's both valiant and brave,
By this little pig,
Who, though not very big,
Will do his best our luck to save.

Fire-Drill. Dodo and staff menagerie escape.

Clockwise: Miss Turton, middle fox; the Bunny, Miss Lord; Miss Jenkins, Jenks, the Peach's Bloom; L.C.M., Miss Maude (?), Elsie; Mlle Guyomar lets fly a book in class; the Pinney Flower, Miss Pinney, Susannah, the adored; and Miss Prain's or Miss Stocks's hands bearing Tout, Thomas Frederick, historian, dead weight. Helen Swain, 1920.

P.H.C.

"FORTES QUI ALIOS VINCUNT"
27th November 1920

Play up! play up!
And keep the cup
And bring it back in glory!
If this you do
We'll all cheer you
From basement to top storey!

A LIBRARY POET

"AND WHERE'S THE WEALTH, I'M WONDERING,
COULD BUY THE CHEERS THAT ROLL
WHEN THE LAST CHARGE GOES THUNDERING
BENEATH THE TWILIGHT GOAL?"

H. NEWBOLT.

You'll play again the immortal games
And grapple with the fierce old friends
We'll cheer your all-undying names
And sing the song that never ends.
Till, when the hard, familiar bell
Tells you that autumn's night is late,
Where long ago you said farewell
You'll say farewell by the old gate.
"Oh Bushey unforgot" you'll cry
"Come you again or come no more
"At P.H.C. we'll keep the CUP
"And hope to always lead the score!"

H. NEWBOLT + A LIBRARY POET.

Debates approach. Now Library wrap up warm to meet the cold.

Dodo — recital — with aplomb.

OUR BLOUSE

Of all the blouses in the world,
There isn't one like ours is.
Its neck is high, its sleeves are long.
Yet no one ever grouses.
Its colour's blue with stripes inlaid
And blue ties down the middle.
To find a blouse that's comfier
That really is the riddle!

Ours is a nice blouse, ours is.
Oh! What a nice blouse ours is!
When we're inside our pretty little sack,
The front's at the front and the back's at the back.
Ours is a nice blouse, ours is.
It don't compare with trousies,
But is neat neat neat,sweet sweet sweet.
Oh! What a nice blouse ours is!

in safety. The weather was perfect, and nothing could have been more delightful than to see the river after the heat and dust of the streets and, finally, to find ourselves in the Park, where much of the beauty of the rhododendrons was still to be seen.

We wandered at our leisure through the Park, until we came to a quiet shady copse. We decided that this should be our dining-room and, having found comfortable tree-trunks, we regaled ourselves with our delicious tea.

Anon.

Juniors were taken to the Crystal Palace—they found the Haunted Castle shut but enjoyed the Hall of Laughter, its distorting mirrors, the music of the band, tea on the verandah—and to Harrow School, where Kathleen Baker's father, George, was cricket coach. The seniors visited the Royal Naval and Military Tournament, Earls Court, where "the fact that the Royal Family was present added additional lustre", and to "cinematographic pictures" at the Philharmonic Hall[11] about Captain Scott and his journey to the South Pole.

A few girls at a time—or the same few—were taken out to concerts, at the Queen's[12] and Royal Albert Halls, the Bechstein[13] and the Grotrian.[14] They heard Fritz Kreisler, Viennese, not yet American, the Belgian Eugène Ysaÿe,[15] violinists; pianists Ignace Paderewski—in 1919 he would be Poland's first Prime Minister—the Italian, Ferrucio Busoni, Moriz Rosenthal, another Pole—he could play by heart all the works of Chopin—the improbable Glaswegian, Eugene d'Albert, who had one by one six wives, Solomon (Cutner), the London child—aged 8 when in 1911 he performed in public Tchaikovsky's Piano Concerto No. 1; and they saw Dr (not yet knighted) Henry Walford Davies and Sir Henry Wood conducting.

The school had as yet no proper orchestra: at best ensembles, which old girls and staff might reinforce. But drama flourished. *The Merchant of Venice*, *As You Like It*—over a hundred girls took parts—*The Tempest*, *Twelfth Night*, *A Comedy of Errors* and *She Stoops to Conquer* were performed before the war. The Goldsmith, 1906, was "zealously rehearsed", Eva Petty's Diggory "convulsed the audience", the dresses looked "exceedingly pretty and becoming", and one small child could not believe that Sybil Isaacson's Tony Lumpkin was "only a girl".

Miss Parker had made it a rule that, in modern plays, girls acting men,

[11] Built in 1907 in Great Portland Street, replacing the St James's in Piccadilly, and enlarged and converted in 1930 into offices and shops.

[12] In Langham Place, next to the St George's, from 1893 till it was bombed and destroyed in 1941. Sir Henry Wood had performed his Promenade Concerts there since 1895.

[13] 1901–17; since then the Wigmore Hall.

[14] The Steinway from 1875 till in 1924 its lease expired and it moved to Conduit Street. Called the Grotrian from 1925, closed in 1938, wrecked in the war, then demolished.

[15] A Brussels *Grand Prix* commemorates his name.

and therefore trousered, wore two aprons, one before and one behind, which ideas of decorum must somehow have explained.

Reviews emphasised spectacle: the sea-nymphs dancing in *The Tempest* wore "very effective shades of blue" and all who saw it thought that *Twelfth Night* was "the prettiest play ever given at the College".

The juniors did *Rumpelstilzchen*, where Lilian Isaacson "had quite mastered the swagger of a youthful courtier" and Georgiana—Georgie—Finch was "capital". What they most enjoyed was murder foul and in 1905 they happily indulged in it.

A new dramatic society has lately been formed among the Junior School, under the name of the Tragedy-Comedy Company, whose plays are open to all members of the School on Saturday evening, in the Recreation Room. Both tragedy and comedy are represented, the method of proceeding being to compose the plot beforehand, while the dialogue is left to the discretion of the actors. The tragedy of Mr Dasher, *the second of the series, was full of the most orthodox horrors—not even in the last scene of* Hamlet *are there a greater number of violent deaths than in this play, where the curtain falls on the two villains gloating over the heaped-up corpses of all the other characters . . .*

A mistress and her form or the Hockey XI or the Old Girls would from time to time offer something tuneful and pretty, or competitive and hilarious, impromptu or secretly rehearsed, ending perhaps with "an exciting game of musical chairs and several lively sets of Sir Roger de Coverley".

A Variety Entertainment
1905

The programme consisted of the inevitable tableaux, music, scenes from Shakespeare, and the breakfast party from The Rose and the Ring.[16] *The scene from* King John, *between Hubert and Arthur, was rendered with great skill and spirit by S. Isaacson and F. von Keudell, the pathetic pleadings of the little prince almost moving susceptible members of the audience to tears, and when the executioner appeared, bearing a red-hot poker, a thrill of horror ran through the spectators, which was deepened when, from the corner in which the instrument of torture had been placed, arose smoke and an alarming smell of burnt cloth. There was a moment of awful suspense; those who were seated in front were preparing to rush to the rescue but, happily, no damage was done and the fire brigade resumed their seats in a state of mingled disappointment and relief.*

Anon.

[16] A comic opera by A. W. Slaughter, 1890, after Thackeray's work thus titled ("or the History of Prince Giglio and Prince Bulbo: a Fireside Pantomime for great and small Children, by Mr M. A. Titmarsh"), 1855.

A pageant was arranged. It began with "Rule Britannia", extolled Britain, its literature, history and empire, with paint, feathers, turbans and "genuine spears eight feet high"—the horse Queen Boadicea rode was also real and devoured the laurel wreath which its groom was wearing—and closed with "Land of Hope and Glory" and the National Anthem.

Opportunity for making costume and dressing up in it was eagerly sought and seized.

1910

Miss Buchanan and Forms VI and Upper V gave a Fancy Dress Masked Dance. The hall was admirably decorated with flags and fairy lights, the front gallery being divided off into delightful nooks and crannies, whither the maskers resorted between the dances.

. . . . .

Two heralds announced each guest on entering the hall and the dance was begun by the maskers forming procession before the Principal.

. . . . .

The national costumes of almost every nation were represented, and queens danced freely with golliwogs, and spirits with gypsies.

. . . . .

The dance music was played by a most accomplished orchestra, the drum being a most important element. At 10.15, after a flourish of trumpets, masks were torn off, and great mirth was caused by unexpected revelations. Festivities were closed with three cheers for the Principal, who left the hall under an arch formed by the raised swords of the cavaliers. The evening ended with three more cheers to our hostesses for one of the nicest entertainments that we have ever had.

J.G. and F.H.[17]

1914

. . . we spent a very enjoyable evening making hats, a competition which was kindly got up by Miss Buchanan. We were told to bring scissors and as many pins as could possibly be found at such short notice; three sheets of newspaper were given to each of us, and then all of us began to make as many fashionable hats as we could think of. At 7.30 the Juniors, wearing their creations, went down to Miss Parker to be judged, and returned in due time, Sybil Carden[18] *being the winner of a beautiful fern. At 7.45 we cleared up the Hall, and Miss Parker, assisted by some of the staff, came to judge the hats. First those below Middle C were judged, Evelyn Bushe winning the prize pot of tulips.*

There were about thirty competitors in the Senior School, and the work of judging was therefore extremely difficult, especially as the majority of

[17] Lt.-Col. Gaisford's Jane, of Dolly's Grove, Dunboyne, Co. Meath, Eire, and Freda, daughter of Mr A. F. Hammond, a retired shirtmaker.

[18] HS19, sister of Kitty, not of Barbara.

them were very ingenious. Some of the hats were large and some small; some were trimmed with big bows of ribbon, some with gigantic feathers and niches, some with rosettes and quills, and some with enormous plumes, so long that they tickled the faces of people who stood close behind them! About half of the competitors were finally chosen and gradually the number was reduced until only three were left in, then two, and at last Nancy Johnston was awarded the prize of a lovely pot of white cyclamen.

Then the bell rang and, reluctantly laying aside our elaborate head-dresses, we gave three hearty cheers for Miss Buchanan and went down to supper.

D.H.M.B.[19]

A main purpose of the many performances of plays, concerts, pageants and bazaars, and of the Literary and Artistic Society, was to raise funds with which to fill the school with more and more reproductions of famous paintings (gloomy brown and grey), to panel the hall with oak, and with oak to replace "the incongruous blue doors". Gifts, meanwhile, steadily accumulated, among them Flossie von Keudell's long-case clock and Winifred—Molly—Reid's barometer. The dining-room was painted green and primrose and year by year the names of the prefects—all the Upper VIth—took their places there in gold.

A Debating Society, top two forms, President always the Head of School, met two or three times a term, speaking once in French—"our enthusiasm for the charming French tongue had just been fired by a delightful lecture we had heard from M. Bouvier, but grammar and sense alike took fright"—otherwise in English. It supported the Monarchy and the House of Lords; feared that education would help return more socialist MPs; disapproved of the suffragettes: woman was not inferior to man and home ought not to be her one and only sphere, but her voice should not be heard in public—she could do without the vote; saw no reason why women sent to gaol needed women warders; opposed co-education; agreed that "girls should be supervised in their reading"; did not believe that war in Europe could be averted; or that aeroplanes would help to remove its threat; approved of military conscription (for men) and of Home Rule both for Ireland and for Ulster; wanted immigration to be curbed and whites not made to share their rights with blacks; condemned fox-hunting but defended vivisection; attributed character to birth rather than to circumstance; believed in ghosts, but not in unlucky numbers; and preferred Athens to Sparta, coming second in Rome to being first in the village, and galoshes to umbrellas. Debates could be "hardly" or "hotly" or "heatedly" contested—"enthusiastic members would rise to their feet, ready to dash arguments to the ground"—and were sometimes known as "fights". The same participants read Shakespeare's plays, from three to six a year, and

[19] Doris Helen Mary Bellamy, who would die aged 28, at her home, Holy Trinity Vicarage, Forest of Dean, in 1924.

girls leaving school were encouraged to join the British Empire Shakespeare Society (object: "to promote greater familiarity with his works among all classes").

The fought debates were not nearly as fierce as the battles waged outside, on the field now free of cows. Lacrosse arrived there either late with Miss Williamson or early with Miss Parker—the school would claim that it was first to introduce it. Miss Beveridge took charge in 1904, who had taught the game at Wycombe Abbey, and her insistence on the short passing which had made that school "such a formidable foe" again proved effective. But the Wycombe Abbey match, which was played "in truly Canadian style", in the snow, "ended in disastrous results . . . the goals being 10–0".

Sybil Isaacson reported how they fared next year: defeat again by Wycombe, 14–2, but three wins and a draw out of four other matches, "one of which was on the enemy's ground"; and that was much, much less than all:

There remains yet to be recorded the most delightful surprise . . . the captain, F. von Keudell, and two members of the team, Violet Lepper and Edith Humphreys, had, with great secrecy, ordered the most charming brooches, consisting of tiny green shields bearing the legend, 'P.H.C. La Crosse, 1906'; and these were presented to the fortunate members of the team, to their great delight, especially as we have often had secret longings for the dainty badges worn by other teams.

Only four matches were played in 1906–07. "In the first", wrote Phyllis Challoner, "our fault was too much passing, and in the second we erred in the opposite direction, while in the third, i.e. that against Roedean, there was not much chance to pass at all." They drew the fourth.

The captain's public comments on her team were candid but kind or kind but candid. In 1909, when Lilian Isaacson found Grace Stubington "inclined to be a little rough" and Freda Hammond "at times clumsy in picking up the ball", she praised their defence; and Marguerite—Rita—Macintyre was "keen and quick . . . but apt to lose her head".

Two years later the College lost against Queen Anne's, Caversham, 1–29, and St George's, Ascot, 3–10, beat West Heath 7–0, then lost 2–7 against Roedean II. Morale, however, soared when about fourteen of the Old Girls, long week-ending at the school, drove over to Bushey with the team for the match against St Margaret's:

The game was splendidly contested, and at half time it would have been difficult indeed to prophesy the result. Finally P.H.C. won by 3 goals to 2. The excitement of the drive home was indescribable and found vent at last in three tremendous cheers as the brakes drove up . . .

The Hockey XI showed fervour and attack, as in 1905, when it met and beat the staff. It too engaged in what were known as "fights" and in 1905, it having lost a hard-fought game 2–0, against Chelsea Physical Training

College, "Hazeline was in great request . . . and bruises were displayed as badges of honour."

Only one match was played next term, away from home, at Wycombe. It was lost 8–0 "but goals might have been trebled had it not been for the splendid play of the goal, and of the backs, who worked together magnificently"; and the valour which the team displayed inspired its captain, Sybil Isaacson, to commemorate the event as did Tennyson the ill-fated charge of the Light Brigade at Balaclava.

The Wycombe Abbey Match

Damp lay the ground beneath,
Clouded the heaven.
On to the Abbey field
Marched the Eleven.
"Play up!" the captain said;
"Show not a sign of dread,
Fight till you're all but dead,
College Eleven!"

"Play up!" the captain said.
Was there a girl dismayed?
Not tho' the whole team knew
Faint were their chances.
Theirs not to turn and fly,
Theirs but to win or die,
Theirs . . . but the whistle sounds;
Ealing advances.

Slashes to right of them,
Slashes to left of them,
Shots aimed direct at them
Volley'd and thundered.
Stormed at with stick and ball,
Fiercely they hacked (and well),
Straight on the ball they rushed,
Only to fall back, crushed—
Luckless Eleven!

Streamed to the winds their hair,
Flashed all their sticks in air,
Laming the centre, there;
Charging the forwards, while
Sadly they wondered
When would *the whistle go?*
Right thro' the line they broke
Once, then, exhausted,
Reeled from the hostile stroke,
Wounded and breathless.

Then they fell back, but not,
Not *as they'd started!*

When shall the story fade
Of the vain stand they made
'Gainst foes unconquered?
Pity their fruitless fight,
Pity their conquered plight;
Hapless Eleven.

Wycombe Abbey won again in 1908, 5–0. The event was discontinued, but six less formidable teams were played next year and beaten, including the Swanley Horticultural College and some Italian mixed vegetables, the Olla Podrida. On the whole the school enjoyed success and Edith Stubington and later Ida Rand kept sweet the taste of it with a hockey-stick-and-ball gold brooch for each of the players.

The scholars being mostly athletes and the athletes mostly scholars, they did not affect disdain for swots or "flannelled fools" and "muddied oafs",[20] as Evelyn Ashdown, as athletic a scholar as any or as scholarly an athlete, showed in 1908 when she wrote her Cambridge Letter:

The events at Newnham which remind us more than anything of school-days are perhaps the inter-hall cup matches in hockey, tennis and fives; the enthusiasm is intense, and the rivalry between the halls is, if possible, even keener than that between the forms for which we used to play.

Muriel Gamble, of the same college, wrote exultantly next year:

It is with feelings of great pride for P.H.C. that I begin my letter, for I must first of all tell you the news which has caused great excitement in Hall this afternoon—that Kathleen Allen has beaten the College champion at tennis, and has won back for Old Hall the cup, which for eight years has been absent from our Hall . . . this is our third cup won in three days; we beat Sidgwick in the final Hall Hockey and our Fives champion won the Hall Fives Cup.

I wish you could have seen the *(for us) match of the year, which we played against Girton a few weeks ago. We expected a severe defeat, as we thought they had a better team, but whether it was the sheer force of desperation or that we astonished them by our hard pressing, when the whistle went the glorious fact was known that though Girton brought the cup they were not to take it home again, and after we had cheered them down the road we welcomed the cup back with the ringing of the fire-bells after its four years' absence.*

[20] Rudyard Kipling: "flannelled fools at the wicket . . . muddied oafs at the goals". From his poem, *The Islanders*, published in *The Times* in 1902, then in 1903 in his *The Five Nations*.

The same enthusiasm was shown for cricket, as on Tournament Day in 1907, when prowess overawed:

The Old Girls were very formidable and when we saw such heroines as R. Maas and E. Bunny going to the wickets, we trembled for our prospects! Our fears were justified . . . and boundaries began to multiply exceedingly, until the spectators grew fearful of their personal safety.

In 1909 Cecily Read found Bertha Burleigh "clumsy" and "too many ducks disfigured the pages of the scoring book". Only one girl bowled overarm in 1911: Faith Heslop; this was shameful. Beryl Jenkins, however, tried her best and so did Evelyn Mangin: "too much inclined to slog straight balls but a powerful hitter" (who went on to play tennis at Wimbledon and with her sister Madge won the All-India Doubles). They were all keen and perhaps Mary Cathcart—Molly—was the keenest, who had arrived late, aged 17, drawn only to the cricket, which no other school in reach could offer her.

Miss Parker encouraged games if they aroused *esprit de corps*, but she could not approve of golf, which you only played so that you yourself might win and for the sake of which too many acres were wasted of precious countryside.

The Fire Brigade, as much a team as the XI or the XII, consisted of thirteen players, namely Hydrant, 1st Hose, 2nd, 3rd, 4th and 5th, Branch Pipe, Spanners, four First Aiders and a Captain. It had dry practices about twice a week, but some say once a fortnight, others every day—old girls forget and routine must have varied—the Head of School swinging her bell and calling through a megaphone, or shouting, that a fire had broken out in the gymnasium or the Lower VIth or the library, and a wet one once a summer on the top field with the Ealing Brigade ("real firemen"). As with hockey and lacrosse, the captain reviewer exposed the weaknesses of everybody else, each College Magazine. Marjorie Beaumont, called Madge, was "rather slow" in 1909, Freda Hammond did not always listen for orders, Iris Harding could be slack, Doris Matthews too often lost her head. But each was also praised; being one of the Brigade was artfully projected as an honour due to those you could depend on; and girls won colours, who with hose-pipe had excelled.

Fire-drill for all, which Helena Lowenfeld had so much enjoyed, the slide in the chute from a top-floor window, happened two or three times a term. It was intended to be a snap test but the girls were forewarned if the games mistress did not appear for dinner wearing evening dress; and when she rushed about the corridors and stairs, blowing her whistle, they were all ready to forsake bed, slip cally over nightdress, grip a towel between their teeth, hold hands, walk—not run—downstairs and gather outside, in the dark and often cold, while the élite coupled hoses.

The eagerness and pride of the Brigade XIII outlasted school. "It is the ambition of most Freshers to be chosen to fill the places in the ranks . . . left vacant", wrote Muriel Gamble, in her letter from Cambridge, and to play

Memories of a certain Match
The Catch of the Season

or work with any kind of team made her heart beat faster. But Phyllis Challoner, a student at Oxford, the same year, did not include the LMH Brigade in her list of "the innumerable advantages and delights" an undergraduate enjoyed. It was not something you had chosen to belong to, you were "caught while very fresh", which was to say "induced"; and at 7.30 a.m., when the bell disturbed your slumbers and you had to spring out of bed "and search wildly for hockey-skirt and sweater . . . *supposed* to be laid out every evening in readiness", and creep downstairs and join the rest of the sleepy team, exposed to "the rebuking eye of a wide-awake captain", you did not feel happy.

A Drill Display took place each year, causing "breathless excitement" inter-form, with figure and step-marching and exercises with skipping-ropes, canes, wrapped in green and gold, balls, hoops, flags; Flossie von Keudell and Georgie Finch performed "a grand salute of the French school of fencing"; and at least two of "the highest jumpers" (they jumped from a springboard), Clarice Hall, daughter of the Matron of the Cuckoo School in Hanwell,[21] "whose good style Miss Woodward particularly commended", and Betty Mellanby, were each awarded a gold medal.

But Tournament Day remained the Year's Event. No other gave such pleasure in advance or would evoke so much nostalgia. Its framework still consisted of cricket and tennis, the day-girl "oppidans" matched against boarders and parents; or the College, day and board, against the OGA. Tea was provided on the red path, shaded with limes. Visitors gave out prizes, for bowlers, batsmen, fielders, tennis-players, photographers, one for the best low-table decorator, from Lady Frances Balfour,[22] and Miss Hope's and later Fräulein Goerke's for the best-kept garden; then would make a speech in the middle of the field, where stood the great white poplar.

Lady George Hamilton[23] approved there of games, if games did not interfere too much with work; Sir Joseph Savory, Chairman, and Sir William Dunbar approved of them anyway; and so did the Bishop of Kensington, who emphasised the need to foster ideals, recommended being useful, to ensure a happy life, and cited Princess Helena as the best example; a Mrs Crowder said that games helped make girls more polite to one another and somehow prepared them to run the house and home; Maj.-Gen. Sir Edward Pemberton-Leach warned them not to dress like men, which was unbecoming, or to adopt their speech, which was rough,

[21] A Central London poor-law school, 1856–1933, built on the Cuckoo Farm estate and hill, hence Cuckoo Avenue, Dene and Lane; now the Hanwell Community Centre. Charlie Chaplin, one of a thousand or so pupils there, must have known Mrs Hall. Comfort was scant, diet meagre and ophthalmia rife.

[22] Daughter of the eighth Duke of Argyll and wife of Prime Minister Balfour's younger brother, Eustace; churchwoman; and eloquent suffragist. Norman Maclean, *DNB*: "A mistress of invective, she wielded the dagger of sarcastic wit with the same zest as her ancestors had wielded the broadsword."

[23] Maud Caroline, youngest daughter of Henry Lascelles, third Earl of Harewood, and the statesman's wife.

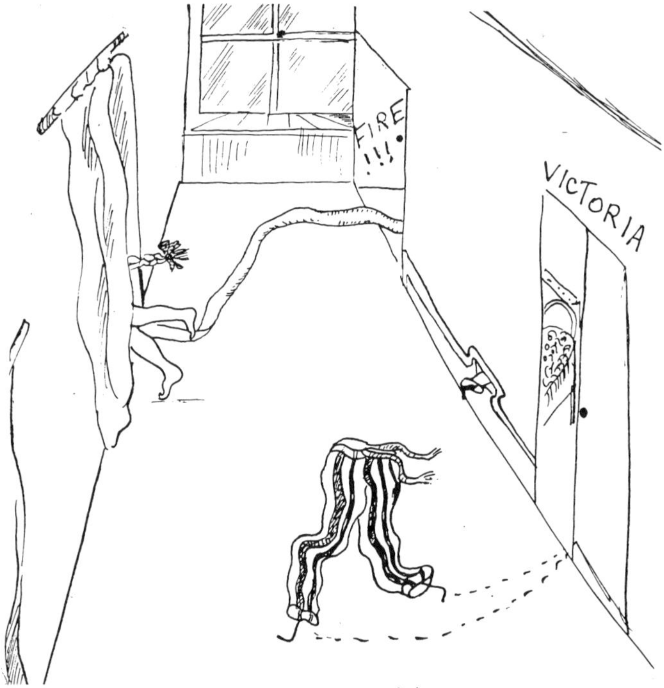

Events Overtake Pyjamas

Mrs C.G. considers it very unhygienic that our toothbrushes should stand about the room all day.

or their manners, which men too often lacked; and Lady St Helier, hitherto Lady Jeune, thought how lucky everybody was to be taught in the twentieth century: "The present is the day of high ideals"—it was 1915—"and great ambitions for girls, and it is wholesome to live up to a high ideal."

More speeches were made each end of Autumn Term, when prizes and certificates were presented, the prizes more green-leather-bound, gold-tooled books, most coveted and handsome of which were the Princess Christian—Helena—for Advanced Pianoforte and the Award of Merit for the Head of School. Princess Helena herself came and gave them away in 1902, with as guard of honour the Middlesex Volunteers—"Tea arranged by Harrod"—and again in 1906, greeted as always by the National Anthem but with now a special verse, sung by Grace Raikes, and with a "hearty cheers" farewell from all the girls—their cheers were always "hearty".

The Royal President made no speech. Nor did Lord Brassey, who failed to arrive, stuck in the fog at Notting Hill. The Bishop of Kensington, however, did, who urged self-discipline; and Sir James Crichton-Browne:[24] the College stood "fully abreast of the best girls' high schools", it had pioneered reform and had prepared its pupils, not only for careers, but to be "good, cultivated, self-controlled, healthy-minded, compassionate women" and "centres of household order and refinement"; Dr Joseph Wood, Headmaster of Harrow:[25] the education of girls had been transformed, from "deportment and accomplishment" to "real training for life" (applause), Miss Parker's girls equalled his boys as scholars, outshone them in grace, refinement and speech and, unlike the "tender plants in hothouses", in many a nineteenth-century novel, always swooning, how free and wholesome was their effort on the games-field! The Ven. Mr Ferrar Sharpe, Archdeacon of Middlesex, valued work more than prizes: a prize could be a tonic, it could also be a drug; Mr C. C. Clarke[26] "gave a very entertaining address"—not a word of it was printed; the Rev. Mr (later Dr) Edmund Pearce, Canon of Westminster,[27] connected Lady Ramsay[28] with Princess Augusta and both of them with God; a wise Mrs Creighton wanted girls to be taught how to learn, acquiring the necessary tools; and in 1913 the Right Hon. Lord George Hamilton, MP, saw games as a means to

[24] An eminent physician and psychologist, then ninety years old, of his allotted ninety-eight; he had campaigned for open-air treatment of tuberculosis, control of venereal disease and improved housing for the workfolk.

[25] 1899–1910. A man whose kindness was admired and criticised. The school has him to thank for the green fields, now its *cordon sanitaire*, which he snatched from the grasp of the advancing philistines.

[26] Perhaps Charles Cyril, future Chairman of the Board of Colston School for Girls, 1924–57.

[27] Master of Corpus Christi College, Cambridge, by 1914, and Vice-Chancellor of the University, 1921–24.

[28] Patricia, 1886–1974, second daughter of Prince Arthur, Duke of Connaught, Queen Victoria's third son, and Princess Louise of Prussia.

promote good health, self-discipline and team spirit, but also seemed to warn that they should not become a fetish.

After Prize-Giving 1906, and throughout the years of war, the Royal Princess kept less in touch with the school and from 1904 to 1918 she attended only one meeting of its Council. Her brother, King Edward, died in 1910. The girls heard the news from a newspaper boy calling "Death of the King!" in the street outside, early one morning in the Summer Term, as they dressed. Sir Joseph Savory wrote assuring Princess Helena of the grief the College felt; and Miss Parker read the girls a letter in which Her Royal Highness ordered them to mourn her brother's death wearing black bands on the sleeves of their (boarders only) white serge suits and on their boaters.

A party of seniors went to Hyde Park to watch the funeral procession: king after king—Europe in 1910 was still full of kings—their mounted retinues and the military bands. Joyce Dennys long remembered it: the girls all wearing black on blue—for the day of sorrow the autumn-to-spring-term blue must have seemed less incorrect—filling two motor-coaches, and mildly but rather unbecomingly elated; the sixpence in each one's pocket; the packed sandwiches; and the labels bearing their names and school address, tied to their camisoles, lest accident befell, which intensified excitement. They were told that they were not to visit the loo till they returned—the honour of the school appeared to be exposed; or talk to strangers; or faint—"You will not faint"—though they had to stand and wait for a good four hours—others might, and many did, so thick was the crowd and the weather so hot. All of them heard the bands and the running commentary of those who were tallest or who stood in front—"Look! There's the Kaiser! Look! See the little dog? He's called Caesar"—and some could glimpse the Kaiser's helmet and the tops of other illustrious heads, which they did not recognise; but only Kathleen Nesbit saw the spectacle entire, a man in the crowd having raised her aloft—he had picked her pocket, then underwent a change of heart and gave her back her sixpence.[29]

Her Royal Highness had already lost her eldest son, Prince Christian Victor, who had died in the Boer War in 1899, of enteric fever, and to commemorate his name she had bought a site in Windsor and had there had a nursing-home built which she endowed and herself organised. Her other son, Albert, lived, but not in Britain: adopted by his uncle, who had sided with Prussia in 1864, he had grown up German; became a German Army officer in 1914, serving at the War Office in Berlin; and in 1921 inherited the title of Duke of Schleswig-Holstein.

Prince Christian died in 1917, who had attended fifteen meetings of the council since 1886, some with and some without his wife. The Council, having met, "desired most respectfully to convey to their Gracious President the assurance of their most sincere and heartfelt sympathy" and "earnestly prayed that Divine Consolation might sustain her in her time of

[29] Correspondence. See also *And Then There Was One*, 1983.

grievous sorrow". But his death went unrecorded in the College Magazine. There remained two daughters: Princess Helena Victoria, a spinster, and Princess Marie Louise, 45, now the disappointed wife of Prince Aribert of Anhalt.

From year to year the news had been published of the last of Miss Williamson's girls overlapping with Miss Parker's of before the first world war. Vera Jenkyn had married Mr Gerli in New York; Josephine Elsdon, the Austro-Hungarian Baron Lothar Vranyczany Dobrinovic—like him she mountaineered and had conquered the Schreckhorn in the winter of 1906, after many another Alpine peak; Elizabeth Hitzmann, Herr Meyer, somewhere; Ruth Abbay, called Nancy, Mr Burdekin, in British Columbia; Flossie von Keudell, Baron Fritz von Offenburg of Kidule, Jurbarkas, in Lithuania, at a church in St Petersburg, now Leningrad; Emma Hughes-Hallett, Captain Webber, of Skinner's Horse, in Jhansi, Uttar Pradesh; Olive Lush, Emma's brother, in Buenos Aires; Winifred Woolbert, Lt. George Waller, of the 44th Merwara Infantry, in Delhi; and Ethel Fausset, called Norah, Mr Bingham, in Kandy, Ceylon.

Margaret Seymour, Anna Colvin, Joan Robinson and Florence—Flossie—Gubbins were in turn presented at court; Molly Read set herself up as a book-binder and leather-worker; Grace Raikes took a course at the Colonial Training College, Wantage; Bertha Burleigh wrote for *The Daily Telegraph* and as war correspondent in Belgium for *The Queen*; Irene MacBeth studied German in Dresden and French in Paris and would teach at Wycombe Abbey; Kathleen Allen taught the daughters of the Chinese Ambassador; Margaret Ashdown stayed *au pair* at the Villa Torrance, near Bonn; and Lilian Isaacson and Winifred Hammond completed their training in the gymnasium run by the sisters Beatrice and Evelyn Bear.[30]

In the last full year of peace Josephine Peake wintered in Sweden, Beryl Jenkins in Prague, Josephine Campbell in Neuveville in Switzerland, Edith Stubington in Lisbon and the Canaries and Marjorie Crichton in Rome, while Kathleen Klingender settled in Goslar. Many other girls had studied French in France or German or music in Germany or taught in private families in many a noble city or estate, all over Europe.

In 1915 Flossie von Keudell wrote a long letter to Miss Parker (who had altered Flossie's name from "von" to "de", to make it sound less foe). A battle had been fought on her estate in Kidule. She was now in Russia; her husband, Fritz, had been interned and she had waited for him at the Hotel Volga, in Moscow, translating from Chekov, until he was released.

What a ghastly war this is! We have had a full taste of its horrors, and after countless vicissitudes have finally landed at Kazan. It is north-east of Moscow[31] *. . . an interesting old town . . . formerly the capital of the Tartar kingdom. There are still a great number of Tartars to be seen about,*

[30] Included in the house for women students which opened at Kensington Gore in 1887; then called Alexandra House; Alexandra's since 1910.

[31] Due east would be almost correct.

which gives it an oriental appearance. Since the last few days, however, the streets are full of Austrian officers brought from Premysel. They look all exceedingly well fed and beaming, and not as if they had been through a hard six-months' siege. Poor, dear Kidule is again in the hands of those dreadful Germans, and they are continuing their work of havoc and devastation there. The saddest thing I have experienced was to see one's home being wrecked before one's eyes and not being able to lift a finger to save it. We came in for a battle, which was rather terrifying, and the shrapnel whizzed over our house for twelve hours. When machine guns and cannons fire at the same time, the noise is, to the uninitiated, perfectly demoralising, for days afterwards one hears the sounds buzzing in one's ears. Fritz has been through the most unpleasant adventures but is now here safe and sound.

Her school in Ealing remained unscathed and hardly at all disturbed. Guns could be heard there, firing at the Zeppelins, and the whine of a shell overhead, as the girls took refuge in the cellars wearing nighties or pyjamas and wrapped in eiderdowns (Miss Parker had preferred nighties, but pyjamas were now recommended, and soon became the rule, a girl having stepped on her nightie in the dark and fallen downstairs). But routine changed little. The same staff taught, mainly women, and a few men, too old to be conscribed. The contest was explained. Maps were displayed and at the first school party of the Autumn Term 1914 both girls and staff were encouraged to identify naval and military commanders and the main types of warplane and ship.

News of the sinking of the German battle-cruiser, the *Scharnhorst*, off the Falklands, with Admiral von Spee himself on board, came early in the war, but Miss Parker's reading of it to the girls did not arouse the kind of fighting spirit which they had shown in debate or on the field, and in one of them at least, Barbara Allen, its effect was the opposite:

Perhaps it was Miss Parker's drooling patriotism, the sanctimonious unction with which she gloated, but suddenly I heard myself saying, "But after all, Miss Parker, it was *three against one," and almost instantaneously found myself bounced out of the room and up the stairs to ignominious bed.*[32]

The Vicar preached a sermon on Christian Warfare and its Weapons: prayer, bible-reading and holy communion, at the Old Girls' Week-End. Emil Cammaerts[33] came and spoke about Belgium and its army, whose morale was even better in the trenches than it was at base. Prof. Albert Pollard,[34] whom the girls heard speak at University College, dealt gently

[32] Unpublished memoirs.

[33] Professor Emeritus of Belgian Studies and Institutions, University of London; he had lived in England since 1908.

[34] The eminent historian, a Fellow of All Souls, Oxford, and contributor of about five hundred lives to the DNB.

with the Germans: it was only the Prussians who were bent on war; Alsace-Lorraine should become an independent buffer state—the French ought not to have it; and the Kaiser should not be treated as a scapegoat. Miss Margery Fry[35] spoke guardedly of patriotism, which in everybody's life now ran "red hot". It was easy to sing patriotic songs, when battles needed to be fought, but it was deeds, not words, that would count, and the truly patriotic woman would not stand idle, when peace had been restored, and when thousands more children would die, neglected, in the big industrial cities. A Mlle Orange Colombier lectured in French on French military verse and recited the "Marseillaise" holding the *Tricouleur* in her hand "to make it more dramatic". Lady Flora Lugard[36] exposed the wicked Germans, grinning as they killed, like the Prussian lancer, who had speared a baby and ridden with it sticking to his lance, in evil triumph, and told about the woman refugee whose friend's Prussian husband had spat into her tea when he was angry with her: "A man who can do that is capable of everything." The world fought for a prize which the girls, now in the rosy dawn of life, would inherit: a better world, where grew the fruits of liberty. Dr George Parkin[37] foresaw that when the war had been won a quarter of the globe would be British and would look to the Motherland for liberty, justice, guidance, while thirteen million Britons would still live in slums, where it was hard to live a Christian life. "I beseech you, girls, . . . teach yourselves to demand of men, not costly jewellery, but service and devotion of better, higher kinds . . ." The Lord Mayor of London, Mr Charles Hanson,[38] arrived fully robed and plumed, with his sheriffs all in scarlet and cocked hats, and in "a cheering address" he called upon all present to support the men in France.

In 1916 a list was compiled, eighty-seven names long, to honour "Special Work of Old Girls in Connection with the War to Assist the Empire". It included those of many nurses and War Office clerks—Kathleen Klingender among them, who had returned from the Harz when war broke out, Edith Stubington, appointed "sub-forewoman in Kew Gardens of the Alpine department", Edith Leapingwell and Gladys Richardson, chauffeuring father's car, Kathleen Baker, with the Forestry Corps—"such a jolly camp life"—at Petworth, felling trees with axe and saw, Sybil Isaacson, who worked for the blind, and those who replaced

[35] Warden of University House, Birmingham, she was soon to work in France with the Quakers' War Victims Relief Mission and later and in turn as Honorary Secretary of the Howard League for Penal Reform, Principal of Somerville College, Oxford, and a Governor of the British Broadcasting Corporation.

[36] Head of the Colonial Department of *The Times* and wife of Sir Frederick, Governor-General of Nigeria in the years of war and first Baron Lugard by 1928.

[37] Author of many books, including one intended to be used in schools, *Round the Empire*, 1892, and a biography of Edward Thring, Headmaster of Uppingham, 1898. He was knighted in 1920.

[38] Knighted in 1918 and to be similarly honoured in Austria, France, Italy, Greece and—Order of the Rising Sun (Third Class)—in Japan.

men in offices and banks or helped in canteens or with concerts, or who stayed at home and prepared bandages for Serbs or knitted socks for soldiers or mittens for sailors or bedjackets for Frenchmen or body-belts and shirts for Belgians.

On Bastille Day next year a "Motion of Sympathy", composed by the VIth Form, was sent to the French Ambassador; he thanked them for their *gracieuse pensée*; the girls assembled, the Union Jack and again the *Tricouleur* were held aloft and France got three more cheers, while the VIth collected money—£6–10s.—for the French Red Cross.

The school contributed to many a new good cause, benefiting soldiers and sailors and their families, hospitals, Belgian children and Russian prisoners of war; girls, mistresses and servants between them knitted 216 socks of size 11, from wool which the Russian Embassy had supplied; the Ambassador wrote thanking all the knitters and Miss Parker read out his letter at assembly.

Miss Parker admired the Russians and the French and she detested the Germans. The country was "plunged in a life and death struggle with her deadliest foes", they were "barbarous" and "savage" and the longer the war dragged on the less could the Russians and the French do wrong or the Germans—Huns—do good. But God gave help, who supported the Allies, and so did Rupert Brooke, with his patriotic verse, and John Oxenham, another faithful bard, fuller than was Rupert of talk of race and fame, who had presented a book to the College.

Propaganda intensified. A display of arts and crafts at Burlington House, including cartoons by the Dutchman, Louis Raemakers,[39] impressed everyone: "These powerful pictures gave us a good idea of the frightfulness of the Germans and the great courage with which the troops of the Allies combat it." What the country needed now was verse and art for victory, whatever might be said for art and verse for verse's sake and art's.

And so it was with music. More patriotic songs were sung than the school had ever known: "To the Navy", "Hearts of Oak", "Soldiers of the King", "The Gunners of London", and perhaps, already, "O Land of Britain, Best of Noble Islands"—they sang it in the twenties—the British National Anthem as before, with the Russian, the French, and even the Rumanian, Rumania having come into the war at about half time, responding to the lure of considerable booty. Miss Parker's ban on German music curtailed the Monday evening repertoires; and one young pianist found her ruling difficult, who could only play a short and simple prelude by J. S. Bach; given out, however, as a piece by Tchaikovsky, it impressed Miss Parker and she smiled and applauded it.

The Russians being allies of the British and the French, it was time to find out more about their culture and ideals. "The language is purely and essentially European, with a grammar slightly more difficult than

[39] His complete *Cartoon History of the War* appeared in 1919.

German", Miss Parker understood, "and which English people have infinitely greater facility in acquiring than have our enemies, and which, as a rule, they pronounce much better." The German lessons had been stopped anyway, Fräulein Goerke resigning her post when war broke out—no more would now be said about the prize for the best-kept garden—so Russian dictionaries and text-books were acquired instead, novels and other works of history and travel. The music of Russia, which Dr Ernest Markham Lee[40] came and lectured on, was already well known and admired, easily confused though Tchaikovsky sometimes was with J. S. Bach; also its ballet, which the curriculum now included, and its art. A Mrs Howe, Russian born, outlined its history and a White Russian *émigré*, Prof. Mikhail Vasilevich Trofimov, who would write text-books, attempted to correct what he had heard described as the Englishman's "abysmal ignorance" of its language.

The Professor began by flattering his audience: their own tongue was "the noblest of the Scandinavian Teutonic group", as was French within the Latin, and his own within the Slav. But the approach failed. The girls ragged him and, although Miss Parker intervened, little was learnt, and even the brilliant Muriel Dodds found that, after eighteen months, almost all that she could say in Russian was "I cannot understand".

German aside, the curriculum had continued undisturbed and the only danger which the war exposed it to did not arise from enemy action but from three British Army officers, who, on the 27th of June 1917, arrived in a motor-car outside the school's front door and asked to see the Principal.

As Miss Parker complained in her report to the Council, they had not given their names, and did not, when she appeared, see fit to introduce themselves. The College was included on a list they had compiled of sites for hospitals, they would now inspect it, and not until she had asked who led them did they say that it was Col. Rowe[41] of the Requisitioning of Sites Department, Eastern Command.

The officers demanded and were given and removed the plans of the school, asked about numbers, then discussed among themselves how best they might adapt it to their needs and where to build some huts. Were houses empty in the street nearby? No, none. But that did not matter, an officer replied; if there was anything he wanted, he could always requisition it.

A fourth officer arrived, perhaps an engineer. One of the others introduced him to the rest but not until he had himself suggested it did they introduce him to Miss Parker, and they continued to think it unnecessary either to address Miss Parker as Principal or to communicate with her employers.

Instead they went outside, measured the grounds, came back indoors

[40] Professor of Organ, the Guildhall School of Music. Author of works on Brahms and Grieg.

[41] Rowe, Octavius, retired, aged 61; Egyptian Expedition, 1882.

and asked about the drains and the supply of water. Miss Parker showed them round and they discussed how they might use the dormitories and form-rooms, adapt the kitchen, add some doors and introduce more gas. Col. Rowe then said that he would have to write his report to the War Office and that he expected to commandeer the buildings.

With the same absence of notification, Miss Parker enquired, as had been their inspection? It was likely, the colonel replied, that a period of notice would be given of about two months.

But nothing happened. Miss Parker wrote and complained to the Board of Education, supported by her Chairman, Sir Joseph, himself no doubt supported by Princess Helena, and the College was reprieved.

A few months later the Armistice was signed; crowds filled the streets and sang and cheered. Miss Parker appeared to have forgiven Col. Rowe, or forgotten him, and called upon her pupils to switch on all the lights and make as much noise as they liked, rejoicing.

But their feelings were mixed; as Barbara Allen was quick to understand, even though her father had been too old to volunteer and her brother too young:

for many of us the marrow froze in our bones. Those with loved ones among the fighting forces, shocked with relief, wanted to behold their peace and healing in quietness. Those of us who had no such contacts felt only the artificiality of such a finale to the vast overshadowing we had taken for granted since our childhood; and as we gazed from our dormitory windows at the brilliant pyrotechnics over London, tears and prayers found silent expression in our hearts in a way which would have earned Miss Parker's undisguised contempt had she but known.[42]

Celebration, however, was already somewhat muted. Influenza, which had spread across the world, caught Ealing and the school. Prize-Giving had to be postponed and Princess Helena's visit cancelled—her first, it would have been, since 1906.

Earls Haig[43] and Beatty[44] were approached in 1920, the Rev. Dr Charles Gore, Bishop of Oxford,[45] Mrs Winston Churchill, a Mrs Davidson, and Sir Clement Montague-Barlow,[46] who all said no, Sir Clement having first said yes. But Lady St Helier, Vice-President, agreed to appear, Princess Helena's Lady-in-Waiting, who told her audience that, although men on the whole outdid women, women deserved to be allowed to take degrees at Cambridge (now that Oxford had relented); they excelled caring for others; and should always strive "to do their best in the

[42] Unpublished memoirs.

[43] Douglas, first Earl, C.-in-C., British Army in France, 1915–17, whose trench-war strategy caused hundreds of thousands to die in vain.

[44] David, first Earl; C.-in-C., the British Fleet, 1916–19.

[45] Author of *The Prevention of Conception, Commonly Called Birth-Control*, 1927.

[46] MP for Salford South and Minister of Labour.

position in which Providence had placed them and, by their example, to bring up their children to the glory of the country".

The Earl of Balcarres and Crawford, PC,[47] followed, who approved of posts for women in public life; and in 1922 Miss Bertha Phillpotts,[48] Mistress, newly appointed, of Girton College, Cambridge.

. . . it gave her great pleasure to be there. She was sorry that our head-mistress was ill as everyone who had had to do with education had heard of her, and she had looked forward to making her acquaintance. She [Miss Phillpotts] had many links with the College. It was the old school of her friend, Miss Compton[49] *. . . Also, since taking up her work at Girton, she had found two P.H.C. old girls there, Rosamund White and Muriel Dodds.*

Most people, she said, in her position wanting to make a speech would try to remember what had been said on similar occasions in their school-days. She, however, had never been to school. She had asked the whole of the members of the Girton Staff, but although they had all been to school and to prize distributions, they could not remember what was said. Some said that the girls were told about the importance of good manners, and the youngest member of the staff said that a bishop had once come to her school, and he had told them to remember to darn their socks.

Miss Phillpotts, having hoped that she would now do better, urged everyone to pursue knowledge, not only to pass examinations or to obtain employment, but for its own sake—as in Iceland, she had found.

The school which the prize-giving visitors had addressed was smaller than Miss Williamson's. Miss Williamson in her last six years had mainly relied on day-girls, about three in every four; Miss Parker took fewer: from about three in five before the war to about one in two thereafter. The intake, day and board, remained professionally middle class to upper, more successful than grand. As at most London or almost-London schools it would grow more cosmpolitan. It did not, unlike Roedean, impose a Jewish quota. A Sechiari, a Mosbacher, a Ricardo arrived. The Christians included Presbyterians; Danish Lutherans; and Erica Fraser, a Christian Scientist from Penrhyndeudraeth, North Wales. Miss Parker once told Lissa Birchall-Wood that she would never accept any girls who had attended a convent school, having found them underhand; but Roman Catholics had also been enrolled, even boarders, who were allowed to worship at their own church, escorted by Ma'm'selle.

Of two girls noticeably different, one, Mary Mercedes Fisher, is said to

[47] David, tenth Earl of Balcarres, twenty-seventh of Crawford; also Baron Wigan of Haigh Hall, where in 1830 the Lindsays applied for a governess but could not be found one. Formerly MP for Chorley and from 1916 to 1922 in turn Lord Privy Seal, Chancellor of the Duchy of Lancaster and Minister of Transport.

[48] Educated at home, all but a term at a private school in Hampstead; then at Girton, where she caught the eye, sailing by on the Huntingdon Road with a sheet of canvas fastened to her bicycle.

[49] Not known.

have been teased and even shunned. She had arrived from Las Palmas, Gran Canaria, in 1917, aged 14, tall, rather dark, with big brown eyes; they called her "the horse", for she was said to be clumsy; and she left for home after only two years. "We were all revoltingly cruel to her," wrote Barbara Allen in 1983,[50] "with the worst of British stupidity and snobbery. It will be a black mark in Heaven against all of us. She was utterly lonely. We were all merciless." But some think that Mary was better received than Barbara remembered or imagined.[51] The other, Rose Hives,[52] everyone called Rosie. Her face looked sad whenever it was photographed, but she played for the Lacrosse 1st XII, so must have felt admired, and she made and kept good friends.

Inspectors returned at the end of the first full year of peace and reported their findings to Princess Helena. The house and grounds had delighted them. Miss Parker's "ability, tactfulness and character" earned "profound admiration"; and the school's financial health owed much to her cleverness in choosing staff, "taking young mistresses who required less salary because they were gaining experience".

So far, so good. But the juniors had to have more room indoors, where they could run about, or a separate annexe or school; compulsory medical inspections were needed, which anyway the law would soon enforce; the contrast between the hall, beautifully furnished by the girls' own efforts, and the cramped and ill-stocked library was "deplorable"; the girls should not start French till they were 9 or Latin till 11; "the absence of any serious science teaching" (botany seemed not to count) "was the most grave shortcoming in the curriculum"—"the girl of the present day and of the future will require to be equipped with a knowledge of science if she is to take her place [we do not read where] as an educated woman"; and Miss Parker's salary would have to be improved—capitation fees were obsolete.

A month or two later the Board of Education declared the school efficient; it acquired an Army hut, where a master at the Latymer Upper School, Mr Ernest Goddard, whom the boys called Botch,[53] taught two

[50] Muriel Dodds (Dr Hood), 18.2.1984: "I note that you quote both Miss Milvain and Barbara Allen—both these ladies have colour and imagination rather than veracity as their strong points; and I should treat anything they say with some reserve."

[51] Barbara Allen (Mrs Priest), 30.4.1984: "Don't set *too* much store by Muriel Dodds!! To be 'outrageous' was to bolster up her conviction of superiority—she came to P.H.C. at nearly sixteen (with me). Mature, sophisticated, travelled, speaking perfect French, exceedingly clever both academically and musically—she was the much-indulged only child of elderly well-to-do parents—her father was a wealthy lawyer in Limerick who left her a fortune. She was most unpopular at school (naturally!) but, like Lord Curzon, being a Superior Perzon has carried her through life! She can be inaccurate—we had japanned *tin* hot-water cans, not brass!!"

[52] Mother of General Sir Richard Worsley, Chief of Staff, Far East Land Forces, 1969–71, and a member of the Board of Governors.

[53] A name carved on his laboratory door at Latymer. He maintained the clock for the Methodist Church next to his school and rode an ancient bicycle.

hours of chemistry and elementary physics on Saturday mornings, with which little help some clever girls progressed to university degrees and science careers, including medicine; a separate preparatory school was planned for the infants; it duly appeared; meanwhile a giant's stride was erected in the playground; and Miss Parker's salary, about £350 a year, rose to £500, paid in three end-of-term instalments.

The salaries of staff had all crept upwards after 1902. A teacher of French earned £70 a year by 1917; a classicist, £85; and a living-out geographer, £140. Pensions and nationally agreed (Burnham) scales were not introduced until the late twenties.

In 1923, when Miss Parker's salary was still unchanged, her deputy, Miss White, received £200, the young Miss Prain, History, £140, and Miss Richardson, assistant matron, £100. Mr Goddard did better. His hourly rate of £1–10s. was a handsome fee, given what it bought, and more, *pro rata*, than was needed to employ Miss Parker and the same three colleagues. The teachers fully earned their "board and lodging free", so accessibly on call were they all, by day and in the night, and with so many duties to perform outside the classroom. Miss Parker had continued to do the work of two. The Council congratulated her on the drawing-up of the balance sheet and in 1922, when she reported to it that £500 had been repaid on the mortgage account and produced a copy of the endorsement made upon the deed, their fully-employed servant must have seemed, to those who saw and understood, to be an underpaid factotum drudge.

We are not informed how the inspectors found the quality of work, but good examination results were achieved and at least seventy-eight of Miss Parker's flock went on to university in the almost thirty years that she was Head: six of them to Oxford, and to Cambridge twenty, where Newnham alone took twelve; and at least nine read Medicine, after Winifred Fawsset in 1910, though Winifred herself did not complete the course. Muriel Dodds won the Higgins Scholarship to Girton in English and French, got a first, misprinted in the College Magazine as "in the Medical and Modern Language Tripos", then her Ph.D at the Sorbonne; Kathleen Sissmore, reading Law, got three firsts in a row; Mary Savery, HS20, a first in Theology at Oxford; Joan Barlee, another, in Mathematics, at Trinity, Dublin; Beatrice White, at Cambridge, took on Sanskrit and Pali, with success; and Gertrude Trevelyan won the Newdigate Prize for Poetry at Oxford in 1927, with her poem, "Julia, Daughter of Claudius". They had relied on mascots or pretended that they did: "anything, always", Mary Savery said, for all her theology: a four-leaved clover or white heather or a squeaking dog.

Musicians in ones and twos excelled: the young, Eisteddfod prize-winning sisters Davies, Dorothy—piano?—and Claire, HS03, the cello, also Dorothy Skerry, reported to be studying music under Carl Weber (but Weber, Carl, was 83 years dead). Three artists were elected to the Royal Academy; Flossie von Keudell and Anna Colvin had apprenticed them-

selves to Mr Frank Brangwyn,[54] who painted, etched and lithographed; and at least six more found places at the Slade.

Athletes continued to be scholars and scholars athletes: Theodora Boys captained Newnham at hockey and represented Cambridge; Kathleen Allen captained Newnham at tennis; and Irene Gamble played for Cambridge at lacrosse, prompting Phyllis Challoner, a rower, to write to Miss Parker that she hoped to confer as much lustre on the letters PHC at Oxford.

The girls who had valued and enjoyed their years at school did not, at university, grow languid or *blasé*. Muriel Gamble, in her Cambridge letter:

Up here, as at P.H.C., work is delightful, and play is delightful, and to any of you who are hesitating as to whether to go to College or not, we, who have tried it, would most emphatically say, "If you want to find a place where your outlook on life will be broadened, your interests developed in every direction, your mind stimulated, then come to Newnham, and here, with the full swing of life, and with the memory of P.H.C. days fresh within you, if you are not one of the happiest girls on earth, you ought to be.

The staff were scholars too and they could teach. Miss Parker, it is claimed, hardly ever appointed a dud. And having picked good staff she seldom if ever interfered with their methods but allowed them to teach as they themselves knew best. Some married, so had to leave; but most of the rest remained till they retired or were promoted.

Miss Boys became Headmistress of St Margaret's (and provided a cup for lacrosse for which her two schools frenziedly competed till in the 1960s it gathered dust in Bushey); Miss Chapman, a lecturer in Classics at Liverpool University, then Principal of Westfield College, London; Miss MacKay, Senior Mistress at Bedales; Miss Adams, Headmistress of Macclesfield High School; Miss Shepherd, of the Richmond; Miss Stokes, of the Guildford, then of Bournemouth; and Miss Pode of the Eveline, Bulawayo, in Rhodesia.

It was rumoured that Miss Pode had given up her post of head and had eloped with the Vicar, he well supplied with all the parish funds. The story was one which the girls rather eagerly accepted, she having incurred their mistrust (and ridicule) as well as earned respect. "We all knew she was a Catholic," wrote Mary Channon. "Miss Parker did not." And Muriel

[54] A Welshman born in Bruges, where a museum bears his name. Knighted in 1941. A sensible collector and a painter who felt, and vehemently said, that the artist's name mattered less than his performance. "I didn't care a *damn* who it was by!", he shouted, as he told of a committee which had sent him back a painting it had asked him to exhibit, refusing to accept it as a genuine Sorel. "The fact *was* and *is* to this day that it was a noble picture of that period." (Count William de Belleroche: *Brangwyn's Pilgrimage: the Life Story of an Artist*, 1948.)

Dodds: "A compulsive liar but a very fine teacher, to whom I owe my scholarship to Cambridge."

The senior musicians tended to be men: Mr Grimson, violin, who retired taking with him his portrait in oils and a purse full of gold; Dr Yorke Trotter, Principal of the London Academy of Music, but with time to spare—he originated the (or a) rhythmic method of teaching, but no one now seems ever to have heard of it; and Mr J. Cliffe-Forrester, composer and pianist, whom Princess Helena's daughter, Helena Victoria, would present with a cheque for £60, which in 1934 would have bought him a new motor-car, thus gratefully acknowledging his fifty years of service to the school.

Almost all the rest of the staff were women. Miss Boys, Miss Buchanan, "the Buke" ("I am not telling you to *stop* whistling—just suggesting you might whistle in tune") and Miss White stood out, much loved, in turn Miss Parker's deputies; also: Miss Paget-Kemp, as devoted to the girls as to her mother old and sick—in the Spring Term of her twenty-first year spent teaching them art she died of pleuro-pneumonia; and Miss Chorlton, English and the Shakespeare play, whom Barbara Allen so adored:

Sandy-haired and spectacled . . . she would gaze upon her fascinated form . . . sometimes with far-away dreaminess, and . . . allow a fine white handkerchief constantly to glide through the fingers of her exquisite hands; this had a mesmeric effect upon her young hopefuls and lulled them into an imprudent state of repose. Then she would pounce . . .[55]

Miss Naylor taught needlework—she topped Miss Parker, standing 6′4″ tall, the smallest member of a family of five—her stitches were as dainty as her fingers were huge; Miss Fryer, Gymnastics, the much admired in her gym-slip navy blue, which barely hid her knees; Miss Turton and Miss Williams, Latin—Miss Williams introduced its new pronunciation, only Welsh, and was known as "Bill", "Willy Wirtus" and "Crash Bang", her habitual comment when a desk-lid fell shut; Miss Pinney, English, and Miss Lord, Mathematics, two devoted Anglo-Catholics; Miss Jenkins, called "Jenks", junior work and Guides—*cognoscenti* fed the rumour that Miss Lord and Miss Jenkins were lovers (they could only have had in mind a crush or bosom friendship); Mlle Guyomar, "Ma'm'selle", taught French: elderly, plump, and who, if impatient, threw books about in class.

The Russian course had long ago collapsed, but not until 1930 did demand revive for German, which Russian had replaced. A teacher of the subject had again to be found. A vacancy was advertised. At least one applicant appeared and as Guendolen Sherrard would recall, writing to the school fifty-four years later, Miss Parker looked pained when her visitor had left and she and her VIth Form pupil met, in the hall outside the Study:

She emerged from her private cloakroom and said, as she had had to interview a German teacher who had put out a hand which, manners

[55] Unpublished memoirs.

decreed, she should shake, she had been off to clean her hands. I gathered that one mother had requested German lessons.

Fräulein Schoppe was appointed, a visiting member of staff, whose hand, it may have been, Miss Parker had accepted, with enough pupils to provide her with an income of £11 a term.

Lectures were arranged as well as lessons, entertaining or instructive or both, on Art, ancient and fairly modern, Music and Literature, the Bible and the Church, Parliament, Newspapers, the Empire, the Empire and the Empire, Astronomy, the Buried Past, Wonders of the World, Pond Life, Dinosaurs—from Prof. Rowntree[56]—and on the Dog and how he had Helped to Win the First World War.

The Rev. Mr Jocelyn Perkins, later Dr, but still called Polly, drew customary cheers for his talk about Westminster Abbey;[57] the Rev. Mr William Draper, Master of the Temple, dealt with nineteenth-century novelists; a Dr Bowen-Armstrong, with Shakespeare; Prof. del Re,[58] with Dante; Mr L. A. G. Strong, critic, biographer and novelist,[59] with writing as a career; the Rev. Mr Theodore Wood,[60] with "cwustaceans"—lobsters, "cwayfish" and "cwabs"—and with ants and bees, using five blackboards, where he drew in coloured chalk, using both his hands at once and with basin, soap and towel all within reach (the ant stood next to man intellectually and had 12,000 eyes, it celebrated funerals, gave half an hour a day to sport and was keen on all-in wrestling); and an author-ornithologist, Mr John Walpole-Bond, imitated bird-calls.

Reports on the lectures choked the Magazine, summary and verbatim. Sixty-seven were recorded in 1921, a few of which had been given outside school—the poet, Walter de la Mare's, and the antarctic explorer, Shackleton's—the rest at the College, where more were arranged in Miss Parker's last ten years than in the previous one hundred. Flossie Gubbins's father, Sir Launcelotte, a surgeon-general, came and spoke about the Afghan Wars. Evans of the Broke followed him, the hero of Jutland and the South Pole; Prof. Wilden Hart,[61] who warned against Bolshevism and called upon the girls to help alert the public to its threat; Dr George Lloyd, Bishop of Saskatchewan—"he believes Canada to be the future master of

[56] Arthur, almost certainly, Headmaster of Bootham, 1899–1927, thereafter a busy itinerant lecturer, and a Fellow of University College, London.

[57] A minor canon there for at least forty years; chaplain, for a while, to a hospital somewhere for "Ladies of Limited Means"; and an assistant master at St Saviour School in Southwark.

[58] Cavaliere Arundel del Re, a lecturer in Italian and-or English Literature in New Zealand, Oxford, King's College London, Tokyo and Formosa.

[59] For twelve years a master at Summer Fields Preparatory School, Oxford.

[60] Vicar of Mary Magdalene, Wandsworth Common, Rural Dean, a prolific writer on natural history and a renowned collector of British beetles.

[61] Historian and lecturer, an authority on the influence of the Bible and Shakespeare on the English language; Poland; and the effect of athletics on students in Japan.

America and that it rests with us whether this mighty power shall be one united English nation: if only a few of the many superfluous women now in England would emigrate this great work might be accomplished"; Dr Aylward Blackman, the Egyptologist, who talked about Tutankhamen's tomb; Miss Alice Bacon, the first British woman pilot: when she looped the loop at Hendon, she had viewed the earth "as if it were up in the sky"; and travellers many, with exciting news to tell about China and Tibet, the Himalayas, Unknown Asia, the South Seas, Malaya, the Nile, the Niger, the Sahara, the African Jungle and Big Game, Swamp and Bush, the Amazon . . . and a Mohawk Chief, Os-ke-non-ton, came fully fledged, with tomahawk and tom-tom, and with dry sticks, from which to rub himself a fire, setting light to what he called a mouse's nest.

The Bishop of London, Dr Arthur Winnington-Ingram, disclosed the five secrets of influence (modesty, purpose, sincerity, humour, faith) and invited five of the girls to come and play tennis with him at Fulham Palace, his lovely Thames-side house and gardens, where he surprised and delighted them, emerging from a secret, book-case door. It is likely that he won, as the girls deferentially allowed his team to do when they met at hockey.[62]

Prof. Arthur Hadrian Allcroft, author-archaeologist, who had drawn, measured and described in print almost every ancient camp and barrow in the land, lectured exhaustively on Greek, Latin and Italian literature, ancient Egypt and mediaeval drama, from 1910 or so till the week of his death in 1923. "I have told you," he began, raising his eyebrows at the girls and wrinkling his forehead, "but I dare say you have forgotten . . ." No doubt they had. But they did not forget how he once rocked too far backwards on his chair and fell right off, when nobody dared to laugh, or how tattered was his gown.

Prof. Sumichrast—Frederick Caesar John Samuel Roussay de Sumichrast, but preferring to be called Mr Sumi—arrived in 1912, aged 68; Belgian-born but Edinburgh and London-educated, and thought to be a Pole, he had lived in Canada, where he edited *The Halifax Morning Chronicle*; and from 1887 to 1911 was Professor of French at Harvard, much acclaimed. The British Government employed him as its envoy to France, with the task of pouring oil on waters which the Dreyfus case had troubled, and to the United States, where he needed the police to protect him from the Irish. A declared feminist, he doted on the girls and for twelve years entertained them with his lectures, on French history and literature and sometimes on America.

He filled the school with gifts: book upon book, more than two hundred all at once in 1922, many leather-bound, gold-tooled; *terra cotta* busts of Molière, Racine, Corneille, Voltaire; beautiful prints and original documents, in particular a *Lettre d'État*, signed by the *Roi Soleil* himself—

[62] He played both games till in his seventies and golf till almost the end of his days, in 1946, when he was 87 or 88.

all have vanished; and in 1927, when Gertrude Trevelyan won the Newdigate Prize for Poetry, he sent to the school in her honour a palm-leaf crown tied with green and gold ribbon.

The Professor retired in 1924. He was eighty years old, but loth to say goodbye, and as a letter shows, which he wrote to Miss Parker in 1931, if ever again he could help in any way he would respond:

This is a memorable week for me. Dr Grey consents to my giving one lecture a week. And the girls will come to me. Is not this wonderful? In my 88th year to be still able to teach acceptably. Beats the psalmist hollow with his moans and regrets.

He had also taught scripture but disturbed some of the pupils in his class, one of whom, Rosamund Ashby, found him "most irreverent", he appearing to mock church practices and hymns: "never before had such ideas been put before me . . . I used to wonder if Miss Parker knew about it."

But Miss Parker revered him, as a scholar and as a person: "our dear old friend the Professor . . . a great teacher and profound student of the Bible . . . to whom the Gospels were the Bread of his life . . . a beautiful and saintly influence in the College—like Abraham . . . a veritable Friend of God", she wrote in her obituary of him, the longest and warmest which the College Magazine had ever contained.

Dr Compton-Rickett, novelist and critic, of the lavender tie stabbed through with jewelled pin, lectured and wrote on everyone and everything of note in English literature, at Cambridge, London and Oxford, first, then from 1915 till 1936 at the College. Did the girls notice how advanced were his views? We read in his memoirs[63] that the mother of a girl of thirteen, at perhaps another school, once asked him to exclude *Romeo and Juliet* and *Othello* from his course or her daughter from his class. He does not record his answer. What it was it would be difficult to guess. On the one hand he disapproved of censorship: "You will only get from a book what you take to it; and by establishing a Bluebeard chamber in literature you do far more harm than by putting on no restrictions whatever." His advice to Miss Parker, on the other hand, was to beware of John Masefield, whose work was sometimes much too coarse to be included in the library.

The girls valued his approach. Scholar though he was, they did not feel spoken down to.

Yet another learned man about the school was Mr Harold Hodge, who agreed in 1920 to be Chairman of the Council, replacing Sir Joseph. An Oxford classicist, translator of the Histories of Tacitus, barrister, a London County Council educationalist, like Miss Phillpotts a Governor of Westfield College, and retired editor of *The Saturday Review*, he had

[63] *I Look Back: Memories of Fifty Years*, with a foreword by J. Ramsay MacDonald, 1933.

Left to right: Prof. Mikhail Vasilevich Trofimov, called Trophy; Prof. Frederick Caesar John Samuel Roussay de Sumichrast, called Sumi; Dr Compton-Rickett; and Prof. Arthur Hadrian Allcroft.

written a book, *In the Wake of War: Parliament or Imperial Government*,[64] and was a keen entomologist.

Mr Hodge approved of Science; he rejected the view that it was not practicable to give girls quite the same education as boys—differences of character between the sexes did not need to be developed until after school age; but he still approved of Latin, which he hoped the sciences would not

[64] London and New York, 1917.

displace: it was preposterous that anyone should claim to be educated who had never read a line of Virgil or Caesar.

It is unlikely that the girls came to know Sir Joseph Savory, *éminence grise* for thirty years, more *grise* than *éminence* (his death passed little noticed in the College Magazine); Mr Hodge made much more impact: it would be mainly thanks to him that the staff got pensions and Burnham scale salaries; and he took the prefects out for treats, to performances of Shakespeare, at the Old Vic, and to the Natural History Museum in Kensington, where he could point to his favourite butterflies, to newly-discovered ones, not yet named, which Sir Bertram Thomas had collected in the Arabian Desert, and to his favourite dragonflies.

Mr Moran, called Moran, the school knew even better: a huge Irish-Canadian, or seeming to be huge; its drains-and-boilerman; he also cleaned the girls' brown shoes for games—they themselves had to clean their indoor black—though some of them said that all he did was throw them into water, then lodge them on the pipes and bake them so hard that everyone got blisters; oiled their lacrosse-sticks; hauled trunks up and down the stairs; walked Miss Parker's dog; posted illicit letters, in return for cigarettes; and claimed to have played lacrosse against Red Indians.

Mr Thompson too, called Thompson, tall and bearded, could not be overlooked: gardener from 1885 to 1922, when he retired with a 10s. a week pension from the school, *ex gratia*. His wife, "Old Cookie", ran the kitchen for the first thirty-four of these thirty-seven years and was then allowed to stay and feed the hens, gather eggs and carry meals upstairs to patients in the sick-room, in which time she too received a weekly 10s.

Dr Savery physicianed; a greyer shade of *éminence* than Mr Hodge, a brighter than Sir Joseph, he would be better remembered for his daughter Mary's dark-red hair and first-class brains, and for his black veteran Renault, with its polished brass and oil-lamps, than for his medicine. Miss Moore was matron, so doctor and matron were sometimes pharmaceutically referred to by the girls as Savery and Moore's mixture.

The school relied on games to promote good health, on crocodile walks, when rain stopped play (to Perivale, its fields and lanes, if they were not too muddy—the Great West Road had yet to be built), and on fresh air in class, where Miss Parker was known to appear fur-coated and have cardigans removed and windows opened wide. But minor ills continued. And one grew rifer. The rule about changing out of black stockings into games-field brown, then out of brown and into black, having failed or lapsed, stockings, damp ones, were accused of causing chills, the brown were discarded and bare and purple legs resulted and more chilblains. But girls got chilblains anyway, the dormitories upstairs being arctically cold, and they had often to plunge and soak their aching toes and fingers in hot water mixed with camphorated oil to relieve the pain.

Coughs and running noses were endemic. A nose could be wiped. But coughs had to be stifled. Miss Parker allowed no one to cough at assembly, in class or at church—"My girls do not cough" (though she herself would

often clear her throat before she spoke)—and, if girl ever did, she would wait for her to stop or tell her to leave the room and not to come back till she had pulled herself together. There was no quick cure. Matron would provide a small white pill or brush girls' throats with iodine, but the iodine hurt and made them feel sick and the pill seemed not to work.

If they would only think about their motto! It took three generations, Miss Parker said, to make a gentlewoman, a woman being gentle who had learnt self-control. "If you are ill you are a nuisance to yourself and to everybody else." We are told that she meant it.

The scene: Miss Parker's drawing-room, where Marjorie Harrison, HS30, has begun to cough. Miss Parker: "Marjorie is obviously delicate. We had better shut the window." Marjorie shuts it. But now Guendolen Sherrard, feeling nervous, has to cough too. Miss Parker: Guendolen is obviously in a state of distress. We must open the window."

It was not school policy to fuss over patients. Mary Bird got jaundice and was made to feel that she was being inconsiderate—a discomfort which, years later, Joan Mackwood understood:

I and two other girls were the first to go down in an epidemic of chicken-pox. It was decided to remove us from the "sicker" in the main building down to the "san", many hundreds of yards down to the bottom of the grounds. We were bundled up in eiderdowns and taken down in the donkey-cart, led by Moran, the general factotum, and followed at a safe distance by M.E.P. and Roy [her second dog].

Not a word was spoken—when we arrived, a stick was waved at the door, we were ordered to enter as though we were beginning a sentence—as indeed we were—outcasts.

Concussion and hay-fever were said to be ignored; also abscess under tooth. But girls and boys exaggerate. Miss Parker visited the two top-floor sick-rooms daily, advising convalescents there (non-infectious) to "bicycle" with their legs—it would speed their recovery; and Margaret Summerford found her "very nice".

Enid Channon, aged 13, died early one morning in 1922, of tubercular meningitis. The guide patrols were at once sent out on an expedition and the rest of the school for a long walk, mystified, all but Gertrude Trevelyan, who had caught a heavy cold and been told to work in the library instead, was overlooked and could hear, then see, what she was not meant to: the men taking Enid away in her coffin. And next day, at assembly, Miss Parker announced that the Angel of Death had visited the College.

The staff—and no doubt parents too—were alarmed. Early morning walks were arranged, as a safeguard, and exercises followed school prayers and continued for it might have been till the end of term, no longer.

Miss Parker had always enjoyed good health. But even she fell ill next year. It was a cold, wet, winter afternoon; two girls, Daphne King and Beatrice White, had promised to walk her dog but had forgotten; so she took him out herself, caught pneumonia, and had to stay in bed for

many weeks, grateful to Dr Savery, who, she believed, had saved her life. Miss White ran the school; Prof. Sumichrast taught Miss Parker's lessons; and Beatrice and Daphne crept into their shells, guilt consuming them.

Infectious disease appears to have been rare. From 1921 to 1926 the sanatorium, as such, stood empty. It was either too big or too small and was especially too small in the great influenza epidemic, in the Autumn Term 1918, when the entire school became a sanatorium. The boarders lay in bed, fitfully attended to by staff, if they did not yet feel too sick to help, and by two hired nurses, one of whom, called "the Ghost", floated softly about, holding a lantern and shining it into the eyes of her patients, and smiled and said, as they blinked at her and moaned, "Don't worry, dear. I only wanted to know if you were sleeping."

Mrs Clare Goslett, whose published works include *Influenza and How to Go Through It*, *Hygiene and Temperance in Secondary Schools* and *Simple Hints for Mothers on the Home Sex-Training of Boys*,[65] lectured almost throughout Miss Parker's years on hygiene, physiology and lady-like behaviour and more of her words have been quoted or misquoted ever since than anybody else's.

"Gairls, gairls, never wear serge." But callies were made of serge. "Bones are made of gristle, gairls. Isn't that wonderful?" "Never marry a man out of pity, gairls." "Gairls, gairls, never drink champagne at a party!" "And remember, gairls,"—or was this Miss Parker?—old girls forget and sometimes disagree—"the woman always pays"—with her good name, committing indiscretions.

Her lecture on "brain hygiene" dealt with diet. It was interesting to know that nervous breakdowns could be caused by too many sweets; and melancholia and irritability by want of fresh air. Cod-liver oil did the brain much good. Few enjoyed it. But Devonshire cream had just the same effect.

Mrs Goslett did not refer to sex but once at least she was thought to be about to, having leant confidingly across her desk and lowered her voice and enquired, "Gairls, gairls, there's nobody here under fifteen?" Anyone who was had then to leave the room. Suspense developed, till Mrs Goslett's nerve seemed to fail and she whispered or croaked, "Never forget to brush your teeth, gairls, before you go to bed."

At least one or two of Mrs Goslett's pupils continued to believe that man childed woman with a kiss. But Miss Parker was satisfied. "Mrs Goslett puts it so nicely."

We cannot tell how much is true that has since been recalled, how much the girls embroidered. Mrs Goslett's dentures may have rattled. Did they once fall out? Did the Head of School then pick them off the floor and hand them over? Did Mrs Goslett, whose subject was hygiene, then cram them back into her mouth, unwiped?

Influenza ran its course; the Drill Display took place in April next term,

[65] 1892, 1905 and 1914.

Says one who knows:
"Flat feet are a misery, gairls!"

when prizes were awarded which had had to be withheld, the bronze and silver stars and the certificates; and in June 1920 the school celebrated its one hundredth birthday and received from HRH a message addressed to "My Dear Old Students and Present Girls" and summarising its history and ideals.

My great hope is that the education and training given in my College will help all its members to grow up into God-fearing, good women, and loyal members of our Great Empire, and that a Princess Helena Girl may stand for all that is good and true. I rejoice to think of the affection that all Old Girls bear to their College, and trust it may always occupy a warm place in

their hearts. The love of their College and pride in it are most valuable assets in helping to maintain great and good traditions.

It was a great source of pride to me to hear of all the splendid work old College girls did during the war. I also rejoice to see in the Magazine, and to hear, how many happy marriages have been made, and to know that the children of old pupils are constantly sent to their mother's old College.

Once again I wish you all every blessing and every success in your lives.

Helena
President

A Thanksgiving Service was held, then a Garden Party, followed by two afternoons of a Pageant of Youth, which Miss Paget-Kemp had arranged. St Peter's Church was packed; the girls took their seats early, the boarders in their white costumes and hats, the day-girls apart, wearing some say white, others callies green and gold, while at the west door Mr Hodge, the Council, Miss Parker and the Clergy stood waiting till Princess Helena's motor-car appeared. The Rev. and Hon. Dr Edward Lyttelton,[66] Headmaster of Eton four years retired, gave a *Respice, Aspice, Prospice* address—"an honourable past and the hope is great"—commending the Spirit of Service to which the hearts of boys and girls leapt up in glad response, happiness being theirs who worked for it in others. The 111th Psalm was sung, hymns and, last of all, the National Anthem (but only the first verse).

About 450 guests, including Sir William Dunbar, Flossie von Keudell's widowed mother's *protégeant*, Lady Cynthia Mosley[67] and Miss Margaret Williamson—but not the still alive Miss Roberts—took tea in the shade of the trees and to music played by the Prince of Wales's band. Magazine: "At five o'clock our Royal President left and we assembled on the front drive and sang the National Anthem"—again—"cheering heartily"—again—"as the car drove past." Exhibitions followed. "After supper we all danced, ending up with Sir Roger."

The pageant, in aid of the Hall Panelling Fund, involved each girl. Sunlight fell from a canopy of leaves and fluttered on their costumes, antique, mediaeval and modern-international, as they filed across the outdoor stage, and Romeo, the College pony (released from his mower) wore a wreath of orange marigolds.

Princess Helena admired her girls. Not all of them, however, admired Princess Helena or had much idea of the debt to her which everyone gathered there owed: "a dowdy, dumpy and dull old lady—like an imitation Queen Victoria", wrote Muriel Dodds, many years later. "The Principal was not allowed to sit in her presence, unless invited to. So, not being

[66] Seventh son of the fourth Lord Lyttelton.

[67] Daughter of Lord Curzon, once Viceroy of India, now Foreign Secretary, and first wife of Sir Oswald Mosley, at the time Conservative MP for Harrow and future leader of the British Union of Fascists.

invited to, she viewed the pageant, from beginning to end, standing by her chair. The girls greatly resented this. To them it seemed bad manners."[68]

It is likely, however, that Miss Parker had done as she herself had chosen, the arrangement reflecting more her own ideas about status than it did the Royal President's.

It was Lady St Helier's turn next day, when all was repeated. Although it rained, no one dared take cover for as long as "the College Grandmother", as she called herself, still sat—*noblesse oblige*—and sit she did, so that everybody watched, from the first scene to the last, feeling damp and uncomfortable.

Princess Helena died in 1923, aged 77. A memorial service took place for her at St Peter's Church, attended by staff, present girls and many girls past, the present wearing black mourning-bands on their costumes white, and by Chairman Mr Hodge, but only three other members of the Council; Betty Stone, Head of School, took a wreath of white carnations, arum lilies, stock, asparagus fern and white and crimson roses, to Schomberg House, in the Mall,[69] where the Princess had lived since her mother, Queen Victoria, had died in 1901; Madge Beaumont took another, rose-pink, on behalf of the OGA; and Mr Hodge and Miss Parker represented the school at a memorial service in the Abbey.

Her Royal Highness had patronised the school since 1868, since 1874 as its President; she had rescued and nursed it and set it on its feet; her attendance at Council meetings had improved, once peace was restored—seven out of twenty in the first three of her last five years of life—and the Equerry in Waiting did not stretch truth when he wrote to Mr Hodge how "perpetual and deep" her interest had been in the welfare of the College.

But her name was more connected in the public mind with medicine than it was with the school that bore her name: with hospitals, the Red Cross, nurses, ambulances, the incurably sick, Army and Navy charities, help for mothers of sick children, an orphanage for girls, a holiday home for boys and the first hospital train which, through her initiative and effort, left for France in 1915.

Mr Bridgeman, Home Secretary, addressing the House of Commons, claimed that the Princess had watered where Florence Nightingale had planted. It was thanks to her that more nurses were employed and better trained, their working conditions and terms of service improved and the benefits of nursing extended to the poor. And *The Times* obituary amplified his tributes:

She had not lived a showy life, but an extremely useful one. Her services, given personally, directly and ungrudgingly over many years . . . were of a

[68] Correspondence.

[69] No. 80, west wing only, of the 1650-ish house. Home of Frederick, Duke of Schomberg, killed at the Boyne in 1690; William, Duke of Cumberland, victor of Culloden Moor; and for fourteen years, till his death in 1788, of the artist, Gainsborough. The façade was restored in 1958.

highly practical kind, and their results could not have failed to give her pleasure as she contemplated them in old age.

Princess Christian chose her career . . . early in life, and pursued it . . . with a thoroughness and love of detail which are not always attained by ladies of high station with similar sympathies. She was helped, we may well believe, by the royal gift of being able to remember events and persons; for few minds, as those who knew her will attest, were more orderly or better pigeon-holed . . .

The buildings at Ealing no longer stand but the school that she had rescued survived, if only just, as did many of her prizes, including the one which was awarded to the girl who had taken the wreath to Schomberg House, a copy of Chopin's *Mazurkas Polonaises*, with the words therein inscribed:

To Muriel Elizabeth Stone, 1920
from Helena
President

It was almost the last. The list of prizes and certificates, handed out or announced, had been whittled down from 201 to 158 in 1917, then again shrank from 124 to 23 in 1922. In 1922 the Award of Merit lapsed and after—and because?—Princess Helena was dead, prize-giving was abolished. Awards continued to be made outdoors, to athletes, individuals and teams. But for fifty years no more was heard of the Princess Christian—Helena—Prize for Advanced Pianoforte. It is thought and may be true that Miss Parker and the Council agreed that unavailing effort should be more esteemed and that gifts, brains and good results were enough boon already and ought not to be rewarded.

Princess Helena Victoria agreed to fill her mother's role of President. She too would be no mere figurehead. Not a single meeting of the Council would she miss from 1923 till the year of her death in 1948. The girls came to know her, at least by sight. She visited the school to see French plays, when everyone looked smarter than ever, but what pleased her most was to meet them caught off guard.

Easter Term
1925

Arrangements had been made . . . that the Princess should not see the girls until they were in their form-rooms after tea; but on her way down to see the bottom field and the sanatorium she met those . . . who had been playing there: the girls were all very muddy and very hot and untidy, but the Princess seemed pleased to see them as they were every day in the week, and remarked on their bare legs, which were, no doubt, the muddiest part about them.

As her sister, Marie Louise, records, the Princess had herself enjoyed games. "She had been so strong and energetic—eighteen holes of golf

meant nothing to her—so fond of riding and hunting . . ."[70] To the family she was Thora. Her brothers called her Mousie. She was also, unkindly, known as Snipe.

Lacrosse results had fitfully improved. War-time matches had been arranged against Chelsea Physical Training College and Newnham College, Cambridge, and lost, but not too badly, and the XII beat Queenswood 19–2. Defeat spread gloom. But victories were often scored against London University Colleges in the mid-1920s, and even later, when numbers were reduced. Jean Rotheram went on to captain Ireland. Beryl Yeld-Stephens played for Wales. But hockey either languished—in 1916 only three matches took place, two against the War Office and one against the OGA—or opposing teams were more difficult to beat; and girls appeared to console themselves not only with teas in the front hall—better than any served at other schools—Lyons iced sponge sandwiches, in chocolate and coffee and pink and white—but with yet more brooches.

Betty Stone—Muriel Elizabeth, HS23—captained in 1921 a rather inactive but undefeated Hockey XI. Jean Mackay promised well but hit too hard and was too fond of going her own way; Charlotte Duncan, called Chattie, from Strathpeffer, Ross, could catch the ball and shoot but was rather short of "dash"; Lavender Norris, though quick and neat, was "very little use against anyone stronger than herself"; and only Betty Riley earned all praise.

Lavender, a girl considered to have been among the prettiest the College had ever enrolled, left school next summer and was still only twenty years old when, in 1926, she was killed, flung from a car being driven by a friend of a friend on the Brooklands race-track.

The Hockey XIs and Lacrosse XIIs were loyally supported by other girls, both present and past, and some, who could not come out and cheer, sent telegrams. "Best wishes . . . Helen Smith . . . Play up, P.H.C. Violet . . . Bun . . . Sybil." Miss Parker's too: "Good wishes to the team. The Principal."

The Cricket 1st XI and its coach, Mrs Cavalier (of the England Lacrosse 1st XII), depended so much on the weather, and the weather was such, that more matches had to be cancelled than were played. But Helen Johnson, HS17, won enduring renown, having swiped a ball from mid-field into the churchyard. "An excellent, all-round player," wrote Barbara Carden, "the most valuable batsman in the team." Jean Mackay had improved her bowling but had yet to perfect her "screws". Marjorie Moir, called Joie, was "too slow on her feet". Christine Trinder's bowling was straight but "too sneaky". The team as a whole in 1929 was inalert, missing "many golden opportunities" and too many of the team collapsed next year "through nerves". Fielding was sluggish. "It should be quite possible", wrote someone, "for every fielder to know where the ball will go before it is actually hit." But Margaret Summerford could hardly have foreseen that

[70] Ibid.

Junior ventures to address Miss Wilmott. "Miss Wilmott, it's the cup match today, isn't it?" W., abruptly: "It is!" J: "Is it hockey or lacrosse?" W., with amazing self-control: "Croquet!" J. perseveres: "Is it home or away?" W: "Why, is the team all wearing hats and coats?"

she would fumble with the ball and it would bounce and lodge inside her skirt. Having found it she appealed and the umpire dismissed the batsman.

Miss Christine Douglass, Old Girl, reflecting the glory of her sister, Dorothea (whose six-year reign at Wimbledon had yet to be surpassed), came and coached the tennis team in 1921, but did not stay long. Only four matches were played that season; all were lost. Sisters Leslie and Beatrice Watson ("of whom we are all extremely proud") made amends in 1930, beating Malvern College in the finals of the Queen's Club Schoolgirls' Doubles, bringing home the Courtauld Cup ("much coveted") and after leaving school they were somehow allowed to play for the Belgian team against England both at tennis and at hockey.

A Sports Day had been held in 1909, pure fun, having little to do with field and track, and would slowly develop till by 1918 it had become the Annual Sports, each end of Summer Term. The girls ran races in sacks or in barrels, running backwards, over treacle-tins, under benches or nets, tousling their hair, through barrels hung from ropes, with trays loaded with tennis-balls or with egg on spoon, or sunshades, or bibbed or lacing their boots or as wheelbarrows, or got into galoshes, raincoat, scarf, best hat, then snatched and opened an umbrella and, one-handed, set up a deck-chair and sat on it, or back to back linked arms, or yodelled or collected potatoes or threaded needles or patted balloons or fed "a hungry sister" with treacle from a spoon, blindfold, or blindfold again whacked a cabbage off a post—*Mors Cabbagaceae*—the cabbage dies—or nibbled the swinging bun, no hands, or with mouth full of biscuit tried to whistle the National Anthem or—the Chinese puzzle—ate jelly using pencils. The staff—all but the old and Miss Parker—walked on stilts, made leek-and-cabbage-leaf hats, clay elephants, had to sing blindfold, two to a song and all at once, as they tried to find their partners, the audience helping, bowled hoops, played tennis dressed for rain, racquet in one hand, umbrella in the other, slow-bicycled, inflated balloons till they burst, or burst them with catapulted stones, walked round in a ring, with ankles tied, wearing tails and jumping on to everybody's tail in front, so detaching it. A shy was raised, where the coconuts wore hats over painted faces. Then came ice-cream, fruit salad or strawberries and cream or cherries or Devonshire splits—cream and strawberry jam in buns—and always dainty sandwiches.

Athletics, after 1912, meant the Running Competition, "a new and important feature in the College events", contested inter-form. Prince barked, and the cheers could be almost deafening, as heats were won and lost. "Most exciting part of all", they decided the final, after which the Lilian Isaacson Challenge Cup was presented to the visitors, its "happy possessors" for at least one year, who carried it off "amidst great joy" and placed it in their form-room.

The Drill Display continued, again inter-form—inter-form was not very "public school" but houses had yet to be instituted—with a three-handled cup to enhance its status, a gift from Lilian Story; "poking heads" and

"open mouths" lost points; but "green-clad damsels"—1922—"with wands outstretched . . . knees deep bent . . . and full of grace" did "glad their patient teacher's eyes" (in Mary Hickey's poem).

The green which clad them was still the cally, their class and games-wear. It had continued little changed. But they altered its length and Miss Parker had often to point her stick at hemlines as she walked about the grounds—the gardener was not to be allowed to see girls' knees—and at belts, hanging slack and low, when fashion lowered waists, hips vanishing, and girls tried to look less like themselves and more like Mlle Desplas, their French teacher of French.

After World War I appeared a white silk frock: high-necked, long-sleeved, either "plainly made", as was prescribed, or thick with tucks and lace, as often happened. It remained till early in the twenties. A gold shantung dress then took its place, embroidered with green, the green and gold said to match the oaken hall, and gathered at the hips; as an after-games alternative to skirt and blouse and for the Saturday evening dance and special treats, it could be worn with any cardigan or jumper on top, but with only low-heeled shoes, and with a sensible vest underneath it, called a spencer, lest anyone caught cold.

It was on Tournament Day that frocks looked right and best. The event had continued throughout the years of war and it now consisted of three main contests: cricket, tennis and the high jump.

1918

The last of these was perhaps the most exciting, keeping the onlookers in a state of breathless anticipation, until finally 4ft 10ins was cleared by Nancy Blankley, who, as she was the winner last year, did not receive the prize; this was given to Dorothy Cathcart, who was second, clearing 4ft 8ins. Miss Fryer kindly judged . . .

Bishop George Frodsham,[71] father of Margaret, gave away the prizes. His "inspiring address" followed; it switched attention from the gamesfield to the soldier, wheeled by or on crutches, "without a limb or with the marks of pain upon his face"; then rambled: from women filling posts which soldiers had vacated, and who dressed like men to perform men's work—"but was their soul to be a man's soul or a woman's?"—to woman and man held together like an arch; unselfishness; the hope which good folk shared: that peace would reign on earth and would last; Schopenhauer, who misunderstood women; the girls of England, in whose hands the future lay of industrial and social reconstruction; and some words by Lacordaire[72] about Duty, Humility and Service.

And yet, despite long sermons in the heat, Tournament Day was still

[71] Bishop of North Queensland, Australia, 1902–31.

[72] Jean Baptiste Henri Lacordaire, 1802–61, Dominican priest, best known for his sermons and funeral orations.

the event which girls, parents and staff most looked forward to and enjoyed and which the College Magazine made seem the most enchanting.

1925

Looking back one has a vague impression of a balmy summer afternoon spent under cool trees; very green trees with a dull red streak between them and many gold frocks moving about. Then exciting and reminiscent conversation; tea, deck-chairs, and the bracing effect of contests going on all round.

M.E.S and R.M.P.[73]

1929

The grounds looked quite transformed; many elegant ladies moved gracefully about in their garden-party frocks, others, more energetic, were busy trying to show that once upon a time they used to be able to play cricket!

Anon.

Less charming than Tournament Day, as exciting, more hilarious, were the parties. The Head of School would read the girls a telegram announcing that a mistress and her form invited everybody else for tea and games. Games, indoors, were like the outdoor sports. Contestants might have to pin a tail to a paper donkey or pig, blindfold, or sing like a coon, or grip a floating apple with their teeth, or gather peas between two pencils, or perform as a band with spoons, tongs, combs, or guess which mistress's hand cast shadows from behind a screen—her groans were meant to help—or which baby in the photograph was now which girl, or restore the jumbled names of motor-cars or trees or flowers or the fragments of a post-card.

1927

The Hall was gaily decorated with balloons and wreaths and streamers of coloured paper, and in the corner stood a Christmas-tree.

When we had all gathered in the Hall, the stage curtains suddenly parted and a chef appeared, wearing a large white cap and apron and carrying an enormous plum pudding. This was carved with great ceremony and was found to be hollow, containing various small charms which were distributed among us.

V.P.[74]

Decoration had begun with ferns and coloured paper; it developed and improved until in 1928 the girls felt as if transported to the Arctic when they stepped into the hall: icicles hung from the galleries, a big snow-

[73] Mary Elizabeth Stephenson, of Albecq, Guernsey, and Rachel Marianna Powell, of the Mansion House, Brecon, two daughters of solicitors.

[74] Dr J. Farquhar Philip's Veronica, HS28. Six years later, in Vienna, a qualified masseuse.

covered bough from the ceiling, and a small motor-car occupied the stage, "almost certainly a 1928 show model", where the snow had not yet fallen.

The Sketching Club and the Artistic and Literary Society expired, but only in name: outings took their place, junior, senior, form and school, either planned and calendared or announced as surprises—"It being a fine day . . ."—or hastily arranged when games had to be cancelled: to the Chelsea Flower Show with Miss Parker, to Kew with Miss Chorlton or Miss Stocks or Miss White, where the orchids and the rhododendrons bloomed and the storks nested, to St Paul's "interesting . . . beautiful . . . most wonderful . . . marvellous" Cathedral, and the Tower, where the girls riveted their gaze on instruments of torture.

An outing entailed packed lunch, or tea at a restaurant or café, the Kardamolo or the Oak or Lyons or Dickins and Jones or Derry and Toms, where ices were served and orangeade and where, so long as no one asked them which orphanage they had come from, the girls left happy.

The Royal Tournament—at Olympia now after Earls Court—they never missed. Horses there pranced and camels loped; Highlanders marched to the pipes and drums; cadets imitated clockwork soldiers; the Romans fought their Picts and Scots and the Templar Knights their Saracens; the Army and Navy and now the Royal Air Force competed at tug-of-war; every size and shape of gun was displayed, oxen drawing one and an elephant another; the first world war continued to be lost and won: a searchlighted Zeppelin was destroyed from the ground—"the German pilot came down in a parachute and was immediately taken prisoner"—and a grand finale mock assault was launched—"this was very exciting indeed"—on German trenches.

The girls behaved themselves gratefully and thoughtfully. "We somehow managed to get to our 'buses"—three double-deckers—and to currant buns—"and so back to P.H.C."—sandwiches and cocoa—"there to see how quietly and quickly we could all go to bed." J.R.[75]

Expedition to Windsor

1924

On Thursday, July 12th, the Senior forms went for the most lovely expedition we have ever had. We set off at 2 o'clock in three large charabancs. The ride was glorious, especially as we were then in the middle of the heat-wave. We went through Northfields, Hounslow, Coldbrook, Datchet, and then into Windsor. We went straight to the Castle as it was already 3.45 and the State apartments shut at 4.0.

On the terrace we met West Heath girls, who were also having an expedition. After a short wait we were admitted and shown round the Castle. The rooms were most attractive and so were the rock gardens and fountains. Several of us took photographs.

We were then allowed to go to the shops and get ices and lemonade,

[75] Jean Rotheram, Crossdrum, Oldcastle, County Meath, Eire.

which was much appreciated, not only because it was hot but because we had never been allowed to do such a thing before.

After this we re-embarked and drove to Runnymede, where we had a lovely tea, provided by Miss Dick. To our astonishment we found it was after 6 o'clock and time to begin the homeward journey.

We came back by a slightly different route and arrived at P.H.C. by 7.30. Everyone agreed that it was the nicest expedition we have ever had and those staying on hope it will be repeated next year, in fact that it may become a tradition!

B.S.[76]

A ride in anything on wheels produced excitement: the bus, called a shandrydan, the tube train and the one last hansom cab which, if they were lucky, stood waiting to collect them at Ealing Broadway.

In March 1927, and "for the first time in the annals of P.H.C.", girls aged at least 16 were taken to the boat-race.

It was kept a secret until the day before, but some of us heard a rumour that we might be going.

. . . . .

On the way, cars decked in dark and pale blue ribbons flashed past us; small children shouted encouragement and all London seemed to be wending its way to the river.

We took up good positions along the top steps of the terrace, where we could see up and down the river, then at a given word opened our luncheon packages and tried to eat large sandwiches genteely whilst the crowd surveyed us.

. . . . .

When at last the boats were sighted the crowds behind gave one mighty lunge forward but P.H.C. stood firm and even managed to take snaps of the crowd with the crews in the background.

N.H.B.[77]

Miss White took botanists to Burnham Beeches, the chalk-pit at Hayes, and Keston Ponds, where, after two pennyworth of sweets from the village shop, they would gaze upon bog myrtle, sundew and bog asphodel; and the entire school to the Philharmonic Hall to see a film about British mountaineers attempting to climb Mount Everest.

"February 26th"—1931—"dawned dull and grey", began "C.B." (Clementine Bell, the daughter of a land-owning farmer, from Mindrum, Northumberland). For some it threatened walks; others, the luckier, looked forward to, then enjoyed, a visit arranged to the Scottish Exhibition:

76 Betty—Muriel Elizabeth—Stone, from Eastholme, Frinton on Sea.

77 Major Baker's Nancy Helen, from Wokingham in Berkshire.

Arriving at Grosvenor House,[78] *many of us saw for the first time somebody in complete Highland dress. One member of the party even walked up and down the stairs in order to see the dirk in the attendant's stocking!*

. . . . .

Most people imagine Scotland to be a very poor country, and [we?] were very much surprised to see the beautiful silver . . . the prettiest of which was a tea-service. Great interest was caused by the equipment of a Highland gentleman, and somebody saw a sporran for the first time. Prince Charlie's claymore was there and also Wallace's.

. . . . .

After we really couldn't find anything more to look at, we had to say goodbye to the past, and hope that we shall see Scotland one day.

Concert-going revived, it appearing to have lapsed for thirteen years, or was at last again reported. In 1929 a chosen few heard Backhaus, Kreisler, Myra Hess and Rachmaninov. But their own orchestral music continued undeveloped, and not for another fifty years would it astound.

The prefects were taken to see the West End shops, including Harrod's, where stood the life-size tiger-and-lion toys, to fashion shows, and other special treats, with sometimes a glimpse of someone famous, as at the National Gallery in 1924—"whom should we see before our very eyes but Princess Mary and Viscount Lascelles"[79]—K.D.[80]—and at a Four Georges Loan Exhibition about six years later another surprise lay in store:

When the Library reached the entrance hall of Sir Philip Sassoon's[81] *house in Park Lane, we all stared at the strangely familiar figure standing there. Then the words, "Car, please, for Mr Baldwin", confirmed our suspicions and, after the departure of the famous political leader,*[82] *we went into the exhibition, amazed at our luck in having seen him.*

M.M. and L.B.[83]

Juniors enjoyed their visits to the zoo, riding elephant or camel, and watching the Lord of the Jungle eat his dinner, or the "Winnie the Pooh" bear, his, or the chimpanzees, their tea; and to the circus, where tigers did tricks—"another very thrilling event . . . they growled every time their keeper made them do anything"—and where more chimpanzees performed, on bicycles and roller-skates.

[78] Built for the Duke of Westminster in 1868 and demolished in 1927.

[79] Daughter of King George V, the Princess Royal, and her husband, Henry, by 1929 the sixth Earl of Harewood.

[80] Lt.-Col. Dobbin's Kathleen.

[81] Conservative MP for Hythe, 1912–39, inheriting the seat from his father, Edward, of a well-known Jewish family.

[82] Between the end of his first two ministries in 1929 and the beginning of his last in 1935.

[83] RN Capt. R. H. R. Mackay's Margaret, Petham House, near Canterbury, and Barrister F. F. Burrowes's Lorna, St John's, Antigua, British West Indies.

A Girl Guides Company began in the Summer Term 1918, to belong to which was not compulsory, though it often felt so. Miss Parker agreed or chose to be Commissioner, encased from neck to foot in navy blue, with white shoulder-cords and with a pudding-basin hat with, on one side, the brim turned up and flat. Patrols, Bantam, Nightingale and Skylark, appeared; then Blackbird, Robin and Swallow; Canary next and Wren, as numbers grew; Kingfisher and Blue-Tit; and they all competed for a Silver Challenge Bowl as if their lives depended on it.

Princess Mary, unofficially "the Guides' Queen Bee", allowed them to wear their own school uniform, the cally, green and gold, instead of blue. Its sleeves accumulated badges: the trefoil, which was confiscated from, or worn upside down by, anyone disgraced, and others denoting skills acquired with rope, tent, bandage, flag, morse, camp-fire and saucepan. The badges helped staff to tell the Stockwell twins apart: Kitty, who lisped, was a Bantam, and Maisie, who had no lisp but imitated Kitty, was a Swallow; only sometimes they exchanged callies. They had been loudly applauded as one of the two sets of twins in *The Comedy of Errors*.

A camp was held at Hassocks near Brighton in the first summer of peace. The party left and arrived by lorry, and returned, it seems, by train, with Miss Pinney and Miss Wright in charge.

Before we started . . . several people took photographs, much to the amusement of the driver, who was thus included in the group. We had a fine send-off from the Staff and caused quite a sensation while crossing London.

They slept in Lady Pelham's barn,[84] all but the two captains and a few others, who camped in a tent in the meadow; in which, however, they could not be found next morning, a cow having thrust her snout inside it, breathing heavily, and frightened them out into the turnip-field.

2.8.1919

The next day we took the train to Brighton, and then the tram to Roedean, to bathe. We had been able to get permission from Roedean School to use its private way down to the beach, so we had a very good time, far away from all other bathers. We all started off laden with food and bathing-dresses, only to discover when we arrived that quite half the provisions—our tea chiefly—had been left behind. Miss Pinney took a few girls down to Brighton to call on Mademoiselle Guyomar and buy buns, while the rest went in the opposite direction to explore Rottingdean. These latter were back at the meeting-place outside Roedean first and presently Miss Pinney and her followers appeared with would-be long faces. They announced that they had not got any buns. Having kept us in suspense for a moment,

[84] A housing estate now occupies the land where the house—Oldlands—and barn then stood. Lady Ruth, a sister of the Anglican Community of the Holy Trinity, Ascot, was the daughter of the fifth Earl of Chichester, who as the Hon. Francis Pelham had been Rector of St Mary's, Lambeth.

Miss Pinney explained that they had taken Muriel Secker home and Mrs Secker had insisted on us all going down to Hove to have tea with her at her flat. We all cheered up at that, and by various stages of trams we reached Hove, and tea. A bountiful spread it was, but our huge camp appetites cleared the plate surprisingly quickly, and Mrs Secker seemed willing to send for more quite indefinitely.

After tea we hurried for our train, and arrived back at the barn, a dusty, tired crowd, demanding supper as if tea had never been.

3.8.1919

. . . we had hot bacon for breakfast instead of the usual cold ham. The wind was contrary and blew the smoke all ways, so the cooks had a bad time that day. We lined up at 10.30 a.m. and marched off to church, causing much excitement in the village. The afternoon—what remained after we had cooked and eaten our chops—was spent in writing and reading in Lady Ruth's garden. After tea some went to church and others for a walk.

4.8.1919

In the evening we lighted a huge camp fire in the middle of the field and sat by it, sheltered from the rain by an old cart with a tarpaulin over it, singing anything that came into our heads. After that we had a torchlight procession round Lady Ruth's house, singing folk-songs that we had learnt from Miss Raikes. The evening finished with more singing and reciting in the barn, for the rain came on harder, forcing us to take shelter.

5.8.1919

We planned to go to Roedean again . . . and accordingly breakfast was ordered for an earlier hour to give us time to catch the train. However, this was not to be, for in the middle of breakfast the irate farmer informed us that the cow had strayed away and it was our fault. Directly after breakfast we started off in different directions, in parties of two or three, in search of this animal. A few of us actually did track her to a field where many other cows were feeding, and the farmer found her amongst them, quite at home. Other parties of searchers then came up, and the cow was driven back in state, with a strong bodyguard of ten or twelve . . . When we arrived the rest had given up the hunt and come back. Two enterprising people had found a cow very like ours, and had begun to drive her in, when they heard our shouts of "Found!"

6.8.1919

Everyone declared it was the jolliest week they had ever had spent and those who were staying on for 1920 began making plans for the next camp. Nevertheless all agreed that no camp could ever be quite so splendid as the first.

Anon.

But each next camp seemed more splendid than the last and jollier: at Coldharbour Farm, near Pulborough, halfway up the Downs, with Mr and Mrs Burra and their two little boys, Mr 3 and Mr 5, who became next year Mr 4 and Mr 6, and where a big white cockerel pecked their legs; in Major Vincent's orchard, near Petworth, where no one could sleep—too many chunks of wood among the shavings in their palliasses—with a brickyard in the nearby field, where Miss Pinney was allowed to make a brick, and a pool not far away at Ebernoe, overgrown with pondweed and lilies, in which they could bathe—mud to the knees and water to the waist; on Lord de la Warr's estate at Withyham; at Goudhurst; and at Baldslow near St Leonard's.

At school in Ealing, between the summer camps, they could spend half of their time in the green and not yet smothered fields reaching all the way to Perivale, playing hide and seek, or in the school grounds, which they helped to keep tidy, and the other half indoors, making toys, including a fully-equipped doll's house to be sent to children in hospital.

Support for charities redoubled, for the benefit of soldiers disabled in the war, other invalids, the Sunshine Home for Blind Babies, the Blinded Soldiers' Children Fund, missions aimed at seamen on the Thames, and at Japanese fishermen, who, it was hoped, would turn to Christ; the girls collected money and raised it selling tickets for the Shakespeare play; made clothes for the children of the poor—Miss Parker eyed each stitch and passed or rejected it—and the boarders adopted a baby girl, Edna Eileen Heeley, whose father had lost his sight at Fleurs in 1916, sending £13 a year towards her upkeep, from 1918, when she was born, till 1932, and on her third birthday a little black cat called Grampus.

Mr Heeley wrote and thanked them for the cat and Miss Parker read out his letter to the school.

I trust that I shall not bore you if I give a short description of my little daughter. She is a happy little soul of two years and eight months and has the distinction of being the first grandchild to both sides of the family tree. From this you will gather, no doubt, quite a fuss is made of her. To myself she has just reached an exceptionally interesting age, being a veritable chatterbox, and possessing, to an almost extraordinary degree, that quality usually characteristic of women, curiosity, it will be observed that her mother and I have quite a good time. Another source of interest to myself is that she is quite a good pedestrian for one so young, and the development of her powers of observation makes it possible for us to take short walks with no other guide. I do not desire that my little daughter be regarded as a prodigy or a phenomenon, but the development of such powers means so much to myself. Maybe I have become a keener student of the human race than heretofore, but that is by the way.

Old Girls had continued to support their own good causes, the Lord Mayor's Home for Cripples, at Alton, and the United Girls' Schools

TH'ORFISERS

Miss Pinney, Miss Jenkins, Captains; Miss Lord, Agnes Smith, Barbara Allen, Lieutenants; and Dodo, District Secretary.

There's a sweet little doggie called Roy,
Very often he's called "little boy",
But although he's not big
He's a bit of a pig
And his appetite none can destroy

Mission Guild, which had founded a settlement in Camberwell, where young working-class women met, played indoor games, acted, sang, debated, were drilled to music, sewed, read books and drank hot cocoa, till as late as half past ten at night, and had provided welfare services, from home-and-hospital visiting and help, to free advice to workers on their legal rights. At Chatham Barracks they furnished a sailor's cabin which took the College's name. And to Agnes Jones they gave a pension of £25 a year; she had taught them the piano for the last nineteen years of the nineteenth century and for the first nineteen of the twentieth.

The girls at school learned more about poverty. Dr Gertrude Willoughby[85] came and told them how it felt to be unemployed; eleven little sons of the unemployed visited the College for a treat; and the VIth Form attended a public meeting where a Father Nigel spoke on "Slums and the Christian Conscience". Mr Frank Briant, however, a Congregationalist and National Liberal MP for North Lambeth, another whom the VIth went out to see and hear, put the problem to them in a new light: the poor resented charity, if that meant patronage, and the state should so improve their lot as to make it unnecessary.

Miss Parker's girls were securely and comfortably middle to upper class and neither argument nor eloquence was likely to disturb what they felt and vaguely thought about applied Christianity. Mr Thompson was a worker and so was Mr Moran and any suggestion that workers should unite and win themselves a bigger share of the fruits of their labour would have seemed to them absurd. But they were not so drilled to conform and acquiesce as to be altogether deaf to new ideas. Mr Hodge encouraged them to keep an open mind. Did they believe what they read in the newspapers? The press could not be trusted; it did not so much reflect the views of the public as it did Lord Northcliffe's and Lord Beaverbrook's: intellectually corrupt and more heedful of profit than it was of truth. "And so, it would be as futile to go to Tory papers, like *The Observer* or *The Morning Post* for a fair statement of advanced internationalism as to go to *The Daily Herald* . . .[86] for the educated viewpoint."

The Debating Society continued to help. It tended to believe that school should be compulsory; but could not decide on private tutors as a sound alternative; disapproved of competitive examinations, which did not properly test knowledge; saw a future for the novel; and no inevitable conflict of poetry with science; did not agree that Spain should have Gibraltar; wanted MPs to vote with their consciences; preferred peace without patriotism to patriotism with war, having earlier supported its country right or wrong; but still thought that disarmament, like socialism, was

[85] Author of a thesis, in French, on wages and conditions of workers in the clothing-trade, in Britain and in France; Paris, 1926.

[86] 1911, 1912–14, 1914–19 (as *The Herald*) and 1919–64. Jointly controlled by Odham's Press and the TUC.

impracticable; voted narrowly for, then narrowly against, the penalty of death; held that mixed marriage was Othello's chief mistake; did not wish Britain to return the Elgin marbles to the Greeks; disapproved of zoos; again approved of vivisection; approved then disapproved of fox-hunting; supported equal rights for women and men; and careers for women in public life; yet would not have let them vote aged 21; thought the best education a woman could enjoy was the one that fitted her best for a role in life subordinate to man's, it being natural; and that women should not be allowed to preach in church; saw tradition all the same as an obstacle to progress; then two years later changed its mind; approved of cinemas and machinery; but voted against a Channel Tunnel; dismissed the idea of a golden age of savages—in 1915 their savage had been happier than civilised man, thanks to the chairman's casting vote, but a few years later it was better to be civilised; agreed with Keats that truth meant beauty and beauty truth; and welcomed attempts to reach the South Pole and climb Mount Everest. About a dozen voters contested each debate, seldom more, but 1923 or 1924 saw a record twenty-six, when Jack of All Trades beat the Master of One, whom the last time round they had tended to prefer.

It is likely that the same debaters and Shakespeare-reading groups were the mainstay of the Classics Society too, which in 1931 had thirty-three members, reading Latin texts and Greek, translated into English.

Creative writers had disclosed in verse their private feelings, in the College Magazine, till 1910. Their antique muse dwelt on the games-field, among wild flowers and in lanes that rang with birdsong; could understand a joke; but then fell silent; or inspired nothing that the editor would accept, until 1922, when it seemed that taste had shifted, towards the land of elves, the sad minstrelsy of Philomel, the clouds asleep o'er dreaming spires, moth-haunted eglantine, gnomes, climbing from the scented bud of rose, leprechauns, wearing green and crimson shoon, flower-cups of nectar for the honey bee, dew on the thorn, bubbling streams in wooded dell, pale moonbeams, through the trees glimmering, wild waves and rugged rocks. Patriotic heroes enjoyed much tribute, as in "After Battle", by Joan Rice (Classics Exhibitioner, LMH), where corn and poppy rise from blood-soaked earth, and in Eileen Darley's "Ode to Nelson", "sublime above all heroes", in Trafalgar Square, who died so that Britain might win renown and stand supreme.

Twenty-five years had passed since Flossie von Keudell light-heartedly endorsed the new school motto. A more serious treatment of the theme now appeared, the work of Pauline Speers, daughter of physician Charles, Donnington, Newbury:

She who riseth every day,
With her first impulse to pray
Unto God, and to Him say
"Let me conquer self";

She who goeth all day through,
Wanting just that thing to do;
Just to keep her pure and true,
"Just to conquer self";

She who cometh home at night
Having tried with all her might
Just to do the thing that's right,
"Just to conquer self";

Always strives in thought and deed,
Always prays in time of need
Only just these words to heed,
"Just to conquer self";

She who teaches good each day,
By her own life—on the way—
Then it is that others say,
"She has conquered self."

Fortis Qui Se Vincit.

Since 1912 the prefects had produced their own magazine, called "Library Lunacy", where they lampooned each other and the staff, all but Miss Parker and her second-in-command, who were allowed to read it, or had to be, and were said to recognise each butt. "Ladies arise and buzz to your baths." "Stop talking at once or you'll be in silence." "Pencils ready, gairls. Don't write till I tell you." "It's absorbingly interesting." "I sink so, sank you." Why such noise? Matron was telling the school to be quiet. And why was the singing class so silent? Mr Colby had told them all a joke.

As for their lacrosse-mates: Dorothy Pearson was idle, deceitful, even vicious; Gladys Richardson, challenging, like an india-rubber ball; Margaret Fraser lumbered; Eileen Hill persevered; Grace Wildman-Lushington, like Gulliver in Lilliput, had to bend too far to reach the ball in time—it was *wildly* alleged that she had accepted a job with Sanger's circus: wearing pink tights, she bestrode a yellow donkey; Joan Dening importuned; Rose Hives could only see her opponent, not the ball; Margaret Bowling was too aggressive and wandered out of place; Molly Cathcart passed the ball to the great white poplar, mistaking it for her own side; and Peggie Coles twittered; but Kathleen G., an ideal player, could find no fault with Gamble, K.

The older girls wasted time learning Russian; they did not take seriously their teacher or their work. Not only did the learned professor smell of hair-oil:

When all else fails we start dictation.
Oh, Russians are an unclean nation!
To clean the board we do not linger,
For he prefers to wet his finger.

And they pretended to deplore the effect, on character, of the teaching of arithmetic, which encouraged cheating and a mercenary outlook, and called upon Parliament to abolish it.

Mrs Goslett "came every Tuesday at half past three . . . with her feet so flat, in a long pink dress and a large black hat"—she advised them to go to an open window if they had to blow their nose—and Miss Wilmott's backless satin dress excited comment. But the main target of their prose and verse with illustrations was Miss Pode, who at a staff dinner had worn a vivid green, looking rather like a pea-pod, or so they chose to think, and had once read something to the class about a rolling pea and was thereafter condemned to be known as "Pode" or "the Pode" or "Pea-Pode" or "Podey-Wodey".

Her Majesty's Inspectors incurred their gentle fun. Mary Savery had watched them come and go:

Children, do ye see them,
on the College ground,
how the three inspectors
prowl and prowl around?

The Library Fairy!

Left: Mrs Clare Goslett, Hygiene. Right: a Miss "H'yes . . . H'yes . . . No . . . No . . . H'yes" — Mary Norrington: "It could be Miss Twemlow . . . a rather Bohemian lady with advanced ideas." Middle two: Miss Pode (whom Kathleen Pakenham-Walsh's pen and brush teased best) at school and on holiday.

Children, up and answer,
though they all should ask:
"What's the French for dancer
or the Greek for task?"

Children, do ye feel them
in the atmosphere?
Tidiness a mania,
gone our festal cheer?

Children, never tremble;
never be downcast;
tidy all your cupboards,
your grief will soon be past.

Most of the rest of the humour was banal, but the more they wrote about staff, and the less about each other, the more it improved. Punctuation was poor, vocabulary splendid, and almost all the water-paint and ink illustrations charmed.

At times they so forgot themselves as to seem to respect staff, acknowledging the value of Prof. Sumichrast's insistence on punctuality, Prof. Allcroft's advice to them to think before they spoke, Mlle d'Orliac's, not to speak out of turn, Mrs Goslett's, to remember the children of the poor, and a distinction drawn by Mr Wood between true humour and false. But they doubted the benefit of Racine's *Iphigénie* to the younger girls performing it: they could hardly have understood what it meant, their pronunciation was more English than French and they had giggled.

The Library's "News of Old Girls" echoed banter of the kind more and more to be expected when students reported on each other to their school:

three . . . are up at Cambridge; there they are leading wild and dissipated lives, swept along by a tide of pleasures, without the courage to stand out against their moral ruin. We deeply grieve for the fresh and innocent lives that went forth from us last term—to think that they should ever have come to this! We have not yet disowned them, for, like Mrs Green,[87] *we live in 'opes that our letters may restrain them in however slight a degree from their final plunge into that dark abyss over whose edge they are hanging suspended by a single thread.*

We cannot tell how much true feeling their laboured wit concealed. Mary Savery, however, addressing posterity, mixed sentiment with fun, doing neither any harm.

To Those Who Come After Us

γίγνωσκε δὲ ὡς ὀφείλεται πᾶσιν ἡμῖν ἐξιέναι.[88]

(Greek quotation inserted out of pure swank by the H.o.S. Kindly translated into dog Latin by the Faithful Puppy.)

Hoc scis, omnibus nobis est discedendum.

Those of you who follow after, in the centuries to be,
Will you ever think, we wonder, of the former P.H.C.?

Sometimes, p'raps, you will remember, at your work and at your play,
Billie, Betty, Faith and Dodo, and the rest, all passed this way.

[87] In Evelyne E. Rynd's *Mrs Green*, 1901, and *Mrs Green Again*, 1916.

[88] Adapted from Euripides's *Alcestis*, lines 418–419, which in English read: "Depend upon it, in the end we all must die." Where Euripides has "die", Mary's Greek and then her Latin have "depart".

As you wend your way through Georgia, as you hasten to the Spa,
Don't forget that many others also dwelt where now you are.

If at times you feel dejected, thinking of the Friday dish,
Don't forget that, long before you, other people fed on fish,

Ate the sausages and treacle, cheese and stodge, and seemed to thrive,
Lived according to traditions of the VI and UpperV,

Had encounters with the Thistle, got reported by the Fox;
When they wished to shorten lectures boldly altered all the clocks;

Passed and failed in Higher Local, never knew their maths or French;
Lined the field to cheer at matches, never never *bagged a bench.*

You, when sitting on Hamilcar, worried by your many ties,
Don't forget that Heads before you sat there and can sympathise.

Though you do not know the Bunny, L.C.M. is but a name,
Don't forget that they both lived here long before you ever came.

Lady White and Posh and Vyvyen, when they too have had their day,
As the Boy and Babe before them, so they too must pass away.

When the Pinney Flower has faded, when the Peach's bloom is o'er,
Other staves will take their places, yet the school stand as before.

Still she governs, still she teaches, still her work continues, though
All her many many children come and go and come and go.

All must go—but grieve not, reader. Listen, think, and you will see
You are one with those you followed, one with those who yet will be.

The Faithful Puppy was Roy: a black cocker spaniel, *alias* John the Baptist, heir to the late Prince; Billie, Mary Savery herself, who altered all the clocks; Betty, Muriel Elizabeth Stone; Faith, Faith Malden; Dodo, Muriel Dodds; Georgia, a floor or wing for Staff and VI; the Spa, the bathrooms; the Thistle and Vyvyen were each Miss Prain—some saw in Miss Prain a rather prickly Scot; Miss Turton was the Fox, known also as the Turtle Dove—a dove perhaps in foxen clothes;[89] Hamilcar, the library chair where sat the Head of School; the Bunny, Miss Lord; L.C.M., Elsie someone—the someone could be Maude; Lady White, *Miss* White; Posh, Mlle Guyomar, who had inherited the nickname from Mlle Pochard; the Boy, Miss Hadley, teacher of gymnastics; the Babe, Miss Wright; the Pinney Flower, Miss Pinney, Susannah, the adored;[90] and the Peach's Bloom, the beautifully complexioned Miss Jenkins.

In her unpublished memoirs, *Birthdays and Bedsitters*, Barbara Allen—"Ba" and "the Infant"—writes of other girls in Mary Savery's time. They included, from Kelso, two of her life-long friends: Agnes Smith, HS21, called "Touie", a little short for Toucan, "because when she was good she

[89] Barbara Allen, Mrs Priest, 29.11.1988: "Yes, Miss Turton was called 'the Fox', she could be a very mean sneak!"

[90] Barbara, 26.2.1990: "Tall, with fair curly hair, startlingly blue eyes and a charm to fetch the birds from the trees!"

had soft pink feathers and when she was bad a very sharp beak'; and Violet, her sister, only two years older than Barbara: "A Titian-haired prefect for whom I swooned with love during the whole of my first year, 'a daughter of the gods, divinely tall and most divinely fair'.[91] I wrote poems to her and remember one was about cheese which she had made me eat at supper."

"There were also fleeting attractions, a sentimental interlude with a blue-eyed flaxen-haired siren"—Cecily Daniel—"who, after creating a scene of dramatic jealousy, flung me from her for ever. My sniffs and gulps, however, were short-lived . . ."

Her days filled more with laughter than with tears. "How, all along the way, it is the laughter I remember best! How we laughed!"

Norah Hanson too was happy. "I think that the thing I remember most"—fifty-five years later, in 1983—"is how nice we were to one another."

The school became family and home for girls like Barbara, with estranged parents, and she more than anyone felt outcast, bidding it good-bye:

And now the years had come and gone. There is always an emptiness when one rises for "God Save the King", and the show's over, and it's Home Again; but for me it was an aspect fraught with special desolation and apprehension. What lay ahead? What renewed developments of past anguish and fear? To what was I returning with the walled and turreted refuge of school gone for ever?

The last evening—the last morning. School Prayers. You could always tell who was leaving by the gradual cessation of those senior voices which were the usual mainstay of high notes and difficult passages. Only the lesser voices were left now to tackle,

> *Let Thy Father Hand be shielding*
> *Those who here will meet no more.*

How often we had sung it, mourning the departure of our divinities, our heroines! But now it was us*! It was for* us *the school was singing now. It was upon* us *the doors of that passionately loved place were now closing for the last time.*

Nay, we even heard them shut and we were outside, *as the carefree voices of our happy juniors soared up to the most famous high note in the annals of the schools of England,*

> *Tho-o-o-ose returning make more faithful*
> *Tha-a-a-an before.*[92]

Like Shakespeare's world the College was a stage; the curtain rose and fell; each girl, each mistress—"demon" or "dote"—had her entrance and her exit. But many lived near and could be found years after, performing in a concert, tableau, play, or sitting in the audience. And as fully paid-up

[91] "A Dream of Fair Women", *Poems by Alfred Tennyson*, 1832 or 1833.
[92] Unpublished memoirs.

members of the OGA they enjoyed four rights: to belong to the Artistic and Literary Society (while it lasted); to arrange "an entertainment" in the hall once a year; to challenge the College to a hockey match in winter and to a cricket or tennis match in the summer; and to participate in any of the school's expeditions.

Participants were mostly day-girls. Departed boarders lived hours, days, even weeks away, by train or boat, from the College and their friends. Day-pupils kept more easily in touch. The school served somewhat as their London club.

It would not so serve much longer. In 1922 Mr Hodge proposed, and the Council and the absent Princess Helena agreed, that day and board should no longer mix. It was "nowadays . . . impossible", the parents were informed, "to combine a Boarding School with a Day School". Conditions had so much changed and day-pupils were denied the advantages they would enjoy at a school for day-pupils only. So: if their daughters were in one of the top three forms they might remain and complete their education; the rest would have to leave after one more term or have to board. Girls under 10 had already been transferred to Miss Johnson's preparatory school in the nearby Presbyterian Hall and, of the fourteen day-girls enrolled that Autumn Term, all were to leave within the next eighteen months.

It is hard to believe that it was mainly for their own good that day-girls had to go. More likely reasons spring to mind: that boarders resented the freedom and home comforts which day-girls enjoyed—hence: "She's only a day-girl" or "a day-bug" (though good for running errands); that Miss Parker objected to parents living near: mistrusted their influence; depended on their help too much—they had to fill in cards indicating how long their daughters had taken over preps—and could punish girls more fairly and with less ado if parents did not walk in and out and complain, remonstrate or cajole; that she feared their sons; that epidemics, like mumps, were difficult to control, if day-girls came and went, infected and infectious; and that boarding was felt to be much more "public school".

It was an ill-timed change. Ealing as a catchment area could then have been likened to a Kensington or Hampstead; the day-girls especially tended to be bright; and it was boarders, not day-girls, that the school would less attract, as London swelled and overran it.

New dormitories were built: the Patricia,[93] for juniors who had lately been transferred to the sanatorium, and the Elizabeth York,[94] the colder of the two, with its three outside walls. A form-room upstairs had become the Augusta,[95] a three-bed room for seniors. But only a hundred boarders were envisaged, not nearly enough to continue to attract a high academic quality

[93] After Lady Ramsay.

[94] Elizabeth Bowes-Lyon, later Queen, newly married to the Duke of York, George VI to be.

[95] Augusta, Princess, Mrs Williams's employer.

of staff and pupil or fulfil Miss Parker's dream of "the building up of a great public school for girls".

The beauty of smallness was still to be enjoyed. Day-girls must have always felt less fostered but they and the boarders remained one brood. Miss Parker remembered them almost all, however long ago they had shaken hands goodbye and left the College. Theodora Eyton-Jones: "Few Headmistresses could boast of such a big family, personally kept in touch with for so many years." Her mailbag filled with news of their engagements, weddings, children, and sometimes deaths, their travels, courses, medals and careers.

Claire Davies, the cellist, became for a while a "Lady Inspector of Factories"; Noel Hughes, called Nellie, would in 1944 receive the freedom of Athens for her work with child refugees; Nellie Anderson—Classics at Newnham—was appointed Warden of the Women's University Settlement in Blackfriars; Ida Rand founded in Canada a branch of the United Girls' Schools Mission; Kathleen Browne went as a missionary to India; Violet Ashdown worked for the blind—of the rest of the earlier of Miss Parker's girls—and so did Nancy Blankley, the high-jumper, who died aged 35, after years of failing health; Violet Smith, the Titian-haired beauty whom Barbara Allen had adored, a Quaker pacifist, became a Sanitary Inspector and Warden of the University Settlement in Glasgow; and Margaret Brown, an Inspector of Children Boarded Out. Many nursed. Diana Beyts, however, who at school had befriended all new girls, walking them arm in arm about the hall, dealt too patiently with her patients, could not complete the work on time and was failed. But she qualified instead as a doctor and with her husband, the Rev. Mr Cecil du Heaume, ran the Leprosy Mission in Jordan. She had endured much sadness. Her mother died young; Dorothea, her sister, had been killed falling from a haystack; her father in India had been mauled by a leopard; and she herself, as a child, had been badly burned and scarred.

At least another five of Miss Parker's dwindling flock read and practised medicine: Elizabeth Bunbury, called Doris—the telegram Bun—daughter of a missionary doctor in Canton, who with her child psychiatrist husband, Dr Hilliard, acquired and restored the house in Bath where William Herschel had discovered Uranus, also Beckford's Tower nearby; Barbara Carden, a naval chaplain's wife: missionary, first, then university professor, in Iran; the Rev. Dr Arthur Claye's Aileen—and surgeon Lord Moynihan's niece—an anaesthetist; Elizabeth Dundee, a "medical officer's" daughter from Belfast; Winifred Edmunds, her father with the British and Foreign Bible Society and her husband an Army chaplain in Allahabad—medicine and the church were repeatedly connected; and Janet Mary Lyle Hamilton, called May, whose early marriage disposed of her career.

Others taught: Joan Bloxam, the artist, who had left as a pupil in 1903 then returned as staff in each of the two world wars; Evangeline Lloyd-Williams, called Grace, at Wycombe Abbey; Theodora Boys, at St Paul's;

Dorothy Allen, at Roedean, Johannesburg; the Ashdowns: Evelyn, senior historian at St Paul's, missionary in India, Lecturer at the University of Lahore and Headmistress of Queen Mary School in Delhi "for high-class Indian girls of all creeds", who spent a fortnight in a life-boat in World War II, when the ship bringing her to England was torpedoed; Margaret, briefly, with a family in Russia; Violet—again—whose nursery school at Cowichan was believed to be British Columbia's first; Ethel Chamier, the daughter of a High Court judge in Allahabad—she became an HMI, somewhere in mid-India; Katie Espinasse, Oxford MA in French, at a mission school in Ranchi, Bihar; two at schools which they themselves had founded: Grace Raikes at Irwin House and Kathleen Griesbach at Portsdown Lodge—Grace, fuzzy gold hair, buxom and fun, having taken a form at PHC; Margaret Trembeth, headmistress of a school for Jewish girls, in Jaffa, under the Church Mission for the Conversion of Jews; Anna Colvin, in Sweden; Cecily Read, to be Principal of the Bedford Physical Training College;[96] Maud Farquharson, at her own school at Half Way Tree, Jamaica, whose father had sent the College a crate full of grapefruit, the first which almost everybody there had ever tasted; Molly Mellanby, for thirteen years a housemistress at Roedean, then Governor of the Borstal for Girls, Aylesbury, and later Assistant Commissioner of Prisons; Kathleen Rowney, art and violin at Tudor Hall, earning fame short and small in World War I making tons of jam for the soldiers—they all said tons; Margaret Waite, art at Wycombe Abbey; Lissa Birchall-Wood at Heathfield, violin and biology; Evelyn East, HS17, like Miss Parker a Newnham historian, Headmistress, in Kottayam, of another Church Missionary School; Muriel Dodds, Lecturer in French at Durham; Betty Stone, mathematics at her old school—a Governor of Bedford College, London; at Christ's Hospital: Daphne King; Bridget Andrews, a surgeon-captain RN's daughter and an American Army captain's bride: Housemistress, Fauconberg, at Cheltenham Ladies' College; Brigit Hutchinson, at Roedean: French, Italian, Spanish, German and Swedish, as required; Guendolen Sherrard, at the Mahbirbia School, another of those for high-caste girls, in Hyderabad; Nora Stapley, Principal of an Indian College of Education in Nairobi; Rosamund Ashby, perhaps the last of her school's hundreds of governesses, with a family in Scotland; and Joan Barlee, who returned to PHC from St George's, Ascot.

Many wrote books: Muriel Bussell[97]—*Peacocks and Primroses*, about Disraeli's novels, and *Seven Against Edinburgh*, about early women doctors, were two of her many; her year-mate, Flossie Gubbins, who had worked as a secretary at 10 Downing Street, *Grass on the Downs and Other Poems*, some prose sketches, *The Wilds of Kensington Gardens*, and *Wind*

[96] Author of *Vaulting for Women and Girls* (n.d.).

[97] Mrs Charles Masefield, war widow 1917–85; MA in 1920, when Oxford at last gave women their degrees.

in the Trees, where she refers to her schooldays and to the pleasure that she found, outside class, in the works of George Macdonald:[98]

a schoolgirl of thirteen, I would take his novels and lie under a tree in the school grounds beside the little patch allotted to me as my garden until I was routed out and made to go and play a reluctant game of cricket. That his books were full of sermons and piety did not offend me then for they were all out of the mouths of shoemakers and countrypeople and not from pulpits; neither were they stereotyped with orthodoxy. Instead he fed one's hunger for spiritual thoughts in an arid wilderness of theology . . .

—not everyone was wild about games; Joyce Dennys, a play, *The Bells Ring*, and *Kookaburra*, a play become a musical, her first instalment of illustrated memoirs, *And Then There Was One*, with a chapter about the College, "an Enclosed Order", its Principal "the Park"—"sounds grander than it was"—outside and up the stairs it was "imposing" but "the rest of the school was fairly shabby"[99]—she was now 90—and a second two years later, *Henrietta's War*; Irene Gamble, a book of sketches, *Scenes from the Life of Long Ago*; Molly Cathcart, another of the pupils of the sisters Bear and masseuse to the British Olympic swimmers at the Empire Games in Canada, who contributed to *Punch*; Joyce Rowley, as R. A. Dick, *The Ghost and Mrs Muir*, which was filmed; Rosamund White, histories, mainly; Mary Molony—another Mary called Molly—the last winner of Princess Helena's Advanced Pianoforte Music Prize—a book about George Herbert; Gertrude Trevelyan, winner of the Newdigate, about ten books, among them *As it Was in the Beginning*, a breathlessly erotic story, rather daring for 1934; Jean Pratt, *Lovely Peggy*; Barbara Allen, *A Far Bell*—war-time adventures in Central Africa; and Guendolen Sherrard, *The Golden Road*—travel—and a book of the poems that she wrote when from 10 to 17, called *The Dawning*, a few of which had first appeared in the College Magazine—one, about tulips, flaming, pink, white, mauve, all perfect, echoes Keats: "the beauty of immortal things abides".

Joan Bloxam wrote and illustrated *Walks Around London*; Flora Mitchell,[100] *Edwardian London* and *Vanishing Dublin*—they now fetch princely sums; Rudyard Kipling admired Bertha Burleigh's drawings, *An Artist at the Zoo*, which Lord and Lady Hailsham exhibited at their home in Portland Place—Queen Mary accepted a copy and Princess Helena Victoria gave another to the two Princesses, Elizabeth and Margaret, who and whose mother, then Duchess of York, said how much they had enjoyed

[98] A Victorian Scot, 1824–1905; allegorist (verse and prose), his readers mostly children, including his own eleven; preacher, C. of E., but tilted to Rome.

[99] Letter to Barbara Allen, 1983 or later: "Faith [Malden] . . . was rather cross with me about the book and said I made P.H.C sound like Dotheboys Hall! I didn't mean to."

[100] Born on a cattle ranch in the American West and wife of William, great grandson of the J. J. Jameson who founded the Dublin whiskey distillers which her father directed.

it; Mabel Green did enamels and the Queen bought one; Natalie Secker's paintings found fame in South Africa, like her sister Muriel's golf; and Mabel Semple, Lady Wigglesworth, illustrated books.

Rita Macintyre became a concert pianist; Beth Ealand, MBE (for her work with the WVS), excelled with piano and cello; and Marjory Lucas wrote music for children—*A Sylvan Glade*—and for the church. No more, of note, is recorded of musicians.

The Lithuanian Consulate employed Alice Sawers to correct the English of its outgoing letters and translate into English from the Spanish and the French. Rachel Powell was appointed Chairman of the Welsh Broadcasting Council; she spoke no Welsh but was the Dean of Brecon's wife. Stella Powles and Patricia Coulson were presented at court and Theodora Eyton-Jones was somewhere and by someone dubbed a Knight Commander of the Holy Sepulchre, a title which impressed, being little understood. Violet Ashdown—and again—took a course in Oxford on how to run a teashop and slept one night alone in a weird Californian desert, beneath the starlit sky; Beryl Jenkins flew aeroplanes; Elizabeth Stephenson sold antiques for many years at her shop, "The China Hen", at Bradford-upon-Avon; Mary Savill—"Dormouse"[101]—saw the Pope enthroned; Jenny Sechiari hunted tigers; and Catherine—Kitty—Carden, sister of Barbara (not of Sybil), took a gardener's training course at Thatcham. At least five of the 140 or so of Miss Parker's girls who wrote her their news kept poultry—"Natalie Glennie, with a friend, has started a smallholding of four acres of grassland to keep cows, poultry and pigs, and she wishes to take pupils"—and at least eleven were Girl-Guide captains and ran or helped run camps.

Phoebe Lawes, brought up without religion by her parents, went up to Newnham (but by way of St Paul's), where she embraced the Church of Rome, then became a Carmelite nun. Mrs Lawes: "Oh, darling! When we gave you perfect freedom to choose, we never meant you to choose *that*!"

Flossie von Keudell had kept in touch. The house and estate in Kidule being requisitioned by the government after the war, and converted into an agricultural college, she and her husband, Fritz, had moved to Willkischken in Memelland,[102] then returned to England, homesick, in 1935. Two years later Fritz died; and Flossie, for most of the rest of her life, shared a house with her schoolfriend, Maud Hamersley, at 3 Southwell Gardens, Hampstead, and at Seven Acres, Long Crendon, Thame (where, thus glory fades, only half an acre of the seven now remains). Another world war followed; Maud earned herself the MBE, with the FANY, but the gifted Flossie, said not to stick long at anything, stood still.

Kathleen Sissmore, HS16, and Helen Johnson, HS17—the hard-hitting batsman—were awarded the same honour as Maud's for their work with

[101] She had memorably dormoused in *The Mad Hatter's Tea-Party*.

[102] Territory including the port of Memel, now Klaipede, in East Prussia. Lithuania acquired it in 1923, Germany again in 1939 and in 1945 the USSR.

K. Sissmore

We are curious to know if Miss Sissmore is in perpetual fear of her clothes falling off. Also if she wears an insecure wig, as both these seem to cause her constant agitation – especially in class!

MI5,[103] briefly with Kathleen Stewart, HS12, in and after World Wars I and II. It was Kathleen Sissmore, by then Mrs Archer, who in MI5 initiated Mr Hollis, its future head, Sir Roger, and who alone came near to exposing as a spy Mr Kim Philby, her superior, already a colonel in the KGB, before he fled to Russia in 1963, as the colonel (later general) himself records, in his book, *My Silent War*,[104] and Mrs Jean Collard, her step-daughter, more than once heard Mrs Archer say within the family how sure she was that Mr Philby was a communist.

Miss Parker's mailbag steadily filled with news of "my old girls", the words appearing thrice in the foreword that she wrote to the College Magazine, 1914, and in 1933 146 old girls and staff were named, working or travelling, at home or overseas. Marriage dispersed them far and wide, from Allahabad, Antigua and Auckland, to Valletta, Vancouver and Vina del Mar—there, in 1930, Joie Moir became McCoy (who as youngest boarder had presented the bouquet to Princess Helena), then died next year of rheumatic fever, aged 21; Southern Africa, Ceylon and India absorbed them most and in 1927 seven were in touch with one another in Malaya.

No news was published of Miss Parker's little boys till Mr Christmas Humphreys told her his, who would claim to be her oldest. As a Buddhist he believed that all life was sacred and that none should be taken; as a Queen's Counsel, future Judge, he successfully prosecuted Mrs Ruth Ellis, the last woman in Britain to be hanged, and Mr Timothy Evans, who was first hanged and then found innocent.

Another well-known figure in public life, Miss Mary Allen, the thrice-gaoled suffragette, returned to the College and talked to the girls about the Women's Police, which she and a friend had launched. Sixty years later, in 1983, Marjory Lucas had still not forgotten the extraordinary visitor who "appeared large and important" in uniform, hatted, "and sort of marched about". But Miss Allen had yet to espouse the Fascist cause.

A day-girl ward appeared in 1922, fourteen years old, tall, fair, sharp-nosed and softly spoken, called Margaret Romanoff. Her father was registered as "(Schoolmaster) (Russian)" and her mother, it seems a widow, of 17 Gordon Road, Ealing, as an old girl of the College. But Margaret claimed to be a royal princess, whose family had fled from the Bolsheviks in 1917, when her sister died of the ordeal. Her school-mates all believed her, especially when a hymn was sung which shared a tune with the Russian National Anthem and filled her eyes with tears. She left, 18, in 1926, one of those among Miss Parker's brood nothing more of whom would ever be recorded.

Old Girls' Week-Ends, begun in 1909, at the end of Autumn Term, were repeated year by year. Miss Parker welcomed the guests as they

[103] Helen, 1989: "I went for my interview while still at P.H.C. (and wearing school uniform) as Miss Parker had been asked to send along suitable leavers in the First World War!"

[104] London, 1968.

arrived, helped by a roaring fire, then tea. Music and dancing followed, a sketch or two—votes for women the subject of the first, in 1908—meant not to rally or inflame but to amuse—and in 1912 was performed a full-length play: Goldsmith's *The Good-Natured Man*—"a very merry meal", with "a grand display of crackers", "Auld Lang Syne"—Miss Parker's Roy continued singing after everyone else had stopped—he fatter grew and fatter and waddled and stank—Form VI took the blame, who had treated him to biscuits for his birthday, every day of every term—and he snorted and snored—the National Anthem, "Forty Years On", loud cheers for Princess Helena, Miss Parker, the College, and a collection for the United Girls' Schools Mission to the Poor in it was either Camberwell or Peckham. The Rev. Mr Austin Thompson, Vicar of St Peter's, stood up and preached. Womanliness was his theme in 1910: the ideal woman was someone you could trust and look to for advice, who discouraged gossip—"drawing-room libels"—and who worshipped God in church on Sunday.

Miss Parker dreaded boys but enjoyed the company of fathers, husbands and fiancés ("All my girls marry") and men were invited from 1920 onwards. Their black coats enhanced the girls' gay frocks; "the beautiful hall, with its now completed panelling and fine display of challenge cups and pictures, formed a perfect setting"; and the fine oak floor seemed better than the Ritz's. In 1927 a gentleman was heard confiding to his partner that he had been dragged there by the scruff of his neck—men too exaggerated—not knowing what to expect; next year "it was amusing to compare the nervous waistcoat-pulling and tie-fingering of the first-timers, apprehensive of any function at a Girls' School, with the here-we-are-again air of the second, third and fourth"; and by 1929 "dancing partners were plentiful and . . . there seemed to be fewer shy men than usual". Miss Parker surveyed them from her Royal Box, where Roy and her sister, Dora, kept her company. The scent of tangerines drifted upstairs and mingled with the perfume.

There was no Week-End in 1922, when Miss Parker fell seriously ill. To have gone ahead would have seemed bad form. Tables were laid for 135 in 1926. Someone prayed silence; Miss Parker said grace. Turkey was served (a treat), plum pudding for a sweet, and a din of conversation arose which reminded Theodora Eyton-Jones of the thunder of the Trummelbach Falls, punctuated by the snap of the crackers and the shrill noise of the whistles they contained, with funny paper hats. A respectful hush made way for Prof. Sumichrast, whose address, nearly 5,000 words long, on "the Spiritual Element in Education", was reported verbatim in the College Magazine, and Miss Wilmott took a class in the newly-built gymnasium.

It was good to be back, exchange news and meet old friends. Boarders returned to their dormitories for the three nights, Friday to Sunday, allegedly misbehaved and gave each other order-marks. The younger of the old had now become more frivolous, cutting long hair short, bobbing their shingled and shingling their bobbed, surprising one another, and one or two of them may have felt disgraced, who had absented themselves from

Holy Communion on Sunday and had worshipped God in bed instead of in St Stephen's.

Miss Parker's Royal Box was now expanded to provide a musicians' gallery. New floors were laid, all polished oak. *Hymns Ancient and Modern* was abandoned for *The Public Schools' Hymn Book*, perhaps not so much for its hymns as for its title. An emblem was proposed, in 1928, which Letters Patent approved, "a daisy erect slipped and leaved between two sprigs of genista [broom] in saltire proper" (a corner-to-corner cross like the St Andrew's)—but only the daisy was new—and a Coat of Arms or Seal designed by the Richmond Herald, which the College of Arms conferred under special licence from the King. The Coat of Arms alluded to Princess Helena's (improperly adopted in 1882) and to her daughter Princess Helena Victoria's: in heraldic terms "per fesse gules and azure, in chief a representation of the Coronet of Her Highness Princess Helena Victoria or, and in base an open book argent, edges and clasps gold, inscribed with the words *fortis qui se vincit* sable, all between two flaunches also argent, each charged with a cross couped between two roses in pale also gules barbed and seeded proper"—a pompous rigmarole which Madge Beaumont, the hydrant "rather slow" in 1909, and now School Secretary, attempted to interpret:

It is difficult to translate . . . but perhaps one may say that this shield is divided horizontally into two halves, the upper red and the lower blue. On the upper half is the Coronet of Princess Helena Victoria, and on the lower half the open book with its motto on either side; the shield is again divided vertically by a segment of a circle, the portion between the segment and the outside of the shield being white (or silver), and on each of these segments are St George's Cross and two red roses, one above and the other below the cross.

Miss Beaumont did not like it. "I think it has little character and is too stiff and niggly. When reduced to a usable size, for any purpose, it just becomes a collection of spots and dots."

Facilities improved. The juniors acquired a playroom, though not until Miss Parker's last full year, with window-seat lockers topped with cushions, brown and orange, ping-pong (as they called it), a gramophone and, set on the mantelpiece, a musical box, "patrols" (chickens, penguins, dogs), a group of riders and a quaint little man, Prince Bulbo (of *The Rose and the Ring*), who could walk; while the youngest of them all acquired a playground see-saw, then shared it with the older.

Individual girls, prefects, forms, parents and staff, all grateful, continued to equip the school and embellish it, with desks, tables and chairs; a fire-stool appeared—"This stool will be much appreciated when the cold weather comes again"—clocks: marble, oak, mahogany, cuckoo and chiming; pictures, vases, an embroidered book-marker for Miss Parker's bible ("as the other one had worn out"), screens, book and show-cases, notice-boards, silver-mounted inkstand, barometer, magic lantern,

pianos, curtains, table-cloths, one red, to brighten the library, a Union Jack ("first unfurled on Empire Day"), with its flagstaff, the antlers of a deer Mrs Swann, mother of Elsie and Elizabeth, had herself slain, many other trophies and gifts, almost all of which have disappeared, it seems unnoticed, but not Flossie von Keudell's long-case clock or Esmée and Margot Preston's mother's intricate, four-fold, Indian screen, too big to slip into a bag or pocket.

The school museum filled with curios from throughout the world: fossilised tortoise, imprint of Buddha's foot, grass skirt from New Guinea, Balimda dagger, shoes of Finnish child, lacquered cards, from Orissa and Bihar, dead wild life of every kind, shells, butterflies from Malaya and South America, the Milligans Winifred and Muriel's rug, skin of the corpse of a grizzly bear which had been shot by their own brother, and stuffed Indian cobra at grips with stuffed Indian mongoose. Mr Secretan, father of Julie and Pearl, gave his precious Roman coins; no doubt they have survived in a collection somewhere. In the war appeared two gas-masks, a Turkish cap and haversack and, from Prof. Sumichrast, the cap of a shell which had only just missed fame, having almost hit and killed the Belgian Queen.

The gardens had matured. Snowdrops blossomed first, then crocus, daffodil and tulip; in the Summer Term the bluebells, laburnum, mock orange, chestnut, lilac, may, pillar rose, California poppy and Spanish iris. An orchard—once waste land—had filled with apple, Siberian crab, quince, French blackberry and loganberry, enclosed by a hedge of bramble. Mr W. J. Bean, revered Curator of the Royal Botanic Gardens, Kew,[105] advised on trees and, thinking them dangerous, as experts often do, had eighty-three black poplars felled. But the view over Harrow improved and limes were planted in their stead, copper beech, apple, plum, Japanese maple, buddleia, magnolia, rhododendron and azalea. The great white poplar on the field still stood; in June the seed-pods burst and rained white cotton. A pergola arose, leading to a stone seat, guarded by two stone storks; a sun-dial followed it, with engraved brass plate—*tempus*, it warned, *fugit*—and a crazy path with a bird-bath in the middle.

The twentieth year of Miss Parker's headship had been generously marked, gifts being heaped upon her from pupils, old girls and staff: a late eighteenth-century French escritoire, a tortoise-shell paper-knife and a beautifully tooled, brown-leather blotter and inkstand, with two, glass, barrel-shaped pots. Now ten more years had passed. Miss Parker, 64, with her mother, 99, sat and watched her last school play as head. She was about to retire.

Two hundred or so Old Girls attended her last Week-End, having groped their way through a London fog, from every corner of the land—wives, it was claimed, abandoning their husbands and mothers their babes.

[105] Author of *Trees and Shrubs, Hardy in the British Isles*, 2 vols, 1914; eighth edition, 1988.

The Bishop of London came and talked about the need for Christian service. He had broken a rule, never to undertake an engagement outside church on a Sunday. Miss Parker accepted a cheque from Una Bird, her first Head of School, for £285, a book filled with the cut-out signatures of all who had subscribed, beautifully illuminated by Dorothy Reid, and bound volumes of the College Magazines from her first year onwards.

From the splendour of the College rooms and gardens, Miss Parker withdrew with her sister into a small house called "Tiga" in de Warenne Road in Lewes. A room was set aside for old-girl visitors. Dog Roy still stank but a few years later he mercifully died and the guests were taken out into the garden, to be told, "That is my little man's grave and the netting is to prevent the cats from digging him up."

Girls present had given her a wireless and girls departed were to send her "a hamper of good things", year by year, Old-Girl Dinner by Old-Girl Dinner, till her life's end, and have her portrait painted and displayed in the hall.

In 1937 Miss Parker set out from Liverpool for the first of three grand tours, from Quebec to Vancouver, from Egypt to Ceylon and from Kenya to South Africa, with Dora twice and then without, all within a year and a month or so. A box lay waiting in her cabin when she boarded her ship, the *Duchess of York*, full of lilies of the valley, and many a telegram to wish her *bon voyage*.

The lions of South Africa appeared to avoid the retired Principal, who sought them high and low, but she stayed with or met twenty-eight of "my old girls"—"one of the very great pleasures in visiting South Africa"—and the diaries or notes that she kept yielded fourteen pages of lively travelogue for three successive issues of the College Magazine.

Miss Parker continued writing letters to the school, all in her own hand, till 1958, when she was ninety-one years old. Her niece, the author, Frances Faviell,[106] then wrote on her behalf: "Aunt Mary is very anxious to go up in an aeroplane and we hope to arrange it for her on a really good day."

Betty Stone and Lissa Birchall-Wood visited their old headmistress next year, bringing fruit, flowers, a chicken and wine, on behalf of all her grown-up children.

She was sitting in her winged arm-chair in the drawing-room when we arrived, wearing a soft green wool dress with a bright scarf at the neck and there was a new green rug over her knees. We particularly noticed her quiet white hands with several rings on them as of old. Her gestures, too, were exactly those we have always known. The tips of her fingers pressed lightly together as she talked—a sudden leaning forward with piercing gaze, ending in a twinkle.

Not again would there arrive "a hamper of good things". That night Miss Parker suffered a stroke and she died next day. She was 92. Her mother had lived to be 101.

[106] *The Dancing Bear*, 1954, and *A House on the Rhine*, 1955.

"Miss Parker", wrote Miss Prain, her colleague and next but one successor, "was a headmistress of the old school, dignified, rather austere and, to those . . . not fortunate enough to get to know her, forbidding." She had looked the part that she was called upon to play, dressing sombrely, in grey or navy, but with many an interesting change of blouse, and on Sundays picturesquely in long soft silks. Her skirt sweeping the floor made her seem to float as she walked erect inside it. The pearl, ruby and sapphire on her fingers caught the eye, as did the silver coach-and-horses ring into which she rolled her napkin, and the silver stand, holding the glass that she drank hot water from at meals. If she tried she could startle, as on Tournament Days, when her hats especially provoked sharp comment, such as "Here comes Merry England, with most of the British Isles on top!" Otherwise, however, she wore only two: a summer and a winter. And Mabel Semple felt rather disappointed when she stole a glimpse of her, a guest at her parents' house in Woburn, sitting up in bed, as the maid brought in her breakfast. "I knew what interest would be shown next term . . .Alas! She looked exactly the same, her hair neatly plaited, and in a long-sleeved nightdress buttoned to the neck."

Did the face with the eyes that twinkled ever smile? Mary Savery believed that it did: seldom perhaps, though sweetly. She had something not unlike a sense of humour; to some it seemed sarcastic and to others dry. "Your mother was a Scot, Mary Hickey, and your father is Irish. If you could develop the good manners of the Irish and the common sense of the Scots, instead of the other way round, you would do better." But few remember, or only Faith Heslop, that Miss Parker ever laughed.

She spoke her mind, as thus with Barbara Allen's mother, so Barbara's unpublished memoirs read, Mrs Allen arriving for the Shakespeare play:

"Oh, Miss Parker! How are you? And how is darling Baba?"

"Barbara, I regret to say, is an extremely tiresome little girl. I only hope that in time we can improve her."

"Oh, but Miss Parker! You mustn't make her too *good . . . or no one will ever want to marry her!"*

"That, *Mrs Allen, will be quite the least of my future worries."*

If she disapproved of anyone or anything, she raised an eyebrow; if ever she was angry, the gold pince-nez and chain, pinned to her bodice, either shook or seemed to shake. Mary Hickey and Patricia Duncan were two of many girls whom she frightened; Iris Norrington another: "Miss Parker . . . used to appear unexpectedly during lessons and had a paralysing effect—on me at any rate—while she sat there listening." And some felt worse than frightened, like Rosemary Mole, who could not forgive what she felt to be the harm which Miss Parker had done to her morale; this rankled:

I did not like Miss Parker, nor she me. Never in five years did I ever once feel at ease in her presence. When I unexpectedly gained exemption from

Matric with enough credits in School Certificate papers, she sent for me to say that this was proof of my deceitful nature, since I had appeared not to be working well, whereas to have achieved this result I must have been doing so secretly. She then said that I mustn't infer from this success that I was intelligent; I had quite an ordinary brain. I am still puzzled that any headmistress could so savagely deflate and destroy the confidence of a very timid girl at her first and only school triumph.

Elizabeth Bunbury, Dr Hilliard, agreed. "The only reason I should like to go to heaven is to meet Miss Parker and tell her what I thought about her."

And yet Miss Prain spoke for many, even most, when she recalled how "warm, whole-hearted" was the interest she took in the girls who had been trusted to her care, lasting years after they had left. It had surprised Joan Mackwood: "When I went into her sitting-room to say goodbye, the evening before I left P.H.C., she kissed me on both cheeks and informed me that she had a soft spot for the rebels—I wished that I had known!" "She knew more about us than we had guessed," wrote Margaret Brown.

The older her old girls grew, the more they understood that a shy Miss Parker underlay the chilling look—"one of the shyest people I have ever met", she had seemed to Peggie Coles—and the more did they forgive, admire and even love her. Her rules had been no stricter than was then usual. She had applied them fairly. In Barbara Allen's words: "like Dr Arnold: a beast but a just beast",[107] and a generous one, too, who would reimburse the train and taxi fares of the less well off among her old-girl visitors.

The tributes multiplied. "I was so fond of her." "For forty years I wrote each year and got a reply." "I never knew anyone so awe-inspiring . . . so kind . . . she was unique." "A woman", wrote Marjorie Harrison, HS30, "of really great moral and intellectual calibre". Veronica Philip, HS28: "You ask how she won the hearts of most of her pupils. I think because we knew we were immensely important to her—she knew (and deplored) our many weaknesses but she was On Our Side." And even Muriel Dodds, ever candid to a fault, could see in her "the selfless dedication of the Mother Teresas of this world" and "a woman who could admit to mistakes".

A Memorial Fund honoured Miss Parker's name with a complete set of the *Encyclopaedia Britannica*, other handsome books, and garden seats, and by pure chance an Old Girl, Cherry Hyde-Johnson, bought the house that now stood empty in de Warenne Road in Lewes.

[107] Correspondence.

Chapter Seven

1931–1935

Miss Gladys Milvain, who had taught German at Roedean, the subject she had read at St Hilda's, Oxford, now replaced Miss Parker. Having spent the last six years in Cairo, as Head of the Sarich Teacher Training College, she enjoyed what she had missed and now discovered: "The lot is fallen unto me in a fair ground: yea, I have a goodly heritage":[1] "the tradition . . . of an English public school", also trees, flowers and well-cut lawns, which a cat, called Timothy, patrolled.

It would have been hard to find a lovelier spot in which to enjoy again all the beauties of Spring at home than the College garden with its snowdrops and daffodils—and *its crocuses, even though Ealing sparrows seem to be fiercer than other sparrows in their onslaughts on crocuses. Is this because, in Marshall's*[2] *words, "The birds have been encouraged"? And does this refer to the extensive bathing facilities provided for the birds, or to the sternness with which Timothy's bird-hunting propensities are discouraged by even his most devoted admirers? Be that as it may, the P.H.C. garden did indeed offer to a traveller returned "a refuge green and cool and tranquil as a dream"*[3] *and its beauties seemed to increase . . . as the lilacs and the fruit blossom succeeded the daffodils and were themselves succeeded by the roses and all the glories of the herbaceous border.*

In her published memoirs, *Gay Memories of Egypt* (1949), Miss Milvain refers to her new school but does not name it and has little if anything to say about her duties or its work. It was the school outdoors that she remembered best: "the loveliness of bare trees . . . veiled in a soft blue mist", which greeted her in winter, the sweet and many blossoms of an English May and the spring and summer nights and daybreak.

I used to sleep out on a balcony, to the amazement of my staff—"We cannot imagine how you can do such a thing!"—huddled in mackintosh covers against the dew, sometimes awakened by heavy showers and sent hurrying indoors to the shelter of my second bedroom, and I can still feel the ecstasy of those May mornings, the curtain of young green around me, the joyous chorusing of the birds as they heralded the dawn of another Summer's Day, and the lovely cool, calm feeling, physical and mental, which sleeping in the open brings.

[1] Psalm xv.
[2] Marshall, C. J., Head Gardener, 1922–61.
[3] Unidentified.

Ealing afforded her "seclusion" and "an ideal taking-off point for jaunts into Town to taste the joys of the ballet, theatres, concerts, shops . . ." Her feet seem hardly to have touched a classroom floor. But she claimed to have opened girls' ears and eyes to choral and orchestral music, if not their eyes and mouths to the many "gay repasts" that she enjoyed in Soho restaurants. The party that she took to hear Bach's *St Matthew Passion* at the Queen's Hall, on "a wonderful Sunday in Lent", "seemed . . . quite hushed . . . overawed by the magnitude of it all—it was something of which they had had no conception." A visit was arranged to the Albert Hall, where Malcolm Sargeant conducted *Hiawatha*, and the Prefects were treated to Noël Coward's *Lilac Time*. Princess Helena Victoria approved, especially when, at a concert given by the cellist, Pablo Casals, in the Grotrian Hall, Sir Henry Wood conducting, she could see "my girls", easily identified, wearing cloaks green, over shantung dresses gold, and a few days later she telephoned Miss Milvain to say how much it had pleased her to know that the school enjoyed such opportunities to hear good music. The girls might have agreed. Not only did they hear, with their own ears, they also saw, with their own eyes, Rachmaninov and Schnabel.

At the Old Vic a party admired a red-haired Romeo. A visit to *Macbeth* followed, which the Lower IVth had already done in class. Their spokesman wrote:

We loved it, and the new garden cloaks helped to make beautiful witches. You can guess, then, what was our excitement when Miss Milvain told us that if we were very *good for the next fortnight, Miss Cohen should take us to see* Macbeth *at the Sadler's Wells Theatre. We nearly burst with goodness, and could hardly believe it was true when we found ourselves seated in the theatre waiting for it to begin. Some of us had never been inside one before, but in spite of that we behaved better than some schools there, who would rustle paper and whisper. There isn't room enough in the whole of this magazine to tell you how much we loved that expedition.*

Mr Young, father of Betty, gave them their first radio-gramophone. Miss Milvain found a room for it, "a worthy setting, swept and garnished . . . with a pleasing colour-scheme in blue, black and grey", where concerts and dance music became "a regular and delightful feature of the life of the school" and where girls might sit, wrapped in their eiderdowns and ready for bed, a luxurious privilege, a memorable joy, and once or twice not to have to go upstairs till the clock had struck eleven.

The girls took to their new Principal. She established the School Council, for which they had asked. They enjoyed her German tea-party. She allowed, indeed she introduced, Easter eggs, hard-boiled, with painted shells, Miss Parker's "heathen relics" and "excesses", and "Cyrus, King of the Persians", her kitten, they adored. But some at least missed the discipline of old. A deputation of seniors went to her and said so.

Debates lapsed but the Shakespeare plays continued to be read. Acting flourished. Form V on its own did *King Lear* in 1932. Lacrosse drooped.

The Roedean and Wycombe 2nd XIIs and even the Wycombe 3rd beat the College 1st. Diana Wadeson, Captain and Head of School, seemed almost to despair as she reviewed the team's performance. Mary Bown could intercept but her stickwork was "slapdash" and her passing inaccurate and slow; Jocelyn Sweet, who had improved her shooting, was "weak and ineffective", being "slow to use her brains and feet"; and Dorothea Abrahall "too lazy".

The Cricket 1st XI fared no better. But games offered more than failure and success, as they found when in 1933 Chairman Mr Hodge had arranged for them to play against St Mary's, Wantage.[4]

We lost the match by 49 runs, but even this could not entirely cloud our great enjoyment. Some of us had not seen the school before, nor had the experience of the drive through Oxford and the Berkshire Downs. We arrived home at 9 o'clock after a long but happy day.

Miss Milvain simplified the uniform. A new green gym-tunic and blouse replaced the old serge cally. The public was thought to admire the garden cloak, just right for girls and witches. The shantung dress remained. Rooms everywhere were painted gold and green, green desks appeared and in dining-room and bedrooms yellow china.

A Founder's Day Service was held, the first and last but one, incorporating a Founder's Day Hymn, with words by Doreen Goodwin, about patience, perseverance, honour and vision, and a vow of loyalty, which the girls had all to repeat:

I will pledge myself to remember that at all times and in all places I am the School's representative.

I will therefore strive to refrain from any word or deed which may bring discredit upon it.

I will endeavour to be always loyal to the Staff and to all my School-fellows.

I will ever seek to be worthy of the School, to add to its lustre and to cherish its highest traditions.

I will try to play my part in transmitting it to others, not less, but greater and better than it was transmitted to me.

More trophies filled the school's museum. It acquired a sambur's head, what remained of a beast which Dorothy Stephen's husband had killed, somewhere in Africa. And a miniature London Museum Exhibition was arranged in the front hall, including two mid-Victorian dolls, Ethel—"Best Ethel"—and Madgie, with each an extensive wardrobe, much of which had already been displayed at a *grande exposition* in Paris.

[4] Founded in 1872 by the Rev. Mr William Butler, Vicar of Wantage, and run by the sisters of the Anglican Community of St Mary the Virgin, till in 1975 they withdrew.

Miss Parker had supplied the Magazine with news drawn from her swollen mail-bag, uniting girls present and past with each other and with staff. Princess Helena Victoria kept some in touch. Beryl Agate met her in Jamaica; in Antigua Lorna Burrowes, the Antigua Brownies' Brown Owl, and Doreen Goodwin, writer of the hymn ("she retained my hand in her own all the time she was asking questions about P.H.C."), with her past girls mother and aunt ("my mother had about twenty minutes' conversation with her, during which she spoke nearly the whole time about the College").

Miss Milvain did not stay long. After only three years and a half and, in Miss Beaumont's words, "young, gay and impulsive", she returned to Egypt's bright blue sky and warmth, too soon to serve as the next link with and focus for "my old girls", but loaded with their and her colleagues' gifts of books: Coward, Maugham, Edith Sitwell, Virginia Woolf and T. E. Lawrence; and a set of records of Schnabel playing Beethoven. She became Principal of the newly-founded English College for Girls in Alexandria; remained there till in July 1940 its Governors asked her to resign; continued teaching, in the Egyptian public sector; and throughout the war kept somewhat open house, "Aunt Milly" to the soldiers.

Chapter Eight

1935–1958

Eaton Rise, where the school had stood since 1882, already sounded neither countryside nor town, and when the housing boom of the 1930s lifted Britain from the slump, and Ealing ("the village", as girls and staff still called it) sprawled, parents choosing boarding-schools began to look elsewhere.

A new abode was needed. Lady Hailsham, now Chairman, sought it, inspecting about fifty properties for sale, in easy but not *too* easy reach of London—Princess Helena Victoria herself eyed two—and in 1935 she at last found and acquired, at Preston near Hitchin, on a northern ridge of the Chiltern Hills, an estate and house called Temple Dinsley.

Edward the Confessor had owned the site. From Edward it passed to William Rufus, from William to Bernard de Balliol, forebear of the Scottish kings, and from him to the Knights Templars, who in 1147 built a temple there to Solomon. The Templars remained, misbehaving, till in 1309 Pope Clement V disbanded them. It is likely that they hoped to return, and the legend could be true, that their treasure still lies buried in a nearby pond, well, wood or field. The Knights Hospitallers of St John of Jerusalem took their place, charitably employed till Henry VIII dissolved the order. Sir Ralph Sadleir, one of Henry's principal secretaries of state, thus came by Temple Dinsley and with Sadleirs it remained for about two hundred years. Benedict Ithell, a London merchant, bought it in 1712; he had the old house taken down and a new one built. More Ithells, then Dartons,[1] Harwood-Dartons and Pryors followed, de Vine Pryors, Barrington Whites; in 1909 Mrs H. G. Fenwick,[2] when Lutyens added wings and Miss Jekyll did the gardens; Mr Douglas Vickers, the aircraft manufacturer, who had Lutyens return and build him arches and more rooms; and lastly Almina, Countess of Carnarvon,[3] whose family brought mummies with them from the pyramids, which villagers, either squeamish or superstitious, refused to help unwrap.

Lady Hailsham visited the school and broke the news of departure to the few remaining pupils, who in October had numbered only sixty-four; appealed to the oldest to stay another term or two; then shook them by the

[1] On the 14th of November 1794 Haydn visited their tenants, Lord and Lady Forfar, bringing with him as a gift for Lady Anne two *divertimenti* for two flutes and a cello.

[2] Violet, born Perkins, a wealthy and seemingly compulsive buyer, occupant and seller, of stately homes.

[3] Widowed in 1923 by George, fifth Earl; and married again within five months to Lt.-Col. Ian Denison.

hand each one and said goodbye. The girls, after three cheers for Lady Hailsham and the College, returned to their classrooms, trying hard to imagine what moving school entailed. *Fortis qui se vincit*, they would do their best; and Miss Beaumont, their exemplar, noted stout hearts, as well as disappointed ones, and missionary zeal:

The idea of leaving our present home . . . was naturally a sad thought, but we were so impressed with the realisation that to us was entrusted the task of rekindling the spirit of Princess Helena College in the new building, and of making the College in its new and lovely surroundings a wonderful success, that we put any die-hard instincts behind us.

Miss Vyvyen Alice Prain became Principal: a Scot—George Watson's Ladies' College, Edinburgh, and Edinburgh University; a former member of the staff, 1919–25, when she already dreamt of following Miss Parker; till 1929 chief historian at Wycombe; thereafter Headmistress of the Ladies' College, Guernsey; called Vyvyen at Ealing, she would now be known as Vap.

A taxi brought her from Hitchin railway-station to the Temple Dinsley forecourt, with a housekeeper and two maids. Her quarters would always be minimal: a small bed-sittingroom and a big bathroom, the bathroom to be shared with her colleague next door. At least it would be clean, tidy and quiet. Meanwhile the house was full of noise and dust. She had no hot water or electric light and it did not seem that within eight weeks all would be ready for her pupils and staff, as she picked her way or groped it over planks, ladders, paint-pots, boxes of screws and nails, tools, coats, boots. And even if it was, could enough pupils be enrolled to support their education? She too would do her best:

I hope that all Old Girls will help by recommending the College to friends who are looking for schools for their daughters. Those abroad may be interested to know that I am prepared to take complete charge of children, and see to their clothes, holidays and so on. Those of you who can make the opportunity of visiting Temple Dinsley and seeing it for yourselves will be very welcome, and will, I know, appreciate the advantages such a place has to offer.

The old upstairs was converted into dormitories; the lighting disconnected and the plumbing, then restored; and a new kitchen with dining-room installed. But workmen were still about when term began, sawing and hammering. A staircase, two floors high, had to wait until Christmas; the west-wing roof, another year, when Mr Felix Lander, the architect, had it car-jacked higher, giving space in which to provide more beds; and the art studio and music wing, till 1937. It cost rather more to buy the house, then enlarge and adapt it, £48,712, than the Ealing house had fetched, £43,000. But the school had won a breather. It lived. The old wives' tale about the gypsy's warning, that never would an eldest son inherit Temple Dinsley, could have nothing to do with Miss Prain, her staff

and pupils, and four years later, when Britain had again declared war on the Germans, the move seemed providential.

Miss Parker and forty of her Old Girls braved snow and ice-bound roads and fog to enjoy their next Week-End, then unfroze before the great log fire in the entrance hall, now drawing-room. "Next morning", someone wrote, "with a Christmas-card effect, the sun shone on a white landscape as we walked through the garden to the little church just beyond the gates—a church as white and simple as one always expects a village church to be."

Miss Beaumont had comforted in verse all those who felt that they had lost their school. *Plus ça change* . . . It had only changed its address. But Temple Dinsley lay off the beaten track and you could lose it in the snow and fog. Miss Parker's past pupils veered to London instead, to either the Berners Hotel, where the din they made was so intense that the waiters stuck their fingers in their ears, or the Ivanhoe or the Rembrandt.

King George V died in January 1936, when the girls had all to wear black arm-bands on the sleeves of their outdoor coats. Mourning was decreed for the next six months and the school's official opening had thus to be postponed. A Garden Party was arranged, for the end of Summer Term. Princess Helena Victoria attended it. Lady Hailsham could not appear, for her husband had just died; Kathleen Sissmore took her place—Mrs Archer, now, of MI5. HRH may have wondered what the room had become in which, a year ago, the furniture was stacked and a space had been cleared where she could picnic-lunch. Miss Prain introduced her to the staff. The band of the Cameronians played in the orchard and danced on the lawn to the music of the pipes. Tea was served in a big marquee and after tea came out the sun.

Temple Dinsley looked its very best. The house was swept and garnished, the dormitories were immaculate, flowers brightened every corner—and a particularly interesting decoration was the telegram of good wishes from P.H.C. Rhodesians, which had arrived that very morning . . .

In the boxed yew hedges, where the Ealing storks now stood, girls mimed, acted and sang.

The storks were two of the mementos which old girls recognised. Victoria, the Great White Queen—her marble bust—occupied the loggia. The smile of the Laughing Cavalier greeted them in the hall. Miss Beaumont had built a model of the Ealing school. The old oak panelling had been taken down and stored. Miss Beaumont and Miss Stone—Betty—appealed for "contributions big or little . . . Everyone helped to panel the Hall—please help now to Hall the panelling." The Honours Boards were sold or destroyed but not before Joan Bloxam, artist and author, had transferred the names there displayed to it must have been the last of fifty years of volumes leather-bound, gold-tooled. A wall in the back yard took the Ealing foundation stone, but not the jar it had concealed, with inside it copies of *The Times*, *The Morning Post*, *The Middlesex County Times*, 17.12.1881, the report on the College for that year, and the

slip of paper signed by the two foremen builders.[4] Miss Parker returned at least twice more, from her home in Lewes, and Miss Milvain once, before her boat set sail for Egypt.

Mrs Fenwick's house had changed: bare wood had been exposed under white paint; bird-cages had disappeared, perhaps long since, which Lutyens had housed in windowed cupboards; and the lily-pond outside would soon be a swimming-pool. Miss Jekyll may have turned half over in her grave, where she had lain three years, and Lutyens may have winced. But the Queen Anne house, and the wings and gardens of 1909, stayed otherwise intact—the forecourt, terrace, arches, the flights of steps to the sunken lawn, rose-beds, loggia, the vine-clad pergola, gazebo, orchard, and the woodland path, leading to the Dower House. Miss Prain invited a company of Guides from Vauxhall to come and enjoy it all, camping on the gamesfield, each end of her first five (peace-time) summer terms. Parents joined them on the last full day, deck-chaired, listened to the gramophone, watched the College do a sketch or two and Betty Baeza dance. Their children sailed boats on the pool, fell into it or swam, swung on the swing, or slid down the slide in the gymnasium, hunted treasure, played musical chairs-and-bumps, picked and embraced huge bunches of flowers and devoured more—and harder—green cooking-apples than they could painlessly digest, leaving not much room for sticky buns, going home in the bus. Miss Prain:

as always we felt, when we waved goodbye to the cheery friendly crowd . . . how well worth while these short personal contacts are, when we become real people to each other, instead of just "they".

An outbreak of whooping-cough prevented Princess Helena Victoria from attending the Garden Party in 1938. She returned in the autumn, when girls, lacrosse-sticks raised, formed a guard of honour. Informal contact was what she still preferred; and it was difficult, wrote someone, to curtsey on the stairs when you chanced upon "a real princess".

In Ealing meanwhile most of Miss Parker's school had been demolished, making room for flats. The tall white poplar, having aged and lost some boughs, was felled. More flats appeared on the bottom pitch, where once had grazed the farmer's cattle. Allotments filled the top. The gymnasium and part of the new wing survived till after the war, but only just. And all that then remained was two gate pillars, where the College's name was chiselled, and a brass altar-desk in St Peter's Church, commemorating the forty years in which the school had worshipped there.

The intake rose until numbers stood at not much more than a hundred pupils, aged 11 to 18. Many of the fathers were officers or clergy. A few had old-girl mothers; their total increased from five to twenty after fourteen years, then halved in half the time, as a new clientèle emerged. Ability was mixed. Miss Prain dispensed with Common Entrance. Yet almost as high a

[4] John Bolt, James Darvall, with Messrs Bray and Pope, 42 Market Street, Paddington.

proportion of her girls went on to university, even in science, including medicine, as did Miss Parker's, though two at least went up to Oxford by way of other schools, Miss Prain acquiescing.

In 1938 the inspectors were pleased. Every subject had been well taught. Miss Prain herself taught best: scripture and history in all forms, comparative religion in VI, with mathematics here and there—and she also took the village children's Bible class on Sundays.

Routine had somewhat changed. At 7.30 a.m. a maid walked a hand-bell through the corridors upstairs and shook it a hundred times, so that all would hear it at least once and could plead no excuse for being late—there was a roped bell too, which tempted passing hands. Once everyone had washed, dressed and stripped her bed, a ten-minute silence followed, so that all could think or say their prayers and read from the Bible. Girls in any way misgrown did remedial exercises with Miss Wooldridge, feeling punished. The rest, not listed sick, pulled on their lacrosse-boots and ran to the Lodge Gate and back, about half a mile, or hid in the music wings or in a cupboard. Having then made their beds and eaten breakfast, they marched in step to the big west-wing room, where they stood for hymn and more Bible, knelt on its hard oak floor and again prayed. Brushes and combs were checked on Mondays, footwear on Tuesdays, laundry and clean sheets passed to and fro elsewhen, and chests of drawers were inspected at random, where only five articles at a time might be kept on top. Staff gave out no letters till end of morning school, which postponed excitement or intensified it. At morning break the village baker arrived and, after hot currant buns, cocoa or in summer orange-juice, everyone had to go outside and freshen her lungs. Meals were conducted much as hitherto: after silence had prevailed throughout the first two courses, hubbub mounted, at all tables but the one in the room next door, where girls spoke only French, coaxed by a mistress or her *assistante*. The rule still applied that no one asked anyone for anything. "Would you like me to pass you . . .?" continued to mean "Would you please pass me . . .?"

At the end of the day Miss Prain read a chapter of a book to each form, some twenty minutes each, while they sat, knitted or sewed. Form III, the youngest, went to bed first, at half past seven, and the prefects last, at half past nine.

Houses were instituted "as in most public schools"—Windsor, Gloucester and York—red, white (later yellow) and blue—and each chose its own Housemistress and competed at games and in deportment and tidiness, to see who could win Miss Prain's Cock House trophy, "a silver cockerel, crowing triumphantly". Each afternoon but Wednesday (hobbies) and Sunday (the Sabbath Day, the Lord's, kept holy), was a games afternoon, as at most boarding-schools.

On Saturdays the girls mended their clothes, under Matron's watchful eye, and washed their hair; played matches; repeated work which staff had marked "unsatisfactory"; danced in the evening or attended a lecture illustrated with lantern-slides. On Sunday they worshipped at St Martin's

Church nearby; wrote letters home; spent Silence Hour as at Ealing, on the same oak benches, where they rhubarb-rhubarb-memorised and recited to the wall their collect or epistle, eating sweets—but the ration had increased, they could now eat sweets on any other day; and after tea practised hymns, often after two much cake for someone's birthday, when diaphragms had tightened and vocal chords felt messy.

The Fire Brigade had disbanded but fire-drill continued: at night, when blazer was slipped over nightwear and bath-towel hung over head, and by day, when each girl had to lower herself from window above to earth below, on a pulley and sling, called the Davy. If the Davy stuck, she might hang and wait aloft, swaying, for what felt like hours, but usually it worked, and Miss Wooldridge, Games, was quick to assist anyone tearfully frightened or hysterical and launch her from the sill, shoving hard.

Uniform changed little from Miss Milvain till the war. Miss Prain kept the green gym-tunic, which Betty Baeza, looking back, thought dashing, with its v-neck and pleated skirt, worn with a green poplin blouse, long-sleeved, and the green, gold-striped tie. A thing or two less was worn for games; and after games a gold poplin blouse with a green cardigan. A flowered dress appeared at the week-end. The girls had still to wear a spencer underneath it to keep them warm, as Matron made sure, who stood at the top of the stairs eyeing suspects approaching. In winter the hat was a green pudding-basin; in summer, the old panama.

Behaviour grew more difficult to control, it being easier to skive in fields or woods than in the Ealing house and garden; also sillier, girls pip-squirting or playing knock-and-run at the staff-room door. Punishment still shamed: a nuisance might be told to stand behind her chair in the dining-hall, or sit there with juniors, an ordeal Jean Dobson narrowly missed, sub-prefect though she was, having argued with Matron, or wait with her face to the wall outside the Study till Miss Prain arrived, in the morning break or lunch-hour. More treats were arranged, therefore more could be cancelled, a visit to a concert-hall or theatre, a dance or week-end film. Betty Baeza lost her place in a team, having knitted all through Latin, where at last she was exposed. Even week-end leave could be forgone, which did not please parents; but parents similarly trained would not demur. Others disobedient or tiresome or rude could be sent to bed hours early; or, one at a time, spend Saturday confined to the sick-wing, feeling horribly fit, with nothing to read or listen to; or write out lines; or learn by heart a psalm or collect. And if anyone swore—said "damn" (bad) or "bloody" (appalling)—she got a tablet of quinine and had to stand sucking it for a whole hour outside the staff-room door, with nothing to remove its bitter taste, until her mouth was cleansed.

Prefects, it is said, punished oftener than staff. A girl might have to write and read them an essay, or walk up and down the terrace, where again Miss Prain would notice, or jog up and down the drive or do extra housework or untangle knotted string, breaking her fingernails, or unmake and make her bed six times.

Girls writing home to complain about a punishment they thought unfair had the punishment redoubled. Betty Forbes, however, who had written on behalf of her sister, Christina, felt for ever grateful, Miss Prain having made her recite, daily and for six weeks, the thirteenth chapter of St Paul's first epistle to the Corinthians, "Though I speak with the tongues of men and of angels, and have not charity, I am become as sounding brass, or a tinkling cymbal", all the way to "And now abideth faith, hope, charity, these three, but the greatest of these is charity".

Miss Prain disapproved of swollen heads but she did not deny the children her esteem when they deserved or needed it. Magazine Foreword, 1956:

I rejoice as much as anyone in brilliant achievements, and am very proud of the successes of our talented members, in whatever sphere they are gained. But P.H.C. has never set out to collect distinctions: if some are slow in academic subjects, they often have much to give in personality, or on the artistic side, or in games. What we ask is that each shall try to make a contribution, according to her talents, shall do her honest best in matters she finds difficult, and by developing a healthy sense of humour, shall learn to follow a middle way between the self-depreciation and self-conceit which so often rob individuals of both happiness and usefulness.

Miss Parker was a daughter of the Empire heart and soul; Miss Prain felt more thankful, than proud, to be British and a Scot. Both were historians but Miss Prain's ideas owed more than did Miss Parker's to her knowledge of the causes and results of World War I and to her dreading of the outbreak of a World War II even more frightful than the first, and she did not despise other faiths or nations.

Miss Prain may have noticed that the younger of the school's old girls knew Europe better—an improvement overdue. Only nine had been reported on holiday in France, or *au pair*, from the armistice till 1931; no one, at least in the published news, had studied music abroad till in 1923 Barbara Noel went to Brussels; and Germany appeared to be completely shunned. But in the next eight years, up to 1939, six were to be found in France; Patricia Duncan travelled to Berlin, Würzburg University, Heidelberg, and enjoyed a German Christmas with a student friend at Speyer am Rhein; others followed: Oberammergau drew four; Eileen Wade lived with a family in Hilchenbach. Diana Wadeson spent a happy year with the family of Princess Reuss, at her home, Schloss Jankendorf, Ober Lausitz, in Berlin and Vienna, and on their boat sailing the Danube, then travelled on and worked *au pair* in Paris, Normandy, Silesia, and at Vac in Hungary. The German scene, unaffectedly tuneful and homespun-picturesque, won many hearts.

Mary Allen's book appeared in 1936: *Lady in Blue*.[5] A staunch Fascist,

[5] An account of the development of the Women's Auxiliary Police, which she and a friend had founded.

she admired Franco and Goering; and Hitler she adored: his "passionate, forceful voice", "hypnotic gestures" and "visionary eyes" held her "spell-bound", "absolutely entranced", when she met him; as his audience helped prove—"the lined faces" that "shone with sheer worship", the "bald heads pink with excitement" and the "irrepressible, growling cheers"—he was the greatest orator the world had ever known; "charming" in private, "courteous, patient", with "steadfast eyes" and "unflinching mouth", reflecting his "sincerity and fixity of purpose", "an enduring friend of England . . . a blood-brother of the ordinary decent people of Europe, whatever their nationalities"; he alone served as "the barrier holding back the tide of Communism".

Miss Prain saw in Europe "a world gone mad" and "a nightmare" on its way. Her pupil, Christine Fenton, echoed her foreboding: newly left and in Vienna, a student there of German, French, and Diplomatic History, she had witnessed the arrival of Hitler's troops and the intense joy with which the Austrians had greeted them.

The village of Preston had been designated safe, but the school took precautions. Its Tudor cellars were cleared of junk, swept clean and white-washed, making bomb-proof shelters, where girls could sleep and gas-masks hang. A sing-song was held there, "Cellar-Brations in Honour of No War"—it was September 1938—"between 10.0 p.m. and 10.0 p.m.", on the night when the clocks were put back an hour, and the verses were sung:

Eensy-weensy sirens
Sound loud at dead of night.
Down come the school-girls
And pack in cellars tight.
Out come the gas-masks,
The coffee and the choc.,
When the raid is over,
Back to bed we flock.

Two hundred and seventy-nine windows and nine skylights had now to be blacked out. Miss Prain herself sewed all the curtains. The rooms downstairs became dormitories and classes were moved from the ground floor to the top. Girls took turns to occupy the cellars, in hammocks or in bunks. Palliasses were not as comfortable as mattresses but talk about fleas was only talk and it was not true that you could tell which feet had not been washed on bath-night.

After France fell, the gardeners roofed over a chalk-pit in the wood nearby, to be known as Hitler Hall, where the girls and staff and plenty of tinned food could be housed, and they installed electric light. The Hall was never used, but three bombs landed on fields not far away—one burst, the rest were duds—an abandoned German aeroplane or two, and three V-1 rockets.

Evacuees had been accepted in the village; Miss Prain lent them the art studio; and her own girls, if their homes were in a danger-zone, she allowed

to spend the holidays with her at the school, with a sister or brother, or with visiting parents, or with nurses whose London hospital had been bombed, or with airmen from overseas, or with children of parents in the French resistance, and with year by year a party of boys from Watford Grammar School, employed to harvest crops on nearby farms. The boys wore holes in their trousers, which Miss Prain patched, and in their socks, which she darned. Mrs Holbrook, with her daughters, Monica and Anne, worked hard to satisfy their appetites. Frail chairs collapsed, a rabbit decayed, which had been left behind on the roof above a window, and some foul eggs emptied a dormitory.

The girls gave concerts in aid of "War Weapons Week" and "Wings for Victory", the VIth acted *Lilies of the Field*[6] for the convalescent soldiers at St Paul's Walden,[7] and they all helped out on the farms, uprooting charlock, thistles and other weeds competing with the turnips or clover, or at school, sticking peas, thinning spring onions, carrots and sugar beet, pulling radishes or lettuce for the kitchen, picking gooseberries or apples (none to be eaten till the last five minutes, when they ate too many and again bellies ached), watering what thirsted, rubbing shoots off stored potatoes (a boring job, so Miss Syvret read them stories while they rubbed), clipping edges of lawn and stacking logs. Each Autumn Term, for a week, a lorry returned them to the fields to pick potatoes and, all the way there and back, everyone yelled her loudest a song then popular about a girl who would wear pink pyjamas, as she came through the mountains, pink pyjamas, pink pyjamas.

Their own small plots yielded little. Jo Tubbs in Magazine:

We planted a packet of peas and radish seed but we had no radishes and only about six peas.

Housework now occupied them all. Cleaners, known as servants, not yet domestic staff, had plied the brooms and cleaned their rooms before the war, and maids, called maids, uptitled since as dining-room assistants, had cleared and laid the tables; the girls had only to darn their stockings and make their beds. But now that maids and cleaners had left to perform more essential war-time duties it fell to the teachers and girls to dust and sweep, wash up and dry, Miss Prain leading them, who rose at 6.0 a.m. each day and swept the stairs.

For some tasks, like marking out tennis-courts, gathering grass from the mower into heaps, washing jam-jars or other girls' socks, and coaching weaker friends in mathematics or French, they were rewarded with national savings stamps. Again Jo Tubbs:

Washing socks is very hard work but very profitable; one's knuckles are very raw by the time one has done sixty pairs, but afterwards one is a shilling the richer.

[6] A comedy by John Hastings Turner, novelist and dramatist, first performed at the Ambassador's Theatre in 1923.

[7] Birthplace, 1900, of Elizabeth Bowes-Lyon, Queen Mother.

Miss Prain saw virtue as more its own reward. Housework built character. Magazine Foreword, 1942:

This year has seen a new development . . . we now do the bulk of our own housework . . . and our lives are none the poorer . . . the splendid achievements of heroes often grow out of faithful and intelligent self-discipline in the preliminary training life offers . . . and so we accept with thankfulness the opportunities that come our way . . . washing dishes and dusting rooms . . . weeding turnips and gathering wood, to gain that strength and readiness for the greater chances which come, as our school motto tells us, through self-mastery with its roots in Love.

The school and its premises remained unscathed until April that year, when Canadian soldiers took down and made away with a lead gazelle, one of two surmounting the main-gate pillars. Its partner was rescued, to be stood beside the arches pond where in later years visitors stalked it.[8] The Gazelle Drive thus lost its name. Next year the house was almost requisitioned. As in 1917 the governors found friends; measles may have helped, the worst epidemic Miss Prain had ever known; and the buildings were reprieved, all but the Lodge, and some land next to the gamesfield, which filled with army vehicles and mobile guns. The soldiers entertained the girls with gun-drill and the girls interested the soldiers, who eyed them as they played their tennis and lacrosse.

When the war in Europe had been won, girls and staff lit a bonfire, where an effigy of Hitler was burned, made of black-out curtains, and all marched round it, singing any song they knew. But Miss Prain seemed more relieved than exultant and more sceptical than relieved. No peace had been declared in the hearts of men, where the seeds of war had sprung:

The aftermath . . . is terrible, as we see all too clearly. Worse than the material and economic ruin is the spiritual and mental damage done, old standards of right and wrong overthrown, the acceptance of violence and greed and ambition as normal, of suspicion and hatred and revenge as natural. These things will take years to pass away . . .

The girls did not see Germans till 1947, at St Mary's Parish Church in Hitchin, where prisoners of war had gone to hear the *Messiah*. Roseann Canon, who reported the encounter, was intrigued:

*they were probably interested partly because Händel [*sic*] was of their own nationality, and, moreover, the Germans are noted for their love of music.*

When the bass (Donald Munro) sang "Why do the nations so furiously rage together?", I wondered what thoughts entered their heads.

Only one Old Girl was reported killed: Gertrude Trevelyan, the Newdigate prize-winner; she died taking a bath when a bomb destroyed her London home. Prof. Sumichrast, long dead, was spared the savage

[8] In 1989 it too would be stolen.

news. Anne Sydney Smith, HS42, came home, who had spent most of the war interned in Japan, near Nagasaki, and had witnessed the immediate effect of the dropping of the atomic bomb.

The first few years of peace proved deadlier than war: Joan, sister of Anne, was killed, thrown from a horse at Minden, in Germany, where she had worked for displaced persons; and Pamela Ross, HS50, aged 16, who from June to July sat four subjects for the Higher School Certificate, two years early, was killed in August, hit by lightning, as she and her mother walked the moors at Glen Urquhart, Inverness. A garden bench commemorated Joan; a trophies cupboard, Pamela.

Miss Allwright, Music, had retired, with an antique walnut bureau, a gift from Lady Hailsham. Miss White, Senior Mistress under three heads, taught almost till she died, sick in mind and body; Miss Miller was invited to return, and she agreed, but was dead within two weeks, of influenza, pleurisy and pneumonia. Miss Wilton took their place, who not only could and did teach almost any subject, need arising: she knitted, sewed, swept, scrubbed, polished and nursed; and also ran the Guides. £200 was collected for her when she retired. She too fell hopelessly ill. Her family spent the money on some bookshelves for the school and on Cancer Research. That was in 1960. Mr Moran said goodbye (called "Moran" to the last), gardener, lodge-keeper, furnace-man and cleaner of girls' shoes after muddy walks, 1918–43, given £88 from past and present staff and pupils, and a letter of thanks from Princess Helena Victoria, which he treasured. Miss Beaumont followed him. No greater love could friend show friend than Miss Beaumont's for her school. Mr E. C. MacIntosh, called bursar, took her place: a Cambridge engineer and a Scottish tennis international, he had taught the Watford boys German, and would now teach tennis and sometimes mathematics; inventor, film projectionist, stage manager, Jack of all trades and master of many—again and again the cry was raised, "Let's ask Mac!"

Problems he could solve. But could solutions be financed? Not all. Arrears of maintenance had accumulated, pot-holed roads, boy-battered furniture, worn carpets, bedsheets the warp and woof of which were said to be imprinted on the flesh of girls and staff, cracked plates, cups handleless. A lady bursar followed, more at home with décor than with boilers. Mary Beattie cooked, a young Old Girl, who would live to chair the Board. Matrons and housekeepers were difficult to keep, eight of whom arrived and-or departed in the year from September 1956. More teachers flitted in and away than in Regent's Park or Ealing.

In 1947 Princess Helena Victoria died. The Duchess of Gloucester succeeded her as President. She visited the College in 1952, elegant and friendly. Only two girls to a form had been allowed to take photographs but she posed and waited for all who could run and fetch a camera or had brought one anyway.

Again school uniform had changed. It now included a long-sleeved dress, with matching belt, yellow, green and salmon pink (rather busy), and

a tweed suit. The war had eliminated brown lisle stockings and lacrosse-wear fawn—unmourned—socks having eked out rations, and the green silk tie, gold striped.

Miss Wooldridge, who never seemed to tire and could not bear to see a girl look bored, or even sitting still, unoccupied, still taught games. It was she who had willed the XII to win when they brought back home the cup from St Margaret's, Bushey, then wreathed the Whitehall (white-walled corridor) clock with laurel and took them out to see Deanna Durbin in a film at a cinema in Hitchin. In 1949 the team lost only once, against Roedean, in the All-England Tournament at Merton. At Merton again, three years later, "in an unexpected blaze of glory", it reached the finals. The Royal School for the Daughters of Officers of the Army, Bath, won 1–0 but Miss Wooldridge was delighted: her girls had shown "toughness of spirit and good fighting quality" and "those not naturally gifted with fleetness of foot did marvels in speed and agility". Her innings was to last from 1937 to 1968, a long stretch for staff chasing up and down pitches.

At tennis too the school at times excelled: Aberdare (All-England) Cup semi-finalists one year and finalists the next, early in the fifties. Hockey had expired in 1933 and cricket in the war. Sports Day had lapsed but was revived. A huge buffet tea began it, events followed, ice-cream, then more events. Staff ran a "curriculum race"—they squirmed, dangling worms, as they ran to their biology; girls cast as steeds in "The Charge of the Light Brigade" somehow almost suffocated; and "the school obtained much fun out of watching the finalists endeavouring to squirt gargle through straws onto blotting-paper, after having eaten an exceedingly dry biscuit". Miss Jekyll's lily-pond had become the swimming-pool. It was small, but full of water, albeit icy cold. Miss Prain allowed the girls to swim there naked on the last night each end of Summer Term. Eyeball to eyeball they encountered frog and newt. Hot sausages revived them. Tobogganers found slopes and a gramophone was placed on the frozen pond, where skaters could dance to a Strauss waltz. The Guides continued, no longer however wearing green and gold, but regulation blue, which did not stick out at rallies. Another three patrols were formed: Chaffinch, Bullfinch and Sparrow, making ten, with each its own hut in the nearby wood; Sea-Guides, for a while; and a company of Rangers. They camped in the orchard near the Dower House, ate stew and semolina, drank cocoa, discovered nature and collected badges. Temple Dinsley offered more than did the ruined fields of Middlesex. It found a place in the College Magazine, where moon shone silver in verse and prose, the sticky buds were bathed in dew and winter's icy fingers gripped the land enchantingly.

Either all or almost all still enjoyed school parties, wearing head-dress or mask, with fancy clothes, watching someone blindfold feel her finger dipped into the witch's eye—a hole cut into a soggy orange—at Hallow E'en (Miss Prain was from Edinburgh), or a blindfold pair, trying to spoon a soft ice-cream into each other's mouth, or skits, where code-word jokes instantly succeeded, like "vinegar" and "stodge".

Miss Bunch, Drama and Speech, arrived in 1943, whom Miss Prain doted on. She produced from seven to seventeen plays a year, often Shakespeare, and sometimes G. B. Shaw. The VIth Form wrote to Mr Shaw and asked him for advice on the pronunciation of French names in *St Joan*. He replied that they should keep it as English as they could.

Rehearsals for staff plays—drawing-room comedies, thrillers and highly improbable romantic tragedies—excited the curiosity of the girls, who eavesdropped from the sick-wing, with an upturned mug wedged between their ears and the floor. Miss Prain almost always took a part, as an inspector, a husband, a nun, a dissolute priest or a Noah's Ark brown bear, and she designed and sewed the costumes, making do with what little she could find, including a stout, striped cloth like Bedouin blankets, which had started as curtains in a royal palace a hundred years ago at least, then had cubicled the Victoria beds at Ealing.

Mrs Hardy taught ballet. Her class, which Miss Prain had frocked, wove green, pink and blue Greek patterns on Garden Party day, when the court of the King of Hearts, fawns, maidens, athletes, Pan, villagers and gypsies leapt and skipped, milkmaids, washer-girl and shepherdess, till in 1957 they danced wearing raincoats and red berets, under raised umbrellas, Leonora Collett watching, 87 years old, who with Daisy Dobson had gone to the Palace in 1891 bringing flowers for Princess Helena.

Visits were arranged to King's College Chapel, Coventry Cathedral, Blenheim Palace and Hatfield House. Manners were exemplary. "Thank you, Miss Prain, for allowing us to go." Musicians attended concerts, Easter Bach, more Christmas Handel, a Solomon recital, but little else. The school showed films. Girls who could not go home for their mid-term break were taken to London; in 1937 to a News Theatre—Mickey Mouse—Lyons Corner House: ice-cream, then curry, the waitress's mistake, and to *Jane Eyre* at the Queen's Theatre, where Miss Taylor bargained with the manager and got 12s.–6d. stalls for only 3s.–6d. each, and where everyone felt secretly relieved when the curtain fell, so gruesomely exciting was the entrance of the maniac.

Miss Prain herself took parties—mainly VI—to parliamentary debates, political meetings, the theatre, Wimbledon, the scant remains of the old School House at Ealing, and St Peter's Church, and walked them back to school from the station once, at midnight, over four miles of drifted snow to the pantry and hot soup. She escorted them abroad: to Paris, where a friendly shop assistant asked whether all nine girls dressed in green tweed suits were her own daughters; to Schloss Hard, Ermattingen, in Switzerland, with its violet and cowslip meadows, and the clanging bells of railway-station, church and cow, where the townsfolk seemed to regard them, still in uniform, as zoological specimens; down the Rhine, in a paddle-steamer; to Paris again, and a less-than-luxury hotel called the Pax, where they were welcomed with champagne but had to sleep three to a room, some on camp beds, with furniture stored in the bath and a chair

slung from the shower; and to Germany, Austria, the Austrian Tyrol, Oberammergau and the Passion Play.

They remembered the poor, filling stockings with clothes and toys for a family in London or collecting money for the inmates of a displaced persons' camp. Many of those who did went on to nurse or worked with the Samaritans or helped the blind. Others taught: Christina Forbes at Charterhouse, Flora MacLeod at Roedean, Ann Kirwan at Benenden, musicians all three; Janet Norton, Games at Cheltenham; archaeologist Clare Goff, English in Turkey; Hester Fellowes, HS52, Science, after Girton, till at Harrow she became a master's wife; and Kirwan, Elizabeth: offered scholarships at Girton and LMH, she preferred LMH—or Oxford to Cambridge—got a first in PPE, specialised in Economics at Nuffield College and lectured on it in Delhi. Cecily Darwin, by way however of the Perse, did research at Oxford into X-ray crystallography, with the Nobel prize-winner, Mrs (later Prof.) Dorothy Hodgkin, establishing the molecular structure of p-bromonitrobenzene, and later, at the Institute of Cancer Research in the United States, of potassium gluconate. Fay Stranack wrote *The Normal and Pathological Morphology of the Kidney*. Patsy-Jeanne Lachelin won an Open Exhibition to Girton, read Medicine, and became St Thomas's Hospital's first woman-resident gynaecological and obstetrical registrar, and later a doctor in Nigeria. Stranack, Gillian, a successful A Level scientist, read English at Cambridge, then followed her sister to St Thomas's and nursed. Margaret Ley, HS39, pianist, and Jean Dobson, contralto, won acclaim. Barbara Moseley got a licence to fly. Heather Chasen partnered Mr Douglas Fairbanks in a film, *The Pleasure of his Company*. Her sister, Christine, directed the Raffles Museum in Singapore. Annabel Scotland, daughter of a rear-admiral, interpreted at the Olympic Games in Rome, Philippa Clauson, a brigadier's, assisted with productions at the BBC, and a colonel's, Jacqueline Conder, painted.

Miss Prain did not refer to them as "my old girls" but they felt themselves hers no less than their elders had felt themselves Miss Parker's. She had led by precept and example. The example shone, as Joan Bloxam saw, noting "every moment of the spare time that she has not got". And so did her precepts, included in her forewords, magazine by magazine. Examinations mattered. They spurred us on to make an effort to succeed and, without the clarity of thought and writing which they necessitated, the world would only stumble deeper into the fog of its confused ideas and purposes. But scholars were not always a school's most valuable members. It was more important for the lesson to be learnt of give and take, which boarding-school provided.

In 1957 Miss Prain decided that the next school year should be her last:

the time has come to hand over my work . . . to someone younger and fresher than I am after forty years of teaching . . . I have another year's work to do . . . I'm glad to say, for in one sense I am dreading the time when the final good-byes have to be said. But I want to begin my retirement while

the description given of me ten years ago, by a recently left VIth Former, still applies: "very elderly, of course, but still quite active"! I want to be able to strike new roots, develop new interests, make new friends, and have a life which is full, though not so strenuous as one at the head of a school is bound to be. But, whatever happens, I shall always thank God that so many years of my professional life have been connected with a school like P.H.C. From my very first term at Ealing, in 1919, I loved it: the traditions, the spirit, the keenness in work and play, the friendliness and cheerfulness, the wide and varied interests, the simplicity and sincerity, the desire to serve, and to do something worth while with life, the loyalty with which so many Old Girls kept in touch many years after they left school—these were precious things to meet, and even more to live with for so many years. These are the treasures we take from a good school . . . far more important than amassed knowledge or examination honours, or popularity, or successful careers. These, if we can keep them safe from the moth of carelessness and the corroding rust of cynicism, will be a real sense of strength and inspiration to us all our days. God grant they may be yours as well as mine.

The girls gave her an electric sewing-machine; the OGA., a lizard-skin handbag containing £261; and the Governors, a gold watch.

In 1961 Miss Prain was appointed Registrar of the New College of Speech and Drama in Anna Pavlova's old house in London, where she worked for seven years—a familiar sight in Highgate: "the old lady who bicycled"—and hardly had she seemed to have fully retired, to Wenhaston in Suffolk, with Miss Bunch, than she was busily involved there with the Women's Institute Committee, its meetings, suppers, jumble-sales, bazaars, recitals and plays, yet again making costumes, including, once, twelve mortar-boards.

In 1982 Miss Bunch took her life, bequeathing Miss Prain her house and all its contents, thus enabling her to be properly looked after at a nursing-home in Beccles, till 1983, when she died aged 87.

At a Memorial Service at St Martin's Church, on the morning of the next Garden Party, Old Girls read from her store of wisdom; a favourite end-of-term hymn of theirs was sung: "God be with you till we meet again"; the choir sang Mozart's *Ave Verum* and Miss Palmer and the organ played, as it were for Miss Prain herself, "The Robbers' March" from *Chu Chin Chow*. The school inherited Miss Bunch's many books and Miss Prain's electric sewing-machine.

Temple Dinsley

Preston, near Hitchin, a Hertfordshire retreat.

Vanguard remnants from the Ealing School

William — Rhodesian mining engineer — Peile's Mary, HS36; Patricia, daughter of the Hon. H.E. Nixon, rubber planter, Malacca Straits; and seated: Maj.-Gen. F.W.G. Wadeson's Diana, HS35.

Epilogue

Miss Thicknesse, meanwhile, had been appointed head: Sibylla Gratiana, known as Grace. It is alleged that she encouraged pupils to rebel, though more against their parents than against school rules, and that a pig that she had won in a village fête, and housed in a nearby field, often kept her busy when visitors arrived. Miss Thicknesse stayed two years and died, still young, of cancer, in 1969.

A governor knew someone who knew about a teacher at St James's, Malvern: Miss Joyce Stratford. Miss Stratford agreed to take the job. She did not, as a socialist, approve of independent schools, but she understood, and could sometimes help, the kind of girl for whom the little college had begun to look ideal: the troubled parents' troubled child. Retired about a year, she too would die of cancer.

The school ran short of pupils, the treasurer of fees. A decorative past ensured no future. Its relics had already mostly disappeared. The house in Regent's Park had been long ago demolished. A new headquarters for the Royal College of Physicians of London would occupy the site: anything but Nash and as hideous behind as in front it looked incongruous. Miss Horden's Chippendale and Hepplewhite remained; a Georgian book-case pair, all but a separated, lower half, superbly crafted, where kitchen staff kept loaves; Miss Roberts's Sheraton bureau, removed to the cellars, its drawers full of tools; and Victoria herself, the Great White Marble Queen, whom someone must have toppled: her nose, not all of it replaced, oozed glue. Stout wooden benches and many screws and nails had splintered the mouldings in the Ealing-oak-panelled hall and the unwary stumbled over holes and knotty bumps in the parquet floor outside it.

The less the girls felt happy, the more they looked unkempt, chewed gum, swore filth, spread litter. At least a few smoked cigarettes. Not many of the less well parented learned manners from the best. Form VI wore what they liked all day, a privilege, they understood, enabling them to bridge an awkward gap from school to university or employment.

One day the empty beds would fill, accommodation expand, comfort and facilities improve, the paintwork gleam; good staff again teach pupils bright and eager; manners please. But the pendulum wriggled as it swung. Worship continued; religion, the subject and its uses, waned: no more had anyone to learn by heart, as prep or punishment, from the Bible or the Book of Common Prayer. "Too little of God", a parent now complained, "and too much Mozart." At four o'clock, each week-end afternoon, television ruled and sated, no need for children to have first been good, till a fortnight later they with goodness almost burst. Entertainment ran like water from a

tap. The youngest knew things that Miss Parker's eldest could never have suspected. No longer did picnics offer memorable treats. Traffic and pop music roared. The fields had mostly lost their grass and almost all their butterflies. Hardly anyone tried to bare her soul in verse. But the orchestra enraptured. And friendship would always develop, root and last, where boys did not incessantly intrude. The school which Madame Pompeati—Teresa Cornelys—and Giacomo Casanova had destined to emerge, when they embraced in Venice in 1753 and when Sophia Wilhelmina Williams was born, still stood. It had deserved to be rescued and survive.

Index

Names of persons and other creatures
either still alive or remembered or of note.